Governing Urban America
A Policy Focus

Bryan D. Jones

Wayne State University

D0002796

Little, Brown and Company

BOSTON TORONTO

Library of Congress Cataloging in Publication Data

Jones, Bryan D.
    Governing urban America.

    1. Municipal government—United States.
2. Federal-city relations—United States.
3. Political participation—United States.
4. Policy sciences. I. Title.
JS331.J58 1982   320.8′0973   82–14938
ISBN 0–316–47284–0

Library of Congress Catalog Card Number 82–14938

ISBN 0-316-47284-0

9 8 7 6 5 4 3 2

ALP

Published simultaneously in Canada
by Little, Brown & Company (Canada) Limited

Printed in the United States of America

Cover photo: Model of a mixed use redevelopment project in downtown
Louisville, Kentucky by the Broadway Project Corporation. Planning, urban
design, and architectural services by Sasaki Associates, Inc., Watertown,
Mass. Model photographer: Sam Sweezy.

Photo, pp. 84–85: Chicago Tribune Photo by David Nystrom. Used with
permission.

PREFACE

I have tried to do three things in this book. First, I have organized the material to illuminate five central issues: limited government, local autonomy, democratic accountability, governmental effectiveness, and policy distribution. These are issues of central concern in political science, and in that sense they are key issues of political theory. They are introduced in Chapter 1 and reevaluated in the last chapter.

The second thing I have tried to do is to integrate as much of modern research in urban politics as space and the limits of my ability to read and absorb this literature have allowed. Much of this literature is directly relevant to the five key issues. The public choice approach to governmental organization, while deeply rooted in economics, is quite articulate on the issues of limited government and local autonomy. The modern quantitative research into the effects of local governmental forms speaks directly to the seeming inability of governments to maximize responsiveness and efficiency simultaneously. The modern literature on intergovernmental relations and policy implementation bears directly on the issue of local autonomy. The community power structure literature obviously has important implications for democratic accountability and popular control. The emerging literature on bureaucratic behavior and street-level bureaucrats can be directly linked to democratic accountability and the issue of policy distribution.

There is no better place to understand these key issues than in the study of urban politics. There the issues have been better stated and the existing research better designed to illuminate these issues than in any other subarea of political science. The close proximity of citizens and government in cities thrusts up the key issues for critical examination, and the rich variety of cities in America offers a superb natural laboratory for doing so.

Finally, I have attempted to integrate the modern policy analysis literature in the study of urban politics and public policy. I have adopted a process approach to policy analysis; the reader will not find separate chapters on criminal justice, education, transportation, and so forth. There are certain commonalities in these policy areas that are far more important to grasp than are the specifics of each area.

Local governments play a special role in the American policymaking process. In the first place, they are independent, policymaking units in and of themselves. In the second place, they serve as administrative units and implementing agencies of higher levels of government. Finally, local governments are enmeshed in a system of policymaking that I have termed "off cycle," to indicate the limitations of the stage theories of the policy process in describing their policy activities.

Integrating the policy analysis literature without losing sight of the five core issues proved to be a difficult task. Part of the difficulty stems from the nonuniform treatment of the policy process literature in the modern political science curriculum. Some universities offer separate courses in public policy. In others this material is covered in the basic introductory course. In still others, it is covered in the urban course. Even where separate courses in public policy exist, they are not always prerequisites for the study of urban politics. At Wayne State, for example, the urban course and the public policy course are parallel courses, each requiring the introductory American government course as a prerequisite, but neither requiring the other.

My solution to the problem of integrating the policy materials in this book was to include a separate chapter covering the basic techniques of the study of public policy early in the book (Chapter 2). If students have taken a public policy course, this chapter can serve as a link; if they have not, more time may be spent here. In Chapter 3, following a suggestion by Fred Kramer, I have set out the distinctive nature of urban policymaking.

A number of scholars reviewed the various drafts of this book. While I did not always agree with the solutions they proposed, these reviews were far more helpful than I would have imagined in helping me catch misleading or inappropriately organized sections. I would like to thank Robert H. Binstock of Brandeis University; Fred A. Kramer of University of

Massachusetts, Amherst; Elaine Morley of Southern Illinois University, Edwardsville; Michael B. Preston of University of Illinois; Bernard H. Ross of American University; and Harmon Zeigler of University of Oregon for their very useful criticism. I have accumulated other debts in the process of completing this work: Jim Murray convinced me that the project was worth doing, and then prodded me on to the end; Carol Wasson patiently typed and retyped drafts of the manuscript.

I had hoped to dedicate this book to my daughter Laura, then four. When I asked her if she would like to have her name in Daddy's book, she said no. Why? I asked. Not a very interesting book, she said. Why not? I asked. Not enough pictures, she said. Wait on the reviews, I told her.

CONTENTS

CHAPTER 1

Introduction

Americans, and their counterparts in most of western Europe, today face a critical turning point in the histories of their countries. For the first time since the dawn of the Industrial Revolution, the population of cities has declined in the absence of war, famine, plague, or economic depression. Yet in the developing countries of the Third World, cities continue to expand at phenomenal rates, severely straining the abilities of governments to provide proper services for the new residents.

Reasons for the decline of American cities are not hard to find. Birth rates have declined, so that urban residents are not replenishing themselves at the rate they once were. Far more significant, however, is a general deconcentration of economic activity. Cities, once the economic centers of the nation, have seen their economic functions gradually siphoned off, first to their own burgeoning suburbs, then to the small towns of the hinterland and to the growing towns and cities of the Sunbelt. Even where cities are growing in America, principally in the South and West, they grow not as central cities but as sprawling housing tracts and shopping centers, both signs of the growing deconcentration of American urban life.

In this milieu governments must react to rapidly changing demands for policies and services, while still searching for resolutions of five classic issues of governance: limited government, democratic accountability, local autonomy, efficient government, and equitable provision of policies and services. Just how urban governments struggle with these classic issues of political theory is the subject of this book. In this chapter we shall look briefly at the role of government in urban society, and then set out the five core issues that will concern us throughout this book.

Urbanization and Government

For centuries the world's cities have offered special opportunities for people. Even though cities are often depicted as grimy, hostile, corrupt, and forbidding, the recent history of the world has been marked by the movement of population from the countryside to the city. Farmers, peasants, and small-town dwellers migrate to the city seeking opportunities for economic advancement.

The migrants often do not feel emotional ties to the city. The French farmboy in Paris plans to save his money and buy a farm in Provence; the worker in the factories of Cleveland, Detroit, or Chicago gets off the shift at 4:00 P.M. Friday and drives nonstop to home and family in West Virginia for the weekend; the Yugoslav worker in Stockholm never feels at ease in the cold, foreign city. But they come nevertheless, seeking a chance to better their lives and those of their families.

Growth and decline and government

These migrations pushed the great cities of the world to unmanageable size, creating strains on existing governmental structures. In many countries experiencing rapid urbanization, governments grew gradually in response to the demands of agrarian, insulated societies. In America, a tradition of local autonomy in government meant that urban public policy would be made on a piecemeal basis, with each city government dealing with local demands and paying little attention to the national implications of urbanization.

Today the New York urban region contains more than 16 million people. According to United Nations estimates, however, Mexico City will overtake it as the world's largest urban area in less than twenty years. As is the case in many Third World cities, so many Mexican villagers and peasants are moving to Mexico City so quickly that no one can estimate accurately how many there are. Today, some eighteen urbanized areas in the world contain more than five million people each. These include four American metropolises: New York, Los Angeles, Chicago, and Philadelphia. In 1790, shortly after the basic relationships between the national government and the states and localities were specified in the United States Constitution, the entire country contained fewer than four million people. The country had about as many people as the Boston metropolitan area does today, and very few of these people lived in cities. Government, of course, has changed in the past two centuries, but changes in governmental form lag far behind changes in the economic and social structure of cities.

The whole process of governing America's cities has been complicated enormously by the strong tradition of local autonomy. As cities grew, many migrants moved away from congested city cores. Too tied to the city economically to return to their rural or small-town roots, they tried to disassociate themselves from urban life psychologically and governmentally by establishing suburbs. In America, suburbs sprang up not long after the little colonial towns became great industrial cities. In the rural tradition of local autonomy, these suburbs set up separate governments. The metropolis was an integrated economic system, yet it was to be governmentally fragmented. Whether this has led to poorer urban policies is currently a matter of lively debate among political scientists, as well as among the residents of central cities and suburbia.

Now, after two centuries of being called upon to formulate public policies for growing cities, many local governments are experiencing the pains of population decline. In many parts of America and Europe, cities are no longer growing as fast as they once did, and some metropolitan areas are actually losing population. This is nothing new for some central cities; many older ones have been losing population to their suburbs for more than two decades. But now entire metropolises are beginning to lose people, and many suburbs are facing a future of declining populations, vacant houses, closed schools, and underutilized public facilities. These changes have profound implications for the government and politics of American cities.

Figure 1.1 diagrams the course of American urbanization in the twentieth century. It graphs the percentage of the population living in urban places (places of 2,500 people or more; this United States Bureau of the Census definition was more useful when America was predominantly a rural country). The figure also graphs the percentage of people living in places of 100,000 people or more.

Urbanization in the United States increased steadily from 1900 to the present, with two exceptions. The first was a leveling off of growth during the 1930s, when the Great Depression limited economic opportunity for all Americans. There was little sense in moving to the city if no jobs were available when one got there. The second exception has been the 1970s and the early 1980s. After the early 1970s the growth of America's cities leveled off. The percentage of Americans living in cities has stabilized, but at a very high level; over three-fourths of Americans now live in urban places.

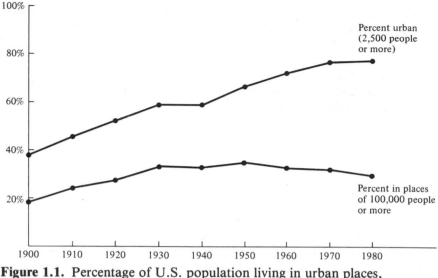

Figure 1.1. Percentage of U.S. population living in urban places, 1900–1980.

Source: John F. Long, *Population Deconcentration in the United States* (Washington, D.C.: Bureau of the Census, November 1981), Table 1, p. 9.

Figure 1.1 indicates that large cities (over 100,000 in population) began to decline in population long before the growth of smaller urban places ceased. There has been no real growth in (large American) cities since about 1930. Much of this decline can be explained by suburbanization; people were moving to smaller cities economically connected with a larger city. The rest of the decline can be explained by the penchant of Americans to move to small and medium-sized cities rather than metropolises, which became very evident after 1970. These factors, taken together, are termed *population deconcentration.* They have very important implications for urban politics and government, as we shall see.

Urban problems, government, and politics

If cities offer great opportunities, they also pose serious problems. Cities are places where large numbers of people are regularly in close contact, and this can threaten public health and order. Until the relatively recent advent of modern sanitary engineering, cities were regularly swept by plagues. Fire was a constant threat until the advent of modern building standards and adequate water systems. Moreover, people working alone could not build the transportation and communications systems necessary for the intense human interaction taking place in cities.

Cities are also heterogeneous places. Migrants from near and far bring their own customs, mores, and understanding of social life. The lack of standard sets of customs governing the behavior of residents of the city can lead to clashes of opinion and misunderstandings.

To solve the problems posed by urbanization, people turn to government. Some of the problems of urban life can be solved or at least alleviated by government action; others cannot. Some of the difficulties faced by urban dwellers cannot be solved reasonably *without* government. A code of laws to govern the diverse behaviors of citizens can be established only by government. Without government, it is unlikely that citizens, working alone or together, will build a sewer system or a water system or a fire-resistant city. Other problems can be dealt with without government, but the results may not be desirable or fair. For example, even if government did not provide for the education of citizens, there would still be schools, but it is unlikely that the poor could afford them.

In some cases, citizens in cities would be better off without governmental involvement. In particular, government housing programs have had a checkered past. In St. Louis, the Pruitt-Igoe public housing project was demolished by the government that built it long before the end of its expected useful life. In many cities, federal home-ownership programs established in the 1960s led to housing abandonment and decay in the 1970s.

The Components of Urbanism

Because of urban heterogeneity, differing interests are more likely to arise and express themselves politically in cities. Governments must both provide necessary services and resolve disputes among contending interests. But what constitutes an "urban place"? The U.S. Bureau of the Census defines an urban place as any place with a population of 2,500 persons or more. By this definition, in 1980 almost 75 percent of Americans lived in cities. And by this definition, Brundidge, Alabama, and New York City are both cities—though they are affected by very different trends and social forces.

An alternative definition of cities centers on the concept of a metropolis. Metropolitan areas generally consist of a *center city,* the municipality that serves as the core of the area, along with a ring of *suburban communities* that are connected to the center city both economically and socially. Further from the center city is an *urban fringe* (sometimes called the exurbs), a patchwork of homes and vacant land that is also connected to the rest of the metropolitan area. If the metropolis continues to grow, the exurbs will be fully developed and become *suburbs.* The United States government tries to define urbanism through the concept of the *Standard Metropolitan Statistical Area* (SMSA). An SMSA is a place that is interconnected economically and socially and has a "large" population center (50,000 people or more). More than 70 percent of the population of the United States lives in one of the country's 279 SMSAs.

Many smaller towns and cities suffer from what many urbanists term "the urban problem" (or, when things get bad enough, "the urban crisis"): declining business districts, increasing concentrations of the poor, deteriorating housing, crime. Basing a definition of urbanism on size alone, then, is not very fruitful. This fact does not mean that it is not useful to distinguish between large cities and small ones. It does mean that studying only large places may exclude much of what we have in mind when we think about urban politics.

Two other components of urbanism are density and integration. *Density* is usually measured by the number of people who live within a standard measure of area. For example, Charlotte, North Carolina, has about 3,173 persons per square mile, while Dayton, Ohio, which has about the same number of people in total population, has 6,360 people per square mile of area. If density is an indicator of urbanism, Dayton is more urban than Charlotte. *Integration* is the extent to which the different parts of urban areas are interconnected, both economically and socially. It is indicated by such measures as the frequency of trips between two points (how many people go from a suburb to downtown, for example). A city whose constituent parts are tightly bound together could be classified as more urban than one whose parts are more loosely linked.[1]

Urbanism as the use of space

The three components of urbanism—size, density, and integration—are important in distinguishing among urban places. Some cities are larger, or more dense, or more interconnected than others, and this has important consequences for their politics. To take but one of many possible examples, a dense city with many high-rise apartment buildings is likely to have many citizens who use public transportation, if for no other reason than the difficulty of finding a place to park. But in a city of the same population that has more single-family houses than large apartments, fewer people may make use of the public transit systems. So the politics of transportation will differ in those two cities.

The three components of urbanism do not, however, distinguish between urban activities and other forms of human activities. One clue to the distinctiveness of urban activity is provided by Oliver P. Williams, who defines ur-

[1] These components may be compared to Louis Wirth's classic definition: "A city may be defined as a relatively large, dense, and permanent settlement of socially heterogeneous individuals." [Louis Wirth, "Urbanism as a Way of Life," *American Journal of Sociology* 44 (July 1938): 5.] An excellent collection of articles on urbanism from a sociological perspective is Sandor Halebsky, editor, *The Sociology of the City* (New York: Scribner's, 1973). This book contains Wirth's article.

banism as the use of location to provide access to valued objects.[2] What this means is that physical space is used to achieve human goals, at least when these goals stress access to valued objects. The closer a person is to a desired object, the better off he or she is. For example, being close to a major shopping area, a school, a country club, a place of employment, a public transit stop, or the street where the wealthiest people live, all can make a person better off. Being far from those things, or being close to such places as the city dump, the worst-polluting factory, or the highest crime district makes one worse off. We will follow Williams and define urbanism as the way in which humans use physical space to achieve their goals.

Five Issues

Observing urban politics is similar in some ways to the blind men describing the elephant. American cities exist in seemingly infinite variety. Each city has its own history, culture, and politics. Savvy individuals can describe the politics and government of each in fascinating detail, and each tale seems far removed from the others. Dallas is light-years from Chicago in governmental form, in political life, and in the way in which government is used to solve city problems. Moreover, the two cities are treated differently by their state governments, and they are affected very differently by the urban policies of the federal government.

It would be easy to write a book stressing the political uniqueness of America's cities—or at least to start such a project. Who has detailed knowledge about enough cities to carry that project to a satisfactory conclusion?[3]

Yet if one described all cities in their fascinating political variations, he or

---

[2] Oliver P. Williams, *Metropolitan Political Analysis: A Social Access Analysis* (New York: The Free Press, 1971), p. 12.

[3] This point is underscored by the general paucity of books thoroughly describing the government and politics of a single city. Many studies of single cities are undertaken not in the interest of thorough description but to test some theory of politics or other. Some of the best single-city treatments are: Frederick M. Wirt, *Power in the City: Decision-Making in San Francisco* (Berkeley, Calif.: University of California Press, 1974); Wallace Sayre and Herbert Kaufman, *Governing New York City* (New York: Russell Sage, 1965); Milton Rakove, *Don't Make No Waves, Don't Back No Losers* (Bloomington, Ind.: University of Indiana Press, 1975) (Chicago); Robert Dahl, *Who Governs?* (New Haven, Conn: Yale University Press, 1961) (New Haven). The lack of thorough material on single cities makes sound comparative description even more scarce. See, however, Edward Banfield, *Big City Politics* (New York: Random House, 1965). The most ambitious attempt at comparative urban political description was undertaken by the Joint Center for Urban Studies of Massachusetts Institute of Technology and Harvard University in the early 1960s. The richness of this approach is reflected in Edward C. Banfield and James Q. Wilson, *City Politics* (New York: Vintage, 1963). Note how dated most of these materials are.

Students of urban geography are more fortunate. A large-scale collaborative project describing major American metropolises was undertaken in the 1970s. See John S. Adams, editor, *Urban Policy-Making and Metropolitan Dynamics* (Cambridge, Mass.: Ballinger, 1976), and the companion volumes on specific cities.

she still would not have a satisfactory description of urban politics and policymaking, any more than the blind men adequately described the elephant. If one has a guide to the important uniformities of urban politics and policymaking, however, he or she is in a much better position to enjoy the variations. The reason is that the differences among cities can be put into an overall context, facilitating understanding.

Five critical issues arise over and over again in the study of urban politics and policymaking. Every action taken by urban policymakers affects the resolution of these issues, and the ways in which these issues have been dealt with in the past influence the actions taken by policymakers today. Moreover, there are no final solutions to these issues. What is appropriate for one generation of citizens will be deemed inappropriate by another. Contemplate briefly the differences in citizen attitudes toward government in the 1960s and the 1980s. As numerous public opinion polls have shown, public attitudes toward government were far more favorable in the 1960s than today, and the nature of political activism has reflected these differences. In the 1960s government was to be used to solve the great social problems, especially the urban problems, the nation faced. In the 1980s many believe that government ought to be severely limited in its actions. In the future Americans may again feel more benevolent toward their governments—federal, state, and local—and a new period of government activism may begin. Whatever the case, an important issue is involved: What limits are to be placed on government actions? And the issue of limited government is the first on our list of critical issues. The five critical issues are:

1. The issue of limited government
2. The choice between local autonomy and effective government
3. The issue of democratic accountability
4. The tradeoff between efficient government and responsive government
5. The issue of policy distribution

Let us examine each of these issues briefly.

Limited government

The first critical issue is the extent of public intervention in modern urban society. How much government do we want? Should the powers of government be limited to certain objectives? If so, which ones?

Many cities have passed ordinances, or local laws, that prohibit an owner from selling his or her home prior to a city inspection. If the city inspection turns up any violations of the city codes, then the defect must be repaired at the owner's expense before the home can be sold. The mandatory inspection protects prospective buyers, but—and this is a big but—it interferes with property owners' ability to do what they wish with their property. Is mandatory inspection a legitimate infringement of the prerogatives of the owners?

Modern cities are very complex social systems. The actions of one citizen have become far more likely to affect others, and the actions of one individual may harm numerous innocent bystanders. Carrying further the example in the last paragraph, suppose several unscrupulous individuals engage in "tenement trading," the practice of selling a slum property over and over to escape legal action. Not only are the tenants in the building affected, but the owners of better-kept buildings in the neighborhood are adversely affected. In order to protect the rights of other property owners and tenants, perhaps the city will pass an ordinance requiring inspections and compliance to city codes when a property is sold. Again, is this a legitimate infringement on the prerogatives of the owner?

Government intervention is more crucial in urban societies than in rural ones, simply because there are more people to get in one another's way. Some government policies are necessary to protect the rights of citizens; the more complex the society, the more necessary are such policies. Yet not all government policies are desirable, and some are actually harmful. Many are harmful because they impose limitations on the liberties of individual citizens without really yielding any gains for the entire community. Deciding just where the line is to be drawn is not a simple enterprise. We will look at the issue of limited government in more detail in chapter 3.

Local autonomy and effective government

There exists in urban America a basic tradeoff between local autonomy and effective government. Suppose for a moment a major central city, say Philadelphia, passes the mandatory inspection ordinance discussed above, but its suburbs do not follow suit. A prospective owner who does not want to be bothered with inspections and compliance when he or she sells property will simply not move to Philadelphia. This will lessen the demand for property in Philadelphia, and owners in the city will have fewer opportunities to sell their properties. They may become discouraged and stop repairing them, falling further out of conformity with the city codes. It is not impossible, then, that the condition of housing in the city would actually decline because of a law attempting to upgrade properties. (All this depends, of course, on the way buyers are influenced by the law. Buyers may view the law as a benefit to them if they do not plan to sell in the foreseeable future.)

There would be no problem if the city of Philadelphia included all of its suburbs, or if there were none. Then buyers and sellers would have no choice but to comply with the ordinance, because they could not take their business elsewhere. In that case, however, Philadelphia would become more than twice its present size, and many say the country's fourth largest city is already too big to be called a "local" government.

Local self-government can be realized only when local units of government are, first, relatively small (don't contain too many people) and, second, have real governmental powers (are not simply administrative units of larger units of government). Yet the smaller the local unit of government, the less likely that it will be able to solve the problems it encounters, for two reasons. First, problems are larger than the governments trying to solve them. What is to stop a criminal living in Berkeley, California, from robbing a bank in neighboring Oakland? Are the citizens of Metairie, Louisiana, to pay for bridge and street improvements made necessary by commuters traveling to work in New Orleans? Such problems that spill over from one unit of government to another must be handled by larger units of government or be negotiated by the affected governments. The second reason that small units of government are less able to solve problems is that they often do not possess the necessary resources. Often poor local governments have the problems while wealthy units of government have the resources to solve them. We will encounter this tradeoff between local autonomy and effective government in chapter 9 and again in chapter 13.

Democratic accountability

The third critical issue is democratic accountability. Politics is the struggle for control of government, and government is the policymaking apparatus for society. Do the democratic institutions—popular elections, freedom to organize, freedom of expression—ensure that popular control of government will result from the urban political process? One must not confuse democratic accountability with local autonomy. Many arrogant elites have established themselves in small towns and cities. Indeed, political scientists have no evidence that large cities are less democratically governed than small towns. We will explore this issue in Part II of this book.

There is a second important aspect of democratic accountability. In the modern urban society, it has become difficult for elected leaders to control the activities of those government employees directly responsible for delivering services to citizens. Even if democratic institutions work perfectly, elected leaders may be unsuccessful in imposing their policies on government bureaucrats and workers. In this case, accountability fails. We shall look at this aspect of democratic accountability in chapter 14.

Efficient government and responsive government

As we shall see in chapter 10, efficient governments are not necessarily responsive, and responsive governments are often not very efficient. A responsive government is a government that tries to satisfy as many of the demands placed upon it as possible. An efficient government is one that tries to carry out the duties assigned to it using the smallest possible amount of the taxpayers' resources. If a government takes on too many responsibilities by being responsive to too many demands, it may not be able to perform any of them efficiently. It may even try to perform contradictory tasks, as the federal government does when it subsidizes tobacco growing while issuing warnings against smoking.

To complicate things a bit more, a responsive government, by catering to the politically active, may produce policies that the majority of citizens (who are not often very politically active) do not really want. We will take a look at this problem in chapter 7.

Government efficiency is always a goal of reformers. Since at least the era of the municipal reformers, during the early part of this century, those who would improve government have called for efficiency. Unfortunately, there is almost always a tradeoff between responsiveness and efficiency. Responsiveness must generally be sacrificed if efficiency is to be increased.

Policy distribution

The fifth and final critical issue concerns who benefits and who is harmed by urban public policies. All policies have *distributional* effects. Policies, in a word, often treat different people differently (and sometimes they treat similar people differently). In some instances this is the way the policy is supposed to work. Wealthy people are not supposed to receive welfare; employed people are not supposed to receive unemployment compensation. But at other times the distributional effects are not intended. We say that they are inadvertent consequences of a policy. Finally, some policies deliberately discriminate against certain people.

What makes policy distribution an especially critical issue for the study of urban public policymaking is that so much distribution occurs without anyone realizing what is happening. This occurs because of the tendency of similar people to cluster together in cities. One of the first things that strikes an observer of an American city is the spatial segregation that invariably occurs. Whites and blacks live in different neighborhoods, as do the poor and the middle class.

This means that, for example, the location of a public facility (highway, park, bridge, and so forth) will automatically affect different people differently. If the city dump is located adjacent to the slum, then the environment of the poor deteriorates even further, while the well-to-do are not troubled. Deciding where to locate the city dump has distributional effects.

This locational component is so important in urban areas that location is a key element in the definition of urban public policies. Urban policies are not simply policies that are pursued by cities; both the national government and state governments have urban policies. Nor are urban policies simply policies that affect large cities. Many small to medium-sized cities are experiencing the problems that are often termed urban problems: crime, economic decay, housing deterioration, racial hostilities. One major component of urban policies pursued at all levels of government is that they affect, directly or indirectly, the location of homes, businesses, and industries.

Issue Resolution in Urban Society

Problems that involve these five critical issues are continually being resolved and then reopened and then resolved again without anyone thinking about the issues directly. Candidates run for office, groups and individuals press their claims on governments, governmental officials make decisions, bureaucrats implement these decisions. All are playing a game of the moment; very few think very seriously about the effects of what they are doing in terms of the five key issues. The issues are dealt with as a by-product of the urban policymaking process.

Not infrequently political actors support their claims on government by extolling the virtues of one side of an issue (local autonomy, for example) without thinking about the inevitable tradeoff on the other side of the issue (less effective government, for example). Hence the issues are resolved and re-resolved on what amounts to a case-by-case basis. Local officials applying for federal grants for their cities spend little time thinking about issues and tradeoffs, yet their actions bear directly on them.

Although policymakers and citizens alike generally do not recognize it, their actions in demanding, formulating, implementing, and opposing various public policy proposals affect the extent of governmental intervention in society, the degree of local autonomy, popular control, governmental efficiency, and the distribution of policy benefits. Just how this process occurs is the subject of this book.

PART I

Urban Policymaking

Policymaking in all sorts of governmental organizations, from the national government to the smallest school district in the country, from the Department of Defense to the smallest municipal departments, has certain distinctive features. Political scientists have described these features in writings on the policymaking process.

Yet is is abundantly clear that there is no single public policymaking process in America. The mere existence of many governments—local, state, and national—means that the relationships among these governments will heavily influence what public policies we have. Further, the existence of many governments is more important in some policy areas—urban policies, for example—than in other areas—defense policies, for example. The participation of many governments, each with at least some autonomy, means that urban policymaking will be extremely complex. It also means that urban policymaking will exhibit some pronounced differences from idealized descriptions of the policy process.

That urban policymaking is both similar to and yet distinct from idealized descriptions of the public policymaking process means that both the idealized model and the specifics of the urban policy process must be understood. In the three chapters that compose Part I of this book, we will examine both the general policy process and the unique elements of that process as it operates in urban America.

Chapter 2 covers the basic concepts of the study of public policy. Only in passing do we refer directly to urban policymaking, yet this material is essential for its understanding. Chapter 3 presents the reasons that urban policymaking is different from the idealized policymaking process, reasons that are directly related to the basic issues of government that were discussed in chapter 1. Chapter 4 is a discussion of the urban policy environment. The social and economic characteristics of cities provide the grist for the urban policy process mill, supplying it with the problems and issues that activate it.

CHAPTER 2

The Policy Process

Political scientists have described certain characteristics of policymaking that are similar for all governments. This general policymaking process applies with little modification to the American national government, to the government of Spain, to the state of Ohio, to the municipality of Los Angeles, and to the Cedar Rapids, Iowa, school district. The issues that these governmental units deal with differ, of course, as do the political institutions that handle these issues. These differences should not be allowed to obscure the similarities. In this chapter we will examine the general policy process, modifying the approach only slightly to conform to our objective of understanding urban politics and government. Chapter 3 will detail what is distinctive about the urban policy process.

The five issues described in chapter 1 are settled, reopened, and settled again through this policy process. The major issues are settled, however, as an indirect consequence of the use of government to solve the problems that groups and individuals in society are experiencing. A recent federal task force established by the Justice Department spent much time considering the problems of crime and the criminal justice system, and recommended that the federal government spend a massive $2 billion to rebuild state prisons. Yet the panel spent very little time thinking about the effects of such a program on local autonomy or on popular control.[1] Such effects are indirect consequences of the public policy process. Only by understanding the policy process as it is used to solve particular social problems can one understand the resolution of the major issues of governance.

Components of Public Policies

Some political scientists define a public policy as any action that a government takes. The word *policy,* however, implies something more. A public policy has four components: (1) it is a line of action; (2) it is directed toward a goal; (3) it involves resource commitment; and (4) it is pursued by a government. Let us examine these components one at a time.

A line of action

A policy is not the same thing as a decision. Although a decision may contribute to a policy, a policy is composed of several different decisions, often taken by different people at different times. Each decision contributes to the line of action that constitutes the policy.

The importance of the line-of-action criterion can be seen most clearly when there is a breakdown in the line. Because decisions affecting a public policy are often made by many individuals in many different organizations and all these people must somehow cooperate in their decisionmaking to produce a public policy, often these separate decisions do not end up contributing to a single line of action. This is a particular problem in urban policymaking, because so many different government bodies affect life in cities.

Goal directed

Policymakers have some goal or goals in mind, however vague, when they enact public policies. The policies they enact may or may not actually contribute to the goals they envision. The policies may even have other effects that have nothing to do with the stated goals of the policy. Such effects may be counterproductive or beneficial. All we require is that the policy have goals. After a policy is put into effect, there is often debate over whether the policy does or does not contribute to its goals. Such debate is indicative of how crucial this purposive, or goal-directive, component is.

[1] Aaron Epstein, "Panel Calls for New State Prisons," *Detroit Free Press,* August 18, 1981.

Resource commitment

For an action to qualify as a public policy, there must be some resources—money or obvious effort—committed by the government to achieve the announced goal. Governments do not always back up policy pronouncements with resources. Many policies are announced grandly, only to die quietly from lack of funding. Without resource commitment, the line of action that characterizes public policy cannot be established.

This criterion holds even for such policies as deregulation, or removing government regulations and restrictions on private actions. This process involves changing the direction of government action, and normally a great deal of effort will have to be applied to change this direction. Just announcing a change of direction will not accomplish it.

Government

By public policy we mean governmentally created (or at least condoned) policy. Urban policies are made daily by many different government bodies, from federal courts to local mosquito abatement districts. In many cases these policies are simple ratifications of decisions made by groups outside government. Regulatory agencies at the federal, state, and local levels have at times simply adopted the viewpoints of the industries they have been responsible for regulating. Industry proposals were uncritically accepted and implemented. Even though the policy is simply passed through a government agency by powerful interest groups, the policy qualifies as public policy. By putting its stamp of approval on the proposal, the regulatory agency has put the full authority of government behind the proposal. So whether the policy qualifies as a public policy turns less on who is responsible for the policy and more on whether government (or, at least, some government agency) acts formally on the policy.

The Stages of Policymaking

Public policies come into being through two very different processes. In the first place, major public policy changes come about only after traveling through a number of stages. These successive stages are known as the *policy cycle.*

The transition from one stage to another is an important event in the life cycle of a policy proposal. Not all issues successfully complete the cycle; many issues never become true policy proposals and many proposals are never enacted into public policy. But most major enacted public policies have moved through a series of characteristic stages.

The stages of policymaking are characteristic of major policy initiatives. But the policy cycle does not describe all policymaking in urban America. Indeed, the bulk of urban public policymaking in America occurs off the policy cycle. These are minor alterations in public policies that are made continuously. Nevertheless, such minor changes can result in major policy changes over a relatively long period of time. These changes do not follow the sequenced stages of the policy cycle; they are made according to a very different process.

The difference between on-cycle and off-cycle policies is related to the amount of public attention they attract. Public policymaking in the glare of public attention is fundamentally different from policymaking away from the scrutiny of the media and the general public. Hence off-cycle policymaking tends to be far more routine and stable than on-cycle policymaking. We will return to an examination of off-cycle policymaking later in this chapter, after examining the policy cycle.

The cycle

Major public policy initiatives go through a cycle of action characterized by seven distinct stages: problem, issue, formulation, enactment, implementation, impact, and evaluation. This cycle (diagrammed in figure 2.1) describes how problems are (sometimes) translated into public policy. The cycle does not invariably operate on all problems, because of the six transition points between the stages. Not all policy proposals are enacted into public policy, and those that are enacted may not be implemented properly. Even if a policy is properly implemented, it may not yield the desired impact. Whatever the impact (or lack of it), people will evaluate the policy, perhaps positively, perhaps negatively. If the policy is malfunctioning, it may become a problem for so many people that government relief is sought.

The picture of policymaking as a well-behaved cycle is an abstraction. It is a way of simplifying and understanding an extremely complex process. The

Figure 2.1. The policy cycle.

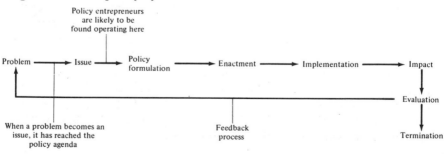

value of viewing the policy process as a cycle is threefold. First, the policy cycle aids us in understanding the translation of problems into social issues, into policy proposals. This part of the cycle shows just how a problem gains enough public attention to be taken seriously, and just how the issue gets framed so that government can consider it formally.

Second, the policy cycle suggests that there are several places in the policy process where proposals can be blocked or drastically altered. Opponents of a policy proposal may be able to stop the issue from being taken seriously. Failing that, they may be able to block formal consideration of the issue by government, or to defeat the proposal when it is considered by government for formal enactment. For example, they may be able to defeat the proposal when it comes up for a vote in the legislature or other policy-enacting body. If the proposal is passed over their opposition, all is still not lost. Opponents may be able to prevent meaningful implementation of the proposal, for example, by denying the new policy enough funds to operate.

Third, the policy process cycle incorporates *feedback*. Policies can create future problems for government. The impact of the policy, both intended and unintended, is evaluated by individuals. They may perceive that the policy has caused them problems and make further demands on government to rectify the situation. The policy process has now begun a second cycle. During the second (and subsequent) cycles, policy may be modified significantly. It is even possible for a policy to be terminated, but this is a rare occurrence.

Wheels

There is no single urban policy cycle in America. Policy cycles occur at all levels of government, in a variety of different governmental agencies. If the policy is social security, the relevant political system is the federal government. The policy could be a rule change by the state education agency. It could be the decision of a police department to change from two-person to one-person patrols. Or it could involve the decision of a municipal government to close down its public hospital for the poor.

A second important point is that different governments may be involved at different stages of the policy process. For example, federal domestic policymaking often works in this manner. A national objective is established by Congress, and money is made available. This money is granted to local governments, with certain conditions attached. The conditions established by the federal government are supposed to reflect national goals. The local governments can use the money as long as they conform to the conditions. The amount of discretion available to local governments depends on the particular policy, and is a matter of lively debate between the two major political parties, with Republicans tending to favor more discretion and Democrats tending to favor more supervision by the federal government. In either case, the national government is involved in the policy-formulation and policy-enactment stages of the cycle, and local governments are implementing organizations; the extent of local discretion determines to what extent national policies will be modified at the implementation stage. Domestic policies put into effect in this manner include federal grants for welfare, health, and urban development.

Perhaps the best analogy for all this would be "wheels within wheels." Imagine a system of wheels, some large and some small. The wheels are geared so that some spin faster than others. Some of the wheels spin freely, but most are locked together. The largest wheel represents the federal government; state and local governments are represented by smaller wheels. In particular, when one of the larger wheels spins, several of the smaller wheels spin. It is also possible for the smaller wheels to drive the larger.

As this analogy suggests, the policies of one government affect the policy-making processes of others. The picture can convey only a vague idea of the complexity of urban policymaking. This complexity stems from the multiplicity of local governments that operate in any city, along with the fact that other levels of government also affect the policies of local governments. We return to this governmental complexity in Part II.

Social Problems and the Policy Agenda

The policy cycle is an idealized model of the way in which social problems are translated into public policies. The first transition point in the movement of a problem through the policy cycle occurs when the problem captures the attention of a sizable segment of the public and becomes an issue. According to Anthony Downs, public problems tend to go through an "issue-attention cycle" characterized by differences in how much attention the public is paying to the issue.

> American public attention rarely remains sharply focused upon any one domestic issue for very long—even if it involves a continuing problem of crucial importance to society. Instead, a systematic "issue-attention cycle" seems strongly to influence public attitudes and behavior concerning most key domestic problems. Each of these problems suddenly leaps into prominence, remains there for a short time, and then—though largely unresolved—gradually fades from the center of public attention.[2]

[2] Anthony Downs, "Up and Down with Ecology—The Issue-Attention Cycle," *The Public Interest* 28 (Summer 1972): 38.

We may think of the issues that serve as the focus of public attention as a policy *agenda* for government. They are the problems that, because of public concern, government must consider seriously for policy action. Policy action may not be forthcoming on an issue, because opponents of policy action on the issue may be able to defeat the proponents of action at some point in the policymaking process. But the problem will at least experience a public debate, and it is likely to be ignored in the absence of such debate.

Social problems

Social problems, according to Charles Jones, are "human needs, however identified, that cannot be met privately." He goes on to argue that "human acts have consequences on others, and some of these are perceived to create need to the extent that relief is sought."[3] Problems are social because they arise when people interact with one another. Another term for a social problem is an *externality*. More precisely, an externality is a harm imposed on one citizen, or a group of citizens, by other citizens, when the harmed citizen has not agreed beforehand to bear the burden.

In many cases citizens, either explicitly or implicitly, agree to bear the cost of a harm imposed on them by other citizens. A person may be willing to take a job that is risky, but he will probably want to be paid more for assuming the risk than he would demand if the risk were not present. Another person may be willing to buy a used car, but she will not pay the same price as she would if the car were new. She realizes that there is risk in purchasing the car, a risk she would not be willing to assume in purchasing a new car. Or, to take a final example, a person may be willing to assume the burden of caring for an elderly parent. Such burdens or costs (or *risks* of burdens) are essentially private matters between "consenting adults," so to speak.

When an individual bears a burden that has been imposed without his or her consent, we have an externality. Externalities are the primary grist for government action, as people turn to government to relieve themselves of burdens they are not responsible for. But people have externalities imposed on them every day, and they bear them without complaining. Thus, not all social problems gain the attention of policymakers. What characterizes those that do? Under what conditions do people turn to government for aid in eliminating the externality?

This is not an easy question to answer. People must, of course, perceive themselves as being harmed, but this just pushes the question back one step. Just why people perceive themselves as being harmed is more a question of psychology than politics.

[3] Charles O. Jones, *An Introduction to the Study of Public Policy,* 2d ed. (North Scituate, Mass.: Duxbury, 1977), pp. 15–16.

A public problem is an externality that affects a sizable number of people. If many people are "externalized on," the basis for joint action is established. They may organize and try to get government to "do something." At this stage just what that something is may not be very well defined in the minds of the demanders. They just know they have a problem.

When a public problem becomes actively controversial, we refer to it as an *issue*. This means that, at present, a large number of people are concerned about the problem and have differing views about it. When a public problem is transformed into an issue, we say that it has reached the policy agenda.

Explaining just when and how a problem reaches the policy agenda is difficult. It is not always true that objective conditions, such as the actual quality of air or water, are deteriorating when problems reach the policy agenda. In some cases, objective conditions are actually improving. What has changed is people's expectations about what problems government should tackle.

But simply because people are concerned about an issue does not mean that government is actually considering action. Cobb and Elder distinguish between the *systemic* agenda, which is the set of issues that are actively controversial, and the *formal* agenda, matters on which the government is presently considering action.[4] In order for policy action to be taken, it is necessary that the problem be set for governmental action on the formal agenda. All problems on the systemic agenda do not reach the formal governmental agenda. Indeed, opponents of action on a problem may be able to keep an issue off the formal agenda. If they can do so, they will be able to forestall action on the issue, since action requires formal consideration. If, however, a problem remains on the systemic agenda, that is, is actively controversial, it is unlikely that government will be able to ignore it for very long.

Crisis.   If objective conditions deteriorate very rapidly, we have a *crisis*. Crises are very likely to reach the policy agenda quickly. Two classic cases of crises causing an urban problem to reach the policy agenda immediately are the urban civil disorders of the 1960s and the financial crises of cities of the 1970s.

The urban disorders of the late 1960s, which were especially severe in Los Angeles, Newark, and Detroit but which occurred in many cities with substantial black populations, brought the problems of northern blacks to the attention of policymakers. Prior to these disorders, efforts to improve the condition of blacks had been focused on the South, where segregation occurred by law (*de jure* segregation). After the disorders, the civil rights

4 Roger Cobb and Charles Elder, *Participation in American Politics: The Dynamics of Agenda-Building* (Boston: Allyn & Bacon, 1972).

movement turned north, focusing on the primarily *de facto* segregation in the large cities.

A rapid deterioration in conditions also was responsible for putting the financial crisis of cities on the policy agenda. After a decade of financial mismanagement, New York City's fiscal house of cards fell apart in 1975. The city could no longer borrow money to pay its bills. The underlying problem was quickly exposed: New York was deeply in debt and was not receiving enough income to cover operating expenses. The sources of the financial crisis were far deeper than financial mismanagement. New York, like many older northern cities, had been losing industry and middle-class residents to its suburbs and to other regions for years. At the same time, new migrants were coming to the city—primarily poor blacks and Puerto Ricans who consumed city services without contributing to the tax base. Finally, the demands of public employees for increased benefits were granted by the city during the "boom" periods of the 1960s without much regard for the future financial strain on the city.

As in the case of concern for urban blacks, the fiscal crisis of cities was rooted in social forces that had affected cities for years. A rapid change in objective conditions was responsible for putting the problem on the policy agenda.

Penetrability

Although it is true that not all problems that reach the policy agenda result in policy action, reaching the agenda is a precondition for action. In his study of the response of municipal governments to the problem of air pollution, Matthew Crenson found that it was difficult for industrial corporations, the chief opponents of municipal regulation of air quality, to block action once the issue was put on the policy agenda. But getting the issue on the policy agenda, where it was taken seriously by policymakers, was a difficult process for supporters of regulation. Moreover, industry had more influence at that stage of the process.[5]

The ease with which an issue can reach the policy agenda, where it will be scheduled for serious consideration, is known as the *penetrability* of the political system. Some political systems are more penetrable than others; in these systems it is easier for citizens to get a hearing. In addition, some issues are more likely to penetrate the system than others.

Penetrability is determined partly by the nature of the issue, partly by the credibility of the individual or group raising the issue, and partly by characteristics of the political system itself. In Detroit, when socialist city

[5] Matthew Crenson, *The Un-Politics of Air Pollution* (Baltimore: Johns Hopkins University Press, 1971).

councilman Kenneth Cockrell proposed that the city buy and run electric generating plants from Detroit Edison, the proposal was not really considered seriously; Mayor Coleman Young quickly rebuffed the idea. Certainly there was no widespread public concern with the issue. But when Mayor Young proposed using some of the city's future federal grant money to secure a bond issue that was used to build a parking garage to serve the new Joe Louis Arena, the issue was not only taken seriously by the city council but quickly passed, albeit with lively debate.

Displacement

Issues get off the policy agenda for three reasons. First, they get solved—or at least people perceive them to be solved—so that they no longer concern people. Second, even in the absence of governmental action on an issue, people may lose interest in it. Maintaining public concern on an issue is not easy; people have interests that are far removed from politics and may simply become disengaged. Finally, issues may get crowded off the agenda by concern for, say, inflation, which may in turn get displaced by a foreign policy crisis.

Figure 2.2 illustrates issue displacement. It graphs the percentage of people naming a given issue "the most important problem facing the country today." The line labeled "social issues" includes many of the problems we

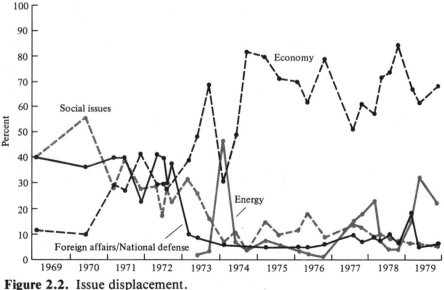

Figure 2.2. Issue displacement.

Source: Data from the Gallup Organization. Figure appeared in *Public Opinion* 3 (December/January 1980): 40. Copyright © 1980 by the American Enterprise Institute. Reprinted by permission.

think of as urban problems—crime, delinquency, riots, demonstrations, and so forth. In the late 1960s and early 1970s, these problems were on the public's mind, but by 1973 economic problems had displaced the urban problem from center stage. This does not mean that governments were not working on urban problems. It does mean that such work was going on out of the limelight of public attention. Moreover, in some places (for example, central cities in the Northeast) urban problems may have remained at the center of public concern. Remember that many separate policy cycles characterize urban policymaking.

Policy Formulation

In order for specific governmental action to be taken on a problem, an *exact* proposal for action must be specified. Translating the issue into a concrete policy proposal is known as *policy formulation*.

Someone must take on the responsibility of translating issues into proposals, and then shepherd the proposals through the often complex maze of the *formal* policy process (the actions that government takes on the policy). These shepherds of policy are known as *policy* (or issue) *entrepreneurs*. Robert Eyestone has characterized them in this manner:

> Along the line from issue generation to governmental response and issue resolution, there must be a number of critical people who facilitate movement in the issue translation process. Though their actions would not be sufficient to bring off the whole enterprise by themselves, these "issue entrepreneurs" are necessary parts of the process.[6]

Issue entrepreneurs exist inside and outside government. Inside, they may be politicians, such as mayors, city councilors, or members of Congress, or bureaucrats, such as agency heads, bureau chiefs, or legislative staff members. Outside government, they may be business people with a stake in the policy or lobbyists for interest groups, or citizens with an intense interest in an issue.

The responsibility for policy entrepreneurship may be individual or collective. In the former situation, a single individual, often with the support of others, serves as the primary entrepreneur. California businessman Howard Jarvis served this function for the tax limitation amendments to the California state constitution (known as Proposition 13) passed in 1978. The bombastic Jarvis stumped the state, decrying governmental wastefulness and getting signatures on his petition to put Proposition 13 before voters. Then, over the opposition of every major state politician, Governor Jerry Brown included, Jarvis raised the finances necessary for mounting a major public

---

[6] Robert Eyestone, *From Social Issues to Public Policy* (New York: John Wiley, 1978), pp. 88–89.

campaign to sell the proposition to voters. The proposition passed overwhelmingly.

In other cases, a number of people may take collective responsibility for policy formulation. When policy proposals come from government itself, often a task force will be established to formulate policy in a manner that can be presented to the formal policymaking branches of government (the chief executive and the legislative branches).

Sometimes a decision maker at one level of government will serve as an entrepreneur for an issue being considered at another level of government. For example, Carl Levin, then President of the Detroit City Council, became interested in the problem of home insurance redlining. Homeowners in many city neighborhoods were being denied home insurance (or being charged higher prices for reduced coverage) by insurance companies, based on neighborhood characteristics of the house to be insured. City government could not act on the problem, however, because insurance regulation is handled by state government. Levin organized city council hearings on redlining, pressured the State Insurance Commissioner to hold a formal fact-finding hearing, formulated the initial policy proposal, with the collaboration of concerned community groups got state legislators interested, helped shepherd the proposal through the legislature, and helped negotiate the compromise bill that finally passed.

Policy entrepreneurs are recruited from what Robert Dahl calls the *political stratum.*[7] This is a relatively small group of individuals for whom politics is a highly salient enterprise. Members of the political stratum are more rational in their approach to politics than are members of the apolitical strata. They have more information about politics than their nonpolitical counterparts; they communicate with one another; and they participate at far higher rates than do less politicized Americans. It is from among the members of this group that policy entrepreneurs emerge.

Policy Enactment

Once formulated, the policy proposal is ready for formal enactment. This stage is by no means automatic. First, the proposal must be scheduled for

[7] Robert A. Dahl, *Who Governs?* (New Haven, Conn.: Yale University Press, 1961), pp. 90–94.

Cleveland City Council President George Forbes presides as the clock above him reaches midnight, the hour at which the city defaulted on its legal obligations. On-cycle policymaking often takes place in an atmosphere of high drama.

Source: AP Wirephoto, December 17, 1978.

debate, or put on the formal governmental agenda. Then the period of intense formal scrutiny of the proposal begins. Now is the time for pure politics: negotiation, political pressure, conflict, compromise. During this period the proposal may go through substantial modification as leaders search for a form that will attract the support of a winning coalition. On the other hand, in some cases a proposal may move through the enactment stage without major modification.

Many policies do not survive the enactment stage. Once they get to the

---

Box 2.1: The High Tide of
Welfare Reform

On August 8, 1969, President Richard M. Nixon announced to the nation that he was proposing to Congress the establishment of a guaranteed income. This was the most ambitious attempt at welfare reform in the thirty-four years that had passed since the establishment of the basic system of welfare by Roosevelt's New Deal coalition. Nixon's Family Assistance Plan (FAP), as it was called, would have replaced America's patchwork welfare system with a single system. Every individual would have been guaranteed an income "floor." If a person earned no income, he or she would be paid an amount equal to the floor. As the individual earned more money, the payments would be reduced until at some point, which was called the "break-even point," the individual would receive no government support.

The idea of a guaranteed income, or "negative income tax," as it was called, had been discussed seriously in governmental and academic circles for some years. It appealed to liberals, who saw an opportunity to extend basic welfare guarantees to the "working poor." It also attracted significant support among conservatives (or at least among conservative economists) who believed that the existing categorical welfare system produced severe work disincentives. Gradually reducing welfare payments, rather than abruptly removing them, could ease a person off the welfare system and into the productive economic sector.

The Family Assistance Plan attracted strong opposition also. Most opponents were rural conservatives who held powerful posi-

Source: See Daniel P. Moynihan, *The Politics of a Guaranteed Income* (New York: Vintage Books, 1973).

enactment stage, however, they usually are not laid to rest without considerable clamor.

We have an irony here. Many policies that traverse the policy cycle this far sail through the enactment stage unscathed, but few die quietly. This is because the political mobilization necessary to get an issue this far continues to the enactment stage and cannot easily be sidetracked. Opponents may mobilize to fight the issue; if they do, we may observe a political "battle royal" (see box 2.1).

---

tions in Congress. They objected to "paying people not to work," as they put it. They generally felt that categorical assistance, such as Aid to Families with Dependent Children, and Aid to the Blind, was justifiable, because it covered those who could not work. But they did not favor extending welfare to the able-bodied poor.

FAP also generated liberal opposition, primarily from social work professionals, who saw guaranteed income as a threat to their jobs, and welfare rights organizations. These groups argued that the guarantee levels (income floors), which were keyed to family size, were too low, and they objected to the provision that any person receiving welfare would have to register with a state employment agency and accept suitable employment if offered. Some blacks feared that such a provision would be used to force blacks into demeaning jobs.

Under the steady stewardship of Wilbur Mills, Chairman of the House Ways and Means Committee,* FAP sailed through the House of Representatives by a two-thirds majority. FAP was sent to the Senate Finance Committee for action. The Nixon administration was able to persuade the Committee Chairman, Russell Long of Louisiana, to support FAP, although never with enthusiasm. The key vote on whether to report the bill to the full Senate was scheduled on November 20, 1970. An alliance of rural Republicans, southern Democrats, and liberal Democrats doomed welfare reform in a dramatic 10–6 vote. Of the six committee votes in favor, only one was from a northern Democratic liberal—Abraham Ribicoff of Connecticut. The bedrock opposition had been from rural conservatives, but liberals apparently undecided up to the last minute held the balance of power on the committee. Then a raucous demonstra-

---

*FAP was technically a revenue measure and had to originate in the House and be considered by the Ways and Means Committee.

Policy Implementation

With enactment, public attention to the issue often fades. Yet policy success is not guaranteed with enactment, as many mayors, governors, and even presidents have found.

Implementation of public policy involves two distinct aspects.[8] First, new

[8] A rich literature has developed around the concept of policy implementation. See Jeffrey Pressman and Aaron Wildavsky, *Implementation* (Berkeley, Calif.: University of California Press, 1973); Eugene Bardach, *The Implementation Game* (Cambridge, Mass.: MIT Press,

---

tion at the Senate Office Building organized by George Wiley's National Welfare Rights Organization seems to have tipped the balance against the bill for Fred Harris, a liberal from Oklahoma. With Harris went the vote, since he carried two proxy votes to the committee room with him—those of McCarthy of Minnesota and Gore of Tennessee. Had these votes been cast in favor, FAP would have been reported to the full Senate for debate. Apparently Harris also influenced the nay vote of Anderson of New Mexico. In an orgy of irresponsibility, Hartke of Indiana, another liberal, neither voted nor cast a proxy.

Welfare reform reached its high tide in the Senate Finance Committee on November 20, 1970. Neither before nor since has welfare reform occupied such a high priority on the national political agenda. But this did not mean that welfare reform was dead; it just moved off cycle. In the next several sessions of Congress, several very important changes in the welfare system were enacted—changes that passed almost unnoticed by the press. One was the passage of *Supplemental Security Income,* which consolidated several categories of aid (aid to the disabled and the blind and general assistance for the elderly), and provided a guaranteed income for these people. Perhaps even more significant was the institution, at the urging of Senator Russell Long, of the *earned income tax credit.* This is a provision of the tax code that allows families whose income is below $10,000 income tax reduction of up to $500. It is a subsidy of the working poor; a principle that conservatives violently objected to when it was presented to them as a welfare plan. It is not uncommon for principles that have been defeated during the heated political battles characteristic of the policy cycle to reemerge in off-cycle policymaking.

procedures must be established in order to meet the goals set by the new policy. This often means that new government agencies are formed. In such cases, staff must be recruited, office space found, and work routines established. Ties with other agencies, legislative leaders, and chief executives must be formed. Sometimes a policy is implemented by using existing government agencies. This can simplify the implementation process, but if too many diverse programs are assigned to one agency, conflict among the various programs can result. Specific programs must be established to set in motion the specific government action implied by the policy. Usually legislatures enact broad authorizations for action, and it is up to government bureaucracies to translate the broad policy into specific programs.

A second aspect of implementation is securing money for the new policy. Just because a legislature has authorized a new policy does not mean that the funds necessary for implementing the policy will be automatically forthcoming. In America, at the federal, state, and local levels, the policy authorization process (the policy cycle) is separate from the appropriations process. Hence policy enactment is not enough. Supporters of a policy must get funds appropriated in order to put a new policy into effect.

Policy change

Because public attention usually declines after policy enactment, the policy can be changed dramatically at the implementation stage. Out of public scrutiny, policies may be modified in a manner that is not at all in keeping with the initial aims of the policy. Different interests become active at this stage of the policy process, interests that may not have been vocal earlier. Public employees unions, for example, may not be very active during the debate over the adoption of a policy, but may become very vocal when employee work rules are being established in the new agency. Moreover, the officials responsible for implementing a policy may not share the enthusiasm for the policy that its original supporters had. These administrators can subtly (or not so subtly) change the program to suit their interests.

Interests that are influential at the policy enactment stage may lose influence during the implementation stage. This is illustrated by Stone's study of economic redevelopment policies in Atlanta.[9] Redevelopment policies pitted business executives interested in growth and expansion against

---

1977); Daniel Mazmanian and Paul Sabatier, eds., "Symposium on Successful Policy Implementation," *Policy Studies Journal* 8 (1980); Walter Williams and Richard Elmore, eds., *Studying Implementation* (Chatham, N.J.: Chatham House, 1982); Carl Van Harn, *Policy Implementation in the Federal System* (Lexington, Mass.: Lexington Books, 1979); George C. Edwards III, *Implementing Public Policy* (Washington, D.C.: *Congressional Quarterly*, 1980).

[9] Clarence Stone, *Economic Growth and Neighborhood Discontent* (Chapel Hill, N.C.: University of North Carolina Press, 1976).

neighborhood groups interested in policies to maintain and upgrade residential neighborhoods. In the enactment stage of the policy process, probusiness interests enjoyed no advantage over the neighborhood groups. But during the implementation stage, probusiness interests were more influential than neighborhood interests. Even more striking was the influence of business interests during the agenda-setting stage. Stone describes this stage as involving a "demand screening" process in which the possible options are culled to yield a smaller number, which are placed on the formal agenda for government action. This suggests a more general principle: neighborhood interests enjoyed relative advantage when there was heightened conflict and media coverage; business interests enjoyed relative advantage during the quieter stages of policy process.

In general, the relative power of groups can and does change as the policy cycle moves from one stage to the next. This is why a policy as implemented can look so different from the policy either as originally proposed or as enacted.

Implementing federal programs

Many problems in the implementation of federal programs stem from intergovernmental relations. It is often the case that the national government (or state governments) enact policies, leaving their implementation to local governments. Generally, for federal urban programs national policy is established in Washington, but policy implementation is left to the state and local governments. Usually the federal government does not order the states and localities to implement a policy. Indeed, given our federal form of government, it generally cannot do so. Rather, the federal government makes money available to localities if they will adopt the procedures necessary to implement national policy.

Because the federal government deals with separate local governments with significant autonomous power, implementation of federal policies often does not go smoothly. This is especially true if local policymakers perceive local interests to be different from what federal policymakers have in mind.

One area in which different interests between federal and local decision makers have led to conflict over program implementation is manpower training programs. Under the regulations established to implement the Comprehensive Employment Training Act (CETA), passed by Congress in 1974, local governments could hire people, but were supposed either to fund them from the local budget or to terminate the jobs after a limited period of time (eighteen months). This was mandated because the act was conceived as a program that would provide temporary employment while individuals acquired the skills necessary to compete in the job market. Local governments, on the other hand, saw CETA as a way to supplement at no extra cost the services they provide to their citizens. Given these contradictory interests, conflict was inevitable. Mayors complained bitterly as administrators from the Federal Department of Labor, which was responsible for implementing CETA, tried to enforce the time limits for public sector employment.[10]

Policy Impact and Policy Evaluation

Policy *impacts* are differences in social, economic, and political conditions caused by a policy. Does the new program developed by the police department reduce criminal activity in the city? Can federal housing programs stem housing abandonment in the central city? What are the consequences of school integration programs ordered by the federal courts?

Policies can have both anticipated and unanticipated consequences. Moreover, a policy usually has multiple impacts. This means that it affects several social and economic conditions at once. A policy can also change governmental and political conditions. This is often the case, for example, when federal policies require local governments to cooperate in order to implement the policy.

Each consequence of a policy has benefits and costs associated with it. When various groups and individuals estimate these costs and benefits, we say that the policy has been *evaluated*. Normally, policies yield different costs and benefits for different people, so that the policy evaluation process is essentially subjective. The pattern of costs and benefits imposed on different groups and individuals is known as the *distributional effects* of the policy.

There are two issues in the policy impact and evaluation process. The first issue is whether the policy did what it was supposed to do. This is a question of impact. The second is whether the policy yields more benefits than costs. This is a question of evaluation.

Impact

Questions of impact are questions of fact—that is, they are *empirical*. They can, in principle, be answered by careful study. It is not always easy to estimate the impact of a policy, because government policies are not the only cause of the social and economic conditions that policies are intended to af-

---

[10] On the linkage between national priorities and local politics, see Randall B. Ripley and Donald C. Baumer, "National Politics, Local Politics, and Public Service Employment," in Charles Levine, ed., *Managing Human Resources* (Beverly Hills, Calif.: Sage Publications, 1977), pp. 271–94.

The impacts of public policies are seldom easy to determine. The impact of police patrolling became controversial after the institution of foot patrols in. high crime neighborhoods in New York's 23rd precinct. While the precinct commander claimed that the precinct crime rate was down, rank and file police officers contended that the program just pushed criminal activity from one area to another.

Source: The New York Times, June 1, 1982, p. B1.

fect (the *goals* of the policy). Policy goals have many causes, and government policy is only one of these. The situation looks like this:

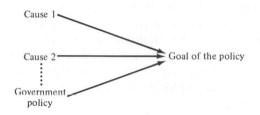

Because so many factors can produce the state of affairs termed the goal of the policy, it is often very difficult to tell whether a particular policy has achieved its goal, or whether other factors are responsible. For example, suppose a city police department initiates a new crime prevention program, and the crime rate goes down. Did the program cause the crime rate to go down, or was it a decline in the unemployment rate? (When the unemployment rate goes down, crime tends to go down, and vice versa.) How about other factors?

A policy can also have multiple impacts. Even if a policy achieves its stated goal, it may also have other, often unanticipated, consequences. These consequences can be desirable or undesirable. An example of such unanticipated consequences may be taken from federal tax laws. Congress has passed tax laws that allow businesses to deduct the cost of buildings, machinery, and other facilities from their federal income taxes. This deduction cannot be taken all at once, but must be spread out over a number of years, the life of the facility for tax purposes. This is called *depreciation. Accelerated depreciation* occurs when the tax life of a facility is shortened by congressional action, which is sometimes done in order to encourage businesses to build new facilities. Thus the government uses the tax laws to stimulate economic activity and promote efficiency.

The undesirable side consequences are these. Older facilities tend to be

A Month of Robberies
In Precinct 23

Data for April 1982
Source: Police Department

110th ST
109th ST
108th ST
107th ST
106th ST
105th ST
104th ST
103rd ST
102nd ST
101st ST
100th ST
99th ST
98th ST
97th ST
96th ST
95th ST
94th ST
93rd ST
92nd ST
91st ST
90th ST
89th ST
88th ST
87th ST
86th ST

Mt.
Sinai
Hospital

Precinct 23
station house

Fire
House
No. 53

Metropolitan
Hospital

CENTRAL PARK

5th AVENUE
MADISON AVENUE
PARK AVENUE
LEXINGTON AVENUE
THIRD AVENUE
SECOND AVENUE
FIRST AVENUE
YORK AVENUE

FRANKLIN D. ROOSEVELT DRIVE

HARLEM
RIVER

EAST
RIVER

Gracie
Mansion
Doctors
Hospital

Guggenheim
Museum

CARL SCHURZ PARK

Types of
Robberies

■ Street
● Indoor
□ Housing Project
▲ Subway Station
○ Commercial
▬ Robbery Overtime
Foot Posts

The New York Times

Edward Hausner/The New York Times

located in older cities. New facilities tend to be built in suburbs. Hence, by allowing accelerated depreciation, the federal government is sponsoring deconcentration and the decline of central cities as old facilities are closed, and generally contributing to the problems of cities.

The situation looks like this:

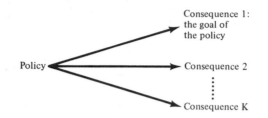

Evaluation

The policy evaluation process, by assessing costs and benefits, involves *values* and is therefore much more subjective than assessing impacts. To decide whether a policy is worth the effort being put into it, we would have to add up all benefits for all people for each consequence of the policy. We would do the same for all costs, and then we would compare them.

There are two ways in which government can evaluate policies. First, it can attempt some comprehensive estimate of the value of the policy by experts in such areas as economics, engineering, psychology, and urban planning. Second, it can rely on the political process, believing that people will react to policies by offering support or placing new demands on government, depending on how they evaluate the policy.

Experts. In the case of evaluation by experts, government officials try to compare the costs and benefits of the policy based on the methods and models developed by experts in policy evaluation. This evaluation can take place prior to a policy enactment, or it can take place after the policy has been in operation for a time. These forms of evaluation are called *prospective* and *retrospective* evaluation.

There are two problems with evaluation by experts. First, the experts can be wrong. Urban social systems are complex, and there is no guarantee that the approaches used by experts diagnose correctly urban ills. One expert in urban analysis, Professor Jay Forrester of the Massachusetts Institute of Technology, has noted that the complexity of urban systems hampers the solution of urban problems because causes and effects can be far removed in time and space:

> In the complex system, when we look for a cause near in time and space to a symptom, we usually find what appears to be a plausible cause. But it is usually

not the cause. The complex system presents apparent causes that are in fact coincident symptoms. The high degree of time correlation between variables in complex systems can lead us to make cause-and-effect associations between variables that are simply moving together as part of the total dynamic behavior of the system. . . . As a result, we treat symptoms, not causes.[11]

Forrester was defending expert evaluation in his comments on the complexity of urban systems. Unfortunately, however, expert analyses are often wrong or misleading in their solutions to systems of human action that are as complex as the modern city.

There is a second problem with evaluation by experts. How are experts going to know what the costs and benefits of a policy are to individual citizens? And, in a form of government purporting to be democratic, does not the opinion of citizens matter? What happens if the solutions to urban problems recommended by experts clash with the expressed wishes of a majority of citizens?

Politics. If we do not trust government to evaluate its own policies, we might turn to the political process. It may be reasonable to assume that people will organize and try to change policies that they view negatively, and defend those policies that they view positively.

There are three problems with this approach. First, different groups have different amounts of power with which to influence the political process. Is it fair to leave policy evaluation up to a power struggle, if resources differ among groups?

Second, individual citizens live in the same complex social system that experts do. They may well be aware of the symptoms of a social problem but be quite unaware of the complex system of social causation that leads to the state of affairs making them dissatisfied. Policies may be demanded that make the situation worse by treating symptoms rather than causes.

Third, who speaks for social benefits and costs? Groups are organized around individual interests and are unlikely defenders of the public interest. Hence, the policies evaluated and adopted in the normal course of the political process may diverge from what might improve things in general. Such a divergence could come about because urban social systems are complex and people do not recognize the potential of achieving a collective good. Or the divergence may stem from the fact that a policy may yield the "greatest good for the greatest number," but the minority that will be harmed is better organized and more effective than the majority that will be helped. In either case, the solution dictated by the political process will differ from that dictated from a more comprehensive evaluation of the potentials of the policy.

[11] Jay W. Forrester, *Urban Dynamics* (Cambridge, Mass.: MIT Press, 1969), pp. 9–10.

There are thus limits to both forms of policy evaluation. Expert analysis can yield the wrong solution and can lead to undemocratic policymaking. Reliance on the political process can yield the wrong solution, and it can fail to represent the public interest.

Policy evaluation in America today is a complex interplay between these two forms of evaluation. It is not necessarily the case that this interplay yields an optimum urban policy. What does happen is that expert opinion becomes a part of the political process, and experts compete alongside other groups in affecting policy outcomes. Economists, engineers, and other experts often testify before policymaking bodies as representatives of the various groups that are interested in instituting or changing a policy. Expert opinion is often divided, and each side can marshall expert opinion in favor of its position. This does not mean that expert analysis is useless, only that it is politicized. Indeed, experts may be better at clarifying urban problems than they are at formulating policy solutions.

Feedback

Policy evaluation is important because it can lead to modification or even termination of existing policies. Government, through its efforts at evaluation, may discover problems with the policy as it is implemented, and try to change it. Or interest groups and citizens may force the issue back onto the policy agenda because of problems they are encountering with the policy. Such reactions take place both inside and outside government. Many times those reacting to a policy will be members of the governmental agency responsible for administering the policy. At other times it will be members of another agency, perhaps at another level of government, who are encountering problems. If the policy is forced back on the policy agenda for serious reconsideration, the policy cycle begins a *second* revolution. When policy evaluation has this effect, we term the process *feedback*.

A second (or third or fourth) revolution of the policy cycle means that the social problem government is dealing with has not been solved. Rather, in trying to solve the problem government has caused more problems, problems that clamor for attention. Aaron Wildavsky has called this phenomenon "policy as its own cause."[12] Each attempt to solve a social problem by government causes more problems, and the larger the policy solution, the more new problems it generates.

As government tries to solve more and more social problems, action by government also can cause new problems for another government (or create new opportunities). This generally happens when the federal government acts, causing all sorts of problems and opportunities for state and local governments, but actions by local governments can also cause problems for federal government.

[12] Aaron Wildavsky, *Speaking Truth to Power: The Art and Craft of Policy Analysis* (Boston: Little, Brown, 1979), Ch. 3.

Off-Cycle Policymaking

Not all policymaking takes place on the policy cycle. Most public decisions are made *off* the policy cycle. *Off-cycle* policies do not receive the necessary public attention to get them on the public agenda. They remain hidden from public view, not because anyone is trying to hide them, but because not very many people are very interested. Off-cycle policies generally affect very few people directly (although their indirect effect may be considerable).

Off-cycle policymaking usually occurs after a government agency has been established to deal with a public problem. After the policy cycle has moved into the implementation stage, the issue usually fades from public attention. This does not mean that government is inactive on the issue. Policymaking does, however, take a fundamentally different form off the cycle. As public attention declines, and the media become concerned with other public issues, the conflict, coalition building, and appeals to abstract symbols are replaced by routine ways of doing things and relatively small changes in existing policies.

Until the recent concern with deregulation, almost all the economic regulatory policies of the federal government could be characterized as off cycle. Normally a city government's allocation of police officers to neighborhoods is not a matter of public concern, yet it represents very critical policy decisions. The federal government's agricultural subsidy and loan programs periodically generate attention, but the attention never seems intense enough to transform this problem into a social issue. Few citizens, except those architects and builders who are directly affected, are concerned with the building and housing codes that local governments enact. Normally government budgeting is conducted far off the policy cycle, but when the size of overall governmental expenditures becomes an issue, budgeting can become highly politicized. (This happened in the spring of 1981 with President Reagan's successful budget reductions.) Then budgeting also is characterized by the sequenced stages of the policy cycle.

For off-cycle policies, popular mobilization has not been sufficient to translate problems into social issues. Policy entrepreneurs are either not active or are not able to generate enough support to place the issue on the policy agenda.

Off-cycle policymaking tends to be both routine and incremental. *Routine* policymaking occurs when all actors involved in the process, actors both within government and outside it, follow standard rules, called *decision rules,* in making decisions. The rules specify in advance how the actors are supposed to behave. Sometimes these rules are written down, but often they are not. Actors generally understand the rules and abide by them.[13]

---

[13] On decision-making routines in government, see Ira Sharkansky, *Routines in Politics* (New York: Van Nostrand Reinhold, 1970).

One example of routine policymaking is the provision of certain federal grants to local governments. Congress has established a set formula for disbursing some grants. The federal decision makers in charge of disbursement need only consult the formula to decide, for example, how much money Memphis is to receive. The formula differs for different kinds of grants. Some are based only on population; others take need into consideration. But the formula governs the decisionmakers' behavior in either case.

Another example of routine policymaking is the provision of municipal services. Once a municipality decides to provide a service (say, fire services), the routines are established to determine who is to receive the service, under what conditions it is to be delivered, and how services are to be made available.

Incremental policymaking is characterized by small changes in existing policies. When a policy is on cycle, political actors tend to "think big." Major government action is contemplated by many people. Although major change may not come about, it is seriously considered. When a policy is off the cycle, however, major change is almost never contemplated. Rather, decisionmakers tend to consider small changes in the prevailing routines. Usually they are motivated to do so because of the problems they are encountering in the way things are working. So they try something a little bit different, wait a while, and check the results.

Just because incrementalism involves small changes rather than large ones does not mean the results are insignificant. Small changes can quickly add up to large ones. The growth of government's role in society, for example, has been basically incremental, interrupted only by abrupt changes in which government takes on major new responsibilities. (The latter are acquired on the cycle.)

Incrementalism carries with it certain definite benefits.[14] First, the action is reversible (or at least more so than the major policy changes taken on the policy cycle) if the new policy fails to correct the problem. Second, compromise is made more feasible by the limited nature of the change. Losers do not lose all, as they may with on-cycle policies. Third, away from the glare of public attention, decision makers are less likely to feel forced to "play to the audience." They can drop the public posturing that often characterizes their behaviors when the television cameras are on and get down to the business of governing. Fourth, incrementalism does not require broad agreement on goals to work. People need only agree that a problem exists and that the new policy will do some good.

Off-cycle policymaking does carry with it one very important limitation.

---

[14] The benefits of incrementalism as a method of making policy have been most cogently described by Charles Lindblom, "The Science of Muddling Through," *Public Administration Review* 29 (Spring 1959): 79–88. See also Aaron Wildavsky, *The Politics of the Budgetary Process,* 3rd ed. (Boston: Little, Brown, 1979).

When policies are off cycle, a very important political advantage becomes available to those interests that are continuously organized for political action. Some groups get organized for the "big fight" over an on-cycle policy, then disappear when the policy moves off the cycle. Others that are always around, making their preferences known to policymakers, have disproportionate influence in the off-cycle policy process.

These continuously organized groups tend to be unrepresentative. They include business and professional groups, such as real estate developers, lawyers, and organized labor. On the other hand, occupants of public housing, renters of tenements, and transient laborers are usually not organized on a continuous basis. One strategy these groups employ is to try to get an off-cycle policy on the public agenda, where they will have more influence. They often do so through protest activities. We return to the role of interest groups in the urban policy process in chapter 7.

Conclusions

The policy process can be viewed as a cycle in which social problems become issues, the issues are formulated into policy proposals, and policy proposals are enacted into law. This does not end the process, however. Policies must be implemented, and the policy may be changed substantially at the implementation stage of the policy process.

Once put into effect, a policy has consequences for people. How they evaluate these consequences, or impacts, determines whether they will make further demands on government. If they do make further demands, the policy cycle may begin a second revolution.

The policy cycle characterizes policymaking in which there is considerable public attention. A substantial segment of the public is aware of the issue, and a number of interested, organized groups are active. Such public attention does not always characterize the policymaking process. Much policy is made off cycle, out of the glare of public attention. There, a very different decision-making process emerges, a process characterized by incrementalism and bureaucratic routine.[15]

---

[15] This chapter has highlighted some essentials of the study of public policies. For fuller (and different) treatments, see Jones, *Public Policy;* Robert L. Lineberry, *American Public Policy* (New York: Harper & Row, 1977); James Anderson, David Brady, and Charles Bullock, III, *Public Policy and Politics in America* (North Scituate, Mass.: Duxbury, 1978); Thomas R. Dye, *Understanding Public Policy,* 4th ed. (Englewood Cliffs, N.J.: Prentice-Hall, 1981), and James Anderson, *Public Policy-Making* (New York: Praeger, 1975).

CHAPTER 3

The Special Character
of Urban Policymaking

Chapter 2 presented a general overview of the policymaking process. For the most part, that overview would fit any policymaking process—within city governments, to be sure, but also within state and national governments, local service delivery organizations, and even private corporations, political clubs, and interest groups. Unless a government somewhere, at some time, at least ratifies the action, of course, the policy would not qualify as a public policy. But if the policy process took place somewhere within government, and if all the legal requirements for government action were fulfilled, then the policy would qualify as a public policy.

What, then, is distinctive about urban policymaking? There are three distinguishing characteristics of the urban policymaking process, characteristics that give urban policymaking its unique flavor. Interestingly enough, urban policymaking is not simply policy pursued by urban governments. State and national governments pursue urban policies, and the United States government has a cabinet-level department whose programs deal primarily with urban policies: the Department of Housing and Urban Development (HUD). Nor do urban policies affect just cities, although they tend to affect them more than they affect rural areas or small towns. Many nonurban places have problems we tend to think of as urban—crime, housing decay—and many urban policies are designed to alleviate such problems.

The three distinguishing characteristics of urban policymaking are:

1. *Urban policymaking deals most directly with the issue of limited government.* Because local governments are the primary deliverers of services (even when the local government is only an administrative unit of a larger government), they must deal more intimately with citizens than the more remote state and national governments. They are also the primary repositories of the *police power,* which grants governments the authority to coerce individual citizens for the good of the general public. Hence local governments regularly must decide, in specific situations involving real people, when and how to employ government coercion.

2. *In the urban policy process, policy distribution is achieved primarily through location.* Costs and benefits that stem from the policymaking process are distributed to citizens through the effects the policy has on the location of residences, commercial and industrial enterprises, and public facilities. A key test of whether a policy is locational is whether the benefits received change when the person receiving them moves. We do not normally conceive of the minimum wage law as an urban policy, because the benefits and costs of that law are passed on to people according to their economic station in life (primarily whether the person is an employee or an employer). A person can move from city to city and still be affected by the law. On the other hand, suppose a city locates a new public housing project in a neighborhood. Someone can reap the benefits of such housing only by moving into it—that is, by relocating. A resident offended by the housing may leave the neighborhood for a residence not so close to the project. He or she has been affected by the location of the project and can change the effect by moving.

   Or take another example. Many states and cities are now engaged in a spirited competition for jobs and industries. Many communities are trying to lure new industry by all sorts of public policies: lower taxes for new industry, job training programs, site clearance aid, loans and grants.[1] These policies are explicitly locational: the goals of the policies are to shift industry around from community to community (and state to state and region to region). No new industry is created; only shifting occurs. Such policies are urban policies.

[1] See Barry Bluestone, Bennett Harrison, and Lawrence Baker, *Corporate Flight: The Causes and Consequences of Economic Location* (Washington, D.C.: Progressive Alliance, 1981); Lynn Bachelor, "Urban Economic Development: Issues and Policies," *Urban Affairs Quarterly* 16 (December 1981).

3. *Urban policymaking is characterized by special relations among units of government.* In the United States almost all local units of government possess real policymaking power. They are not simply administrative units of state or national government. Although legal theory affirms that cities are legal entities within states, in practice states allow a great deal of discretion to local governments most of the time. Policy arrangements among local governments therefore involve a great deal of negotiation and bargaining—normally no unit of government is in a position to impose its will uniformly on other units.

Choice and Coercion: The Issue of Limited Government

Public policymaking results in a temporary resolution of the issue of limited government. Any public policy carries with it, explicitly or implicitly, a theory about the proper level of governmental intervention in the community. When citizens vote on a new school millage to support increased educational expenditures, when the mayor and city council vote to issue municipal bonds to finance new fire stations, when President Reagan supports a reduction in federal aid to states and cities, and when the mayor of Jackson, Mississippi, signs an agreement to provide incentives to a plant that is relocating from Pennsylvania, the issue of limited government is resolved, if only fleetingly.

Each time a resolution of the issue is achieved, one of three things happens: resources are taken from the private sector of society and transferred to the public sector; resources are taken from the public sector and transferred to the private sector; or public resources are shifted so that they benefit people other than those whom they were benefiting previously.

When citizens approve a new school millage, resources are transferred from the private sector to the public or governmental sector. Because governments do different things than do individuals, groups, and corporations acting privately, we get a different *social allocation* of activities. We get, for example, more schools and fewer consumer goods. This is because at any given time, there is only a finite amount of social resources (money, time, effort) available. If there is an increase in support for schools, there must be a corresponding loss in support for some other activities.

When the federal government cuts its support for aid to cities, and lowers taxes rather than reallocating the funds to defense or other governmental activity, resources are transferred from the public sector to the private sector. We get more consumer goods and fewer police and firefighters. When Jackson, Mississippi, offers a package of incentives to a Philadelphia businessman, public resources are shifted from citizens and residents to the business community. To provide the businessman with his incentives, either city services must be cut or taxes must be raised. In either case, the relative distribution of benefits and burdens has shifted.

Finally, governmental decisions can shift resources to fulfill different public objectives. One of President Reagan's first actions as president was to increase spending for national defense while simultaneously cutting expenditures for urban and other social programs.

Government, coercion, and public choice

We live, it is said, in an "era of limits." No longer are we, as a nation, able to do all we want to do. We also live in an era of immense social problems: inflation, stagnating economy, an unstable world order, poverty amidst affluence, deteriorating cities, high unemployment, and strained racial relations, to suggest but a few. Some of these problems probably cannot be alleviated, much less solved, by government. Others were probably caused in large part by government. Some are likely to improve under sustained governmental effort, but not sufficiently to be worth the sacrifice involved. Still others can be alleviated by government and are clearly worth the cost. For these problems, some solutions cannot be implemented because they are not politically feasible; that is, they are opposed by the majority or by powerful organized minority interests.

Simply because there are social problems does not mean that government ought to act. Urban America is replete with examples of problems made worse by government action.[2] Some, but by no means all, government housing programs have actually increased housing abandonment in cities by vesting ownership in individuals who lacked the steady income to pay for continual maintenance. Lovely urban parks have become home to youth gangs. Crackdowns by city health and building inspectors can put small, productive enterprises out of business.

Yet urban America is also replete with examples of problems that were, quite simply, solved by government. Indeed, in most of these cases, the problems could not have been solved in the absence of government action. Perhaps the greatest achievement of American local governments is something taken completely for granted today: the provision of clean water and sanitary sewerage systems. Less than a century ago residents of American cities could count on neither, and experienced the constant threat of typhus and tuberculosis as a consequence.

It is not possible to list the problems that can be effectively and efficiently alleviated by government. If such a listing were possible, we could easily answer the question of how much government intervention to allow. The

---

[2] See Gordon Tullock, "The Social Costs of Reducing Social Cost," in *Managing the Commons,* ed. Garrett Harden and John Baden (San Francisco: Freeman, 1977).

issue of the limits of government intervention is a crucial one because governments possess the power to coerce citizens. Properly harnessed coercion can be used to get citizens to cooperate for the public good. Improperly used, coercion becomes oppression.

Put starkly, a government is a social organization whose reason for existing is coercion. Government is in the business of using force (or the threat of force) to get citizens to do things that they would not otherwise do. The best governments use their power to achieve goals that benefit the community. The worst use their coercive powers to achieve private ends.

If people could achieve their collective goals by freely cooperating, governments would be unnecessary. Alas, they cannot. This basic fact of social life does not mean that human nature is basically selfish and uncooperative. In modern society people have different goals, and in pursuing those goals they often infringe on the rights of other citizens. Governments exist in the first instance to limit these infringements and in the second to channel the energies of citizens pursuing individual goals toward collective goals that will improve the lot of all citizens.

In many cases, government coercion promotes the general welfare. We are all better off, for example, because government establishes and enforces traffic laws. Imagine the chaos that would result if each citizen chose which side of the road to drive on, whether to stop at intersections, and how fast to travel! In other cases, government causes people to act in ways they perceive to be contrary to their interests, and backs up its action by threatening them with loss of liberty, property, or even life if they do not accede. Even this coercion may be in the public interest, since the desires of a minority often have to be sacrificed for the good of the majority. But let us be clear about such situations: government is being used to coerce a minority into doing something it would not otherwise do. Such policies ought to be entered into cautiously. Because such situations involve differences of preferences and values concerning the use of government, conflict often emerges. Such conflict is called politics.

Many social organizations use coercion. Families punish their children, businesses fire their employees, churches threaten their members with expulsion. Two things set government coercion apart, however. First, government generally gives us no choice about whether we comply with its directives. It backs up its commands with severe consequences. If an employee of a private firm is threatened with firing, he or she may choose whether to comply with the order or to search for other suitable employment. Government, however, gives us no choice about whether we pay our taxes. Government can physically coerce us if we do not pay, something that the private business cannot legally do.

The second thing that sets government coercion apart is that citizens generally feel that it is right and proper for government to exercise that coercion. People believe that it is proper for government to jail an individual for not paying taxes; they would feel very differently if a private business incarcerated a citizen for not buying the firm's products. The feeling that governments are the proper instruments for coercing citizens is termed a *sense of legitimacy.* When governments enjoy a sense of legitimacy, people generally obey without having to be coerced. In such cases government power over people, which is rooted in coercion, is referred to as *authority.* Where governmental legitimacy is strong, the link between coercion and authority goes almost unnoticed.

Governments do not everywhere enjoy the support of their citizens. At some places in some times, a substantial number of citizens may feel that government illegitimately coerces them. The sense of legitimacy broke down among blacks in urban America in the 1960s, when widespread violent civil disobedience occurred in such cities as Los Angeles, Newark, Detroit, Washington, D.C., and Chicago. This violence was almost always triggered by an act of government (often a policeman arresting a citizen) that would normally be viewed by most citizens as a legitimate act; but that was not the case for at least some blacks at that time.

Local governments and coercion

Local governments in the United States exert more coercion, on a daily basis, than either state governments or the federal government. Consider some examples.

- They maintain standing police forces for use against citizens, not against foreign powers.
- They enforce complex zoning and land-use laws that tell a citizen how private property can be used, what can be built on the land, what materials must be used in any building constructed on the land, and what animals can be housed in the building.
- They issue regulations prescribing where people can start fires, dump garbage, light firecrackers, drink alcohol, play ball, and park their cars.
- They employ tax collectors who have the authority to take money from citizens based on how much another government official, the tax assessor, thinks their properties are worth.
- They have the power, known as *eminent domain,* to take private land from citizens and put it to public use, being required only to pay a "fair price" for the land. (Fair price is determined by another branch of government—the courts.)
- They can even take away a citizen's property and give or sell it to another citizen.
- They can order a citizen to tear down buildings that he owns.

- Government officials can enter a place of business, inspect it, and order the owner to close operations, depriving him or her of a livelihood.

But government does not spend all its time coercing citizens. Local governments also provide positive services—fire protection, garbage collection, elementary and secondary schools, streets, parks, recreation programs, libraries, a sewer and water system, and a host of other services that are essential to life, health, or public order, plus those that add to the amenities of a limited number of citizens, such as a museum or a municipal zoo.

Even when government provides positive public services such as these, citizens have been indirectly coerced. Governments collect taxes to support their projects and services, and the power of taxation is directly based on coercion.

Three kinds of policies

That the actions of government are based on the threat of force does not mean that people are worse off or oppressed because of government action. It does not even mean that they are less free, in any meaningful sense. Whether they are or are not depends on what it is that government is doing.

Simplifying things considerably, we can distinguish among three kinds of government policies: those that benefit everyone; those that benefit more people than they hurt, but do harm some people; and those that harm more people than they help.

Policies that benefit everyone are clearly desirable. But what about the other two? On the face of it, policies that harm more people than they help would seem to be undesirable. But would your opinion change if the people who were helped were benefited a great deal, and the others harmed only slightly? How do we compare the good done, in total, with the harm done, in total? The second kind of policies, those that help more people than they hurt, may seem desirable. But what if those who benefit are helped only slightly, and those harmed are badly hurt? What if those who benefit are greatly helped, but those harmed are badly hurt? Public policymaking involves just these kinds of choices. For the first kind of policy, there is likely to be little controversy over whether government action should be taken. But the other two depend on who is benefited and who is harmed, and by how much. And governments confront the latter kind of choices more often than the former.

Type 1 Policies: Collective Goods. A *collective good* is any public policy that benefits all citizens, even though some citizens may be benefited more than others.[3] Two basic characteristics of collective goods (sometimes called

---

[3] On collective goods, see Vincent Ostrom and Elinor Ostrom, "Public Goods and Public Choices," in *Alternatives for Delivering Public Services: Toward Improved Performance,* ed. E. S. Savas (Boulder, Col.: Westview Press, 1978), pp. 7–49. See also Mancur Olson, Jr., *The*

public goods or *collective benefits*) are *nonexclusion* and *jointness of consumption*. By nonexclusion we mean that no individual can be barred from the benefits of the policy. By jointness of consumption we mean that two or more people can take advantage of the benefits provided by the policy without exhausting them. Classic examples of collective goods are national defense and lighthouses. Once the national defense umbrella has been established, everybody benefits from it. Similarly, once a lighthouse has been put into operation, all ships can benefit from it. An urban example of a collective good is police protection. If potential criminals are deterred because of fear of being caught, all citizens benefit (see box 3.1). Some

Logic of Collective Action (Cambridge, Mass.: Harvard University Press, 1965), and Norman Frolich and Joe A. Oppenheimer, *Modern Political Economy* (Englewood Cliffs, N.J.: Prentice-Hall, 1978).

Box 3.1: The Leviathan as a Collective Good

One of the collective goods provided by government is an orderly society. The English political philosopher Thomas Hobbes (1588–1679) emphasized this role of government above all others. Without government, according to Hobbes, there was a continual state of war, "where every man is Enemy of every man . . . men live without other security, than what their own strength, and their own invention shall furnish them withall." In such a situation there is "continuall feare, and danger of violent death; and the life of man, solitary, poore, nasty, brutish, and short."

In order to escape from this state of complete liberty, Hobbes thought, it was necessary for people to surrender their individual liberties to a central power, a sovereign individual capable of establishing a framework for a peaceful, cooperative society through a monopoly of coercion.

It might be noted that some individuals in Hobbes's hypothetical state of nature were doubtless faring better than others. The weak had more to gain from the establishment of a centralized government than the strong, since the strong were probably faring quite well in the state of war. This is characteristic of collective goods: even when all benefit from the collective good, some benefit more than others.

Source: See Thomas Hobbes, *Leviathan* (Harmondsworth, Middlesex, England: Penguin Books, 1968). First published in 1651. Extract from p. 186.

citizens, however, benefit more than others. As long as justice is dispensed fairly and in a nondiscriminatory fashion, blacks, the elderly, and center-city merchants, for example, who are more likely to be victims of crime, will derive more benefits than those less subject to crime. Other examples of collective goods in urban areas include public parks, streets and highways, and street lighting.

Many goods are of a private nature, however. This means that the user of the good or service can deny use of it to other people. An apple is an example of a private good. I can keep you from having any, and when I eat it there is none left.

One important aspect of nonexclusion is that the enjoyment of the good or service is not related to the effort a person expends in helping to produce it. "Let Joe do it. If he does it, I can benefit with no effort; if he does not, I will be no worse off than I am now." Any collective enterprise is characterized by what has been called the "free rider" problem. Any time a project is undertaken that provides collective benefits, in that no individual can be excluded from the benefits of the good, there will always be some individuals, the "free riders," who will not contribute their time, energy, or money to the project. They know that even if they don't contribute they can enjoy the fruits of the labors of others.

Suppose a block club or a community organization in a city proposes to residents that next Saturday everybody come out and clean up the local park, which is deteriorating because of neglect. Whether or not a given resident contributes, he can still enjoy the park. No one can keep his children out of the park, and the whole neighborhood looks better. But what if not enough people turn out to do the work?

This illustrates an important point about collective goods. In at least some cases projects that provide benefits for everyone will not get done, because too many potential contributors will opt out, letting Joe do it. If individuals interact voluntarily, and there is no coercion to force them to cooperate, collective goods will be underproduced. There will be too few of them. Everyone could be better off if there were a way of forcing slackers to contribute their fair share.

Suppose a neighborhood is considering contracting for plowing of its streets, because the city does not provide the service. If all the residents contribute, it will cost each person ten dollars. But some citizens will refuse to pay, realizing that they will benefit from the street plowing whether or not they contribute. The snowplow cannot avoid their sections of the street, plowing only in front of contributors' houses. The actions of these individuals will drive the cost of service up for the others, because the contractor has to do all the street no matter how many people pay. If half the residents contribute, the cost per resident would be twenty dollars. It is possible that some residents would pay ten dollars but not twenty. The price would then have to rise some more for the rest. If this were to continue (and it may not; some people may be willing to pay the cost whatever it is), the service will not be provided. We have a strange situation: everyone wants the service and would be willing to pay ten dollars for it. But there is no way to get each individual to cooperate to provide the service, since some individuals will hold out, hoping to become free riders, benefiting from the service paid for by others.

How do you solve the problem? Enter government. One solution is to tax everyone ten dollars and provide the service. All are better off then they would have been if government had not entered the picture. Government coercion has been used to force people to cooperate in doing something everybody wants. Finding out just how much people are willing to give up in taxes for the collective good can be a problem, however. If people are actually willing to pay ten dollars, and government must tax them fifteen dollars to provide the service, the service should not be provided.

Type 2 and 3 Policies: Reducing Externalities. Some actions taken by some citizens directly harm other citizens, even though it was not intended that they do so. Such actions are termed *externalities*. Externalities are costs imposed on others by citizens pursuing private goals. So-called regentrifying of urban neighborhoods offers particularly graphic examples of such externalities.

Chicago's Uptown district is such a regentrifying neighborhood. As housing prices escalated in the city's more exclusive older neighborhoods, such as Lincoln Park, young white, middle-class singles and couples began to move into the tired, old, decaying neighborhood.[4] As the neighborhood became more attractive to the middle class, developers began buying some of the fine, old, once exclusive buildings now inhabited primarily by the poor, the elderly, and the destitute. Often with the aid of government loans, the developers began converting the old tenements back into the exclusive apartments they had been in the 1920s. Many of the buildings were converted into condominiums.[5] "There is no question that Uptown is the hottest place in Chicago right now," commented one developer who has been active in Uptown.

As the middle class began moving into Uptown, the poor were forced out. They could not afford the high rents that owners were charging for refurbished apartments; neither could they afford condominium ownership. Such forced moves are particularly hard on the elderly, who may have severe dif-

---

[4] For a description of Uptown, its problems and prospects, see Elizabeth Warren, *Chicago's Uptown* (Chicago: Center for Urban Policy, Loyola University, 1979).

[5] A *condominium* is an ownership arrangement in which a person owns an apartment in a multiple-unit building; the owners of the separate apartments collectively own the common areas of the building.

ficulties in finding other suitable living arrangements, and numerous older Chicagoans called Uptown their home.[6]

According to developers and Uptown boosters, this is an inevitable cost of development, and not a particularly severe one at that. One supporter of development commented:

> The only way we're going to turn this neighborhood around to what it was 15–20 years ago is to attract a different class of people and push some of them [the poor] out. Those are the simple facts.
>
> Most of these people are transient in nature; they are used to moving around. Most will find adequate or better places to live if they are forced to move.[7]

Quite a different view is offered by a spokeswoman for one of the community groups active in Uptown. She saw a desperate need for housing for individuals of poor and moderate income, and was much more cautious on the benefits of a redeveloped Uptown: "There is a crying need for housing. The rental stockpile is being demolished almost systematically between condominium conversion, slum landlords who milk the buildings dry, arson and demolition."[8]

Private developers, by investing in decaying neighborhoods like Chicago's Uptown, are imposing harm on others, particularly the low-income renters. It is easy to condemn the developers as evil financiers who care little for the well-being of the poor. Not so many years ago, however, these individuals were criticized by many urbanists for taking their money out of the city and investing in the suburbs (a process termed *disinvestment*). In general, investment will flow where investors perceive opportunities for good returns on their money. Whether that happens to be Uptown or the rapidly expanding suburbs is immaterial to the investors. It is not the role of the economic system to calculate the externalities generated by such investment flows. That is the role of the political system.

Some other examples of externalities include a polluting factory; a shopping center that is ill kept and attracts an undesirable clientele, from the viewpoint of the surrounding neighborhood; a "drug pad"; an abandoned building. In each of these cases, the offending individuals prefer to act in manners contrary to the wishes of other individuals. The situation in which some citizens prefer to act in a manner contrary to the preferences of others is very different from the collective-good situation. The offending citizen is not simply holding out in the hope that someone else will provide the effort necessary to produce something he or she actually wants. In the case of

---

[6] "Rebirth of a Neighborhood Is Not Without Some Pain," *Chicago Tribune,* Thursday, June 21, 1979. High mortgage interest rates and a weakening economy have slowed development in Uptown, as elsewhere.

[7] Ibid.

[8] Ibid.

neighborhood snow removal, each citizen wants the project to be undertaken but is not willing to contribute unless everyone contributes. In the case of urban redevelopment, people genuinely have different preferences about what is happening.

As it can in providing collective goods, government can intervene in the situation. By suppressing the externality, it can provide a better environment for the people living in the neighborhood. By regulating the developers, by eliminating the pollution, by closing drug dens and houses of prostitution, government can improve things for some citizens. But in order to do so, it must coerce nonconforming individuals into doing something they do not want to do.

In the neighborhood redevelopment situation, someone is going to be coerced. The poor have little choice other than to leave their homes if government fails to act. If government does act, the developers will be denied an important investment opportunity, the prospective middle-income residents will lose what they perceive as a desirable place to live, and city government will be denied an important addition to its tax base.

Let us take another example of this tradeoff between private and public coercion. Suppose a homeowner in a quiet urban neighborhood maintains her house in a dilapidated condition. It is not only an eyesore to the community, but is actually dangerous to visitors. Other homeowners in the neighborhood feel that their homes are worth less because of the building. Some have experienced difficulty in selling their homes because of it. The offending owner, however, feels that it is not worth the cost to bring her house up to the standards of her neighbors. Perhaps she is an elderly widow living on a small pension and cannot afford extensive repairs.

If government intervenes to force the widow to upgrade her building, significant costs will be imposed on her—in opposition to her preferences. The majority of citizens will have imposed their will on the deviant minority.

If government intervenes at the urging of the majority, the freedom of the minority is limited. If government does not intervene, the majority of homeowners suffer declines in the "quality of life" as well as losses in real wealth as the values of the properties decline.

For the kinds of policies exemplified by the deteriorating house and urban redevelopment, there is no specified rule for determining when government ought to intervene. All we know is that someone is going to suffer, regardless of what public policy is formulated to deal with the problem (even if that policy is to do nothing).

Politics and the public interest

Generally we do not know whether we are dealing with a policy whose total benefits will exceed its total costs, or whether costs exceed benefits. Because of these indeterminacies, and because different people perceive the costs and benefits of policies differently, politics results. Politics involves competition among groups and individuals to gain benefits and avoid costs associated with government coercion. Because these costs are subjective, there is usually no way of adding benefits and subtracting costs rationally to decide on the proper course of action for government.

Politics exists because people have different interests that they pursue in the policy process. An *interest* is a stake in the outcomes of the policy process; it is a perceived benefit that can be derived from the process. We know that individual interests exist; but does a "public interest" or "general good" exist?

Political scientists disagree over this question. Some feel that there does, in fact, exist a public interest over and above the simple summation of individual interests, and that that state of affairs is the ideal that government should strive for in its policymaking activities.[9] Other political scientists, the "realists," think that there is no public interest that is any different from the sum of individual interests. They point out that any group that makes demands on government for some action that will benefit it generally claims wider social benefits for the policy it advocates. Those in the Philadelphia business community who benefit from a revitalized downtown claim that a vital central city benefits all residents of the city, because the activities stimulate economic growth and more jobs for residents. Opposing neighborhood organizations retort that Philadelphia is a "city of neighborhoods," and the good of all would be best served by investing in them.

The debate over the existence of a public interest has at times been fierce, but it has never settled the issue. We do know, however, that the provision of collective goods, those goods that would not be produced by citizens acting without government coercion yet that yield some benefits for all, are clearly in the public interest. Even collective goods benefit some people more than others, but generally, all people are somewhat better off. Unfortunately, very few public policies produce pure collective goods. Most public policies end up benefiting some citizens and harming others. The only way to determine whether such a policy is in the public interest would be to total the benefits provided by the policy, total the costs of the policy, and see if the benefits outweigh the costs—a difficult process given the subjective nature of costs and benefits.

Even if total benefits exceed total costs, however, we are not free to jump to the conclusion that the policy ought to be adopted. The policy may impose severe costs on a substantial minority, or otherwise be unfair to a group. This minority may feel very intensely that the costs ought not to be borne by it. If it does so, it can always engage in political action to try to avoid the imposition of the costs. Politics emerges. Indeed, in a society that permits freedom

[9] For a good discussion, see Emmette S. Redford, *Ideal and Practice in Public Administration* (University, Ala.: University of Alabama Press, 1958), ch. 5.

Emma Harris, here wearing a shirt reading "The Cashew Queen," was arrested in St. Louis, Missouri, for violating a city ordinance against eating on city buses. She was arrested after eating four cashews on a bus. When does government coercion protect the public interest and when does it impose an undue hardship on minorities?

Source: UPI Photo, *Detroit Free Press,* June 17, 1981.

of expression and organization, politics will emerge whenever public policies are considered. Even if a proposed policy were clearly in the public interest, citizens would be free to engage in politics to try to halt or modify the proposed policy. Some urban planners, for example, see their plans, which they feel are in the public interest, destroyed by special interests that will be harmed by the plans. Many political scientists feel, to the planner's chagrin, that politics is most desirable, because no plan (or any single person's conception of the public interest) is infallible. The free play of politics allows adjustments and compromises to be made. These adjustments and compromises can result in policies that are closer to the public interest than was the original plan.

We will return to this point in chapter 15. For now it is enough to point out that these adjustments and compromises are what determine the level of government intervention in society. Rather than the proper level of intervention being established in a philosophical debate over the proper limits of government, it is set by a seemingly infinite number of decisions made in city halls, statehouses, and Washington. In sum, these decisions, themselves the product of politics, determine how much government we are to have.

Policy Distribution and Location

The second characteristic of urban policymaking is that the costs and benefits of policy actions are often distributed to citizens through location. Policy distribution via location does not occur only in cities. Nevertheless, distribution via location affects more people more intensely in cities simply because cities are dense concentrations of people whose activities are interconnected.

The human use of physical space and the location of human activities in relation to one another are key organizing principles of the urban social science subdisciplines. Urban economics concerns the location of business, industry, and labor markets. Urban sociology deals with the use of geographic space to differentiate classes, races, and ethnic groups, and studies the evolution of neighborhoods as social units. One does not have to look far to find a similar concern in the study of urban politics and government. Central cities and suburbs compete for resources on a metropolitan landscape; territory-based organizations, from homeowner associations to urban gangs, form to protect their "turfs" through political action; public services are distributed to class and ethnic groups on the basis of their geographic locations; national urban policies attempt to compensate for the loss of jobs and industry stemming from the freedom of movement that allows citizens and business enterprises to relocate. What characterizes each of these examples is that policy benefits are distributed by the manner in which physical space is used.

Space and location are bound up in the policy process in three basic ways. First, the social problems that are the subject of the policymaking process are spatially organized. Second, the governments that are established to deal with these problems and to provide public services to their citizens are spatially organized. Third, political issues have a spatial component. As governments formulate and implement policies in this spatial context, they invariably distribute costs and benefits to citizens who are themselves spatially segregated.

Social problems: Hard times in Benton Harbor

The connection between location and social problems may be illustrated by taking a brief look at Benton Harbor, Michigan. Benton Harbor was predominantly white and prosperous until the late 1960s. By 1980 it was 90 percent black; unemployment stood at almost 25 percent; between 50 percent and 65 percent of the population was receiving some form of welfare; 90 percent of the downtown commercial property had been abandoned. Across the river, St. Joseph is all white and thriving, as are the suburban communities of western Michigan's Berrien County. Recently, Benton Harbor's last white mayor, who left office in 1973, complained bitterly, "It's nobody's fault but the damn white people. They ran like a bunch of scared rabbits. If the white people had stayed put, you would have a truly integrated city; downtown would be thriving. But once the panic started, the whites just cleared out."

Many people in Benton Harbor blame the city's problems on the state of Michigan's generous welfare benefits. The benefits are much higher than those of southern states, or even the neighboring state of Indiana. This, many feel, encourages poor families to migrate to Michigan, swelling the state's welfare rolls. Benton Harbor's ex-mayor complained, "The wrong kind of people started moving in, people who didn't have anything to contribute." He suggested that Michigan cut back its generous welfare payments to discourage migration.

The director of the Michigan Department of Social Services disagreed. "To discourage such movement by lowering Michigan's benefit levels is an extreme disservice to Michigan citizens," he commented.[10]

Clearly, Benton Harbor's problems are affected by location—the ability of well-off citizens to move, the attractive power of relatively generous government assistance, the relocation of commerce and industry from the city. Public policy solutions, if indeed there are any, must take this locational component into consideration.

Governments

All governments are spatially organized. They occupy physical space, and boundaries separate one governmental unit or jurisdiction from others.

---

[10] This material was taken from Tom Hundley, "White Flight, Hard Times Cripple Benton Harbor," *Detroit Free Press,* March 30, 1980.

A *political system* comprises a government along with certain nongovernmental groups and institutions that interact regularly with the government. Included within a political system are political parties, interest groups, neighborhood associations (when they try to influence government), and citizens (when they vote or try to obtain benefits from government). Because governments are spatially organized, so are political systems.

This spatial organization is especially important in urban areas. The typical metropolitan region contains numerous separate governments, some overlapping. A typical metropolis (if there is any) contains county government, municipal governments (cities, towns, and villages), school districts, and special-purpose districts (such as those established to provide water, sewerage, or mosquito abatement). In the Midwest, one also finds township governments.

In 1977, there were 79,914 different governmental units in the United States: one federal government, 50 state governments, and 79,863 local governments. Some metropolitan areas contain more separate governments than others. We say that these regions are governmentally *fragmented.* Far and away the leader in the number of separate governmental jurisdictions is the Chicago metropolitan area, with 1,214. Philadelphia is a poor second with 864. New York contains fewer still: 362.

The various metropolitan regions contain different numbers of people, so that just counting governments may not be a fair comparison. Another way of measuring governmental fragmentation is to determine how many people, on average, a government in a metropolis serves. The smaller the number of people served, the more the fragmentation. By this measure Chicago is no longer the leader in governmental fragmentation. Table 3.1 presents the average number of people served per government in various metropolises.

It should be noted that these figures are averages and, like all averages, can be misleading. In particular, in any metropolitan area most people are served by several different governments: a municipality, a county, a school district, perhaps several special districts. The figures conceal the variety of metropolitan governments. Nevertheless, they rank cities approximately according to their fragmentation.

The spatial organization of government in a metropolis means that some governments will serve wealthy areas and some will serve poor areas. Figure 3.1 is a map of housing values in St. Louis, Missouri. Clearly, the people served by St. Louis City are much less well off economically, on average, than those served by the suburban municipalities that provide services to the residents of St. Louis County. In the United States, local governments have substantial responsibilities in determining service levels and raising taxes to pay for them. This means that the jurisdictions outside the center city (OCC, as they are sometimes termed) can afford better services than those within the center city. This is true even though need for many services (for example,

Table 3.1. Local government fragmentation: The number of people served by the average government, selected metropolitan areas, 1977

Peoria, Illinois	1,360	
Omaha, Nebraska	2,200	More fragmentation
Pittsburgh, Pennsylvania	3,130	
Indianapolis, Indiana	3,600	
St. Louis, Missouri	3,840	
Denver, Colorado	4,290	
Kansas City, Missouri	4,600	
Houston, Texas	4,690	
Minneapolis–St. Paul, Minnesota	4,950	
Cincinnati, Ohio	5,210	
Seattle, Washington	5,370	
Philadelphia, Pennsylvania	5,560	
Chicago, Illinois	5,780	Less fragmentation
Dallas–Ft. Worth, Texas	6,900	
San Francisco, California	10,050	
Detroit, Michigan	12,660	
New York, New York	26,320	

Source: Calculated from *1977 Census of Governments, Vol. 1: Government Organization* (Washington, D.C.: U.S. Bureau of the Census, 1978), Table 2, p. 13.

fire and police services) is greater where housing quality is low and people are poor. Hence, the spatial organization of governments in the metropolis perpetuates the inequality generated by the economic and social systems. We return to these issues in chapter 9.

Political issues: The snows fall in Chicago

On January 13, 1978, 21 inches of snow fell on Chicago, on top of the 12 inches still on the ground from a severe New Year's Eve storm. A severe cold wave followed, with the thermometer dropping below 0 degrees Fahrenheit day after day. The snow and cold ruined the motors of the electric trains, and the Chicago Transit Authority used only its elevated tracks. During the crisis motorists abandoned their automobiles and flocked to the trains, at a time when fully 40 percent of the CTA's rolling stock was out of service. The train cars were crowded with people, and some passengers risked their lives by riding on the couplings between cars.

As the transit crisis worsened, CTA policymakers decided that the only solution was to reduce service. To reduce the strain on the system, they closed certain stations. Policymakers said they used two criteria for deciding which stations to close: use, with the stations with the lowest riderships

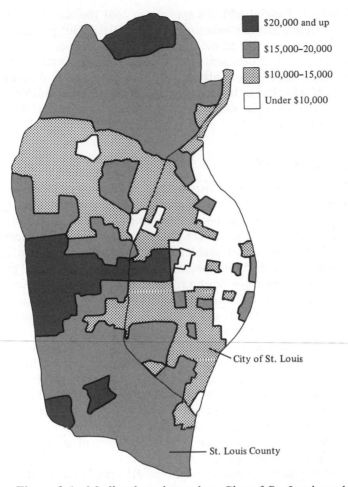

Figure 3.1. Median housing value, City of St. Louis and St. Louis County, 1970.

Source: U.S. Bureau of the Census and Manpower Administration, *Urban Atlas, St. Louis, Mo.-Ill. SMSA* (Washington, D.C.: U.S. Government Printing Office, 1974).

closed, and the availability of alternative transit possibilities, with stations closed on lines where a parallel route could provide service. These were seemingly rational rules. But the result of the rational rules was that every single closed station served a black neighborhood.

Community leaders deplored the situation. Blacks complained of "plantation politics." Federal officials speculated that the closings might have violated the United States Constitution. City officials put pressure on CTA officials. Within the week, all the closed stations were back in operation.[11]

The Chicago transit decision was locational. Close certain stations and you disproportionately harm blacks, not because of direct discrimination, but because blacks tend to live together in Chicago. (*This* tendency may, of course, result from racial discrimination.) Such locational effects are the "stuff" of urban politics.

Locational distribution

Public policies are spatially distributed first because citizens, their social problems, and their social resources are spatially segregated. Hence, to deal with these social problems, public policies must affect these spatial aggregations of citizens differently. In large part, the federal government has an urban policy because social problems tend to be concentrated in cities. Moreover, in order to deal with these spatially concentrated social problems, governments must somehow cause a transfer of resources from places where they are plentiful (such as suburbs) to places where they are not (such as central cities). In large part, the debate over urban policy concerns just how much of this ought to be done.

In the second place, governments are spatially organized. A wealthy suburb can raise much money by taxing its citizens relatively little. A poor city must tax much more heavily to raise the same resources. Hence the suburb can provide more services at less cost to its individual citizens.

Finally, political issues are spatially organized. As a city government tries to deal with the issues that emerge, it must treat different areas of the city differently. As it does so, it treats different classes of people differently, because social classes are spatially separated.

Many urban policies thus have locational effects without policymakers intending them to do so. Locational effects can be unintended consequences of public policies that were enacted to achieve other goals. The situation looks like this:

Numerous federal, state, and local policies have such inadvertent urban effects. Salamon and Helmer comment that "the Federal Government not

[11] For a more complete discussion, see Bryan D. Jones, "Distributional Standards and Service Delivery Decisions," *The Urban Interest* 1 (Fall 1979): 6–15.

only has had an *explicit* urban policy for decades, but an *implicit* urban policy as well, resulting from the frequently inadvertent urban impacts of other federal programs."[12] Such federal programs as highway building, subsidies for constructing housing for the middle class, and a hesitancy to provide funds for mass transit have implicitly promoted residential and commercial deconcentration, adding to the problems facing central cities.

Many urban policies are nonetheless explicitly locational. Community use of public incentives to attract industries is presently the most visible of explicitly locational (or in this case, *re*locational) policies. Other examples include the use of zoning laws to direct the location of commerce, industry, and residences; the use of eminent domain to remove citizens' dwellings and businesses to make way for other, presumably more productive land uses; and the location of fire stations in order to minimize the distance traveled to fires. In each of these cases, public policies are used to direct (or at least influence) the human use of urban space. In each case, moreover, policy costs and benefits are distributed according to locational criteria.

Relations Among Governments

The third characteristic of urban policymaking is the set of special relationships that exist among units of government bearing policy responsibility. The extreme fragmentation of urban governments makes it difficult to work out common problems. Because the various local governments that coexist on a metropolitan landscape are legal equals, they must bargain and negotiate to produce collective goods for the metropolitan area. The fragmentation means, however, that each government can tailor *policy packages,* the mix of government-provided goods and services, to its citizens. Because citizens are spatially segregated, each government will be providing its policy package to a relatively homogeneous citizenry.

Local governments must also deal with governments that are legally superior to them: the state and federal governments. These larger units of government are better prepared to deal with the large-scale social problems that characterize modern urban society, but they are naturally less responsive to local wishes. Hence the relationship between the state and national governments, on the one hand, and local governments, on the other, involves a good deal of bargaining and negotiation as each side struggles with the issue of effective government versus local autonomy. Just how this issue is worked out in practice is discussed in chapter 9, which examines relations

---

[12] Lester M. Salamon and John Helmer, "Urban and Community Impact Analysis: From Promise to Implementation," in *Urban Impacts of Federal Policies,* ed. Norman J. Glickman (Baltimore: Johns Hopkins University Press, 1980), ch. 2.

among local governments, and in chapter 13, which explores relations between local governments and higher levels of government.

Conclusions

The policymaking process presented in chapter 2 is an idealized description. It would fit, with some modifications, policymaking in a variety of governmental and nongovernmental organizations. In this chapter we have looked at three characteristics that distinguish urban policymaking from the idealized model of chapter 2.

First, local governments, particularly those in urban areas, confront the issue of the proper use of public power far more directly than other levels of government. Because local governments are more intimately and consistently involved in the lives of citizens, the application of governmental coercion takes on a personal quality that is lacking at other levels of government. In the second place, urban policymaking distributes the costs and benefits of governmental action through location and the use of physical space. Through land-use planning, zoning ordinances, and building regulations, local governments channel the use of physical space. In this process, some interests are favored (perhaps developers, for example) and some are harmed (low-income renters, for example). Through packages of incentives, communities compete for jobs and industry, and for desirable residents. Federal government policies favor some locations over others. Finally, special relations among governments exist in the urban policy sphere. Local governments must deal with one another, but they must also deal with legally superior governments: the state and nation.

CHAPTER 4

The Social and Economic Environment of Urban Policymaking

Public policymaking always occurs in a social and economic context. This context is called the *policy environment;* it is the set of problems and opportunities that activate policy entrepreneurs and stimulate them to transmit demands to government. As these demands reach the policy agenda, government is forced to deal with the problems that activated the demands initially—if it possesses the necessary resources, and if opponents of government action are not able to stall the action at one of the stages of the policy cycle.

The environment of urban political systems consists of those aspects of the economic and social systems that impinge on urban political life. Two key aspects of this urban environment are particularly critical for governing America's cities. First, in urban areas the physical proximity of individuals, groups, and institutions means that many aspects of the economic and social systems affect politics and policymaking. As we shall see, the social and economic systems of urban areas take distinctively spatial forms, and this affects urban politics. The relative locations of races, ethnic groups, business corporations, and public institutions have a pronounced influence on the urban policy process.

Second, the social and economic trends described in this chapter are national in scope. Urban problems are national problems. Yet the tradition of local autonomy means that local governments with limited resources must play the major role in dealing with these national trends.

The Form of Cities

Cities occupy space, and just how the urban landscape is structured has important consequences for urban governance. Sociologists, economists, and geographers have developed several models of the spatial structure of cities. Such models are abstractions, and they ought not to be judged right or wrong based on any specific situation. They ought to aid us, however, in our understanding of urban spatial development. Three basic models have been developed: the *concentric city,* the *sector model,* and the *multiple-nuclei model.*

The concentric city

Urban spatial models were first developed by E. W. Burgess, R. E. Park, and their colleagues at the University of Chicago during the 1920s. The Chicago school of urbanists termed their approach *social ecology,* because many of their ideas were drawn from the study of plant and animal ecology.[1]

To the Chicago urbanists, cities tended to take a concentric form. At the core was the central business district. Each concentric circle outward delineated a different land-use pattern. Near the central business district, a zone of heavy industry clustered. Nearby, encircling the central business district, was a zone of tenements that housed the poor. Next came a zone of working-class homes, then a region of better neighborhoods. In general, moving outward from the central city, two things happened. First, the residential districts tended to house the economically better off. Second, land use was less intensive. There was more open space, yards were larger, and fewer high-rise developments existed.

In the concentric city there was room for individual variations in the various zones, but the basic spatial character of urban structure remained unchanged. As the city expanded, growth occurred along the outer ring of the city, and the inner rings went through a transition from one land-use pattern to another, generally less desirable form. The zone of working-class homes became slums, and the middle-income neighborhoods became the

---

[1] On the Chicago school of urbanism, see D.I. Scargill, *The Form of Cities* (New York: St. Martin's, 1980), ch. 2, and Keith Bassett and John Short, *Housing and Residential Structure* (London: Routledge & Kegan Paul, 1980), ch. 2.

homes of the working class as those who could afford it moved to the city's outskirts.

The engine of change in all of this was the process of *invasion and succession*. As one group began to expand outward it invaded neighborhoods inhabited by another. These two groups might exist uneasily for a time, but soon the character of the neighborhood would begin to change. The process of invasion and succession still characterizes many urban neighborhoods, as different classes and ethnic groups jostle uneasily on the urban landscape. This is particularly true of racial transition. A fireman in a major industrial city recently commented that "in this city, there are three kinds of neighborhoods—white, black, and changing from white to black."

Although the concentric city of Burgess and other Chicago urbanists depicts many important features of urban spatial organization, it is limited in its ability to describe and explain urban form. In particular, the concentric land-use pattern was probably characteristic of a particular historical period in the development of American cities. The concentric pattern observed by the Chicago urbanists during the 1920s existed in a radically different form before the early 1900s. Since the 1920s American cities have tended to move away from the concentric form, although cities that were built up during the first quarter of the twentieth century still display many of the characteristics of the concentric city.

Cities have always been hostages to transportation systems. Prior to the development of mass transit systems, most of the wealthy in a city lived in the core city, with the poor congregated at the outskirts. In a study of Detroit, Donald Deskins notes that the average income of citizens declined as one moved away from the central business district prior to the development of the city's street railway system in the late 1800s.[2] With the development of convenient transit systems, the wealthy were able to relocate on the city's rim, away from the noise, congestion, and crime of the center city. After the development of the street railway system, the concentric residential pattern emerged. The automobile added to the ability of those economically better off to move away from the center city, but it did not change the basic residential structure of the city.

Sector theory

The economist Homer Hoyt objected to the concentric model developed by the Chicago urbanists, and he postulated a city structure characterized by sectoral development imposed on the concentric structure.[3] Hoyt saw urban

[2] Donald Deskins, *Residential Mobility of Negroes in Detroit, 1837–1965* (Ann Arbor, Mich.: Michigan Geographical Publication no. 5, Department of Geography, 1972).

[3] Homer Hoyt, *The Structure and Growth of Residential Neighborhoods in American Cities* (Washington, D.C.: Federal Housing Administration, 1939).

land-use patterns developing along transportation routes, such as railways or major highways. Once a direction of growth is established, Hoyt asserted, there is a tendency for the directionality to maintain itself. If, for example, high-quality residential dwellings are built on the west side of the city, there will be a tendency for high-quality building to extend westward.

It is worthwhile to reexamine the map of St. Louis presented in chapter 3 (see p. 61). In that map, one can see clear evidence of sectoral development. People with the highest incomes inhabit a band that moves westward from the city. But the sectoral development is clearly superimposed on a concentric development, with higher-income individuals generally living farther away. In this sense, the sector theory is compatible with the concentric model.

Multiple nuclei

In the mid-1940s, Chauncy Harris and Edward Ullman proposed an alternate model of city spatial structure.[4] They argued that urban land use develops not from a single core but from several separate centers, some of which developed early in the city's history, some later. Cities expand outward from these separate centers.

This pattern of growth characterizes many cities in their most recent growth periods. Suburbanization, the development of separate general governmental units on the outskirts of a metropolis as it expands outward, has created residential and commercial centers that are not as tightly integrated with the core city as in the past. Industry has also moved to the suburbs, primarily because of the availability on the city's rim of land at lower prices. With this dispersion of industry, jobs, commerce, and residences, a process termed *deconcentration,* the modern city has tended to approximate the multiple nuclei model more and more, especially with regard to commercial activity. Whereas the central business district once provided a central place for commerce, industry, and shopping, increasingly it has adopted a specialized function, focusing on banking, legal activity, and government. Dispersed shopping centers increasingly have come to compete with the central business district as retail centers. Business firms have also dispersed, and in several major cities one or more suburbs serve as commercial centers of rival status to the central business district. Southfield serves this function for the Detroit metropolis, as does Clayton in the St. Louis metropolitan region.

Suburbs, once primarily bedroom communities for the wealthy who commuted to jobs in the core city, increasingly have become differentiated

---

[4] Chauncy D. Harris and Edward Ullman, "Rival Models of Urban Growth," *The Annals of the American Academy of Political and Social Science* 242 (November 1945): 7–17.

themselves. Today there are working-class suburbs, middle-income suburbs, suburbs that cater primarily to industry, commercial suburbs, and suburbs that serve primarily as retail centers, as well as upper-income bedroom suburbs.

Deconcentration of industry, retail activity, and residences has added a complexity to the modern metropolis that is better captured by the multiple-nuclei than the other models of city growth. Yet the concentric and sector models continue to be very useful in describing many aspects of modern cities. Housing, quality, average income, and other indicators of social and economic well-being tend to increase (perhaps in sectors) as one moves outward from the core city. In industrial cities, heavy manufacturing tends to be located in sectors corresponding to transportation facilities, particularly along railroad tracks. Each of the three basic models describes some aspects of city structure, and no city fits one model exactly.[5] (Figure 4.1 compares the three basic models of city form.)

Immigration

All Americans are, strictly speaking, immigrants; there are no "native Americans." Indians reached the North American continent first, some ten thousand years ago, crossing a bridge of land connecting Siberia with Alaska. European immigration to North America began in the early seventeenth century. Recognizing this essential fact about the people of the United States, President Franklin Roosevelt, himself a member of an old New York family, once began an address to the Daughters of the American Revolution, "My fellow immigrants . . ." (The ladies were not pleased.)

The models of city form based on the concentric growth of cities outward from the central business district are premised on population increases. During much of the history of American cities, population was increasing. The industrialization of America brought waves of immigrants directly to the cities, especially the cities of the Northeast and Midwest (and, to a lesser extent, the West coast). Industrialization occurred first in the Northeast, where it resulted in a concentration of manufacturing activity. (In the 1930s, 72 percent of the manufacturing activity in the United States was concentrated in a belt going east and west between Boston and Chicago–Milwaukee, extending no farther south than Louisville and Baltimore.)[6] Because of the concentration of jobs, immigration from abroad was confined dispropor-

---

[5] The spatial models of city form have been further refined and developed by urban geographers. See, for example, David Herbert, *Urban Geography: A Social Perspective* (New York: Praeger, 1972).

[6] *The President's 1978 National Urban Policy Report* (Washington, D.C.: U.S. Department of Housing and Urban Development, 1978), p. 9.

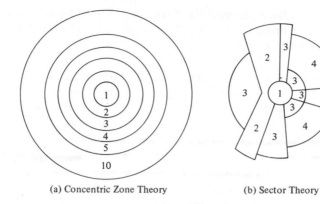

(a) Concentric Zone Theory   (b) Sector Theory

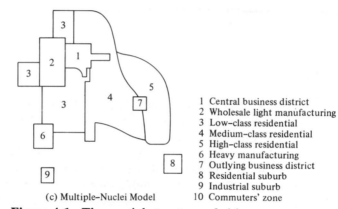

(c) Multiple–Nuclei Model

1 Central business district
2 Wholesale light manufacturing
3 Low–class residential
4 Medium–class residential
5 High–class residential
6 Heavy manufacturing
7 Outlying business district
8 Residential suburb
9 Industrial suburb
10 Commuters' zone

Figure 4.1. The spatial structure of cities.

Source: Reprinted from "The Nature of Cities" by Chauncy D. Harris and Edward L. Ullman in volume no. 242 of *The Annals of The American Academy of Political and Social Science*. Copyright 1945 by The American Academy of Political and Social Science. Reprinted by permission.

tionately to this region. By 1910, New York's population was over 40 percent foreign-born, and another 38 percent were native-born of foreign or mixed parentage. Chicago, Philadelphia, Boston, Cleveland, Pittsburgh, Detroit, Buffalo, San Francisco, Milwaukee, Newark, and other cities contained populations of more than 60 percent first- and second-generation Americans.[7]

As cities boomed, many more migrants came from American rural areas to cities. Many rural areas of the Northeast and Midwest experienced ab-

[7] Howard P. Chudacoff, *The Evolution of American Urban Society* (Englewood Cliffs, N.J.: Prentice-Hall, 1975), p. 91.

solute declines in population, as the natural increase failed to offset the migration to the industrializing cities.

Industrialization and cheap migrant labor stimulated an urban building boom. Cities grew outward, and the pattern of deconcentration began. The core city continued to be a crowded place, however, for as soon as one core-city resident left for the city's rim, several more arrived to take his or her place.

The immigrants brought different cultural traits with them that clashed sharply with those of Anglo-Saxon Americans. Their languages, dress, eating and drinking habits, and, perhaps most important, their religion (most immigrants were Catholics) contributed to culture conflict, a conflict that occasionally erupted into violence.

Foreign immigration to the United States consisted of two major waves. The first began in the 1840s and peaked in the 1880s. It consisted of Irish Catholics, Germans (both Protestants and Catholics), and English and Scandinavian Protestants. The second wave began in the 1880s and peaked between 1900 and 1910. This second wave of immigrants came from Italy, Russia, Hungary, Romania, Poland, and what later came to be Czechoslovakia. They were predominantly Catholic and Jewish.

Immigration declined in the 1920s, when federal law ended unrestricted immigration and established nationality quotas, and it reached a low point during the Great Depression of the 1930s. Since then, immigration has gradually increased (see figure 4.2).

Each wave of immigrants contributed to the ethnic mosaic that American cities were becoming. As time passed, immigration slowed and the ethnics became at least somewhat *assimilated,* or socialized into mainstream American culture. Most of the sons and daughters of immigrants learned the

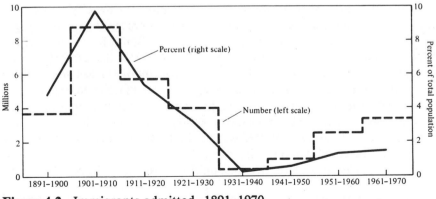

Figure 4.2. Immigrants admitted, 1891–1970.

Source: *Social Indicators, 1976* (Washington, D.C.: US. Department of Commerce, 1977), p. XXXIII.

language, habits of thought, and symbols implicit in that culture. Nevertheless, many American cities still retain ethnic neighborhoods. Although the divisions are weaker than in the past, much of the urban "turf" remains divided among ethnic groups in many cities. Two geographers, Michael Cozen and George Lewis, write that in Boston, a particularly ethnic city,

> Ethnic neighborhoods retain strong identities even as time and family moving thins out the old ethnic stocks. Old Irish neighborhoods, for example, are particularly cohesive, and many residents display a real garrison mentality that finds strongest geographic expression in their urban "turf."[8]

Chicago, another city renowned for its ethnicity, has been described by newspaper columnist Mike Royko as a loosely connected network of tightly knit neighborhood-towns:

> The neighborhood-towns were part of larger ethnic states. To the north of the Loop was Germany. To the northwest was Poland. To the west were Italy and Israel. To the southwest were Bohemia and Lithuania. And to the south was Ireland.
> It wasn't perfectly defined because the borders shifted as new-comers moved in on the older settlers, sending them fleeing in terror and disgust. . . . But you could always tell, even with your eyes closed, which state you were in by the odors of the food stores and the open kitchen windows, the sound of the foreign or familiar language, and by whether a stranger hit you in the head with a rock.[9]

Blacks

After the Second World War, internal migration replaced immigration as the primary source of replenishment of population for the city's core. The movement from farm to city quickened, and an important regional shift got under way as both blacks and whites left the rural South for the jobs of the industrial cities of the Northeast and Midwest. In 1910, just after European immigration to America had peaked, only 27 percent of blacks lived in cities; by 1970, 81 percent did. In a half-century, American blacks had transformed themselves from rural tenant-farming peasants into urban laborers.

The migration of blacks to the industrial Northeast and Midwest began in earnest after 1910 and accelerated during the 1920s. It slackened during the 1930s but increased dramatically during the 1940s, when well over 1.5 million blacks left the South, over one million of them for the Northeast and

[8] Michael P. Cozen and George K. Lewis, "Boston: A Geographical Portrait," in *Contemporary Metropolitan America*, vol. 1, *Cities of the Nation's Historic Metropolitan Core*, ed. John S. Adams (Cambridge, Mass.: Ballinger, 1976), pp. 91–92.

[9] Mike Royko, *Boss: Richard J. Daley of Chicago* (New York: Dutton, 1971), p. 24.

Midwest.[10] For the three decades following 1940, blacks were the major migrant group to northern cities. Then, as suddenly as it began, the internal migration of blacks to the North ceased in the 1970s. Most blacks were urbanized, and the remnants of the black farm-to-city movement were directed at the rapidly developing southern cities such as Atlanta, Houston, and Jacksonville.

Today, 75 percent of all blacks live in metropolitan regions (compared with 66 percent for whites). They are, however, much more concentrated in central cities than are whites: although only 24 percent of whites live in central cities, 55 percent of blacks do. Although 41 percent of whites live in the suburbs of metropolitan regions, only 20 percent of blacks do, and many blacks live in racially segregated suburbs.[11]

In recent years, a third wave of immigration has gained force. Many Latin Americans have moved north of the border, many legally, many others illegally. Like the immigrants in the first two waves, immigrants from Latin America have taken low-paying jobs disdained by Americans. Migrants from Mexico have concentrated in the Southwest. San Antonio, Texas, is over 50 percent Mexican American, and Los Angeles County is home to more than 2 million legal immigrants. South Florida generally, and Miami in particular, has become home to hundreds of thousands of immigrants who left Cuba after Fidel Castro came to power. Puerto Ricans, who are not subject to immigration quotas because their island home is a United States territory, have settled in New York and other eastern cities.

City Growth and Suburbanization

During the late nineteenth century, when many major American cities were experiencing rapid growth, most outlying areas wanted to unite with the center city in order to receive such essential municipal services as water, fire protection, and transportation. But by the early 1900s, many people who had moved to the outlying regions began to demand governmental status separate and distinct from the core city. As the city population expanded outward, city boundaries followed as settled area after settled area was incorporated into the governmental structure of the core city. When the citizens of Oak Park, Illinois, refused to unite with the city of Chicago in 1910, suburbanization was born.

Suburbanization did not alter the social and economic structure of the

---

[10] *The Social and Economic Status of the Black Population in the United States: A Historical View, 1790–1978* (Washington, D.C.: U.S. Bureau of the Census, 1980), p. 15.

[11] *The President's National Urban Policy Report, 1980* (Washington, D.C.: U.S. Department of Housing and Urban Development, 1980), pp. 1–15.

metropolis at all. After the development of electrified trolley systems in the late 1890s, those upper- and middle-income individuals who could afford to do so moved to the rim of the city to escape the congestion, noise, and health hazards of the core city. This migration left the city's core increasingly to the poor. What suburbanization did was to grant those who were economically better off separate political status. This status allowed them to escape the burden, which local government was just beginning to assume, of dealing with the poor immigrants arriving from abroad. They did not, however, save much on taxes, because the building up of the *public infrastructure* (roads, schools, and a system for handling water and sewerage) fell entirely on the taxpayers in the newly incorporated suburbs. (Annexation with the center city had allowed the spreading of the cost of the public infrastructure to all residents of the city.) Indeed, suburbanization was primarily rooted in such subjective motives as the desire for local control and the desire of Anglo-Saxon Americans to escape the unsettling (to them) mix of cultures that the center city was becoming, rather than in a desire to escape the burden of taxation.

Fear of the immigrants crowding the central city was not the only reason that many cities stopped growing through annexation and started growing through suburbanization. In some cities, such as St. Louis and Detroit, city leaders simply thought their cities were big enough. City boundaries were expanded far enough to include all growth for the foreseeable future, and the power of annexation was relinquished. In other cases, hostile state legislatures passed legislation limiting the annexation powers of city governments. Finally, in some situations, such as along the northern boundary of the city of Detroit, the city's legal boundary stopped at a county line[12] (see figure 4.3).

The Urban Underclass

Whatever the motives of the early suburbanites, the consequences of separate incorporation were to concentrate the poor in a governmentally separate jurisdiction, the center city. Today, center cities continue to be diverse places, housing a variety of income classes, ethnic groups, and races. The old image of the city as the home of cultural variety, with its distinct ethnic neighborhoods—black, Irish, Polish, Mexican—still has validity. As we noted in discussing the multiple-nuclei model of the city, suburbs themselves have become increasingly diverse. But this diversity does not

[12] An excellent study of the growth of a single metropolis is Harold M. Mayer and Richard C. Wade, *Chicago: Growth of a Metropolis* (Chicago: University of Chicago Press, 1969). See also Edgar Hoover and Raymond Vernon, *Anatomy of a Metropolis* (New York: Doubleday, 1962).

A. Growth by Annexation

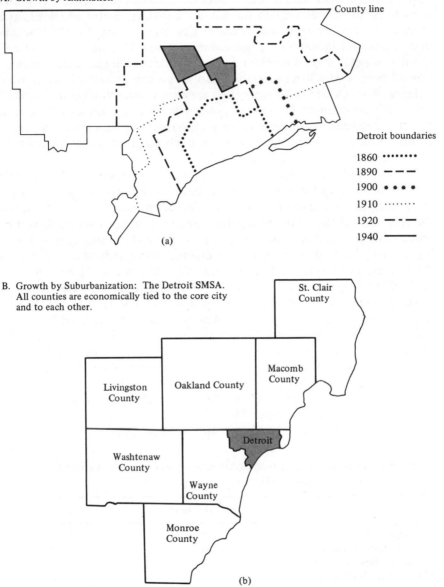

County line

Detroit boundaries

1860	··········
1890	— — —
1900	* * * *
1910	········
1920	— ·· —
1940	——————

(a)

B. Growth by Suburbanization: The Detroit SMSA.
All counties are economically tied to the core city
and to each other.

St. Clair
County

Livingston
County

Oakland County

Macomb
County

Washtenaw
County

Wayne
County

Detroit

Monroe
County

(b)

Figure 4.3. City growth: The case of Detroit.

Source: (a) Compiled from Donald R. Deskins, Jr., *Residential Mobility of Negroes in Detroit, 1837–1965* (Ann Arbor, Mich.: Department of Geography, Michigan Geographical Publication no. 5., 1972), various maps. Used with permission.

obscure some basic social and economic distinctions between city and suburb. Suburbanites are, on the whole, wealthier, better educated, and more likely to be white than their center-city counterparts. In 1978, the median household income of suburbanites was $16,579; that of center-city dwellers was $12,059. When we take into consideration the racial composition of people who live in metropolitan areas, the disparity is even more striking. Blacks who live in center cities are almost three times as likely to fall below the governmentally defined poverty level as are whites who live in center cities, and are five times more likely to be poor than are white suburbanites. Blacks in central cities are more likely to be poor than blacks who live in suburbs (see table 4.1).

Not all people who are poor at any one time are always poor. Many people seem to move in and out of poverty (arbitrarily defined as a particular income level) according to their own personal success and the performance of the economy. If the economy is performing well, many individuals will be able to find jobs and increase their incomes. But if the economy is performing poorly, as it does during a recession, many individuals will find themselves out of work, and the welfare rolls will increase. Hence, the concentration of the poor in central cities is a relative matter. The extent of poverty in cities is closely connected to national economic trends. Nevertheless, there exists concentrated in American cities a group of hard-core unemployed, disproportionately black, who lack the skills to compete in the modern technical American economy. Economists call these people the *structurally unemployed.* Edward Banfield has termed them America's permanent underclass: "It now appears that the big cities are going to have substantial populations of people who have never had a job and have no expectation of ever having one. They may become America's permanent underclass."[13] This underclass is not within the productive economy and is

Table 4.1. Percentage of households whose income falls below the poverty level, 1978

	White (%)	Black (%)
Metropolitan areas	7.5	28.5
Inside central cities	10.8	31.5
Outside central cities	5.9	20.1
Nonmetropolitan areas	11.2	37.2

Source: Statistical Abstract of the United States, 1980 (Washington, D.C.: U.S. Bureau of the Census, 1980), p. 462.

[13] Edward Banfield, "America's Cities Enter a Crucial Decade," *Congressional Record—Senate,* April 1, 1980, S3376.

dependent on government transfer payments, such as Aid to Dependent Children, food stamps, and supplemental social security income, for support.

Dualism in American Urban Society

Immigration brought wave after wave of people with different cultures, languages, and skin tones to American cities. Most met some form of discrimination from the ethnic groups already established. In the middle of the nineteenth century, many established English employers, when advertising positions, added "no Irish need apply." The Irish, in turn, discriminated against the Italians, who later disliked the Poles. Remnants of this discrimination remain today, embodied in housing preferences, income differentials, and ethnic jokes. Two groups of immigrants, however, met more intense discrimination.

Anti-Semitism

European immigrants often brought an anti-Semitism with them to America, and this anti-Semitism occasionally found fertile soil in Christian America. American anti-Semitism was never as virulent as it was in Europe; nevertheless, Jews did meet significant hostility in the United States. Such devices as restrictive *covenants* in deeds restricted the transfer of property in certain neighborhoods to Christians, until the Supreme Court ruled them unconstitutional in 1948. Both private and public universities employed quotas to limit the number of Jews admitted. One reason for the heavily Jewish character during the 1930s and 1940s of such urban universities as the City College of New York and Wayne State University in Detroit was the quotas maintained by state and private universities. Organizations from country clubs to college fraternities contained clauses in their charters barring non-Christians from membership.

Discrimination in the real estate market and the restrictions of religious practices limited the residential options of Jews. In many cities distinctly Jewish neighborhoods and suburbs continue to exist; in Detroit, for example, the Jewish community is residentially more segregated than other ethnic groups, including blacks.[14] Nevertheless, in a manner similar to other immigrants, Jews have found their place on the ladder of economic mobility in America.

[14] Carol Agocs and Bryan Thompson, "Detroit Area Ethnic Groups," (Detroit, Mich.: Center for Urban Studies, Wayne State University, 1972).

The special status of blacks

Of all the racial and ethnic groups in America, only blacks bear the burden of having been treated as the chattel property of other human beings. Even though great strides have been made in racial relations in the last quarter of a century, blacks still meet from moderate to severe racial discrimination in jobs, in housing, and in human relations.

In 1976, for example, a national sample of white Americans were asked a series of questions concerning racial relations. Thirty percent said that they would object if a member of their family wanted to bring a black home to dinner, and about 40 percent agreed that whites should be allowed to keep blacks out of their neighborhoods. Racial hostility was strongest in the deep South and weakest in New England and on the West coast. Older whites were less tolerant than younger whites; Jews were more tolerant than Catholics, who in turn were more tolerant than Protestants. College graduates exhibited less racial hostility than persons of less educational attainment.

Between 1963 and 1976, however, American whites became a good deal more racially tolerant. Change has taken place in all demographic groups, but dramatic change has taken place among the college educated in the South.[15]

Racial discrimination is most graphically reflected in differences in income and employment between whites and blacks. Blacks are three times as likely to fall below the governmentally defined poverty level. Unemployment rates are proportionately twice as high for blacks as they are for whites. Unemployment rises and falls with national economic trends, but the relative position of blacks changes little. Indeed, the tendency is for blacks, holding a disproportionate number of low-skill jobs, to be laid off first in a recession.

In 1947, the ratio of median black family income to median white family income was 0.51—that is, black income was 51 percent of white income. In 1963, it was 0.53; the situation had remained constant for sixteen years. During the late 1960s, when the American economy was booming and the federal government initiated many new programs to aid the plight of black Americans, the ratio of black to white income rose to 0.63 by 1967. Since that time there has been a slight decline in the economic situation of blacks.

These facts of black economic life reflect a dual labor market operating in American society. Whites and blacks, at least until the very recent past, have been allocated different jobs, with the better-paying jobs going to whites and the poorer-paying to blacks. Two students of the phenomenon commented several years ago:

> [In the northern labor market] the process of allocating jobs to white workers is
> so effectively separated from the process of allocating jobs to Negro workers

[15] D. Garth Taylor, Paul B. Sheatsley, and Andrew M. Greeley, "Attitudes Toward Racial Integration," *Scientific American* 238 (June 1978): 42–49.

that year after year the differentials between white and Negro workers are maintained.[16]

In more recent years, the dual labor market has begun to break down. Blacks today hold jobs that would have been unattainable a decade ago. But blacks still hold a disproportionate number of dirty, low-paying, semiskilled jobs in the American economy. One need only check the racial composition of the local garbage-collection crew to verify this. Visitors to Ford Motor Company's massive Rouge complex, a factory in which iron ore is brought in and finished automobiles leave, will note another aspect of racial dualism. On the assembly line, integration is the order of the day; black and white workers assemble automobiles side by side. But in the foundry, where temperatures regularly reach 130 degrees Fahrenheit, the work force is composed entirely of blacks.

Racial dualism also exists in the housing market. In the past, blacks were denied access to certain neighborhoods. Neighborhood racial segregation was maintained through differential access to mortgage money, with mortgages denied to blacks who wished to purchase in white neighborhoods. In more recent times, racial segregation has been maintained by subtler means. Racial steering has taken place, with real estate dealers guiding whites and blacks to different neighborhoods. Access to mortgages for blacks is still sometimes denied. One real estate dealer noted to the author of this book that not so many years ago, after the practice of listing race on mortgage applications had been discontinued, a small black mark would be made on mortgage applications of blacks. Banks would then deny the mortgage on the supposedly objective grounds of poor credit or low income if the house was located in a white district. There has been an erosion of such real estate practices over the last several years.

Whites sometimes make the mistake of imputing homogeneity to the black community. Even in the worst days of white oppression of blacks, when blacks in cities were consigned to tightly packed ghettos, status distinctions among blacks existed. Professionals such as teachers, store owners, ministers, and funeral directors served as black "aristocrats" in the ghetto. In the white community, professionals and semiskilled workers tend to live in different neighborhoods; increasingly, such a separation is occurring in the black community. But when racial dualism in the housing market kept blacks in the confines of the ghetto, the black middle class lived in close proximity, often on the same block, as the unemployed lower class (see box 4.1).

Occasionally racial tension in cities has exploded in urban disorders that

[16] Harold Baron and Bennett Hymer, "Racial Dualism in an Urban Labor Market," in *Problems in Political Economy: An Urban Perspective,* ed. David M. Gordon (Lexington, Mass: D.C. Heath, 1977), p. 194.

Box 4.1: Ada Street

In the early 1950s, Verne Jackson was a teenager on Ada Street in Chicago's Black Belt. On the west side of Ada Street lived the "Ada Street aristocracy," composed of people who had good, steady jobs. Being a mail carrier, an insurance salesman, a minor clerk in the Loop, a worker in the post office or the civil service, or even "head chef on the rayroad" could qualify one as a member of the upper-class Ada Street. The houses were nice and were owned by the occupants.

On the east side lived the "ratties"—more than 85 percent on welfare. "There was no grass on the east side and only a precious few trees—only a row of 11 two-story, plank-board steel gray houses badly in need of repair," each containing four four-room apartments. There were no bathtubs, and electricity came to the east side in 1948. They were all owned by an Irishman named O'Rourke, who rented them for $11 per month.

> While children of the west side regarded [us] east-side kids with condescension or envy, their parents never looked across the street. . . .
> The "high class peepers" ignored our funerals, our births, our fights,

Source: Verne Jackson, "Several Summers," *Chicago,* July 1979, 104–8. Extracts reprinted by permission from *Chicago* magazine. © 1979 by WFMT, Inc.

have cost numerous lives and millions of dollars' worth of damage to property. Major racial disturbances occurred in Chicago in 1919; Detroit in 1943; Los Angeles in 1964; Newark and Detroit in 1967; Washington and Chicago in 1968; and Miami in 1980. After each outbreak a government report is commissioned; each report points to the economic conditions of blacks and racial segregation as the root causes of the violence, with some specific event, such as a particular action taken by the police, acting as a catalyst for the outbreak. Yet black progress remains slow; 1980 violence in the Liberty City district of Miami points up the still-desperate circumstances in which many blacks find themselves.

Nevertheless, there are some signs of progress. At least some blacks have escaped poverty. Young, intact black families outside the South achieve family incomes that are slightly higher than those of their white counterparts outside the South. For all families in all regions, black intact families earn 75 percent of what white intact families earn—quite a bit better than the ratio of all black families to all white familes (58 percent). One legacy of racism and poverty is the broken family, and black families are far more likely to be

and our great wealth of sociological and pathological problems. . . .
We ratties, young and old, paid the west-side aristocrats no mind. The
old niggers kept on spending their government checks on cheap wine
and craps, and we fought and lived scenes right out of Porgy and
Bess' Catfish Row.

Because of racial discrimination in the real estate market, it was
not unusual for blacks of all classes to live in the same neighborhood. "If they had higher than average incomes, they moved to a
better street or built a nicer house in the same area, but they nearly
always stayed within the confines of Chicago's Black Belt."

By the mid-1970s, Verne Jackson had escaped the ghetto and
lived in an exclusive North Chicago lakefront highrise. In 1972 she
returned to Ada Street. Most of the houses on the east side had been
destroyed or were burned-out shells.

But I was astounded by the houses of the aristocrats. . . . The homes I
had once thought of as veritable palaces now seemed to be quite ordinary, even seedy lower-middle-class residences. . . . Perhaps the
black revolution of the sixties reduced those poor snobbish creatures
on the good side of Ada Street to the proper situations in life, but
who could blame them for trying to keep their heads above the sewer
of slum life just across the street? I no longer feel like laughing when I
think about our aristocrats. They lived in the ghetto along with us.

headed by a female, with no male present. (Blacks are about 12 percent of
the population, but they make up over 27 percent of the female-headed
households.) These families earn far less than the median family income for
whites—or for intact black families. And these families are disproportionately represented in the "urban underclass." Family structure, then, accounts for part of the income differences between blacks and whites.
Although this situation is not good news, it does indicate some crumbling of
racial dualism in the labor market as a factor that maintains black-white
economic differences.[17]

The Two Cities

Some observers have heralded the renovation of some urban neighborhoods
as part of a "back to the city" movement that has the potential to rebuild

[17] See *The Social and Economic Status of the Black Population in the United States: A Historical View, 1790–1978.*

and redirect urban America. The sons and daughters of suburbanites, it is said, are returning to reclaim the city of their grandparents. Yet estimates by the United States Bureau of the Census show that suburb-to-city migrations are but a trickle when compared to migrations from the city to suburbs and nonmetropolitan areas. Indeed, central cities in the United States lost nearly 2.9 million people, about 4.6 percent of their populations, between 1970 and 1977. Although the major losses were experienced by major, slow-growing metropolitan areas, smaller central cities in smaller, fast-growing metropolitan areas also experienced population declines.[18] Moreover, it is generally the more affluent who are leaving. This does not mean that the back-to-the-city movement is nonexistent; clearly, it does exist and has had a significant impact on several cities, such as San Francisco and Washington, D.C. However, the trend is obscured by the same migration patterns that have characterized the city for the better part of the twentieth century: as the poor enter the city, the more affluent leave it for the suburbs. In the past, more people migrated to the city than left it; today more people are leaving the city than moving to it.

A small number of mostly young, professional, middle-class individuals have chosen to live in cities (or, at least to use a phrase coined by Sternlieb and Hughes, a select number of "nonsmokestack cities"—cities whose economies are based on services rather than manufacturing). These "new elites have attracted attention far beyond their numbers. The neighborhoods they renovate contrast starkly with the poverty of the nearby slums." Sternlieb and Hughes have characterized this contrast as the "two cities" phenomenon:

> From the viewpoint of the poor, the city . . . has become the city of redistribution—of transfer payments and welfare. For the elite there is a city—far from new, but increasingly vigorous—of information processing and economic facilitation, of consumption rather than production. Lost between these two poles and fast disappearing are the middle groups who find both the lifestyles and economic opportunities of suburbia (and increasingly exurbia) affordable and more fulfilling.[19]

Neighborhood Development

As cities change, so do neighborhoods. Neighborhood change was built into the models of the Chicago urbanists. The processes of invasion and succes-

[18] George Sternlieb and James W. Hughes, "Back to the Central City: Myths and Realities," in *America's Housing: Prospects and Problems,* ed. George Sternlieb and James W. Hughes (New Brunswick, N.J.: Center for Urban Policy Research, Rutgers University, 1980).

[19] George Sternlieb and James W. Hughes, "The Two Cities Phenomenon," in ibid., p. 178.

sion guaranteed that cities would be in eternal flux as neighborhoods continually underwent change in their class compositions and ethnic characters.

Hoover and Vernon have presented a description of change at the neighborhood level.[20] They postulate that urban neighborhoods go through a succession of five distinct stages. The first four involve neighborhood downgrading; the fifth is a period of redevelopment. The stages are:

Stage 1. Residential development in single-family homes. This stage is the earliest, appearing when an area on the fringes of a city is first developed.

Stage 2. Apartment development. Most of the new housing in the neighborhood is apartments, so that residential density is increasing. The migrants to the area tend to be young marrieds or marriageable singles.

Stage 3. Downgrading associated with conversion. Many of the older units, both single- and multiple-family buildings, are converted to even higher density use. This is the "slum invasion" period; the neighborhood may experience waves of immigration of various ethnic composition. Household size grows as children arrive and relatives or lodgers are taken in.

Stage 4. Thinning out. The density of the neighborhood declines first as a consequence of a shrinkage in the size of households as children leave. In more advanced stages of thinning out, the number of households declines; dwelling units remain vacant, and neighborhoods experience abandonment and demolition.

Stage 5. Renewal. Obsolete older housing is replaced with new multi-family housing. Housing quality increases, but density may not.

Hoover and Vernon postulate two stages of neighborhood development not anticipated by the processes of invasion and succession: thinning out and renewal. These stages can occur only if the populations of neighborhoods (and therefore of cities) decline. Only then will land be available in sufficient quantity (and at reasonable prices) to encourage redevelopment, Hoover and Vernon's Stage 5.

The thinning-out stage is associated with extensive housing abandonment. Many of the abandoned houses become vandalized, homes to vagrants, alcoholics, and drug addicts. At some point, they will be burned, either by accident or by arsonists. It is this late stage of urban development that has come to characterize large sections of many older northeastern core cities. The South Bronx, with its burned-out tenements and blocks of urban land with only one or two buildings standing, symbolizes this stage better

[20] Edgar Hoover and Raymond Vernon, *Anatomy of a Metropolis.*

The classic inner city: a glittering, vibrant central business district surrounded by residential and commercial decay.

Source: Chicago Tribune, May 14, 1981.

than any other part of urban America. It was here that President Carter toured in 1977 to demonstrate his commitment to the problems of the cities. But the South Bronx is not the only urban neighborhood suffering severe blight. In Chicago, vast segments of the South Side have been depopulated, apartments abandoned, the title to the land reverting to city government—soon, one wag comments, Chicago will be a vacant field owned by itself. A 1978 survey of Detroit's Lower East Side found 9,000 vacant lots and 1,000 boarded-up homes out of the 45,000 properties in the area.[21]

---

[21] Jim Neubacher and Ellen Grzech, "Charting the Tragedy of the Lower East Side—A Fifth of It Has Vanished," *Detroit Free Press,* February 10, 1978.

The economist Wilbur Thompson views the depopulation and attendant housing abandonment in core industrial cities as an opportunity for redevelopment rather than a curse. He has called for a reexamination of attitudes toward center-city depopulation:

> Substantial depopulation of the inner city is a necessary prerequisite to recycling for many metropolitan areas. . . . We must find a way to admit, politically, that depopulation is not only a likely and logical consequence of the aging of urban capital, but is actually occurring and demands explicit policy.[22]

[22] Wilbur Thompson, "Economic Processes and Employment Problems in Declining Metropolitan Areas," in *Post-Industrial America: Metropolitan Decline and Inter-Regional Job Shifts,* ed. George Sternlieb and James W. Hughes (New Brunswick, N.J.: Center for Urban Policy Research, Rutgers University, 1979), p. 194.

But recycling, which involves moving from Hoover and Vernon's Stage 4 to Stage 5, is not automatic. Land availability is not enough; the land also has to be attractive to investors and developers for the transition between stages to occur. The attractiveness of land for redevelopment will vary from neighborhood to neighborhood and city to city, and may well not occur at all in many neighborhoods and in many cities. Chicago's Uptown, on the shores of Lake Michigan, seems to be in transition to renewal, but Detroit's Lower East Side, located along the Detroit river close to downtown and the exclusive neighborhoods of Grosse Pointe, shows few signs of redevelopment.

Deconcentration and the Regional Shift

As cities have sprawled outward, jobs have also dispersed to the outlying areas. Between 1970 and 1975, the city of New York lost 2.4 percent of its jobs per year; Chicago lost 2.8 percent per year, Detroit 4.4 percent, and St. Louis 3.6 percent. This pattern was repeated in most northeastern and midwestern metropolises. In most cases, the jobs added in the suburbs offset the jobs lost in the city. (New York was an exception; the New York metropolitan region lost 1.7 percent of its employment opportunities per year during the period.) The result in many northeastern and midwestern urban areas was a no-growth economy. By *no-growth* economy we mean that no *net* increases are taking place. Many changes occur in any economy; new industries and job opportunities are added as old ones disappear. In total, however, the economy is not expanding.

During the same period that the economies of Chicago, St. Louis, Philadelphia, and Detroit were reaching zero economic growth (ZEG), and the economy of New York was declining, employment in the city of Houston was expanding at an annual rate of 6.1 percent per year, and its suburbs were adding jobs at a 5.6 percent annual rate. Other southern and western cities were also growing, although not at the rate experienced by Houston.[23]

These regional differences in economic growth have led some analysts to proclaim a region of growth, the so-called Sunbelt, and a region of decline, the so-called Frostbelt (residents of the latter would perhaps prefer the terms "tropical zone" and "temperate zone"). Table 4.2 presents one measure of these regional differences in economic growth. In regional terms, the Northeast experienced a no-growth economy during the first half of the 1970s,

---

[23] These figures are from Herrington J. Bryce and Seymour Sacks, "Trends in Central City Employment," in *Revitalizing Cities,* ed. Herrington J. Bryce (Lexington, Mass.: Lexington Books, 1979).

Table 4.2. Percentage share of national growth in employment, by region, 1960–78

Region	1960–65	1965–70	1970–75	1975–78
United States total	100.0%	100.0%	100.0%	100.0%
Northeast	14.5	20.7	−0.6	9.7
North central	23.5	27.2	14.7	27.2
South	38.5	33.9	55.8	36.7
West	23.5	18.2	30.1	26.5

Source: The President's National Urban Policy Report, 1980 (Washington, D.C.: U.S. Department of Housing and Urban Development, 1980), pp. 1–9.

while in the Midwest the economy grew slowly. The South and West both grew approximately three times as fast as the Midwest. Since 1975, these regional differences in the growth patterns have continued.

Causes of regional shift

The sources of regional changes in economic growth are many. One source is the relocation in the South and Southwest of facilities formerly located in the North or Midwest. In the Sunbelt labor is generally cheaper, less unionized, and more docile. Advances in communication and transportation mean that industries are free to relocate in other regions and, indeed, no longer need confine themselves to large cities.

A second reason for the regional shift has been the changing nature of the national economy. Manufacturing provides a smaller and smaller proportion of the jobs in our economy, and services a larger and larger proportion. Moreover, there has been a shift in the manufacturing sector from heavy manufacturing, such as the production of steel and the finished products dependent on steel (automobiles, home appliances, and the like; to light manufacturing, such as the production of computers, calculators, cosmetics, and phonograph records. The latter industries are less labor intensive and more technology dependent than the heavy manufacturing that has dominated the economies of the North and Midwest. Much of the regional shift has involved a phasing out of jobs in heavy manufacturing in the Frostbelt and the concomitant opening of job opportunities in different industries in the Sunbelt. Steel plants have not been relocated in the Sunbelt; indeed, both Pittsburgh and Birmingham have lost manufacturing jobs. The steel industry in the United States has not been able to compete with foreign steel, especially steel from Japan and West Germany. The modern plants of these nations, newly built since the Second World War, produce steel that is competitively priced even with the shipping costs added. The aging open-hearth steel plants of Youngstown and Bessemer and Gary are labor intensive, dirty, and inefficient when compared with those of their foreign competitors. They shut down and lay off workers with no corresponding openings in Dallas or Atlanta.

Other national economic trends affect the regional shift. Steel mills were originally located near deposits of iron ore and coal in order to minimize transportation costs. For similar reasons, oil refineries were located near oil deposits. As energy prices have risen, the oil-rich states of Texas, Louisiana, and Oklahoma have taken larger percentages of the national wealth, as has coal-rich Montana. As the energy industry has boomed, so have ancillary services in these states. The ports of New Orleans and Houston serve as supply outlets for the numerous tankers picking up the refined petroleum; drilling suppliers, consulting geologists and chemists, data processing specialists, and others have opened offices in the energy cities of the Southwest.

New sources of wealth, based in the production of energy, the development of communication and information systems, and the delivery of services, have eclipsed the old wealth—heavy manufacturing centered in the older cities of the Northeast and Midwest. These new sources of wealth are centered in the new cities of the South and West.

A final component of the regional shift has been government. Sunbelt states have tended to be low-tax states. They tax both corporations and individuals at lower rates than their northern counterparts. They also provide their citizens with fewer public services. Corporations, however, are generally more concerned about tax rates than about services. Moreover, the priorities of southern cities have tended to conform to the priorities of corporate managers: roads and sewers are built, but provisions for welfare, health, and other human services are not impressive.

The federal government has also contributed to the shift, in two ways. The first is the preference of the Department of Defense for Sunbelt contractors. Major defense contractors are located in California, the state of Washington, and Texas. Many of the producers of planes, weapons, and other heavy equipment have close relationships with the Department of Defense and are awarded large contracts for the development and production of weapons systems.

The second manner in which government has contributed to the regional shift springs from the fact that federal expenditure tends to be redistributive. That is, the federal government tends to take tax monies from wealthier states and redistribute them as government expenditures to poorer states. In general, northern and midwestern states score higher on measures of personal wealth and income than do southern states. Hence, the southern states receive a larger proportion of federal expenditures.

Regional differences

The economic growth of the Sunbelt cities does not mean that they have escaped the urban problems suffered by the cities of the North. The problems of rapid economic growth are as real as the problems associated with economic stagnation and population decline, and perhaps as severe. Economic growth does not spread wealth equally, nor does it necessarily spread it fairly. The abject poverty of many Chicanos and blacks in northeast Houston contrasts sharply with the glitter of the downtown highrises and the burgeoning new subdivisions of west Houston. The attractiveness of the Sunbelt cities to people searching for employment opportunities has meant that housing is in short supply, a problem remedied much more rapidly for the better off than for the poor.

Sunbelt growth rates have not affected economic differences between the two regions to the extent suggested by many newspaper writers. In their study of differences between Sunbelt and Frostbelt cities, Dye and Ammons conclude that:

> Frostbelt cities are losing population; they have higher population densities; they have larger ethnic populations; and they have larger numbers of people living in their surrounding suburbs. More importantly, Frostbelt cities are showing their age: They have much older housing stock on the average than Sunbelt cities. . . .
>
> In contrast, Sunbelt cities, despite their growth rates, have lower median incomes, lower property values, larger proportions of poor people, larger proportions of black residents, and lower incomes and greater poverty among these black residents. In general, Frostbelt cities have greater *economic resources* than Sunbelt cities, but Frostbelt cities suffer the ill-effects of *age and deterioration* to a greater extent than Sunbelt cities.[24]

There is nothing inevitable about the regional shift, or, for that matter, deconcentration in general. The circumstances propelling the move south may change; government may intervene; a major heat wave such as occurred in the summer of 1980 may weaken the perceived climatic advantage of the Sunbelt for service-oriented industries. Watkins and Perry remind us that it is human decision making, not impersonal economic and social forces, that govern the regional shift:

> Throughout the history, regional growth and decline has been governed by the decisions of individuals acting both in their capacity as private citizens and through various social institutions. . . . During each stage, the fate of various

[24] Thomas R. Dye and James H. Ammons, "Frostbelt and Sunbelt Cities: What Difference It Makes," *The Urban Interest* 2 (Spring 1980): 33.

cities rested on the perspicacity or lack of foresight of the dominant economic actors. Human decisions and not the Invisible Hand were the major controlling factor in the past just they will continue to be preeminent in the future.[25]

Zero Metropolitan Population Growth

Central cities in America have been losing population for decades. During the 1970s, several major metropolitan regions also either failed to add significant numbers of residents or actually lost population. People were not simply leaving the center cities for suburbs; they were deserting the metropolis entirely. Pittsburgh has the distinction of anticipating this trend by being the only metropolis to lose population during the 1960s.

The size of cities is a function of four factors: in-migration, out-migration, the birth rate, and the death rate. Of these factors, only the death rate has not changed during the past fifteen years. Migration to metropolitan areas dropped dramatically during the 1970s. Significant numbers of people left metropolitan regions for the small cities and towns where job opportunities are growing. Table 4.3 portrays these dramatic changes in migration patterns. Moreover, the birth rate has dropped significantly, not just in the cities but in the countryside; not just in America, but worldwide, especially in the industrial societies of western Europe. In the United States, the number of births per woman has dropped from 3.5 in the late 1950s to 1.8 for the last several years, the lowest since the 1930s. Changing lifestyles, the massive entrance of women into the labor force, and the increased use of contraceptives and family planning have all contributed to declining birth rates.

Changes in the rate of population growth have important implications for society generally and cities in particular. The average age will increase, as will the proportion of dependent aged. Tax burdens will increase as the size of the working population goes down. Many cities will cease to grow, and those that do grow will do so because of migration patterns alone. There will be increases in housing abandonment, as fewer houses will be needed for a smaller population, although this will be somewhat offset by the existence of smaller households, with each household needing separate living arrangements. Other impacts on the economics and politics of cities can be foreseen only dimly; many others cannot be foreseen at all. What is certain is that changes in growth rates have important consequences for cities, and that alterations in their demographic compositions, economic systems, and political forms can be expected.

[25] Alfred J. Watkins and David C. Perry, "Regional Change and the Impact of Uneven Urban Development," in *Urban Affairs Annual Reviews,* vol. 14, *The Rise of the Sunbelt Cities,* ed. David C. Perry and Alfred J. Watkins (Beverly Hills, Calif: Sage, 1977), p. 52.

Table 4.3. Average annual rate of net migration per 1,000 population by metropolitan size and region, 1960–70 and 1970–80

Size and Region	Northeast			North Central			South			West		
	Net migration		Population 1980	Net migration		Population 1980	Net migration		Population 1980	Net migration		Population 1980
	1960 to 1970	1970 to 1980		1960 to 1970	1970 to 1980		1960 to 1970	1970 to 1980		1960 to 1970	1970 to 1980	
Total regions	1.0	1.1	49,137	−1.4	−2.6	58,854	1.6	11.5	75,349	10.0	13.7	43,165
Metropolitan	−3.9	−5.8	41,716	.6	−4.8	41,166	7.7	12.2	48,697	13.5	12.3	34,415
Metropolitan:												
3 million and over	1.6	−8.3	24,737	.1	−6.8	12,363	17.9	9.3	6,621	13.8	5.9	16,378
1 to 3 million	−3.7	−7.7	4,558	1.5	−6.0	13,855	15.5	16.1	13,913	10.2	19.1	9,338
½ to 1 million	3.0	−1.6	7,349	1.0	−5.0	3,997	5.6	11.5	11,441	4.1	14.0	2,745
¼ to ½ million	−.3	2.3	3,419	−.4	−1.4	4,876	−.1	10.0	9,214	14.5	18.5	3,756
Under ¼ million	.9	1.7	1,652	−.1	−.5	6,076	−1.2	11.4	7,508	8.3	23.1	2,196
Nonmetropolitan	.3	8.1	7,421	−4.6	2.8	17,688	−8.3	10.1	26,652	−3.6	19.1	8,750

Source: John F. Long, *Population Deconcentration in the United States* (Washington, D.C.: U.S. Bureau of the Census, 1981), table 13, p. 59.

Urban Problems in Comparative
Perspective

The trends we have examined in this chapter are shared, to a greater or lesser extent, by other cities in the world. Countries in the world may be divided into three groups, somewhat crudely but not entirely misleadingly: Western, industrialized countries (the United States, Western Europe, and Australia and New Zealand); the Communist world (the Soviet Union and its satellites); and the Third World, a vast and diverse region containing the bulk of the world's countries and most of its population. Urban problems differ significantly among these regions.

Urban affluence, according to data assembled by Robert Fried and Francine Rabinovitz, is concentrated in the cities of the Western world. North America and Europe, with about 18 percent of the population of the world, have three-quarters of the world's telephones and four-fifths of its private automobiles.[26] These differentials are maintained on such *social indicators* as housing quality, accident rates, infant mortality, availability of health care, access to baths, flush toilets, and running water, and access to such appliances as washing machines and televisions. Communist cities are not on a par with Western cities on the quality-of-life indicators listed, but they do far better than the cities of the Third World.

Indeed, it is in cities of the Third World that urban problems are most severe. Third World cities are affected by extreme rates of both migration and natural increase. Fried and Rabinovitz note:

> In Third World cities there are typically at least twice as many births as deaths; in places like Seoul, Teheran, Bangkok, Baghdad, and Manila, there are more than five times as many births as deaths. In advanced cities, births barely outnumber deaths (about 1.7 to 1 in American cities); in Central and Northern European cities like Vienna, West and East Berlin, Budapest, Hamburg and Prague, there are far more deaths than births.[27]

High rates of natural growth combine with high migration to yield genuinely explosive growth rates in many cities of the Third World. Between 1960 and 1967, the population of São Paulo, Brazil, grew by more than 2.5 million people, approximately equivalent to the entire population of the Dallas–Fort Worth metropolis. Migration is estimated to account for about 68 percent of this increase.[28] Such rapid migration also characterizes Mexico

[26] Robert C. Fried and Francine F. Rabinovitz, *Comparative Urban Politics: Performance Approach* (Englewood Cliffs, N.J.: Prentice-Hall, 1980).
[27] Ibid., p. 152.
[28] Ibid., p. 154.

City, Cairo, Bombay, Jakarta, Lagos, and Nairobi, to mention but a few of the Third World cities affected by extreme growth rates.

Rapid growth has led to urban sprawl in Third World cities, but it is an urban sprawl unlike American urban sprawl. In cities such as Calcutta, Ankara, Mexico City, and Rio de Janeiro, from one-third to three-quarters of the residents live in squatter settlements, in wood-and-paper shacks clustered on the open space surrounding the city, without running water, electricity, or sanitary facilities. Water must be gotten from communal wells; no streets (if the rows among the shacks can be called streets) are paved. The public infrastructure (streets, sewer systems, water systems, utilities) has been built up in the core city, but there are at best modest plans to extend them into the squatter slums. Because city amenities are concentrated in the core city, the better off live in the core rather than on the rim of the city, as they tend to do in American cities. Indeed, the opulence of the inner-city residences of the wealthy in the Third World contrast starkly with the squalor of the squatter settlements.

The realities of explosive growth are translated into the social indicators assembled by Fried and Rabinovitz. In Cairo, 141 infants die for every 100,000 live births; in Istanbul, 114; in Recife, 229. At the other end of the scale, European cities lose few infants for each live birth. Some American cities, such as Chicago, Philadelphia, Atlanta, and Denver, have higher infant death rates than most European cities, as well as such Asian cities as Tokyo, Hong Kong, and Singapore, but far lower than the bulk of Third World cities. Housing in Third World cities is scarce and expensive; there are few of the urban amenities that North Americans are accustomed to, and those that exist are concentrated in the hands of a small number of wealthy individuals.

In comparative perspective, the urban problems of America fade. In aggregate affluence, American cities offer the amenities sought by most of the world's population.

On some social indicators, however, American cities do not fare so well. American cities lead the developed world (and much of the undeveloped world as well) in crime rates. One is three times as likely to be robbed in San Francisco or Baltimore as in Taipei, Mexico City, or Toronto. The death rate from fires is far higher in Philadelphia than in Munich or Rio de Janeiro. And as we have indicated, infant death rates in American cities exceed those in most European cities.

Perhaps most disturbing is the disparity in economic resources in American cities. The *distribution* of wealth and income is far from equal; squalid slums exist for a minority even as the majority enjoy most of the urban amenities available, and a few virtually wallow in them. Superimposed on this unequal distribution are urban problems: crime, poor health, poor nutrition, and poor housing go hand in hand with poverty. This unequal distribution of resources is not nearly as pronounced in the United States as it is in Third World cities, but it far exceeds anything observable in Europe and most Communist cities.

Conclusions

Since the first United States census was taken in 1790, save for a brief time during the 1930s, Americans have been moving from farm to city. The growth of American cities began in earnest after the Civil War, during the rapid industrialization that was taking place in the Northeast and Middle West. Philadelphia doubled its population between 1850 and 1860; Chicago tripled its population between 1860 and 1870, and doubled it again between 1880 and 1890. Los Angeles tripled its population between 1900 and 1910, and Detroit doubled its between 1910 and 1920. By 1920, America was an urban nation; more people lived in cities and towns than in the country's rural regions. The vast bulk of this urban population was located in metropolitan regions; by the mid-1970s, almost three-quarters of all Americans lived in metropolitan regions. During the 1970s, however, metropolitan areas (SMSAs) grew at a slower rate (10.2 percent) than did nonmetropolitan areas (15.1 percent).[29]

The great migrations of people to America's industrial cities brought European immigrants of a multitude of ethnic, cultural, and religious backgrounds, and transformed America from a nation composed primarily of North European stock into an ethnic hodgepodge. After World War II, black Americans began moving to the cities, and for three decades they were the most important addition to urban population growth. Although blacks did not find the racial intimidation they often experienced in the South, they did encounter discrimination in employment and housing.

Prior to the development of relatively clean and efficient transportation systems, the wealthy lived near the center of the typical American city. After the electric railway was developed, the wealthy moved to the rim of the city, and the core city became increasingly populated by poor migrants. With the development of the mass-produced automobile the wealthy were joined by the middle class, and the suburban boom was on. During this period, the city assumed a concentric land-use pattern, in which better residences were located on the rim of the city, and housing was of poorer and poorer quality as one moved toward the center city. Cutting through these concentric circles were sectors, or wedges, of manufacturing and commercial activity as factories located along railroads and other transportation routes.

[29] Philip M. Hauser, "The Census of 1980," *Scientific American* 245 (November, 1981), p. 57. The metropolitan growth rate was composed of a sizable suburban increase (18.2 percent) and no growth in center cities.

As suburbanization progressed, suburbs themselves became differentiated. Some suburbs continued to serve as "bedrooms" of the wealthy, who commuted to jobs in the central business district. Others, however, specialized in industrial location, in shopping outlets, in middle-income housing and working-class residences. The metropolis came to approximate the multiple-nuclei model, but with patterns of concentric and sector development still clearly visible.

Modern trends affecting American cities include the regional shift of industry, population, and employment; the increasingly bipolar nature of the center city; and declining population growth, affecting northeastern and middlewestern cities especially. As the American national economy has shifted from an emphasis on manufacturing to a stress on services, southern and western cities have grown relatively faster than northeastern and midwestern cities. Indeed, several older northern cities have experienced zero growth. The new central city is still prone to suburbanization and deconcentration, as industry and people continue to move to the city's rim, but in some "nonsmokestack" cities well-off middle-class professionals constitute a back-to-the-city movement, a trend that has been in progress for several decades but that has accelerated somewhat recently. Some analysts have seen an increasingly bipolar city as a result, with the urban "underclass," mired in poverty, dependent on government transfer payments, and having no real hope for permanent employment, coexisting uneasily with the urban "gentry" hoping to revitalize the city and make it the cultural and commercial center of the metropolis once again.

Interconnectedness

This, then, is the context within which urban public policies are made. In it, one observes both remarkable stability and ceaseless change.[30] Many urban trends are remarkably stable: no major United States city has ever disappeared, and few new cities of any consequence have been born in this century. Other trends cumulate over many years to cause major changes in cities: declining birth rates have important implications for the growth and structure of cities. Yet one also observes rapid change in urban America: the invasion and succession of neighborhoods; the violence of the urban disorders that have occurred in American cities; the closing of a major industrial facility, throwing thousands out of work.

The major problem for urban governance is that most of these trends are interconnected. They affect one another, sometimes intensifying the effect,

[30] Some indication of this stability amidst change may be gleaned by comparing two volumes on urban problems written more than a decade apart. See James Q. Wilson, ed., *The Metropolitan Enigma: Inquiries into the Nature and Dimensions of America's "Urban Crisis"* (Cambridge, Mass.: Harvard University Press, 1968); and Arthur P. Soloman, ed., *The Prospective City* (Cambridge, Mass.: MIT Press, 1980).

sometimes dampening it. The regional shift of jobs and people has intensified the effects of declining birth rates on city growth for northeastern industrial cities, but has muted or even offset them for Sunbelt cities.

Public policymaking involves response to these trends, decisions on which government ought to try to affect and which ought be allowed to run their course. In a democratic society, this must be done in the context of demands made by citizens and groups for change. Such demands must be taken seriously, although citizens will not always voice support for policies that will make the situation better. Demands do indicate problems, however, and deserve some response by government. Yet resource limitations, the tradition of local autonomy, and the realities of the policy process constrain the available responses to these demands. In the next chapters we will examine the sources of citizen demands, how they are made known to urban governments, and how governments respond to them.

PART II

City Politics

Politics, government, and public policy form a triangle that is never broken. Where one finds government, one finds policies. Where one finds policies, one finds politics. Indeed, one common definition of politics is the struggle over the control and use of governmental authority.

In this section we study city politics. Chapter 5 examines the means by which citizens can participate in urban policymaking. Chapter 6 presents an overview of the operation of urban political parties, once an extremely important urban political institution and still viable in many locations. Chapter 7 is an examination of the role of urban interest groups, and chapter 8 examines the structure of community power and the manner in which private power influences public decision making.

In the complex interplay between citizens and government, a critical issue emerges: can political elites (that is, governmental officials) be held accountable to the public? Do the policies they pursue conform to the interests of the general public, or are powerful private elites, narrow interest groups, and political party "bosses" able to subvert popular control? Can urban interest groups and political parties, the only institutions capable of linking citizens to government, be harnessed in the attempt to secure popular control in urban governments? Or are the rituals of a democracy only meaningless shams, manipulated by a powerful economic elite in order to keep the vast majority of citizens passive?

CHAPTER 5

Participation
in Urban Politics

At one time, many Americans particpated directly in local public policy-making. In New England, town meetings set the agenda of public action; in many other parts of the nation, citizens and their government were remarkably close. Yet most Americans were excluded from participating in this system: women, slaves, indentured servants, and those who did not own property. Even among the eligible, turnout was often quite low. Nevertheless, the rural character of the country and the fact that towns were quite isolated from each other meant that local citizens could, more or less directly, affect public policy.

That system of government quickly became archaic. With the growth of cities, with the expansion of the franchise, and with the increasing number of functions performed by government, accountability of government to the governed could no longer be accomplished simply. When they participate at all, most citizens in the urban areas of America participate indirectly in the policymaking process, by voting for policymakers, by forming groups to influence government, or by other means. This is as true of local government as it is of the national government. Indeed, city hall can be as remote from the average citizen as Capitol Hill. Studies indicate that local politics are no more salient to citizens than national politics (although local affairs are followed more closely than state or international affairs).[1]

In this milieu a number of institutions have developed, institutions that have the effect of linking citizens to their government. These institutions include elections, political parties, interest groups, and, occasionally, the government bureaucracy itself. To the degree that these institutions do not provide regular channels of access, or to the degree that they provide access to some citizens and deny it to others, accountability fails.

In this chapter we examine citizen participation in the urban context. Looking specifically at the modes citizens use to influence government, and the institutions associated with those modes, we pose a key question of modern political science: Is democratic accountability being maintained in modern urban America?

Modes of Participation

It is difficult to quarrel with the definition of participation offered by two leading students of the phenomenon: participation includes "acts that aim at *influencing* the government, either by affecting the *choice* of government personnel or by affecting the *choices made by* government personnel."[2] Participation is trying to get the government to do something. According to this definition, participation is not an expression of support for the system, such as might occur in an Independence Day parade. Neither is it participation when citizens gather to express outrage in a protest march. Protest, and expression of support, constitute participation only when they aim to spur government to do something, such as enact a particular law or change an administrative ruling.

There are six different modes that citizens can use in their attempts to influence government: voting, partisan activity, group activity, citizen-initiated contact, mandated participation, and mobility. *Voting* is a choice made by an individual that has collective consequences. When individual votes are added up, they determine who is to run the government. In local elections they also determine substantive public policy, through referenda. *Partisan activity* can involve serving as a precinct captain for a political party. Contributing money, attending meetings, canvassing voters, and soliciting funds for a party also fall within this mode. *Group activity* is participation in which citizens band together in order to influence government.

---

[1] M. Kent Jennings and Harmon Zeigler, "The Salience of American State Politics," *American Political Science Review* 64 (June 1970): 525.

[2] Sidney Verba and Norman H. Nie, *Participation in America: Political Democracy and Social Equality* (New York: Harper & Row, 1972), p. 2.

It includes regular support of an interest association or neighborhood organization; it also includes protest activity. *Citizen-initiated contact* is a form of participation in which the individual citizen contacts government about a specific problem—writes to a congressman about problems in receiving social security checks, or calls the bureau of public works about a pothole in the street. Many urban service agencies spend much of their time handling such citizen complaints. *Mandated participation* is participation that is conducted by government as a part of a program it operates. This can involve required open hearings, citizen advisory boards, or referenda among program recipients. Finally, *mobility* is changing one's residence or place of business in order to affect public policy. It is "voting with one's feet."

Institutions of participation

Each of the modes of participation rests on one or more supporting institutions. Voting, for example, cannot be meaningful without free and open elections. Moreover, unless the electorate (those who vote in a given election) is reasonably representative of all citizens, elections will not reflect the opinions of the mass public. A political party cannot be a meaningful institution for making governments accountable to citizens unless it can compete freely in elections. A party must also be able to control the policies of government once it is put into office. Otherwise what a party does in office will not be related to what happens in an election.

Group activity is not a meaningful linkage mechanism unless citizens can freely organize, and unless government officials pay attention to their demands. For citizen-initiated contacts to serve as a channel of citizen access to government, government must have regular procedures for responding to such contacts. If citizen mobility is to influence public policy, the free movement of people and capital must be allowed. Finally, mandated participation rests squarely on government: unless government provides for it, it will not exist. Table 5.1 reviews the modes of participation and the institutional ar-

Table 5.1. Modes of participation and supporting institutions

Mode of participation	Supporting institutions
Voting	Free elections
Political parties	Elections; party control of government
Groups	Free association
Citizen contact	Government procedures
Mobility	Unimpeded movement of citizens and capital
Mandated participation	Government procedures

rangements necessary for making them meaningful mechanisms for accountability.

The Decision to Participate

The individual citizen must decide whether to make an attempt to influence government. The decision to participate may be viewed as a rational one in which the citizen weighs the costs and benefits of participating and acts accordingly. Clearly many citizens decide that the effort is not worth the cost, since only about 53 percent of eligible voters cast ballots in presidential elections; far fewer engage in other acts of participation. A school millage election that is held separately from state and national elections can draw as little as 10 percent of the eligible electorate. Even fewer citizens engage in the more complex form of participation: campaigning for a party or candidate, working actively in an interest group, or serving on a citizen advisory commission.

Citizens participate because they derive rewards from doing so, either intrinsically or instrumentally. A citizen is *intrinsically* rewarded when he or she receives pleasure from the act of participating itself. Voting fulfills a sense of civic duty, and joining an interest group or engaging in a protest march offers camaraderie. *Instrumental* reward occurs when a citizen participates in order to get government to solve a problem or achieve a goal. Such motivation causes a citizen to contact the building department to complain about an abandoned house. It also motivates a group of business people to approach the mayor for help in clearing land for a new construction project.

Whether the citizen will engage in an act of participation to achieve his or her goals depends on four factors:

1. *Problem and need.* The citizen must perceive that he has a problem. The citizen, then, must be dissatisfied with his existing state of affairs; he must feel a need for government action.

2. *Information.* The citizen must perceive that government can help to solve the problem, and she must understand the connection between an act of participation and a response by government.

3. *Efficacy.* The citizen must feel that the act of participation has some probability of getting the government to respond to the problem. This is often termed a sense of efficacy.

4. *Institutional context.* An institutional context must exist that makes it likely that government will respond to citizen demands. Some institutions inhibit governmental responsiveness; others facilitate it. Some, in other words, are more open to citizen participation than others. Participation is generally greater in the open system than in the closed.

Socioeconomic status, ethnicity, and the activist subculture

The literature on political participation confirms again and again that Americans of higher socioeconomic status participate more in political activities than those of lower status. This holds for each of the modes of participation except one: citizen-initiated contacts. Moreover, the more difficult the act of participation, the stronger the association between status and participation. Verba and Nie found that, in their national sample, there was less difference between low-status and high-status Americans for the relatively simple act of voting than for the much more difficult and time-consuming activity of participating in interest-group activity.[3]

Survey data also confirm that there exists a cadre of very active citizens who have high levels of information about politics and who feel that their activity will be effective. Verba and Nie term these individuals *complete activists*. Studies at the national and the local level show that membership in this activist subculture is related to social status. For example, in a study of four mid-sized Wisconsin cities, Alford and Scoble found that their general index of political involvement correlated substantially with status (particularly educational level), and involvement was also related to membership and activity in organizations.[4]

It would be a mistake to jump from the finding that upper-status individuals participate at higher rates to the conclusion that they predominate in the politically active subculture. Because there are fewer upper-class citizens than lower- and middle-class citizens, upper-status people can still be outnumbered by those of lower status in the activist subculture. Suppose, for example, a community contains 100,000 citizens of low and middle status, and 10,000 citizens of high status. Even if the lower- and middle-class citizens participate at a 20 percent rate and the upper-class citizens participate at a 90 percent rate, the activist strata will be composed of 20,000 citizens from the lower classes and 9,000 citizens from the upper class. As Robert Dahl puts it, "Because the number of Better-Off citizens is inevitably rather small, the *aggregate* activity of citizens with smaller resources is often impressively large."[5] Although upper-status individuals will be overrepresented in the activist subculture, because of their small absolute numbers, they still may not be able to prevail on any particular issue.

Moreover, there are factors in political activity other than socioeconomic status. One of these is ethnicity, which several scholars maintain is far from dead as a motivating factor in elections.[6] In a study of citizens in New York,

---

[3] Ibid., p. 132.

[4] Robert Alford and Harry Scoble, "Sources of Local Political Involvement," *American Political Science Review* 62 (December 1968): 1192–1206.

[5] Robert A. Dahl, *Who Governs?* (New Haven, Conn.: Yale University Press, 1961), p. 284.

[6] Andrew Greeley, "Political Participation Among Ethnic Groups in the United States: A Preliminary Reconnaissance," *American Journal of Sociology* 80 (1974): 170–204; Michael

Differences of opinion are often expressed in America's diverse cities.

Source: Detroit Free Press, June 18, 1981.

Nelson found that both socioeconomic status and ethnic identity were strongly and independently related to local political involvement. He suggests that "ethnic divisions are going to be enduring features of the sociopolitical landscape."[7]

These studies indicate that some ethnic groups will be underrepresented in the activist subculture, and others will be overrepresented. This will occur regardless of socioeconomic status. Within the low-status group, for example, Nelson's New York study indicates that Cubans and Dominicans (immigrants from the Dominican Republic) are substantially underrepresented in the activist strata, and Irish and blacks are overrepresented.

Parenti: "Ethnic Politics and the Persistence of Ethnic Identification," *American Political Science Review* 61 (September 1967): 717–26.

[7] Dale C. Nelson, "The Case for Ethnic Political Culture," *American Political Science Review* 73 (December 1979): 1924–38.

Voting

Voting in national elections always means voting for candidates or parties. Citizens try to support candidates who they feel will enact public policies that are in tune with their needs and desires. In local and state elections, citizens also vote for candidates, but they are in addition regularly asked to approve a variety of referenda on substantive policy matters. In most localities, for example, citizens must approve all increases in the property tax rate imposed by school districts. In some localities, citizens must approve all bond issues, sometimes by "supermajorities." In St. Louis, bond issues must be approved by a 60 percent vote; this makes it very difficult to gain passage of these issues.

Referenda voting and ballot complexity

The number of candidates and referenda that citizens must vote on means that election ballots are often very complex. In the general election held in November 1980, citizens of Detroit were asked to vote on three separate sections of the ballot. Names of candidates for President and most other offices were on the partisan ballot, which designates party affiliations next to the candidates' names. (There was no election for governor or mayor, because election reformers long ago decreed that these offices would be chosen in years in which there was no presidential election. This was supposed to make the choice more independent, but what it actually did was to decrease participation in the off-year elections.) Voters were also to select judges from a nonpartisan section of the ballot. Finally, citizens were asked to judge the desirability of a number of state, county, and municipal referenda, including the following: three statewide, contradictory proposals for shifting the tax burden from property tax (all failed); one statewide proposal for increasing the income tax to build prisons (failed); four county propositions to increase the property tax rate for a variety of purposes (all failed); four city proposals to issue bonds for certain public improvements (all failed); a city proposal to remove from the city charter a provision that promotions in the fire department be based solely on seniority (passed); and a school district proposal to increase the property tax rate (passed). Voters were also asked to rule on the duties of the lieutenant governor, on immunity from civil prosecution for state legislators, and on provision of legal counsel for the Detroit city council. Needless to say, lines were long at the polls that day.

But long and complicated ballots have a consequence far more important than waiting time. Turnout in Detroit in that election was about 60 percent of eligible voters, higher than in many cities (but far lower than in many other Western democracies). Yet many voters, as many as half on some issues, failed to cast votes for the complicated referenda issues, which were difficult to understand. This is called *ballot roll-off*. Since the most educated and informed (and most affluent) voters are the most likely to work their way through the entire ballot, complex ballots can give them disproportionate influence in determining the outcomes of the issues and offices most subject to the roll-off.[8]

In most cities, various groups endorse candidates and issues. Endorsing groups include the metropolitan newspapers, labor unions, business and civil groups, church groups, and political party organizations. These endorsements mean little in presidential or gubernatorial contests, but they can be vitally important in carrying referenda issues. When ballots are long and complex, such endorsing groups wield more influence.

The context of the voting decision

The decision to vote in an election is influenced by *individual characteristics,* such as socioeconomic status and political interest, by the social, political, and institutional *context* of participation, and by *particular features* of the election in question, such as its perceived closeness and the attractiveness of the candidates vying for office. Having discussed the role of individual characteristics in "The Decision to Participate," here we concentrate on the context of voting.

It is possible for contextual factors to affect the voting decision in an opposite direction from individual factors. For example, citizens of higher socioeconomic status are more likely to vote than citizens of lower status, but this does not necessarily mean that higher-status communities have higher turnout rates than lower-status communities. In an analysis of American cities, Alford and Lee found that level of education was inversely related to voter turnout. The higher the level of education in the community, the lower the turnout. This relationship probably stems from the fact that higher-status communities are more homogeneous and are characterized by less social conflict. With a lower level of social conflict, there is less reason for people to participate.

This study found other interesting contextual influences on voting. Turnout was directly related to ethnicity (the higher the proportion of foreign born, the higher the turnout), directly related to the age of the city, and inversely related to the extent of mobility of the population. Moreover, turnout was also related to the political structure of the city. High turnout was associated with partisan elections and with mayor-council governmental

---

[8] A study of a statewide referendum on tax cut amendments in Michigan in 1978 found that roll-off was greater in Wayne County (Detroit) than in nonmetropolitan counties (Patrick G. Grasso, "Voting on Tax Cut Amendments in Michigan: Some Lessons from 1978," unpublished manuscript, Department of Political Science, Wayne State University, 1980).

forms.[9] Where political systems are organized by political parties and where elections for mayor provide a highly visible political context, voter turnout is higher than in nonpartisan cities and those with the council-manager form of government. Nonpartisanship offers neither the free operation of parties, whose job it is to get out the vote, nor the opportunity for the voter to identify psychologically with candidates from his or her party. Council-manager systems do not offer the electoral "drawing card" of a race for mayor. Participation consequently is lower.

Not only is voting turnout lower in such cities, but the *composition* of the electorate is different. As turnout declines, poor and working-class voters drop out more quickly than the better off. Hence low-turnout elections give more weight to the preferences of the middle-class voter, and less weight to poor and working-class voters.

Registration. Governments may manipulate the institutional context most directly through voter registration laws. Most laws pertaining to the qualification of voters are established by the states, but it is up to local governments, primarily municipalities and counties, to enforce these laws. Indeed, local governments are generally responsible for the entire conduct of elections—local, state, and national—within certain limitations imposed by the United States Constitution, court decisions, and acts of Congress.

Registration laws, and other laws regulating the conduct of elections, may affect the citizen's decision to vote by imposing additional costs on the potential voter. In much of the South before 1965, registration requirements were manipulated to deny blacks the right to vote. Poll taxes (a tax imposed as a condition for registration), literacy tests, short registration periods, and periodic registration rather than permanent registration had the effect of limiting the electorate. These devices imposed a higher cost on low-income citizens and, in particular, black citizens. But the real discrimination came in administration. Local officials in many southern counties would use different forms of literacy tests for blacks than for whites. The number of blacks voting in a county was decided largely at the whim of the local registrar. One result of the discretion exercised by local officials was huge variation in the size of the black electorate from county to county. In Alabama, for example, state voter registration laws were administered with reasonable evenhandedness in Tuscaloosa County, but in neighboring Jefferson County, the locus of the city of Birmingham, there was considerable discrimination against blacks. The Voting Rights Act of 1965, as amended in 1970, abolished literacy tests and provided for federal registrars in certain southern counties. The poll tax was abolished by amendment to the United

---

[9] Robert Alford and Eugene Lee, "Voting Turnout in American Cities," *American Political Science Review* 62 (September 1968): 796–813. The relationship between political structure and turnout survived various statistical controls.

States Constitution. The southern black electorate grew rapidly, and quickly elected blacks to local and state offices previously held by whites.

The first systematic examination of the effects of registration laws on voter turnout was conducted by Stanley Kelley and his associates, who set out to explain differences in voter registration in 104 cities in 1960.[10] In this study the investigators reasoned as follows: Registration would be affected by certain socioeconomic factors such as racial composition, class composition, mobility of the population, and the region in which the city was located. Registration would also be affected by registration laws. So their research would have to include both of these sets of factors. The study used a statistical method called *multiple regression,* which relates a number of independent variables (social and economic factors and registration laws) to one dependent variable (the percentage of citizens who were registered to vote). Kelley and his associates concluded that "local differences in turnout for elections are to a large extent related to local differences in rates of registration, and these in turn reflect to a considerable degree local differences in the rules governing and arrangements for handling, the registering of voters."[11]

Since the mid-1960s, voter registration has become easier in most localities. In Detroit, for example, volunteer voter registrars sign up voters in supermarkets and shopping centers all over the city. In an attempt to reevaluate the effects of registration laws on the electorate, Rosenstone and Wolfinger studied the effects of state registration laws (but not local implementation) on the 1972 presidential election. They concluded that registration laws reduced turnout by a full 9 percentage points, but that changing these laws would have little consequence for the character of the electorate. An electorate without registration requirements would be slightly less educated and affluent, but only about 0.5 percent more would be Democratic voters.[12] This study, it must be noted, applies to a national electorate. The outcomes of certain state or local elections may be affected by rigid registration laws, because these laws impose higher costs on poor and working-class citizens than on the middle class.

Location. Where a person resides can, in certain circumstances, become a voting cue. Years ago, V. O. Key noted that voting in some southern primaries seemed to be based not on class or ethnic identity, but on the residential location of the candidate for office. Alabama gubernatorial candidate "Big Jim" Folsom's electoral strength in 1946 was based in his home

[10] Stanley Kelley, Jr., Richard E. Ayres, and William G. Bowen, "Registration and Voting: Putting First Things First," *American Political Science Review* 61 (June 1967): 359–79.

[11] Ibid., pp. 373–74.

[12] Steven J. Rosenstone and Raymond E. Wolfinger, "The Effect of Registration Laws on Voter Turnout," *American Political Science Review* 72 (March 1978): 22–45.

county and the county of his boyhood home at the other end of the state. Key was critical of such appeal, and he attributed its existence to the absence of a two-party tradition or even a system of enduring intraparty factions in Alabama.[13]

Such voting patterns evidently occur also in cities. One must be cautious, however, in interpreting results that show, for example, two precincts voting similarly. Two neighboring urban precincts are likely to be similar in class and ethnic composition, and these factors may determine the voting behavior of residents.

Location can also play a part in referendum voting. A study of voting on several referendum issues (water fluoridation, education, parks, civic improvements, and public works) in several cities showed that electoral cohesion within a social class was greater when the class was spatially segregated than when it was integrated with other social class groups. That is, if the class was concentrated in a single area, it voted more cohesively than if it was scattered throughout the city. Such voting patterns cannot be explained on the basis of class alone; location must also be taken into account.[14]

The Consequences of Elections

Although elections can serve as mechanisms for holding political leaders accountable to citizens, the existence of elections does not mean that there will automatically result a linkage between community leaders and citizens (often termed a linkage between political elites and the mass public). Only under certain conditions will elections serve as a means for translating mass preferences into the public policies promulgated by public officials.

Concurrence

When the actions of leaders follow the policy wishes of citizens, the resulting correspondence is termed *policy concurrence*. This can happen in two ways. First, the electorate may select leaders (political elites) who share its policy attitudes. Then, when in office, these leaders may enact their own policy preferences. In so doing, they will be enacting the policy preferences of citizens. The second way that elections may encourage policy concurrence is for leaders to enact what they perceive to be the desires of the public regardless of their own policy preferences. Elections facilitate this linkage to the degree that political leaders view elections as a potential threat to their continuing to hold public office. In essence, because of the threat of electoral

[13] V. O. Key, Jr., *Southern Politics* (New York: Vintage, 1949), pp. 37–41.
[14] Timothy Almay, "Residential Location and Electoral Cohesion: The Pattern of Urban Political Conflict," *American Political Science Review* 67 (September 1973): 914–23.

defeat, political leaders adjust their policymaking activities to correspond to citizen preferences. The former system of accountability may be termed *concurrence by elite replacement;* the latter, *concurrence by electoral threat.*

Conditions of Concurrence. Susan Blackall Hansen has systematically investigated the conditions of concurrence by elite replacement. Using a sample of citizens in sixty-four randomly selected communities with fewer than 60,000 people, she studied concurrence between leaders and citizens in the salience of community problems.[15] Because this study investigated concurrence in attitudes, it is a study of concurrence by elite replacement. The study investigated neither concurrence in policy choices (elites and masses may agree that urban decay is a major problem but totally disagree over the public policy remedy) nor the actual policies of the communities studied.

Hansen's findings are fascinating nevertheless. Concurrence is higher where elections are conducted on a partisan basis, and where the chief executive is directly elected (rather than appointed, as in council-manager cities). Concurrence is higher where either the Democratic or the Republican party is active, but declines where both are active. Finally, concurrence is higher where elections are hotly contested. (However, this relationship holds only for communities in which there is a high degree of consensus between politically active citizens and the mass of more passive citizens.)

Concurrence seems to be promoted by electoral competitiveness and other facilitating institutional arrangements, such as partisan electoral systems in communities characterized by high consensus. A community with substantial social cleavages and policy disagreements offers no single point of view with which leaders can concur. They can concur with one side or another, but they cannot concur with both at once. In homogeneous communities with high consensus, however, certain institutional conditions do promote leader concurrence with the single point of view that does exist.

Electoral accountability does not have to rest on concurrence between elite and mass attitudes. Elected leaders may agree to pursue policies favored by citizens because they anticipate losing elections if they do not. Joseph Schlesinger has argued that such a theory of electoral accountability rests squarely on the ambition of men and women:

A political system unable to kindle ambitions for office is as much in danger of breaking down as one unable to restrain ambitions. Representative government, above all, depends on a supply of men so driven; the desire for election and, more important, for reelection becomes the electorate's restraint upon its public officials.[16]

---

[15] Susan Blackall Hansen, "Participation, Political Structures, and Concurrence," *American Political Science Review* 69 (December 1975): 1181–99.

[16] Joseph A. Schlesinger, *Ambition and Politics* (Chicago: Rand McNally, 1966), p. 2.

In a study of city councils in the San Francisco Bay Area, Kenneth Prewitt noted four facts relevant to the theory of electoral accountability. First, many city council members had not sought office, but had been appointed to fill vacancies. Second, low turnouts and plurality elections (in the at-large election systems that characterize small-city California) mean that very few votes were needed to get elected. Third, almost no city council members who stood for reelection were ever defeated. Finally, there was a very high frequency of voluntary retirement from office. Prewitt concludes that a *norm of volunteerism* was operating, in which "men enter and leave office not at the whim of the electorate, but according to self-defined schedules."[17] He found that where volunteerism was high, council members were less likely to vote with what they perceived as the majority opinion in the community.

When local legislators serve in office out of a sense of civic duty rather than a personal desire to occupy the office, electoral accountability is lessened. Public policy will be more in the hands of the better off in such communities, both because such citizens have more of a sense of civic duty and because they can afford the low pay and part-time hours that characterize many city councils.

Partisan Activity

Citizens have the opportunity to participate in political party activity in a number of ways—campaigning for a party or a candidate, attending rallies and meetings, contributing money to sustain the party organization, serving as a member of the party apparatus. Yet this basic organization of political linkage has deteriorated considerably over the years, and the greatest decay has occurred at the local level. Many cities (and some states) prohibit parties from being active at the local level by law. In other areas parties are much weaker than they once were. This decline does not mean that local governments are therefore free of politics. Indeed, a different kind of politics occurs, one often dominated by "volunteerism," high participation by the "better off," and low participation by the mass public. Hence the decline of party has resulted in a loosening of the major mechanism of public control of political leaders. This topic is so important that chapter 6 is devoted to it.

Group Activity

The age-old strategy of citizens banding together to influence the course of public policy is guaranteed in the United States Constitution, and continues

---

[17] Kenneth Prewitt, "Political Ambitions, Volunteerism and Electoral Accountability," *American Political Science Review* 64 (March 1970): 5–17 (quote at 10).

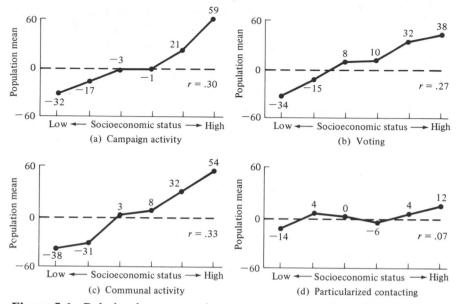

Figure 5.1. Relation between socioeconomic status and participation, by mode.

Source: Figure 8.4 (p. 132) from *Participation in America* by Sidney Verba and Norman H. Nie. Copyright © 1972 by Sidney Verba and Norman H. Nie. Reprinted by permission of Harper & Row, Publishers, Inc.

unabated today. In urban politics, however, the number of groups and the variety of ways they gain access to government have expanded tremendously in recent years. In chapter 7, we examine the various groups that participate in urban politics, the avenues by which they attempt to influence public policy, and the resources they possess to do so.

Citizens who join political groups are not at all representative of citizens generally. Verba and Nie present data that indicate that what they call communal activity, which is joining a group to influence politics, is more tightly tied to socioeconomic status than any of the other modes.[18] In other words, the difference between high- and low-status citizens with respect to group activity is greater than with respect to voting, individualized contacting, or campaigning (see figure 5.1). This participation differential means that upper-status people will have more influence in politics, all other things being equal.

[18] Verba and Nie, *Participation in America*, p. 132.

Citizen Contacts

The most pervasive manner in which citizens make their demands known to government is by direct citizen contact. Many contacts concern broad social issues, but the vast majority involve specific problems. Each day thousands of individual citizens contact local, state, and national government officials about their particular problems. The problems that stimulate them to contact are diverse: citizens contact the local public works department to complain about garbage collection; they contact their city councillors to make all sorts of service requests; they write to their representatives in Congress to demand better service from federal bureaucrats; they contact the police for help in solving problems with neighbors; they file suit in state court to settle disputes with building contractors. The particular government official receiving the individual demand can be a bureaucrat, a chief executive, a legislator, or a judge.

What is common to all of this activity is that an individual citizen contacts government to solve a specific problem. These citizens are not organizing to demand the provision of public goods. Rather, each citizen demands a benefit that is particular to his or her situation. Citizen contacts are primarily designed to demand particularistic, divisible benefits from government. Because the benefits demanded are so particularistic, groups of individuals are unlikely to share collective goals. Hence, group organization is not normally a realistic alternative.

The frequency of one-to-one citizen-initiated contacts means that such contacts are an extremely important method for linking citizens to government. Indeed, Richard Brody has referred to this form of political activity as "the fundamental intersection of the citizen and the polity." [19] Brody notes that some contacts with government bureaucracy are definitely political demands, such as would be the case when an irate citizen calls the police complaining about a nearby house of prostitution. Other contacts are "no more political than buying groceries," [20] as would be the case when a citizen goes down to the health department for a free vaccination.

There are four basic reasons that citizens initiate individual contacts with government. First, they may be interested in influencing policy on a relatively broad issue, as would be the case if a businesswoman contacted her city councilman concerning a municipality's zoning policies. Second, a citizen may request a service or a benefit that he or she is entitled to because of a

[19] Richard Brody, "The Puzzle of Participation in America," in *The New American Political System,* ed. Anthony King (Washington, D.C.: American Enterprise Institute for Public Policy Research, 1978), p. 318.
[20] Ibid., p. 320.

government program. (It is this class of contacts that is about as political as buying groceries.) Contacting government to buy a business license or to apply for Social Security benefits is not an exercise in participation. Third, citizens may contact government to solve disputes they are having with other citizens. Calls to the police, or to municipal regulatory agencies such as the building department, the environmental control department, or the consumer affairs department to complain about the behavior of other citizens fall into this category. Finally, citizens may contact government because they feel that something is amiss in the government service delivery system—the welfare department failed to issue a check that was due, water and sewerage services have been interrupted, the garbage collectors left rubbish all over the yard, or a police officer was abusive. In this final case, citizens are complaining because government failed to deliver what it was supposed to deliver.

Extent of contacting

Although the extent of this form of activity is difficult to estimate with precision, because political demands shade into routine contact with governmental bureaucracy, some disparate figures will suggest the extent of contacting. When Verba and Nie asked respondents in a national sample whether they had ever contacted government officials about particular problems, fewer than 20 percent said they had.[21] Yet researchers at the University of Michigan report that fully 58 percent of their national sample reported getting help from government officials in one or more of seven specific government services (finding a job, getting job training, workman's compensation, unemployment compensation, public assistance, medical care, retirement benefits).[22] In his study of a sample of Milwaukee residents in 1970, Eisinger reports that 33 percent of his sample of whites had contacted government, but only 11 percent of blacks had done so. Moreover, whites had contacted government more frequently (2.4 times per contactor) than blacks (1.2 times per contactor).[23] In a study of citizen contacts in Garland, Texas, an upper-status suburb of Dallas, 44 percent of a random sample of citizens reported contacting city government over some problem or issue.[24]

Other estimates of the magnitude of citizen contacts may be gleaned from the records of government agencies. For example, Chicago's Department of Buildings received over 100,000 contacts per year from Chicago citizens during the 1970s. Even if we assume a considerable amount of multiple contact-

[21] Verba and Nie, *Participation in America,* p. 67.

[22] Daniel Katz, Barbara A. Gutek, Robert Kahn, and Eugenia Barton, *Bureaucratic Encounters* (Ann Arbor, Mich.: Institute for Social Research, 1975), p. 20.

[23] Peter Eisinger, *Patterns of Interracial Conflict* (New York: Academic Press, 1976), p. 120.

[24] Arnold Vedlitz and Eric Veblen, "Voting and Contacting: Two Forms of Political Participation in a Suburban Community," *Urban Affairs Quarterly* 16 (September 1980): 33.

ing, between 3 percent and 4 percent of Chicago's citizens are contacting municipal government annually concerning this problem area alone. Many cities have centralized complaint agencies to handle citizen grievances. Houston's central complaint agency handles from thirty-five to fifty complaints a day, but many more complaints go directly to city bureaucracies.[25] San Francisco's Police Department processed 476,592 calls for service in 1976, or 717 calls per 1,000 persons; Chicago's Police Department handled 2,603,945 (848 per 1,000 persons.)[26]

Who contacts?

When it comes to the individualized, particularistic problems that characterize most citizen-initiated contacts, the standard socioeconomic model of participation, which states that participation increases as socioeconomic status increases, no longer holds. The weight of the available evidence suggests that it is those of working-class and lower-middle-class status that disproportionately contact government. A study of contacting in Detroit shows that citizens living in low- to middle-income neighborhoods contacted city government more frequently than citizens living in the poorest and the wealthiest neighborhoods.[27] Mladenka, in a study of citizen contacts in Chicago, reported an identical pattern.[28] A study of contacting in Dallas and Houston found that poor neighborhoods contacted more than middle-income or upper-income neighborhoods.[29]

These studies indicate that the need for government action plays a more important part in the citizen's decision to initiate a contact than in the other forms of participation. The poor are more in need of government intervention than are the better off; hence the poor initiate more contacts. In other forms of participation, such as voting or campaigning, or joining an interest group, need plays a less important part, so that the decision to participate is influenced primarily by other factors, such as information, a sense of efficacy, or a sense of civic duty.

If this is the case, why do some studies report the highest contact levels

[25] Kenneth Mladenka, "Citizen Demand and Bureaucratic Response: Direct Dialing Democracy in a Major American City," *Urban Affairs Quarterly* 12 (March 1977): 280.

[26] Michael G. Maxfield, "The Politics of Policing and Patrol Allocation in Chicago and San Francisco," unpublished manuscript, Center for Urban Affairs, Northwestern University, Evanston, Ill., May 1979.

[27] Bryan D. Jones in association with Saadia Greenberg and Joseph Drew, *Service Delivery in the City: Citizen Demand and Bureaucratic Response* (New York: Longman, 1980), ch. 2.

[28] Kenneth Mladenka, "The Political Machine, the Urban Bureaucracy, and the Distribution of Public Services" (Evanston, Ill.: Center for Urban Affairs, Northwestern University, 1979), p. 62.

[29] Arnold Vedlitz, James Dyer, and Roger Durand, "Citizen Contacting with Local Government: A Comparative View," *American Journal of Political Science* 24 (February 1980): 50–67.

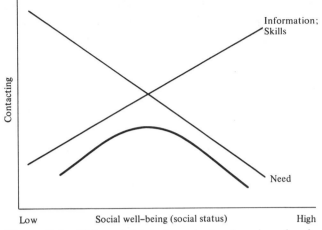

Figure 5.2. Citizen-initiated contacts at various levels of social well-being.

Source: From *Service Delivery in the City: Citizen Demand and Bureaucratic Rules* by Bryan D. Jones et al., fig. 2.2, p. 51. Copyright © 1980 by Longman Inc., Reprinted by permission of Longman Inc., New York.

among middle- and working-class individuals? Primarily it is because the poorest citizens lack the skills and information necessary to engage in even this limited form of participation. Poverty-stricken individuals living in socially disorganized urban neighborhoods often lack even the rudiments of a sense of efficacy. Why call "them" if you don't believe "they" will do anything? Figure 5.2 diagrams the resulting curvilinear relationship between contacting and social well-being. The figure emphasizes that both need and information are necessary to stimulate contacts. The poor have needs but lack information; the wealthy have information but lack needs. Middle-income citizens have some of both.

Citizen-initiated contacts constitute an effective means of citizen access only if government responds to these demands. There seems to be substantial variation in the degree to which cities respond to citizen-initiated contacts. In Houston, Mladenka found that many citizen complaints were simply ignored by the service bureaucracies, but Jones and associates report that every citizen complaint in Detroit received some kind of response.[30] (Whether that response satisfied the complaining citizen is a different matter. We examine the bureaucratic response further in chapter 14.)

[30] Mladenka, "Citizen Demand"; Jones, *Service Delivery.*

Mandated Participation

It seems self-evident that citizens ought to participate in government. This tenet has been the base of the citizen participation movement for decades. This movement, composed of a loose collection of reform-oriented groups, has advocated a variety of mechanisms for increasing citizen influence over governmental decisions. These mechanisms include citizen advisory boards, public hearings, opportunities for citizens to comment on proposed changes in public policies, and a whole substructure of citizen district councils, poverty area governing boards, and other arrangements to increase the access of the poor to government. Because these arrangements are specified as a matter of public policy, rather than arising more or less spontaneously from the interaction between citizens and government, we refer to them as *mandated participation.*[31]

The problem with these attempts to increase citizen participation is that they are premised on a faulty understanding of the motives of most citizens. Mandated citizen participation is based on two assumptions. The first is that citizens should participate in an issue-oriented debate on the merits of public policies. The second is that the existing modes of participation have discouraged the poor from participating in such a debate. According to this logic, the parties and traditional interest groups have not contributed to such a debate because both are too concerned with narrow self-interest. Finally, the belief exists that minorities have been shut out of the system because (1) they lack the resources to engage in traditional interest-group activities; and (2) they lack the numbers necessary to influence parties in a majoritarian system.

The problem with all of this is that citizens rarely participate in politics out of broad, issue-based concerns. Their motives are more narrowly based: How will what government is doing affect my everyday life? Years ago, Banfield and Wilson pointed to the supreme irony of the citizen participation movement:

> The spread of the doctrine that there *ought* to be "grass roots" participation in local affairs has largely coincided with a reduction in real opportunities for citizens to exercise influence in the matters of importance to them; for example, opportunity to "participate" in urban renewal projects has taken the place of opportunity to "fix" traffic tickets.[32]

Whatever one thinks of the opportunity to participate in fixing a traffic ticket versus participating in urban renewal planning, the former is generally

[31] See the special issue on citizen participation in the *Journal of Applied Behavioral Science* (December 1982) for a discussion of a variety of such programs.

[32] Edward C. Banfield and James Q. Wilson, *City Politics* (New York: Vintage, 1963), p. 258.

of more concern to the average citizen than the latter. Because of the lack of interest that most citizens have in planning urban renewal projects, mandated citizen participation is never broad-based. Participation falls into the hands of the active and the interested, as usual. The average citizen simply does not perceive a tight enough connection between participating in such arrangements and what goes on in his or her everyday life.

Many of the attempts to increase citizen participation have limited the rights of participation to citizens living in a particular neighborhood or to those likely to be most adversely affected by a public policy. Because upper-status individuals are excluded, mandated participation in many cities has offered access to a different class of individuals. This opportunity has broadened the base of the traditional system of policymaking to include spokespersons for the deprived. In their study of poverty programs in five cities, Greenstone and Peterson noted the emergence of "professional representatives of the poor," a tiny cadre of individuals claiming to represent inner-city neighborhoods, who dominated the poverty planning boards.[33] These men and women have been able to utilize the new arrangements for participation to gain access to government. One may well applaud this change. It must be remembered, however, that such a process bears no relationship whatsoever to an increase in the level of citizen participation in policymaking. It is still policymaking by political activists, albeit with the characteristics of the activists somewhat altered. Furthermore, these avenues for participation have been most vigorously pursued not by the poor, but by such middle-class groups as environmentalists, who have used the new avenues for access as a way to block both public projects, such as highways, and private projects, such as power plants.

Governments are not always open to the new modes of participation. Often citizen participation is mandated by the federal government as a condition for a local government's receipt of a federal grant. The local governments receiving these grants generally view such mandates as a bother, and they often try to limit opportunities as much as possible. Some governments have become proficient at structuring participation so as to render it ineffective. When the city of Detroit wanted to relocate a number of residents in order to clear enough land for a new automobile plant, it organized a citizens' district council for the area. Such a move was optional, not actually required by law. Then the mayor appointed the district council, with the approval of the city council. The citizens' district council thus appointed was far more docile than the indigenous neighborhood groups were.

In several cases, mandates for participation have resulted in struggles for control of the new avenues for interest representation. Because mandates are often vague in specifying exactly what mechanisms are to be used to ensure

[33] J. David Greenstone and Paul E. Peterson, *Race and Authority in Urban Politics* (Chicago: University of Chicago Press, 1976), p. 37.

participation, conflict results. The best example of this occurred in the community action programs established by the War on Poverty of President Lyndon Johnson's administration (see box 5.1).

Mobility as Political Expression

People who are dissatisfied with the way things are going in their neighborhood have three options: they can tolerate the situation; they can leave the

---

Box 5.1: Community Participation and the War on Poverty

The War on Poverty was the most controversial attempt of the federal government to mandate participation in local policymaking. The Economic Opportunity Act of 1964 established community action programs that were designed to operate separately from existing city bureaucracies in delivering services to the poor, through community action agencies. The community action agencies were supposed to increase the political resources of the poor by involving them in the policymaking process. Consequently, Congress provided in the act that the programs be "developed, conducted, and administered with the maximum feasible participation of residents of the areas and members of the groups served." Congress and the Office of Economic Opportunity, established to administer the poverty programs, left open the question of exactly what constituted participation.

At the local level, controversy centered on how the representatives of the poor were to be selected. Mayors generally wanted to appoint the representatives, but community groups wanted representatives to be selected at meetings of community organizations. In his study of New York, Philadelphia, and Chicago, Paul Peterson found that "at no time did neighborhood groups in any city call for direct election of the representatives to the city poverty council; in place of mayoral appointment, they preferred election at meetings of existing neighborhood organizations. Neighborhood groups, as well as mayors, preferred a means of providing formal representation which they themselves could control." *

*Paul E. Peterson, "Forms of Representation: Participation of the Poor in the Community Action Program, *American Political Science Review* 64 (June 1970): 495.

neighborhood; or they can stay and try to change things.[34] If citizens stay and try to influence government to help change neighborhood conditions, we would of course classify their activities as political participation. Leaving the neighborhood is not normally viewed as political action. When mobility is used in attempting to solve problems, however, it should be regarded as political participation.

There are many reasons why people leave one place and move to another. These reasons can be classified as *pull* and *push* factors. Pull factors are those that are attractive in the future place of residence: better schools, higher status, more open space. Push factors are problems with the prospective mover's present neighborhood. When push factors are more important in a decision to move, mobility can be viewed as political action.

Citizens contemplating moving as the solution to their problems generally engage in a process of rational decision making. Only when problems become acute enough will the decision process be triggered. How acute a problem must be will vary from person to person, of course. Some people are more prone to accept their present condition than others. Even in the face of acute problems, people will consider leaving only if they do not believe that other actions will help them solve their problems. If such forms of political activity as contacting public officials, organizing a neighborhood group around common concerns, and protesting are evaluated by the citizen as unlikely to be effective, then he or she may wish to leave. Whether leaving is possible, however, depends on whether the citizen has the financial resources to move to a neighborhood without the problems that are of concern. The process of deciding whether to exit, engage in political action, or remain passive is diagrammed in figure 5.3.

Figure 5.3 makes one other point clear. Citizens can be passive because they do not perceive problems as existing. Citizens can also be passive because they believe that neither political activity nor exit will help, or that political activity will not work and they cannot afford to move. Passivity, then, can indicate that citizens are satisfied with their fate or it can indicate that they are dissatisfied but are pessimistic about their chances of changing things.

City officials, especially officials in central cities, are quite attuned to the fact that mobility is an expression of political opinion. Moreover, they see that this mobility can affect the well-being of the city. If those most able to move do so, they will not be there to help shoulder the burden of the taxes that will have to be levied if problems are to be solved. Yet a heavy tax burden can be one of the problems that citizens wish to escape by moving. Hence city officials not infrequently find themselves in a difficult position.

---

[34] John Orbell and Toru Uno, "A Theory of Neighborhood Problem-Solving: Political Action vs. Residential Mobility," *American Political Science Review* 64 (June 1972): 471–89.

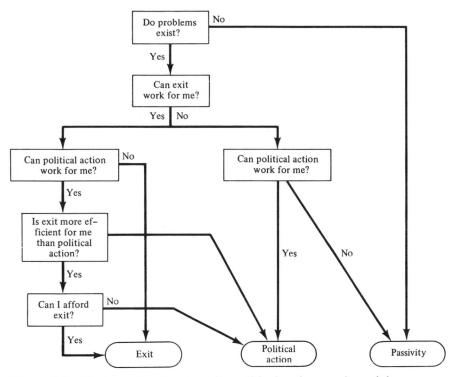

Figure 5.3. Decisions leading to exit, political action, and passivity.

Source: Modified from John Orbell and Toru Uno, "A Theory of Neighborhood Problem-Solving," *American Political Science Review* 64 (June 1972): Fig. 1, p. 486. Used with permission.

If they do nothing, they risk losing the most productive citizens. If they attempt to solve neighborhood problems by imposing taxes, they risk adding to the dissatisfaction of potential movers. Finally, if they provide better services to those who threaten to move, they will either have to provide a higher level of services to all citizens, or they will have to provide fewer or poorer services to those who cannot or do not want to move. Since the movers are generally more affluent than the stayers, this will grant more services to the better off, a situation that many will view as inequitable. We return to this problem of distributing service benefits in chapter 14.

There is a final irony here. Those who move have superior resources, in general, than those who stay. These include financial resources, but they also include education, information, and the other skills that can be used to influence politics. The movers leave the stayers less able to engage successfully in political action to solve neighborhood problems.

Conclusions

This chapter has examined the various modes of participation in urban politics: voting, activity in a political party, group activity, citizen-initiated contact, mandated participation, and mobility. Because of their past and present importance, groups and parties are more thoroughly discussed in separate chapters.

Each of the modes of participation rests on one or more supporting institutions. To be meaningful, for example, voting must occur in free and open elections. The social and institutional context is also important because certain contexts facilitate participation and others inhibit it. The clearest example of this occurs in the case of voting registration laws. If they are severe, voter turnout will be lower; if they are lenient, turnout will be higher.

Any discussion of participation invariably raises the issue of democratic accountability. Voting and elections can establish accountability to the mass public either through elite replacement or through electoral threat to the occupants of public offices. Certain conditions facilitate accountability, such as electoral competition, partisan elections, and the ambition of officeholders to retain their leadership positions.

Accountability is also maintained through the other modes of participation. Whereas elections operate to hold leaders accountable to the active electorate, other modes can operate to hold leaders accountable to other segments of the citizenry. Mobility provides the most obvious example. The possibility that citizens and businesses will leave the city hangs over the heads of city officials like the sword of Damocles. Whether mobility can be stemmed by public policy action is an unanswered question in the study of urban government and politics. Yet city officials perceive people and businesses to be leaving the city because of policies they pursue (primarily those that lead to poor services and heavy tax burdens). So long as they perceive this to be the case, they will be sensitive to the desires of the most mobile citizens.

Accountability in urban democratic society is complex, and no one can say with any certainty when it exists and when it does not. The following three chapters, on local party structures, interest groups, and urban power structures, examine in more detail aspects of this important topic.

CHAPTER 6

Political Parties
and the City

In the not-too-distant past, political parties were a more important avenue of participation in local affairs than they are today. In at least some parts of the country, parties were also extremely important in the urban policymaking process. The decline of that influence has paralleled a decline in the ability of parties to link citizens to government. This decline of party has important implications for the conduct of urban policymaking.[1]

The Changing Role of Political Parties

The American federal government was established on the principle of disunity: separate branches of government, each with the ability to interfere with the prerogatives of the others; different electoral constituencies for each branch of government, ensuring that each would represent a different set of

---

[1] An excellent consideration of these issues is Robert A. Goldwin, ed., *Political Parties in the Eighties* (Washington, D.C.: American Enterprise Institute, 1980).

interests; state governments with independent policymaking powers. The founders, moreover, wanted it all to operate without political parties.

That may have been all right when there was little governing to do (the national government during Washington's administration was about the size of the present municipal government of Poughkeepsie, New York), but the plan courted disaster for governing even a moderately complex nation. Decentralizing forces too greatly outweighed centralizing forces, and no formal mechanisms existed to manage the conflict that was bound to break out. Parties developed, first as legislative factions, then as organizations outside government. These organizations, at least up to the 1970s, provided a web helping to unify the various elements of government. Not only were Senators, Representatives, and the President unified by loyalty to the party, but in addition the President, as head of the executive branch of government, possessed substantial powers of patronage that could help maintain party solidarity by rewarding the party faithful. Similarly, governors at the state level and mayors at the local level could use patronage to promote party unity.

For a variety of reasons, parties have lost much of their unifying power in recent years. These reasons center on (1) the ability of elected public officials to act independently of the political party; (2) the ability of appointed officials to act independently of elected officials; and (3) the decline of loyalty and the rise of independence as a cultural precept. First, politicians are no longer so beholden to the party. Because of the institution during the Progressive era of the direct primary for selecting nominees for office, and its expansion after 1968, a candidate can become the nominee of a party without being tapped by party leadership. Second, communications technology has made it possible (indeed, necessary) for candidates to contact voters without relying on campaign workers, once provided almost exclusively by the political parties. Third, the reforms enacted since 1968 have made it even easier for candidates to run independently of the party. The federal government now provides funds for presidential candidates not only for the general election, but also for the nominating process. So candidates are able to establish campaign organizations independently of the party structure.

Parties have declined as unifying factors for another reason: the loss of patronage. After the Jacksonian era, when American political parties became mass-based organizations, government jobs at the state, national, and local level were patronage positions, to be used to reward the party faithful who had campaigned diligently for the winning candidate. Patronage not only ensured the loyalty of the party worker, but also gave the party leader leverage in public policy matters. If a legislator did not behave appropriately, she could be stripped of her patronage, because legislators have no direct access to government jobs. So long as the chief executive, whether President or governor or mayor, could allocate jobs, he had a powerful method of inducing legislators to pass his legislative program. With the rise of civil service reform, however, the ability of the chief executives to do this has declined at all levels of government. So has the unifying force of political parties.

Finally, the norm of loyalty has declined as a cultural precept, and the norm of independence has replaced it. Regardless of how uninformed they are of public affairs, many voters pride themselves on being independents, "making up their own minds" on the issues. The two parties in America are centrist parties, but they do differ on many public issues of the day. This is true at the state and local as well as national level. Many voters continue to use party labels as cues for deciding how to vote for a variety of candidates; to the extent that they do so, they will seldom be misled. But "independents" have no such beacons. Unless they are very well informed on public affairs (and most Americans, including independents, are not), they will be swayed heavily by irrelevant candidate characteristics and media packaging of candidates. Thus, although the decline of party loyalty in the electorate has weakened political parties, it is not clear that voting is, therefore, more "rational"; indeed, it may well be less so.

The norm of independence has infused legislators as well. Congressional representatives once prided themselves on their records of legislative support for the President, at least when they and the President came from the same party. Today, however, many members of Congress pride themselves on their independence from the President and the congressional leadership as well.

At the local level, independent city councilors pride themselves on their challenge to aging party organizations, and deride their fellow council members for relying on the "boss" for making decisions. Independent aldermen in Chicago point out that a council vote is usually determined by how the First Ward alderman votes. The First Ward alderman has his "marching orders" from party leaders; the other machine aldermen cast their votes accordingly. To independents, this is ludicrous. Legislatures are supposed to deliberate. But having party organizations structure public policy alternatives means that leaders must decide the party position; moreover, there must be followers to accept it.

Local party structure

The disintegration of political parties nationally has been paralleled by disintegration at the local level. Four points about the role of local parties are important.

1. Political parties in the United States have traditionally been rooted at the local level, because most government took place at that level. Most governmental functions were performed locally; moreover, most government jobs were in local government. Hence, patronage-supported parties found fertile soil in local government. Limited federal patronage and the federal structure of government meant that national parties were coalitions of state parties, which in turn were basically coalitions of local party organizations.

2. As the availability of patronage declined, so did the strength of the local party. In states where patronage was weak or nonexistent, parties tended to be weak. In the 1950s, when Samuel Eldersveld studied the party structure of Wayne County, Michigan, he found a viable Democratic organization in fewer than half the precincts, and a viable Republican organization in only about a third.[2] In Michigan, parties had access to little patronage.

3. It is possible for political parties to coordinate governmental functions in the metropolis in a manner similar to the way they have traditionally functioned at the national level. Metropolitan governments are even more fragmented than the national government. The Chicago Democratic organization, for example, has provided coordination for the extremely fragmented governmental structure of Cook County. It is possible for formally fragmented local governments to be informally coordinated by parties, but this requires strong parties, and it also requires that the various governments in the metropolis be run by officials from the same party.

4. In many areas of the country, political parties are so weak locally that they are, for all practical purposes, irrelevant to local policymaking. In many parts of the country, the one-two punch of civil service and nonpartisanship has removed parties from a meaningful role in local public affairs. But because partisanship, once established, was hard to change, many cities that were politically well developed at the time of the municipal reform movement in the early part of this century continue to have strong local party systems. Cities established subsequent to the reform movement almost invariably have nonpartisan systems. In some states, notably California, local nonpartisanship has been mandated by state government. Because of the survival of a number of cities and towns with strong party systems alongside nonpartisan cities, political scientists have been able to study the differences that parties make in municipal affairs.

[2] Samuel J. Eldersveld, *Political Parties: A Behavioral Analysis* (Chicago: Rand McNally, 1964), pp. 103–4.

The Urban Political Machine

Not so long ago, many American cities were governed by a party structure often termed the *political machine*. Several still are. Often based on European ethnic votes and cemented by the politically astute Irish, political machines were peopled by such colorful characters as "Bathhouse John" Coughlin and "Hinky Dink" Kenna of Chicago's infamous First Ward. At times, urban political parties were headed by power "bosses" who were able to control both the party and local government, and whose influence extended far beyond the city to the state capital and to Washington. (A recent example of such a political leader was Mayor Richard Daley of Chicago, who died in 1976.) At other times, however, urban parties disintegrated into intraparty squabbles among more or less coequal "chieftains," none of whom could centralize influence within the party. So not all urban political machines had "bosses."

Although most political machines developed in northern cities, some southern and western cities also proved fertile ground for the machine form of government. The most notable was E. H. Crump's Memphis, Tennessee, organization. Kansas City was for years governed by the Pendergast machine; a machine also developed in Omaha, Nebraska.

Even though Irish politics was characterized by a rural form of organization that resembled American urban machines, it is not the case that the machine was simply imported by European immigrants. Machines developed in cities with few European ethnics. Machine "bosses" were often Americans of English origin, for example the infamous Boss Tweed of New York, Cox of Cincinnati, and Crump of Memphis. They were most prevalent in cities, but machines in rural areas were not uncommon, and occasionally statewide machine organizations have emerged. Huey Long's Louisiana machine extended from the clay hills of northwest Louisiana to the Cajun country of the Mississippi Delta marshes.

Incentive Systems

Out of all this diversity, what do political machines have in common? The common feature of all political machines is their reliance on material incentives to induce party members to contribute to the organization. Clark and Wilson have classified the incentives for participation in any organization into three categories: *material,* which are concrete benefits, such as money or jobs; *solidarity,* which are satisfactions deriving from the act of participation itself—a feeling of belonging to a group, status within the group, or simply enjoying politics—and *purposive,* which are those rewards that stem from the accomplishment of the goals of the organization not tied directly to the individual member's self-interest.[3] Wilson applied this perspective on organizations to political parties in his classic work *The Amateur Democrat*.[4] He defined an *amateur* as a participant in a political party organization who is motivated primarily by the desire to accomplish certain public policy objectives. That is, the amateur participates in politics in order to see certain laws enacted, laws that do not benefit him or her directly. The amateur is driven by purposive incentives. The *professional,* on the other hand, is motivated primarily by material benefits. For the professional politician, politics is a livelihood.

A machine is a form of party organization that induces its members to participate primarily through the use of material benefits. Party workers are marshaled by the promise of jobs; voters are induced to support the party because they believe that they will be favored with government services if their party holds power; leaders contribute because they can advance to better positions if their party is electorally successful. A machine, then, will be staffed primarily by professionals.

Naturally, all organizations will employ a mix of the three kinds of incentives. In particular, almost all organizations use solidarity as a secondary incentive for contributing. Amateurs as well as professionals gain satisfaction from engaging in activities with people having characteristics and motivations similar to their own. But almost all organizations are characterized by a dominant incentive system, and for the machine that incentive system is based on material gain for participants.

The limits of material inducement

During the first third of this century, at least, there were a great many material incentives available to induce party members to contribute to the electoral success of the machine. Most local governments contained numerous patronage positions that a boss could use to reward the party faithful. Civil service systems made inroads into the spoils system, but not all jobs were covered by civil service provisions and not infrequently such provisions could be circumvented. Those in business could be induced to contribute to the campaign chest of the party (and not infrequently the pockets of the politicians) by careful allocation of government contracts and franchises for transportation and utilities. Where machines continue to operate, these features continue to exist, even if in a more limited form.

Material incentives alone, however, cannot explain the urban political machine. There are four major reasons that the politicians who ran the

---

[3] Peter B. Clark and James Q. Wilson, "Incentive Systems: A Theory of Organization," *Administrative Science Quarterly* 6 (1961): 129–66.

[4] University of Chicago Press, 1962.

urban machines never had enough material incentives to extend organizational control deep into the urban electorate. In the first place, many of the urban public services delivered by cities are in the nature of collective goods. It would be difficult, if not impossible, to divide up these services and parcel them out to voters to reward supporters and punish opponents. The growing cities of the early part of this century needed paved streets, sewer systems, street lighting, and fire protection. Such services offered excellent opportunities for finding jobs for the party faithful, and offered the ability to let contracts for capital improvements to contractors and others on the basis of their support for the party. But such services are not as useful for mobilizing voters. If, for example, a party leader decided to punish a neighborhood for its support for opposition candidates by denying the district fire protection or garbage collection, the health and safety of the rest of the city would quickly be threatened. These are collective goods: once the benefits of a sanitary city are established, it is not possible to deny access to the benefits to some citizens without reducing them for others. When a neighborhood contained some supporters and some opponents, it was even more difficult to distribute services to supporters and deny them to opponents. Even a pothole could not remain unrepaired without harming supporters as well as the opposition.

A second reason for limitations on material incentives is bureaucratization. When a change in party control occurred in government, a machine quickly had to replace existing city workers with its supporters. Urban reformers fumed that the spoils system disrupted the machinery of government. That disruption was minimized by the machine's reliance on bureaucracy in government. In order for the inexperienced party workers to operate an increasingly complex urban government, it was necessary that tasks be kept simple and that stable rules govern operations.[5] If the services were not delivered, the voters were not going to be so charitable as to keep the party in power. Indeed, when the Chicago Democratic machine suffered its biggest setback in fifty years with the election of challenger Jane Byrne over incumbent machine-supported Michael Bilandic in 1979, it was because of the widespread perception by traditional machine supporters that city services were no longer being delivered effectively. The necessity of relying on simple tasks, necessitating a complex division of labor, and of stable rules to structure things meant that a political leader would be unable to shift services around according to the behavior of voters. This also meant that a cadre of experts was indispensable to the maintenance of a smoothly functioning organization. In a study of the highway department in a rural Pennsylvania

---

[5] This important point is often overlooked. For a clever discussion, see Michael Nelson, "Ten Ironies That Made Our Nation What It Is Today," *Washington Monthly* (November 1980): 34–45.

county in the 1950s, Sorauf found that the Democrats did not replace technically proficient Republicans for this reason.[6]

In the third place, it always has been difficult to use governmental services to reward supporters and punish enemies, because such a system implies more control over the interworkings of public bureaucracies than the typical machine politician has been able to impose. Establishing lock-step control over the patrolman on the beat or the building inspector or the supervisor in the public works department is not generally possible. The major instrument of control that the party leader had was the ability to fire government workers. But, as Johnson has pointed out, jobs are "lumpy" inducements.[7] You either fire a worker or you do not. Firing for minor violations of what the leader wants can create all sorts of resentment in the organization, and is also a potential source of service disruption (minimized, of course, by bureaucratization of tasks). From the point of view of the boss, it would be far better to save firing, the ultimate sanction in machine systems, for gross failure to perform *political* work. Hence, most political leaders did not expand a great deal of time and energy trying to control the interworkings of governmental bureaucracies, except where absolutely necessary. Moreover, few leaders are able to dispense jobs solely on the basis of partisan merit. In particular, personal friendships and obligations interfere with the allocation of jobs based solely on political productivity.[8]

A final reason for limitations in material incentives is that when the American welfare system was established during the Great Depression, it was the federal government that took primary responsibility. Rules established for eligibility precluded excluding persons because of their political affiliations. The local party structure was unable to deny benefits to uncooperative voters; it had completely lost control of these government benefits.

Machines, then, use material inducements to build a cadre of loyal party activists but cannot rely primarily on such incentives to establish ties to voters. Why do voters support urban political machines? There are many reasons, but perhaps the major one, as Thomas Guterbock has emphasized, is a normative commitment to the political party.[9] Political scientists have long stressed that one major reason voters support one party over another is *party identification,* a psychological attachment to one party over another that is acquired in a manner somewhat similar to one's religious affiliation and other social values, through a process of political socialization. Party

[6] Frank Sorauf, "State Patronage in a Rural County," *American Political Science Review* 50 (December 1956): 1046–56.

[7] Michael Johnson, "Patrons, Clients, Jobs, and Machines: A Case Study of the Uses of Patronage," *American Political Science Review* 73 (June 1979): 385–98.

[8] This is supported by both the Sorauf and the Johnson studies cited in footnotes 6 and 7.

[9] Thomas N. Guterbock, *Machine Politics in Transition: Party and Community in Chicago* (Chicago: University of Chicago Press, 1980).

identification has declined in the American electorate, but it remains a powerful organizing symbol for many voters. Partisan attachments were probably quite strong among urban machine supporters, because party allegiance was reinforced by the tight-knit ethnic character of many urban neighborhoods.

Political Work

The party activists who staff the urban political machines face the same problems as any political activists: first, keep the faithful as satisfied as possible between elections; second, try to lure the marginal and undecided voters into the fold; and third, mobilize the faithful on election day. Because they can rely on government workers to perform political work, machines have a decided advantage in getting these tasks done. Moreover, these workers are not available just on election day; they are available for regular contact with voters year-round. Hence, much of the work of precinct-level party workers involves regular contact with voters, helping them get the government services they want.

One myth about urban political machines that has little truth in it is that the party regularly supplied the poor immigrants with life's necessities, such as the proverbial "bucket of coal," in order to gain votes at election time. Although urban political parties often did supply some necessities to tide over a family in the neighborhood that was experiencing hard times, this was never done regularly. American political parties have never had access to extensive financial resources. Although the party assessed patronage workers regularly, this assessment did not provide enough resources to provide material incentives to "bribe" voters, as it is sometimes put. Harold Gosnell, writing about the Chicago machine in the 1930s, noted:

> Since the political parties in the United States have very limited financial resources of their own, it is necessary for them to rely upon the governmental agencies to supply most of the needs of their constituents who are in want. They act as brokers for the various governmental services filling the gaps left by the red-tape provisions of the bureaucrats. Party workers refer their voters to the proper authorities and try to claim as much credit for themselves as possible.[10]

One strategy of the political party in attempting to overcome the limits of material incentives is to act as intermediary between citizens and service bureaucracies and claim credit for delivering. In machine cities, many voters

[10] Harold Gosnell, *Machine Politics, Chicago Model* (Chicago: University of Chicago Press, 1968), p. 74.

come to rely on their precinct captain as a source of knowledge, information, and influence in dealing with city bureaucracies.

A second strategy used by party workers is to try to influence voters for minor offices rather than push the top of the ticket. Especially when there is a contest for president, precinct captains concentrate on turning out the vote and recommending that voters support their candidates for municipal judges, sheriff, district attorney, and sanitary district commissioner. Voters tend to resent being told how to vote for president, but they will often follow the advice of the party's precinct captain if they know little about the office, especially if the captain has been helpful in the past. This has returns to the party, since many of the local officials who benefit from this strategy control numerous patronage positions.

Urban Party Organization

Urban political parties have seldom been as centralized and hierarchical as mythology would have us believe. Because some machines were centralized organizations dominated by a "boss" and others were decentralized and characterized by intraparty disagreement, one student of urban political parties has been led to distinguish between *machines,* boss-run hierarchical parties, and *machine politics,* a politics characterized by the exchange of material incentives among actors.[11]

Indeed, in terms of formal organization, urban political parties tend to be decentralized. A typical urban party, such as the Cook County (Chicago) Democratic organization, is organized around the ward.[12] The ward is an electoral unit for the election of an alderman, or city councillor.

In other states (Michigan), the basic political unit is the congressional district; in still others (New York) it is the state legislative assembly (lower house) district. The party official for the ward is known as the *ward committeeman.* He or she often holds public office but receives no pay for party work. (This does not mean, of course, that he or she goes unrewarded. Clearly, the party office may be good for his or her law practice or insurance business or restaurant.) The ward committeeman appoints precinct captains to work the precincts in the ward, hence, the precinct captains are beholden to the committeeman for their positions.

The committeeman is the ward's representative to the *central committee,* which in Illinois is based on the county. Suburban representation is based on townships. The central committee is an assembly of chieftains whose basic

---

[11] Raymond Wolfinger, "Why Machines Have Not Withered Away and Other Revisionist Thoughts," *Journal of Politics* 34 (May 1972): 365–98.

[12] On Chicago's party structure, see Milton Rakove, *Don't Make No Waves, Don't Back No Losers* (Bloomington, Ind.: University of Indiana Press, 1975).

functions are to allocate patronage, to slate candidates for office, and to disburse party funds at election time.

Because of the preeminent power of ward committeemen, bosses emerge only when they can centralize enough of the party material incentives to command the loyalty of the ward committee. This almost always means that the boss is himself a ward committeeman and is often the *chairman* of the local party. It also means that he either holds a major governmental position commanding substantial patronage or has associates in such positions. Ward committeemen become reliant on the boss as a source of patronage. They also may rely on him to carry local candidates into office with him to the extent that he is electorally successful.

The inherent decentralization of American urban party structures means that it is very difficult for a centralized machine to survive power transitions. When a powerful boss departs the scene, factional squabbles are almost certain to occur. Such squabbling is occurring in Chicago today. After the death of Mayor Daley, Mayor Bilandic proved unable to control the organization. A combination of gradual social changes, loss of the tight central control maintained by Daley, and simple bad luck led to his electoral defeat by Jane Byrne. Byrne has proved incapable of centralizing the party to date, and a fierce intraparty fight is occurring between her and Richie Daley, Mayor Daley's son. In the general election of November 1980, Daley established a strong base for challenging the Byrne faction by capturing the office of state's attorney (district attorney). The office of state's attorney is powerful both because it commands patronage and because its investigatory powers can be used to embarrass political opponents.

Brokerage

The boss generally does not command a hierarchical organization. Rather, he commands an essentially decentralized organization with many underlings who possess substantial independent power. Ward committeemen command in their own bailiwicks, and this mastery offers the potential of a challenge to the boss. Within the party, then, the boss must act as a *broker of interests,* bargaining with committeemen and settling jurisdictional squabbles among them and within unruly ward organizations.

Because of the numerous ethnic groups jostling for power in most northern cities, and because the decentralized American political structures gave each group a chance to capture a piece of the action, the boss often had to deal with a multitude of chieftains, each clamoring on behalf of his or her constituents. As Jacob Arvey, the past committeeman for Chicago's once heavily Jewish Twenty-fourth Ward, told oral biographer Milton Rakove, the political power granted by the high turnouts of the ward meant that he could go downtown to the party leaders "and *demand* things, not ask for them." [13] Wards that turned out heavy majorities for the party ticket were automatically in a bargaining situation with party leaders.

The boss, however, does not simply broker within the party. In cities dominated by political machines, the entire style of politics came to be infused with the brokerage style. Bargaining, compromise, logrolling (the trading of votes by legislators), and accepting "half a loaf" were characteristic of political systems of these cities. As time went on, various other elements of the community that needed to deal with city government became part of the system—workers, homeowners, real estate developers, newspaper editors, and those who owned factories, small businesses, and transportation companies. Each element of the community found it in its interest to cooperate. By delegating, informally, a little power to the party boss, all elements found that things could be done, projects could be completed, and money could be made. The fact that such a system of bargaining and compromise often led to "side payments" in the form of corruption bothered the participants but little. It did bother the urban reformers who arose to attack the system.

Decline of the broker

The success of brokerage politics rests on two foundations. First, it is essential that economic growth be sustained. When growth is continuing, compromise is easier to enforce than when stagnation is occurring. In the case of growth, a leader has to convince the contending parties to accept "half a loaf" each. In the case of stagnation, the leader may have to ask each participant to give up something.

Second, brokerage politics assumes that no demands are brought to the political system that threaten the set of social values on which the system rests. Many issues that threaten the social consensus are highly symbolic and are perceived by people as being *zero-sum*. These are issues on which there can be no compromise. Like a football game or a game of checkers, there is a winner and a loser, and the loser gets nothing. An example of such an issue is abortion. Many people perceive the condoning of any abortion by the political system as an extreme, albeit symbolic, loss for them. They cannot accept a small number of abortions as a reasonable compromise.

Chicago's Mayor Ed Kelly found himself facing such a position in the late 1940s when a controversy arose over open housing for blacks. With characteristic Irish egalitarianism, he commented that as long as he was mayor, any Chicagoan could live wherever he or she could afford to live. Such a statement was a severe threat to the ethnic groups that were the

---

[13] Milton Rakove, *We Don't Want Nobody Nobody Sent* (Bloomington, Ind.: University of Indiana Press, 1979), p. 4.

bulwark of Democratic support. He was not slated for renomination by the central committee.[14]

The one great urban issue that could not be compromised within the brokerage system was racial integration. As blacks migrated to cities after the 1940s, they became important components of the machine. In many cities they had become one of the jostling ethnic groups, until the integration of neighborhoods became an issue. Invasion and succession had always characterized urban neighborhoods, but when blacks threatened, the ethnic groups responded with intense hostility. Many party leaders wished to compromise and broker this issue in the way they had so many issues in the past, but their ethnic constituents viewed the situation as zero-sum. The result was that many machines remained captives of their dwindling ethnic bases, leaving black voters incompletely integrated into the machine. These voters were available for independent black candidates attacking the machine to mobilize.

In Chicago, blacks have increased their antimachine votes over the years. In 1955, when Mayor Daley was first elected, the bedrock of his support was the wards of black Congressman William Dawson. By 1975 many black voters were voting against Daley, and in 1979 Byrne swept all but one of the black wards (see box 6.1).

This does not mean that machines kept blacks out of power. Indeed, they could not. Blacks made up a sizable proportion of the urban electorate, and in politics, numbers count; and politicians can count numbers. Had the urban party structure not been in such shambles, it would have been a powerful institution for the exercise of black power. Patronage would have obviated the need for "affirmative action," and in the hands of capable black leaders, a new brokerage system would have been possible. Without a strong party system, black mayors have a reduced opportunity to centralize urban power and exercise it on behalf of their constituents. This does not mean that it cannot be done, and, indeed, it has been done. But it is more difficult.

Local Political Parties and the Expansion of Conflict

Political parties are the mainsprings of mass democracy. This is true because they are the *only* institutions with a vested interest in citizen participation. All other institutions work toward systems of limited participation. In politics, if all other things are equal, there is an inevitable decay toward a multitude of virtually independent policy systems, within which policy is set

[14] This was given as the major reason by Jacob Arvey, then county chairman of the party. See ibid., p. 12.

Box 6.1: Support for the Machine

Based on their observations of the Chicago machine, Kathleen Kemp and Robert Lineberry have constructed a typology of wards based on the proportion of eligibles who vote and the proportion of those voting who support machine candidates. Their typology looks like this:

Machine Support

		Low	High
Turnout	High	Renegade	Deliverable
	Low	Independent	Controlled

Wards that are characterized by high turnout and high machine support are called *deliverables*. These are the bedrock of machine support. Wards in which voting is low but machine support is high are *controlled* wards. *Independent* wards are low-turnout wards, and they vote against the machine. *Renegade* wards are high-turnout wards with a high proportion of voters voting against the machine. This pattern usually occurs when a popular local ethnic candidate challenges the machine, siphoning off wards that generally support it.

The real threat to machine domination is in the controlled wards. Voter passivity there is not necessarily indicative of satisfaction. High turnout in normally controlled wards is indicative of a breakdown of that control, and almost always hurts the machine. In modern times, black wards have tended to move from the controlled category to renegade status (when there is a black candidate running), or even to the independent category.

Source: From the essay entitled "The Last of the Great Urban Machines and the Last of the Great Urban Mayors? Chicago Politics, 1955–1977," by Kathleen Kemp and Robert Lineberry in *After Daley: Chicago Politics in Transition,* edited by Samuel K. Gove and Louis H. Masotti, published by the University of Illinois Press (© 1982 by The Board of Trustees of the University of Illinois). Reprinted by permission.

by regular actors: representatives of interest groups, bureaucrats, leaders of legislative committees. This is just as true of local politics as of national politics. It is also true of the so-called public interest and citizen participation movements. Although these movements represent far different interests than those that are typical of policy systems, they operate on principles of limited participation themselves.

Parties must reach out to the mass public because their medium of exchange is votes. They cannot rely on expertise or interest or power to win. Only numbers count.

Actually, in the absence of competition, a political party can become a system of limited participation itself. The statewide machine put together in Virginia by the Byrds was a classic case: exclusion of black voters until well into the 1960s coupled with limited participation by poor whites left the political system in the hands of the Virginia aristocracy.[15] In Chicago, the Democratic organization can rely on about 350,000 votes. Therefore, it prefers elections in which the turnout is below 700,000. Otherwise things become unpredictable; someone else may be mobilizing the votes against the organization.

But parties, at least occasionally, have the incentive to stimulate participation. A losing party has but one option: expand the conflict. Bring in more voters to the political arena. Beat the other party at its own game.

In Memphis, for example, E. H. Crump constructed a machine whose electoral base was composed of the outcasts of Memphis politics. In a fine example of political detective work, Kenneth Wald painstakingly reconstructed the sources of strength of the Crump machine. He found the base to be in black and ethnic (predominantly Irish) neighborhoods. Wald considers Memphis an ideal place to study the bases of machine support because of its small number of ethnics. Yet even in Memphis the base of organization support consisted of those most downtrodden, and the organization served as an institution for protecting and extending black participation.[16] (Although Tennessee was traditionally more liberal than many other southern states allowing blacks to vote, Memphis is a deep-southern town. V. O. Key called it an "extension of Mississippi.") Crump's machine was an irritant to the Memphis establishment until it faltered and passed from the scene in the late 1940s. It was all the more remarkable because it developed within a one-party system. Electoral competition, when it was organized at all, consisted of intraparty factional struggles.

One reason for the decline in participation in America is the decline of political parties as meaningful organizations. No organization can survive as a healthy specimen unless it has access to incentives that it can use to encourage members to participate. As civil service systems, employee unions, national party reforms, and general changes in attitude toward parties have limited the incentives available to party leaders, parties as organizations have eroded. As party organizations have eroded, so have the linkages between

---

[15] V. O. Key's classic book *Southern Politics* (New York: Vintage, 1949) is a study of systems of limited participation, including Virginia's.

[16] Kenneth D. Wald, "The Electoral Base of Political Machines: A Deviant Case Analysis," *Urban Affairs Quarterly* 16 (September 1980): 3–30.

the party and the citizen. With the decline of the only democratic institution with reason to stimulate citizen participation, there has been a decline in participation. Although this decline has not been caused solely by the decline of party, it has been aided and abetted by this decline.

Party Control and Public Policy

Where party organizations are strong, they have the resources to mold public policies to conform to the preferences of their supporters in the mass public. Do they use their resources to accomplish this? Urban political machines, be-

---

Box 6.2: Public Policies and Political Parties in West German Cities

Can political parties affect public policy outcomes in cities? Interestingly, some of our best evidence that they can comes not from the United States but from West Germany. Professor Robert Fried of UCLA studied the impact of party control on a number of public policy outcomes in fifty-three cities in West Germany. According to Fried, "West German cities are quite varied in their policies: some tax their citizens and business firms much more than others; some spend more on welfare; some incur larger debts; some employ many more people." If party control matters, then cities controlled by the Christian Democratic Party should spend less and be less active generally than cities controlled by the more liberal Social Democratic Party.

West German cities, like municipalities in the United States, also have different policy environments. It is quite possible that environmental conditions, such as population density and class composition, account for these differences in public policy outcomes. These environmental conditions could also explain differences in party control, with working-class cities supporting the Social Democrats and middle-class cities, particularly those with large Catholic populations, supporting the Christian Democrats. In such a

Source: Robert C. Fried, "Party and Policy in West German Cities," *American Political Science Review* 70 (March 1976): 11–24.

---

ing brokerage organizations, were far more interested in managing urban conflict than in setting general directions for municipal public policy. It can be argued that American urban parties managed urban conflict relatively well by brokering diverse interests and offering jobs and possibilities for upward mobility to urban ethnics. But these conflict-managing organizations may have been poor vehicles for setting and implementing policy goals.

Some evidence supports this line of reasoning. Machine politicians were generally supportive of the expansion of federal government programs during President Franklin Roosevelt's New Deal, but they were certainly not leaders and not policy entrepreneurs. Many scholars today give machines high marks for their roles in building the public infrastructure of twentieth-

---

situation, party control would have little influence in the policymaking process, as diagrammed here:

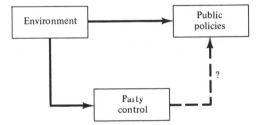

Fried found that party control by the Christian Democratic Party was associated with less municipal activism (higher spending and taxing, and growth in service bureaucracies), less collectivism (public enterprises such as public housing and hospitals), and less expansionism (bureaucratic growth). These effects were *in addition to* the effects of environment. However, Social Democratic control did not relate to higher activism, collectivism, or expansionism. Several factors explain this, including the difficulty experienced by the Social Democrats in establishing party control for periods long enough to make a difference in public policy and the tendency of Social Democrats to be cautious at the municipal level (perhaps in large part from the fear of losing citizens or businesses because of high taxes).

Thus, party control of municipal government can have an effect on policy outcomes, but the effect is limited by environmental conditions and the possibility of movement by citizens and businesses if tax burdens are perceived as being too high.

century American cities. But this involved primarily responding to initiatives from private developers and centralizing power in order to marshal public resources to carry out public works projects. It did not really involve setting public policy directions after a debate before the public. The whole system worked much the way Tammany Hall politician George Washington Plunkett operated: "I seen my opportunities and I took 'em."

European political parties are a good deal more ideological than American parties. They are also less diverse; each party is composed of a more homogeneous group of supporters so that ideology can be pursued with less fear of alienating a bloc of supporters. It is possible that European local parties are better at setting and implementing policy directions than are their American counterparts (albeit at the cost of an obvious loss of ability to manage urban conflict). Evidence from a study of local parties in West Germany indicates that party control does make a difference in policy outcomes (see box 6.2).

Strong party organizations based on either material incentives or European-style ideological solidarity are uncommon in America today. The effect of party decline has been to weaken the popular control of government at local, state, and national levels. Strong parties have the ability to impose some degree of local uniformity in the pursuit of national goals by simply nominating local candidates who will adhere to the policies pursued by the national party. At one time parties in the United States performed this function. Frank Goodnow, writing in 1900, claimed that without strong political parties, "our government would have consisted of a disorderly, uncoordinated, unregulated crowd of officers, each equal in actual power to every other, and each acting according to the dictates of his own conscience or the caprice of his own whims."[17]

Goodnow had hoped to keep parties strong yet make them more responsive to popular will. He writes that "the boss or leader is an absolute necessity" and urged that reformers "not destroy the boss but make him responsible."[18] Reformers did not follow Goodnow's good advice; the result is that local officeholders in America are more "a disorderly, uncoordinated, unregulated crowd" today than they were in 1900.

Conclusions: Patronage and the Local Party

The glue that has held together American political parties has traditionally been not ideology or issues, but patronage. Parties were primary local

[17] Frank J. Goodnow, *Politics and Administration: A Study in Government* (New York: Macmillan, 1900), p. 106.
[18] Ibid., p. 193.

organizations because most government jobs were at the local level. The urban political machine was a party organization that ran almost solely on patronage and other material incentives, avoiding to the extent possible the issue-oriented politics that could divide its supporters.

With the advent of civil service, employee unions, and the cultural norm of independence, local parties atrophied, and so did an important mechanism for citizens to influence government. The decline of party has also limited the resources of chief executives, from mayors to the President, in dealing with legislators. With patronage a city executive potentially could influence legislators to support his or her program. In the absence of patronage, chief executives not only must deal with independent legislators, but also must face bureaucrats who are difficult to discipline.

Parties were not always allies of chief executives. Often local party organizations deteriorated into bickering factions of independent chieftains. But it was always possible for leadership to emerge, if patronage could be centralized. Today legislators do not face the threat of being denied their patronage, and bureaucrats are not threatened with the loss of their jobs for political reasons. But the loss of patronage and the decline of parties has also meant that policy coordination by a strong chief executive is all the more difficult.

CHAPTER 7

Interest Groups
in Urban Politics

Numerous groups actively seek to influence urban policies at the local, state, and national levels. In this chapter we examine interest groups in urban life: what issues concern them, what resources they use in trying to influence policy outcomes, and how successful they are in employing those resources.

Underlying this chapter is a very basic assumption: that political groups matter in the urban policy process. It is, of course, possible that the rich group life that characterizes many American cities is irrelevant to urban policymaking, and that a small cabal of economic notables use their wealth and organizational abilities to determine what city governments do. Before we examine this thesis in detail, however, it is necessary that we map out the major urban interest groups and the strategies they use in attempting to affect the course of urban policy. Then we may turn, in chapter 8, to the issue of urban power structures.

Organized and Potential Interests

Political scientists distinguish between potential interest groups and organized interest groups. *Organized* groups have a leadership structure, and communication occurs between members and leaders. An example would be a labor union, such as the United Automobile Workers. A *potential* group consists of individuals who possess a common interest who are not all members of an organized group that claims to represent that interest. In some cases several organized groups speak for a single potential interest.

Organized groups consistently try to influence urban politics, but that is not the whole story. Often some individuals, not representing any organization formally, emerge as spokespersons for a potential group. The chairman of the board of directors of the largest bank in the community does not need to be the president of the local chamber of commerce to be a representative of downtown business interests. The minister of the church with the largest black congregation in the city may well speak for blacks, even though he holds no formal position in any civil rights organization. Such informal spokespersons for potential interest groups are generally not very effective in national or even state politics, but they can be quite effective in local politics, where they have the opportunity to become known personally and demonstrate individual effectiveness.

Because of the emergence of individuals who champion issues that are of concern to potential groups but who hold no formal positions in organized interest groups, it is possible for a potential group to influence the political process without formal organization. In general, however, for a potential group to influence the policy process, it must include one or more formally organized interest groups, or an informal spokesperson.

Stakes and Resources

Groups become active in politics because they perceive a *stake* in the outcomes of the political process. A stake is a public policy outcome that a group perceives to be beneficial to it. That stake can be something the group wants to gain, but it can also be something the group wishes to protect. Many groups enter politics in order to engage in defensive actions, as would be the case if business owners worked against the election of an antibusiness candidate for the city council in order to forestall action unfavorable to their interests.

The ways in which groups try to influence the urban political process vary according to the resources that the group possesses. Many different kinds of resources may be used to influence public policy outcomes. Some groups exercise political influence by the use of money; some group leaders possess special knowledge; others are especially adept at organizing their members. Any of these may result in increases in political effectiveness.

Some groups command great respect in the community, or within a particular subcommunity, and their endorsements of candidates or ballot proposals can be crucial. These are groups that emerge only at election time, produce a list of preferred candidates, and disappear until the next election.

New York Daily News Photo

Over 30,000 Hasidic Jews mourn the death of Grand Rabbi Levi Grunwald in Brooklyn in 1980. Ethnic diversity continues to characterize urban America and make necessary mutual adjustments among groups with different values and cultural heritages.

Source: AP Photo, *Detroit Free Press,* April 15, 1980.

Other groups claim that their endorsements carry the special weight of expertise; this is especially true of the endorsement candidates for judgeships receive from the local bar association, a professional association of attorneys. These groups claim to speak for the public interest by ruling on the competence of public officials. If this claim goes unchallenged, the group will be able to wield power in the process of selecting candidates for public office.

Newspapers, of course, regularly endorse candidates and take positions on issues, but the mass media are more important because they help shape the community's policy agenda. The media act as the major channel of communication between the politically active substrata and the mass public. Power can stem from access to the communications media.

Some groups or individuals are influential in politics because they have been able to develop and legitimize special relationships to public decision makers. Where collective bargaining is legal, unions representing city employees have this special relationship. A common judicial reform calls for judges to be appointed from a short list developed by the bar association, again a special legitimized relationship for a special interest group. Often state and local regulatory boards are composed of representatives of the trades, professions and businesses that they are to regulate—barbers regulate barbers, doctors regulate doctors, electricians license electricians.

Finally, political scientists have recently recognized that protest and a willingness to disrupt the normal proceedings of politics and government can in itself be a political resource. Such threats can make policymakers accede to demands, but disruptive tactics can also backfire and generate hostility toward the disruptive group. Policymakers may then rely on majority support when they refuse the demands. Because this tactic is both unstable and potentially double-edged, it is generally used by groups that are relatively powerless, possessing few, if any, alternative political resources.

Resource distribution

Political resources in a community may be *cumulative* or *noncumulative*. In a community in which resources are cumulative, the same citizens who possess most or all of one kind of resource possess most or all of other resources. Moneyed groups also possess disproportionate political knowledge, prestige, and the other resources used to influence political outcomes. Although the distribution of resources is more nearly equal in some communities than in others, nowhere are resources completely equal. This means that some groups start out with a political advantage. This advantage may be offset if those groups with less advantage are more *efficient* in translating resources into power. In order for this to happen, however, groups with fewer resources would have to recruit more skillful leaders than those with more resources.

Policy Systems

The urban political arena is filled with numerous groups with different memberships, interests, and political strategies. A pluralism of groups, however, does not necessarily imply group competition, because most groups are active on but few issues, and those groups tend to collaborate rather than compete within their respective chosen arenas. Two of many possible examples will illustrate this. Parent-teacher associations, or PTAs, educational administrators, and local, state, and federal officials concerned with educational policy are all active on issues concerning the financing of schools. At any one time they are more likely to be collaborating on matters of educational policy than conflicting. Similarly, business and labor, traditional enemies in national politics, are typically collaborators on the issue of local economic development. Because separate issue domains exist and few groups are active on a wide variety of domains, groups spend more of their time and energy agreeing on policy matters than disagreeing.

Policies that result from agreement among groups generally stay off the policy cycle, because no active group with a stake in the process has any reason to bring the matter to the policy agenda. The critical questions concerning who is to participate in the policy process have already been settled. Unless some outside force emerges to disrupt the prevailing arrangement, off-cycle policymaking is likely to be the characteristic mode. Such "islands of functional power," as Sayre and Kaufman termed them,[1] have more recently been labeled *policy systems*.

Policy systems generally involve a loosely connected network of local, state, and federal bureaucrats, certain legislators (generally chairpersons of the committees responsible for the policy arena in the city council, state legislature, and Congress), and the interest groups affected by the policy. These interest groups often have a national organization as well as local branches. Local organizations are active in the policymaking system centered in local government; the national organization is active in Washington.

Characteristics of policy systems

In any well-developed policy system, three characteristics predominate. First, public policy is heavily influenced by the views of "experts," individuals who claim special knowledge of a particular issue area. Education professionals claim special knowledge in the areas of public education, as do their counterparts in the areas of housing, urban development, planning, law enforcement, energy, and numerous other domains. These issue specialists

---

[1] Wallace S. Sayre and Herbert Kaufman, *Governing New York City* (New York: W. W. Norton, 1965).

tend to be trained in university programs that cater to their professions. The proliferation of new programs to serve these issue specialists is a measure of the increasing importance of expertise in public policymaking. Many universities offer advanced degrees in urban planning, architecture, law enforcement, social work, fire science, and environmental science, not to mention the numerous subspecialties that have proliferated in the field of education in recent years: special education, bilingual education, educational psychology, and reading.

The second characteristic of policy systems is that the participants tend to be in regular contact with one another at both the local and national levels. "More than ever," notes Hugh Heclo, "policy-making is becoming an intramural activity among expert issue-watchers, their networks, and their networks of networks."[2] These *issue networks,* according to Heclo, are now the primary centers for public policymaking in America.

The third characteristic of policy systems we have already noted: they operate at all levels of government. Indeed, the fact that issue networks of policy experts are national entities partially accounts for the increasing centralization of policymaking at the federal level. It also accounts for the rapid diffusion of *policy innovations,* the process by which new policies are copied by other governments. The word of a successful policy innovation quickly spreads to other political jurisdictions via the issue network. (An example of a well-developed policy system is given in box 7.1.)

Groups and Parties

The power of interest groups in local politics is enhanced where political parties are inactive. This is the case for three reasons. First, where parties perform their usual functions of recruitment for office and mobilization of voters in elections, the electoral power of interest groups is curtailed. If parties fail to act, either because of internal weaknesses or because of nonpartisan electoral systems that prevent them from doing so, these functions must be performed by electoral organizations of candidates. In this situation candidates are more likely to become directly dependent on interest groups to raise campaign funds and mobilize voters, and this help is not likely to be forgotten. In nonpartisan San Francisco, candidates for office frantically rush around to every civic and neighborhood group in the city in a desperate search for endorsements. Without the standard party labels that allow voters to define candidates, candidates must search for self-definition in the group

---

[2] Hugh Heclo, "Issue Networks and the Executive Establishment," in *The New American Political System,* ed. Anthony King (Washington, D.C.: American Enterprise Institute for Public Policy Research, 1978), pp. 105–6.

Box 7.1: Issue Networks and the
Regulation of Buildings

The regulation of building and construction is an activity that traditionally has been left to local governments. Municipalities enact building codes to set construction, occupancy, and maintenance standards. Their authority to do so is granted by the state through enabling statutes or home rule provisions. The activity is justified because it sets minimum standards for the safety of building occupants.

The existing system of local regulation has led to a patchwork of building regulations even within a single metropolitan area. Building standards in one suburb may not hold in an adjacent one. This situation has led architects and contractors to argue for national standards for construction.

Actually, standardization in construction regulations is much more advanced than one would expect based on the degree of local autonomy that exists. The reason is the existence of a national network of groups and individuals who are concerned with building regulation. Several professional associations issue *model codes,* which are suggested building code ordinances for municipalities to consider when writing their building codes. These groups include the Building Officials and Code Administrators (BOCA), the International Conference of Building Officials (ICBO), and the Southern Building Code Congress, International (SBCCI). In addition, the National Fire Protection Association (NFPA) provides a model fire-safety code (fire-safety codes must dovetail with building ordinances and indeed are often considered part of the building code). Each of these associations claims to speak for the public interest; each never-

---

endorsements.[3] Calling something nonpolitical or nonpartisan does not mean that political activity will disappear, only that other groups, perhaps less well equipped to perform the function, will fill the vacuum.

Second, in some cases parties and groups compete directly, and the competition reduces the power of groups. Political machines, for example, rely on patronage in city government to reward faithful precinct workers, but city employees crave job security and predictability in appointments. In Chicago, organizations of city employees have clashed with both Mayors

[3] Frederick Wirt, *Power in the City* (Berkeley, Calif: University of California Press, 1974), ch. 4.

theless represents an association of professionals: fire-prevention engineers, code-enforcement officials, and so forth.

Increasingly the federal government has entered this policy sphere, primarily by attempting to encourage standardization among the various model codes. In 1974 Congress established the National Institute of Building Sciences to conduct studies and issue advisory opinions concerning the safety and economy of changes in building technology (which must be incorporated into local building codes if the codes are to keep pace with technology changes). The federal government has also financed the development of rehabilitation and energy conservation codes. In the House of Representatives, the Committee on Banking, Housing, and Urban Affairs has conducted hearings on the impact of building codes.

Many small jurisdictions simply adopt one or another of the model codes in total, but larger jurisdictions invariably piece together their own building codes from the model codes and the requests from local interest groups. In either case, however, there is essentially a reliance on expert opinion in the policymaking process. The process of building-code revision and amendment in Chicago is illustrative.

In the 1960s Mayor Daley appointed the Mayor's Advisory Committee on Building Code Amendments to advise him on what changes ought to be made in the building and fire-safety codes. Although the committee bears the title "advisory," it is in actuality the policymaking body for building regulation in the city. A Chicago mayor has refused the advice of the committee only once, and that refusal caused the committee to cease operations for three years.

Bilandic and Byrne, the successors of Richard Daley and the titular heads of the Chicago machine. Bilandic was able to beat back a firefighters' union's demand for collective bargaining, which city of Chicago workers lack. The current Mayor, Jane Byrne, promised in her election campaign that she would authorize collective bargaining for employees, but moved slowly because of objections by party officials. Consequently, in the winter of 1980 firefighters struck illegally. As the power of the Chicago Democratic organization declined, the power of unions representing city workers increased.

Third, interest groups tend to be weaker where parties are strong because of the coalition politics that is necessary for party government. Parties can

Since its reinstitution in the late sixties, it has had the field to itself. This does not mean that the mayor's views are not part of the committee's deliberations, because the commissioner of the building department (a mayoral appointee) chairs the committee. Also on the committee are officials from the building department (now the Department of Inspectional Services) and the fire department, along with architects, structural engineers, mechanical engineers, developers, realtors, construction contractors, and building trade unionists.

Once the committee decides on a policy change, it is submitted to the mayor, who passes it on to the city council with his or her endorsement. The chairman of the city council's Committee on Building and Zoning, Alderman Edward Vrdolyak, the only city councilor with any real interest in or expertise on building codes, holds hearings. The hearings are perfunctory, however, because Vrdolyak has already had his input into the process as a member of the mayor's advisory committee and is already "on board." The full council usually passes the changes recommended by Vrdolyak with no debate and no dissension. This includes the independent, anti-machine aldermen. Aldermen are reluctant to interject themselves into an issue that has already been settled by the major participants, especially where they lack professional expertise.

Local regulation of buildings thus displays all the characteristics of a well-developed policy system. A national issue network (actually several overlapping networks) exists; policy is primarily made by experts; and local policy is influenced by both the national network and local interests.

---

capture control of government only where they can construct coalitions of interest groups large enough to win elections. Parties have few interests outside of gaining and retaining office, so they act primarily as brokers of groups interested in substantive policy issues. Unless the party is able to enforce compromise among the diverse interests, the electoral coalition will fly apart. Hence, parties attempt to enforce unity in coalitions by stressing moderation and by deemphasizing issues that might prove divisive. Such actions by parties help to restrain the tendency of pure group politics to degenerate into rancorous conflict. Because parties must create electoral coalitions to govern, they have a *stake in compromise*. Such enforced compromise limits the power of groups in the political process.

Indirect Influence: Money and Organization in Elections

Groups affect the policy process in two ways. First, they involve themselves in electoral politics. By helping to elect friendly candidates and defeat unfriendly ones, they hope to influence public policy indirectly. They also engage in the policy process directly, by lobbying and developing special relations with policymakers, often within particular policy systems. First we examine indirect influence by groups.

Money in campaigns

Money is a liquid resource: it can be translated easily into other political resources. One important use of money in local politics is to finance election campaigns. Campaign expenses for some offices are trivial: a local school board candidate may spend next to nothing in a suburban district. In large cities, especially for mayor and other at-large offices, expenses often run into millions of dollars. Not only are high-visibility offices expensive to run for, some offices that seldom cross the mind of the average voter increas-

---

Box 7.2: Special Interest Money in New York

Just prior to the 1981 Democratic primary election for mayor of New York, incumbent Mayor Edward Koch had collected $1.15 million in campaign contributions. His major opponent, State Assemblyman Frank J. Barbaro, had collected $125,000. The outcome of the election was widely perceived as a foregone conclusion, and Koch went on to an overwhelming victory. The contributions were thus not vital to the election's outcome.

The group bases of the contributions to the two candidates were substantially different. In the absence of meaningful limits to the size of campaign contributions, Mayor Koch received large lump-sum contributions from a number of individuals and organizations involved in real estate and finance. He received at least $200,000 from real estate interests and some $28,000 from a single stock brokerage firm. Smaller contributions came from certain unions,

Source: See Frank Lynn, "Special-Interest Money Aiding City Candidates," *New York Times* (September 3, 1981).

---

ingly require large sums of money for a candidate to mount a credible campaign. Moreover, there are fewer legal restrictions on contributions to candidates for municipal offices than for federal offices (see box 7.2).

Money provided by interest groups to bankroll campaigns is especially important in nonpartisan cities, where political parties are not active in selecting candidates and raising money for campaigns. Candidates become more reliant on support from special interest groups for both money and endorsements where parties are weak. Moreover, in those cities that use at-large elections to elect city council members, groups organized citywide become more important, and neighborhood groups become less important. The candidate for council needs citywide endorsements of business and labor groups, and can ill afford to be viewed as a spokesperson for homeowners or residents of a particular neighborhood.

Access to media is important everywhere, but especially where parties do not perform their voter mobilization functions. And media advertising is expensive, especially in citywide campaigns. Because campaigning candidates can rely on the party for neither workers nor funds, they become especially reliant on interest groups, particularly groups organized on a citywide, rather than neighborhood, basis.

---

primarily the Operating Engineers Union, the International Ladies' Garment Workers Union, and the Uniformed Sanitationmen's Association.

In contrast to the minuscule union support received by Mr. Koch, Mr. Barbaro was almost completely dependent on unions to keep his campaign alive. He obtained sizable contributions from the International Brotherhood of Electrical Workers, the United Automobile Workers, the Drug and Hospital Workers Union, and the Transport Workers Union.

As is generally the case, interest groups contributing to the respective candidates did not expect to receive particular favors from the politicians. But they did believe that the policies pursued by their favored candidates would benefit them. One Koch contributor put it this way: "The benefit for industry and business comes primarily from the city being straightened out." On the other hand, many union officials felt that their members had been forced to absorb the brunt of the financial bail-out measures supported by Koch. Barbaro had been far more solicitous toward unions, and many felt that he merited their support.

Money in referenda

Money can be used to mount public relations campaigns to support particular public policy issues. This is perhaps most frequently done to support or oppose substantive policy proposals that are put before the voters in referenda. Many states have provisions that allow or require legislatures, city councils, or school boards to put issues before voters for decision; such a ballot proposal is termed a *referendum*. Some states also allow citizens to initiate legislation through petition; voters then decide on the issue through a referendum.

The most common public policy issue decided by voters is school millage, when voters decide whether to increase (or renew) a property tax to support their schools.[4] Voters have been increasingly reluctant to support millages, and several groups have become very active in attempting to persuade voters to pass them. Educational interest groups, such as teachers, principals, and PTAs, are clearly affected by the fate of the millage. At times, however, other groups become active, particularly business groups, reformers, and civic "boosters," who see defeated millages as reflecting on the image of the community as a whole.

Beginning with California's 1978 Proposition 13 (from its position as the thirteenth proposal on the ballot), a variety of tax limitation proposals have been put before the voters in several states and localities. Government employees have made common cause with the client groups receiving services to fight the proposals. On the other side homeowners and landlords have mounted major efforts to pass the proposals, with varying success. Because such campaigns rely heavily on the media to contact voters, they quickly become expensive.

Direct Influence

Because so many crucial public policy issues are decided by government actors far removed from campaigns and elections, or by elected officials not facing immediate threat of electoral defeat, interest groups often try to influence the decisions of government officials directly. Many groups maintain paid professional staffs that engage in lobbying efforts before legislatures and city councils when issues arise that affect the group's interest. The staff produces in-depth analyses of issues that are given to legislatures or the general public, testifies at hearings scheduled by

---

[4]Property taxes are generally expressed in mills, or tenths of a cent, per dollar of taxable property; hence the term *millage*.

legislatures or city councils, keeps the membership informed on issues before government, and organizes public relations campaigns on major issues affecting the group.

Increasingly, local affairs are influenced by national trends. Decisions once made almost exclusively by local decision-making bodies are affected by policies made by Congress and the President. Reflecting this trend, many interest groups that were formerly interested primarily in policymaking at the local level have organized on a national basis to influence decision making at the federal level. Municipal employees are often represented by local affiliates of national organizations rather than by purely local entities. The advantages of this arrangement may be gauged by the grateful remarks made by former President Carter when the American Federation of Teachers (AFT) endorsed him for reelection. The AFT had supported Senator Edward Kennedy in the Democratic primary elections, and Carter believed that the endorsement and election work provided by the AFT were crucial to Carter's primary losses in Pennsylvania and New York.

Because so many urban policy issues are decided by the federal government, many organizations now retain representation in Washington. This has been true of nationally organized groups for some time, and recently purely local organizations have found it in their interests to hire lobbyists in Washington.

Finally, the courts, federal and state, have become increasingly important decision-making bodies in the urban policy arena. Courts are asked to decide on desegregation plans for school districts, to determine the validity of government reorganization plans, to intervene in labor disputes between municipal governments and workers, to determine the constitutionality of hiring and promotion plans, and to rule on the environmental impact of highway and public works construction, as well as to decide numerous other issues once left to legislatures and executives. Consequently, many organizations maintain paid legal staffs and funds for court challenges to decisions made by legislatures and city councils.

Corruption: Illegal direct influence

The vast majority of the money and activity that flow into local politics is used legitimately—to organize, to advertise, and to present cases before policymaking bodies. There remains, however, a significant amount of corruption in local politics, especially in some cities.

Corruption in local politics is far less extensive than it was some fifty or seventy-five years ago. Even then true corruption was probably far less extensive than some reformers alleged. George Washington Plunkitt, a New York ward politician and Tammany Hall stalwart at the turn of the century whose "philosophizing" at the New York County Court House shoeshine stand was recorded by journalist William Riordon, carefully distinguished between honest graft and dishonest graft. Dishonest graft involved illegal activities, such as blackmail, extortion, or bribery. Honest graft, according to Plunkitt, involved taking advantage of the opportunities a politician encountered. Buying up land where public improvements are planned and selling it to government at inflated prices, for example, is a tactic that is as old as government involvement in public improvements. As Plunkitt put it, "Ain't it perfectly honest to charge a good price and make a profit on my investment and foresight? Of course it is. Well, that's honest graft."[5]

Corruption does not invariably involve money, but it usually does. Indeed, two students of corruption in local government have defined the phenomenon as "the exchange of money or other material goods for preferential treatment by public officials."[6] Corruption occurs when (1) opportunities for corruption occur, and (2) the benefits of corruption perceived by government officials and those trying to influence the decisions made by government officials exceed the costs of corruption.[7] Opportunities for corruption exist because government has decided to regulate and tax the activities of citizens. In the absence of government attempts to specify or prohibit certain actions by citizens, no corruption could occur, because citizens would not need preferential treatment and government officials would be unable to offer it.

Individuals contemplating corruption engage in a rough cost/benefit calculation to decide whether the action is likely to be beneficial to them. If the benefits exceed the costs, they are more likely to engage in corrupt practices. For example, the owner of a small store will be more likely to attempt to bribe a health inspector if the inspector is threatening to file a major, costly violation against her than if the violation will cost little to correct. She will also be more likely to engage in corrupt practices if she feels that the probability of being caught for the act is slim.

Finally, the cultures of some localities are more conducive to corruption than are others. Although no area of the country is free from corruption, some are worse than others. American mythology holds that center cities are hotbeds of corruption and the politics of suburbs are "squeaky clean," but this is not altogether true. It is probably true that the reform ideology that grips many suburban communities makes corrupt practices more difficult, but many opportunities for corruption exist in suburban communities, especially where extensive development is taking place. There developers may offer public officials an opportunity to "invest" in new projects such as

[5] William L. Riordon, *Plunkitt of Tammany Hall* (New York: Dutton, 1963), p. 3.

[6] John A. Gardiner and Theodore R. Lyman, *Decisions for Sale: Corruption and Reform in Land-Use and Building Regulation* (New York: Praeger, 1978), p. 5. These authors note that this is a narrow definition, but it fits what we generally think of as corruption.

[7] Ibid., pp. 10–11.

shopping centers or subdivisions in return for favorable action by government on the developers' zoning applications.

Gardiner and Lyman conducted a survey of newspaper articles concerning corruption in an attempt to ascertain roughly the dimensions of the problem. Even though newspaper coverage is far better in central cities, about 25 percent of the reported corruption incidences occurred in suburbs or independent cities, 47 percent occurred in central city governments, and 28 percent took place in county government.[8]

Gardiner and Lyman also tabulated the areas of reported corruption in their survey (see table 7.1). Where opportunity exists, corruption follows. Prime areas for corrupt practices included the letting of government contracts; land-use regulations such as building regulations, zoning, and subdivision ordinances; and personnel matters, involving hiring and promotions. Significant incidences of corruption also involved law enforcement and the abuse of welfare and other government benefit programs.[9]

Generally, then, political corruption occurs where (1) the political culture is tolerant of such practices; (2) there are ample opportunities; and (3) the probability of being caught and prosecuted is relatively low.

Contracting. In the letting of government contracts, the stakes are relatively high. Local governments contract for a variety of goods and services, and private firms stand to make considerable profit if they win the contract. Hence, contractors will occasionally pay "kickbacks"—usually some portion of the anticipated profits—to officials who control the letting of the contract. Although most government contracts involve public improvements such as road construction and the laying of water and sewer

Table 7.1. Newspaper reports of local corruption, 1970–76

	Number	*Percent*
Government contracting	112	30.1
Land use	83	22.3
Personnel matters	45	12.1
Other (law enforcement,	132	35.5
abuse of government benefit	372	100.0
programs, etc.)		

Source: See John A. Gardiner and Theodore R. Lyman, *Decisions for Sale: Corruption and Reform in Land-Use and Building Regulation* (New York: Praeger, 1978), pp. 6–7.

[8] Ibid., p. 9.

[9] Of course, reports of corruption by newspapers are not a reliable sample of all incidences of corruption, because they are dependent on what prosecutors, investigative reporters, and reform groups uncover, and on what newspapers decide to publish. The distribution of incidences is nevertheless instructive, and there is no other source to consult.

mains, governments also contract for white-collar services from consulting firms. Management consulting, personnel classification studies, feasibility studies of computerizing service delivery operations, efficiency studies, and the like have become as common in government as in private industry, and they offer ample opportunity for corrupt practices. Kickbacks are definitely a form of "dishonest graft," but what about the situation in which a potential government contractor contributes to the campaign fund of an elected official? Is he engaging in the constitutionally protected practice of freedom of speech by making his political preferences known, or is he trying to buy a contract?

The problems of corruption in government contracting have led reformers to demand that checks be imposed on the contracting process. Most common is tight specification of the job, and a requirement that government accept the lowest bid on the job. But firms clearly differ in their ability to get a high-quality job completed in a timely fashion. Demanding a lowest-bid system means that officials cannot use their judgment in deciding who is best qualified to perform the task. Once again we face a trade-off—limiting opportunities for corruption means limiting discretion that can be used in the public interest.

Building Regulation. The regulation of land and the buildings erected on the land is a function exercised primarily by local government. This is the area in which corruption is probably most ingrained. Local government regulation significantly increases the cost of building, and if the cost of bribing an official to overlook building code violations is less than the money that would be expended to bring the building up to code, the motive is present. In a more spectacular case of corruption, suburban developers of a large shopping center may make large payoffs to city councillors to obtain a favorable change in a zoning ordinance. Finally, building codes are extraordinarily detailed. Almost any building fails to meet all code specifications, and corrupt building inspectors may use the code to extort payments from owners or developers (see box 7.3).

Group Activity in Urban Politics

Because of the existence of a number of different policy systems in the public sector, few groups are uniformly powerful in the urban policy process. Many groups are active, however, and in this section we survey some of the more important groups in urban politics: business, labor, city employees, neighborhood groups, public interest advocates, the mass media, and public officials organized as interest groups.

Box 7.3: Extortion in Chicago

The Department of Inspectional Services in Chicago has a rich tradition of corrupt practices, stemming back to the early 1900s when it was rated as the worst city department by a study commission. Since the 1950s corruption has been curbed in many of the department's bureaus, but in the past few years new scandals have broken out in the electrical bureau, which is responsible for enforcing the city's electrical code; the new construction division, responsible for inspections of new buildings and renovations; and in the license inspection process, which certifies the safety of restaurants, taverns, and other places of public assembly. One-third of the electrical bureau's inspectors were recently convicted of extortion. License inspectors were caught in the act of accepting bribes and making superficial inspections of taverns; their actions were captured on film by a CBS news team during a "sting" operation organized by the Chicago *Sun-Times* and the Better Government Association, a reform group given to muckraking.*

Although the department has instituted a sophisticated system of management control along with an internal affairs division charged with investigating wrongdoing by inspectors, corruption continues to

*See Zay Smith and Pamela Zekman, *The Mirage* (New York: Random House, 1979).

Source: Bryan D. Jones, "Management Control as Public Policy," paper delivered at the meeting of the Operations Research Society of America, Milwaukee, Wisc., October 15–17, 1979, and unpublished files assembled by the author.

Business

In all cities business plays a crucial role in urban politics, but the role it plays differs among cities, and among issues within a single city. In some cities, the business community is strong and united on the direction that it wants the city's political system to take. Other groups challenge business discretion at their peril. For years Dallas's business community has dominated politics through its Citizens' Council, as did San Antonio's through the Good Government League. Aided by reformed political institutions, business values were thoroughly incorporated into the political structure. In recent years, business domination has broken down in San Antonio and has weakened in Dallas. The business community is still important in

be a serious problem. "It's a payoff system," commended one independent alderman. "It's the most corrupt department in city government," said a building department official, off the record. "It's blown way out of proportion," said the commissioner of buildings. "And another thing," he continued, "the problem is more with the public pushing money at our inspectors than anything else. I tell 'em not to take it, but temptation is always a problem."

It is true that most corruption does involve citizens seeking favors. Often bribing a building department official is cheaper than bringing a building up to code. It is far from uncommon for contractors to pay inspectors to ignore new construction that fails to meet city standards, or to pay an inspector to allow construction to continue without properly filing plans and permits with the city. Contractors are perhaps unwittingly encouraged by law-enforcement officials who tend to concentrate their efforts on government officials when corruption is uncovered, allowing contractors immunity from prosecution in return for their testimony. Contractors know that they are unlikely to be prosecuted for their activities.

In some cases, however, city inspectors are bold enough to use the codes to extort money from owners or contractors. An inspector can delay final approval of construction until the money is paid. One young executive at a downtown bank reported the following:

> I own two buildings I bought to rehabilitate. I had them inspected, and the electrical inspector told me to get some work done, and to be sure to get a licensed electrician to do the work. I did just that. When

both cities, but it does not form a unified power structure as it did in previous years.

In other cities business people are important in some areas but not in others. They are crucial actors in urban development, for instance, but do not act in a coordinated way on other issues, if they act at all. Even on issues that concern then intimately, they often must share power with other groups, primarily politicians and government officials, who have independent power bases. In Chicago, politicians backed by the powerful Democratic machine and business people collaborate on issues of urban development and government financing, but the values of business clearly do not dominate the political culture as they do in Dallas.

In most cities, the business community itself is diverse. In almost all major cities it has two main components: businesses with primarily local in-the inspector came back to inspect the job, he said, "This work is not to code." *Owner:* But I got a licensed electrician as I was requested. *Inspector:* I'm sorry, but it is not to code. It will have to be ripped out.

Finally I got smart. I asked the inspector: "How much is this going to cost me?" The inspector said: "One half of what it would cost you to replace the work." I said, "No way"; then we negotiated, I ended up paying. I don't remember how much. I shouldn't have, but I did."

The electrical bureau was the most corrupt in the department; inspectors not "on the take" were ridiculed by the rest. The assistant chief of the bureau, who had served with distinction in the Second World War, boasted openly about the money he had made through engaging in corrupt practices, a fact taken into consideration by the federal judge who sent him to prison for a lengthy jail term.

In an attempt to control corruption, Mayor Jane Byrne reorganized the former building department into a Department of Inspectional Services, and made a former police commander with no substantive knowledge of building regulation commissioner, with a single mandate: control corruption. The chief of the electrical bureau quietly retired, and management control operations were extended into the formerly recalcitrant electrical bureau. After all these administrative changes, a plumbing inspector, bent on confirming the axiom that "plus ça change, plus c'est la même chose" (the more things change, the more they stay the same), was caught by the FBI accepting a bribe from a contractor.

terests, such as banks, department stores, and local law firms; and businesses with a national outlook, such as corporations whose headquarters just happen to be in New York or Atlanta, or wherever. The local branch of the business community is often intimately involved with politics in the community; the national branch generally stays out of local politics and in return wants to be left alone.

National Corporations. It is not true, however, that the nationally oriented businesses are not important in local affairs. Often national companies claim to act out of a sense of "civic betterment" in their local political arenas. United States Steel in Pittsburgh, Ford Motor Company in Detroit, and Coca-Cola Company in Atlanta all have been active in local city politics.

Civic betterment is not the only reason for business action. Important business interests may be threatened by what is happening in cities. Karen Orren has noted:

> The inner city and the tremors of social disorder are the most constant threat to the status quo between big business and the forces of the state. This threat is a fundamental reason why corporations undertook the ghetto projects of the late sixties and early seventies.[10]

Decisions made in corporate board rooms in New York can affect urban politics in San Diego or Phoenix or Toledo. If a consortium of investors in New York decide they ought to invest in Denver, or if General Motors decides to build a new plant in Tennessee, one can be sure that the configuration of local politics will be altered. So even when national corporations make strictly economic decisions, they can affect local politics without directly intending to do so.

Local Businesses. Diversity also exists within the local business community. A commonality of interests does exist on some issues, such as economic growth, but this united front disappears on other questions. Not all business people, for example, favor policies to revitalize the center city. Many have committed themselves to suburban locations or locations in the outer city, and see the revitalization of the central business district as a threat. Owners of existing apartment buildings are not particularly enamored of policies encouraging the construction of new buildings. Construction contractors, on the other hand, prefer policies facilitating new construction to those facilitating rehabilitation, which is more likely to be done by the building owner or independent contractors. Whether business is united or divided depends very much on the issue.

Organized labor

There are two kinds of labor unions: *industrial* unions, such as the Teamsters, the United Automobile Workers, and the unions affiliated with the Congress of Industrial Organizations (the CIO of the AFL-CIO); and *craft* unions, such as the organizations of plumbers, electricians, and carpenters. Although the interests of these two kinds of union often correspond, in local politics they can and do differ. It is not so much that the two compete as that they are incorporated into different policy systems. Craft unions tend to be interested and active in making and enforcing building codes, fire codes, and professional licensing procedures, which affect their

---

[10] Karen Orren, "Corporate Power and the Slums: Is Big Business a Paper Tiger? in Willis D. Hawley, Michael Lipsky, and others, *Theoretical Perspectives on Urban Politics,* (Englewood Cliffs, N.J.: Prentice-Hall, 1976), p. 46.

livelihoods directly. Industrial unions have little interest in such matters, leaving the field to their craft brethren.

Industrial unions are very important in national political life, and in the politics of many states. They are, however, less active (and less successful) in local politics, for two reasons. First, local politics offers lower stakes to the mass-based industrial unions than the politics of state and nation. Such items of vital interest as minimum wage laws and legal guarantees of labor's right to bargain collectively are the province of the national government and the states; localities have little power there. In the second place, labor union members are also homeowners and taxpayers, and they may vote for conservative policies and candidates in local affairs while supporting liberal measures in the national political arena. Moreover, labor unions, especially industrial unions, are ethnically diverse. Urban politics often involves conflict over residential and educational integration, and any position taken by union leadership may alienate either black members or white. From the perspective of union leaders, it may be better to stay out of local politics and concentrate on state and national issues that can rally the diverse membership.

Neighborhood groups

Neighborhood groups are formed on the basis of physical proximity rather than other shared characteristics of members (occupation, religion, race, and so forth). Just as there are all kinds of neighborhoods, there are all kinds of neighborhood associations. Associations of property owners in an exclusive neighborhood may join together to improve the local school; poor renters may demand that city hall enforce the housing code against the absentee landlords who own the buildings they inhabit. Working-class residents of a neighborhood of modest cottages may be concerned about improving city services to try to keep white residents from moving away, thus forestalling integration.

The one thing that unifies neighborhood organizations, whether they are composed of rich or poor, black or white, renter or owner, is their concern with the delivery of services to the neighborhood. Richard Rich has indicated that neighborhood organizations play three distinct roles in the delivery of services.[11] First, they act as *demand articulators* to demand services from city government. On the theory that collective action is more effective than individual action, neighbors band together to place demands before government. Second, neighborhood organizations can serve as *alternate producers* of services, as when the organization establishes a child care center or main-

[11] Richard C. Rich, "The Roles of Neighborhood Organizations in Urban Service Delivery," *NASPAA Urban Affairs Papers* 1 (Fall 1979): 2–20.

tains a vacant lot as a local park. Relying on neighborhood sources rather than government, the community produces its own services.

Finally, community groups can act as *coproducers* of service. Service is produced only when citizens and government cooperate. The neighborhood watch program, in which city police enlist the aid of citizens in regular surveillance to detect potential criminal activity, is an example of city service departments attempting to harness the energies of citizens in helping to produce services. Other coproductive efforts may be less formal: the removal of fire hazards by neighborhood groups, encouraging the use of adequate garbage containers to decrease litter, and a clean-up campaign for the neighborhood park all are examples of coproductive efforts of neighborhood organizations.

How effective are community organizations in these roles? We have surprisingly little evidence. In a study in Chicago, however, Jones found that community organizations served as an alternate channel for citizen demands for housing code enforcement. However, community groups were unable to stimulate demand beyond what would have existed in the absence of the organization, were unable to influence city officials to deliver more service than they would have delivered according to their standard operating procedures, and did not coproduce services by influencing landlords to keep up their buildings.[12] In Chicago, neighborhood organizations must compete for citizen loyalty with the machine, so the results from this study may not hold in other cities.

Neighborhood organizations lack the resources that would make them stable influences in city politics. They rely primarily on volunteer labor; only the most successful have any paid staff at all, and even then the number of workers is small. Lack of immediate success causes many volunteers to lose interest in participating in the organization. The heady volunteers who gather to picket an unscrupulous landlord seldom show up in housing court to testify against him. Perhaps most damaging to neighborhood organizations is the fact that they are based on geography rather than occupation, class, or race. When people move, they do not normally change other aspects of their social station in life, so they are still union members, members of a particular religion, and so forth. But they leave their community organizations behind. Even the possibility of mobility hurts the ability of many organizations to mobilize residents.

Protest as a political strategy

Neighborhood organizations differ in the strategies they use in attempting to influence government. Some try to develop a traditional interest group

[12] Bryan D. Jones, "Party and Bureaucracy: The Influence of Intermediary Groups on Urban Public Service Delivery," *American Political Science Review* 75 (September 1981): 688–700.

strategy by forging coalitions and developing expertise in dealing with city agencies. Others have developed more radical styles to dramatize their grievances.

Neighborhood groups, of course, are not the only groups to employ protest. Civil rights groups, feminist groups, antiwar activists, antibusing groups, and groups fighting freeways have all used protest in an attempt to secure their goals. Paul Schumaker sees protest groups as normally excluded from the interest group politics prevailing in a community. He defines *protest groups* as "groups of citizens who do not normally interact with government officials, but who, under certain conditions, organize on an informal, issue-specific basis to make demands on public officials through pressure processes." [13]

As Michael Lipsky has pointed out, groups engage in protest activities primarily because they lack more stable political resources.[14] Indeed, protest strategy hinges on a complex theory of influence. Most protest groups, lacking direct access to the councils of policymaking, hope that their protest activities will attract the attention of third-party reference groups, groups that do have resources and have sympathy with the aims of the protesters. By making dramatic gestures, protest groups hope to activate third parties on their behalf. Civil rights demonstrators in the deep South in the 1960s had scant hope of influencing such southern police chiefs as "Bull" Connor of Birmingham, but they did hope to focus the attention of northern liberals on the plight of black southerners. This, they hoped, would stimulate liberal groups to bring pressure on Congress and the President, who in turn would initiate action in favor of powerless southern blacks.

To capture the attention of a third party, however, requires that the attention of the mass media be captured. Only the media can elevate the grievances of protest groups to the policy agenda. Protest strategies are always directed, first and foremost, at the media. The complex process of using protest as a political resource is diagrammed in figure 7.1.

Protest is generally an unstable and unreliable tactic of political influence because of the number of links separating the protest group from the target of the protest. But a second problem exists, because the protest group cannot control exactly who receives the media message it hopes to generate. Third-party reference groups can receive the message, but so can inactive groups who are potentially hostile to the aims of the protest groups. Such groups can become active to oppose the aims of protest groups.

Some indication of this potential of negative reaction toward protest groups is indicated in a 1970 survey conducted by Peter Eisinger of blacks and whites in Milwaukee. Eisinger found substantial differences between

[13] Paul D. Schumaker, "Policy Responsiveness to Protest Groups," *Journal of Politics* 37 (May 1975): 490.

[14] Michael Lipsky, *Protest in City Politics* (Chicago: Rand McNally, 1970), ch. 1.

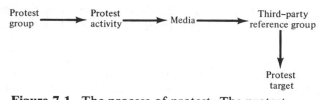

Figure 7.1. The process of protest. The protest group must generate "newsworthy" activities, hoping that the media will report them, causing a sympathetic third-party reference group to influence the target of the protest (often government).

whites and blacks in their understanding of the nature of protest behavior. Blacks tended to think of protest as instrumental activity, activity designed to accomplish concrete policy goals; whites tended to view protest as activity by "troublemakers." Table 7.2 presents figures from Eisinger's study attesting to the dramatic differences in understanding of the meanings of protest behavior.

In order to study the effectiveness of protest group behavior, Paul Schumaker measured the extent of such behavior and the responsiveness of policymakers in a number of cities. As one might expect, the support of community groups (potential "third parties") was important in explaining community responsiveness to protest group demands. But the attitudes of both elected government officials and city bureaucrats were also important in explaining protest group success. Schumaker indicates that in the appropriate milieu, protest groups can appeal directly to protest targets (government officials) without having to rely on activating third parties.[15] His data also indicate that radical strategies are less successful than more moderate

Table 7.2. Attributions of motivations for protest behavior, Milwaukee

	Blacks	Whites
Instrumental reasons ("to win demands")	56%	36%
Expressive reasons ("to express outrage")	20	15
Negative reasons ("troublemaking")	8	37
Other	1	1
Don't know	15	12
	100%	100%

Source: Peter K. Eisinger, *Patterns of Interracial Politics: Conflict and Cooperation in the City* (New York: Academic Press, 1976), table 6.1, p. 128. Reprinted by permission.

[15] Schumaker, "Policy Responsiveness."

strategies, primarily because they provoke hostility in the community at large.

City employees

Political scientist Edward Banfield has written, "Because of their numbers, and because nearly two-thirds of them (in the largest cities almost 100 percent) have joined unions or professional associations, city employees are—and will surely be in the future—the single most powerful interest group on the local scene." [16] Once the cannon fodder for the powerful urban machine, city employees are now an independent force in local politics.

Public sector unionism has been far more successful in recent years than has private sector unionism. Although the percentage of public sector workers who are unionized has grown, the percentage of private sector workers who are union members has dwindled. In 1955, 24.4 percent of the total labor force in the United States was unionized, but by 1976 the figure had declined to 20.3 percent. These figures are for the labor force as a whole, and mask two different trends: the decline of traditional union membership and the explosive growth of public sector unions. Public sector unions also organize a far greater percentage of their potential membership than do private sector unions: in 1977, 47.8 percent of state and local employees were unionized. [17]

Collective Bargaining. City employees are influential in city politics because they have important stakes in policy outcomes—their livelihoods are determined by city policies—and because they possess important resources. These resources stem primarily from the collective bargaining process, increasingly used as a model for labor relations in the public sector. In *collective bargaining,* a union is designated as representative of workers to negotiate a contract with management, covering matters of wages, salaries, fringe benefits, working conditions, and grievance procedures, that is binding on both labor and management for the duration of the agreement.

There are important differences between the use of collective bargaining in the public sector and its use in the private sector. In the private sector, management is responsible to the owners of the corporation (usually stockholders represented by a board of directors). Management's primary responsibility is to make a profit, and labor negotiations are influenced by that aim. In competitive industries, at least, wage settlements that are higher than those of other companies in the industry will mean that the prices

---

[16] Edward C. Banfield, "America's Cities Enter a Crucial Decade," *Chicago Tribune,* March 23, 1980.

[17] U.S. Bureau of the Census, *Statistical Abstract of the United States 1979* (Washington, D.C.: U.S. Government Printing Office 1979), pp. 421 and 431.

charged for the product will rise relative to the prices charged by other companies, and profits will fall as consumers buy competitors' products. In the public sector, however, management is composed of elected officials, officials who generally want to retain their positions. Municipal employees are a potent electoral bloc, and elected officials are sensitive to their potential influence in upcoming elections. Moreover, municipalities are not in business to turn a profit, and wage settlements are negotiated without such a constraint. As more cities find themselves in fiscal difficulties, however, officials have taken a tougher stand on wage settlements.

Strikes. Not all states allow state and local workers to bargain collectively. In many southern states, and in areas such as Chicago where machines are still strong, workers do not have collective bargaining rights. Almost everywhere government employees are flatly prohibited from striking. This prohibition has not stopped teachers, firefighters, sanitation workers, and police officers from engaging in illegal work stoppages. Every fall the nation is treated to the spectacle of numerous strikes by teachers that keep tens of thousands of schoolchildren from their classes. Several years ago firefighters in Memphis struck in a bitter labor dispute, as did those in Chicago. Police in New Orleans struck during Mardi Gras, engendering strong hostility on the part of the community and giving Mayor Ernest Morial the opportunity to break the strike. Sanitation workers recently struck in Atlanta, and black mayor Maynard Jackson refused to budge on the demands from the predominantly black sanitation workers' union. In Bessemer, Alabama, sanitation workers struck and demanded solidarity from that city's numerous steel workers. The South is no longer free of public sector labor disputes, and this pattern is likely to accelerate in the future.

The number of strikes by public employees is not excessive when compared with strikes by private employees. In 1977 there were 5,535 work stoppages in the United States, causing a loss of over 310 million worker-days. Only 413 occurred in the public sector, with 18 million lost worker-days. About 0.32 work days were lost per worker due to private sector strikes, but only 0.15 work days were lost due to public sector strikes.[18] Public sector strikes, however, affect large numbers of people who are not parties to the negotiation. Strikes by police, firefighters, and sanitation workers can seriously threaten the health and safety of many people, and therefore must be taken more seriously than most private sector strikes.

Arbitration. Because of the impact of public sector work stoppages, a number of methods have been tried to avert them. *Mediation,* in which a third party brings parties together in the hope of resolving issues, has

[18] Ibid., pp. 430–31.

generally not worked very well. A second method of resolving labor disputes is *arbitration*. An arbitrator has the authority to write the final contract that is binding on both management and labor, with the only recourse being appeal to the courts. Currently, arbitration is gaining popularity as a method of resolving disputes, presumably because of its resemblance to the judicial process.

Arbitration has severe problems, however. It encourages the parties to make extreme demands and refuse to negotiate seriously, because they assume that the arbitrator will just split the difference. This practice has led to a system called *final offer arbitration,* in which the arbitrator must accept either labor or management's last offer. This system governs labor relations concerning firefighters and police in Michigan cities. The 1970 law providing for arbitration lists the factors that arbitrators are to take into consideration in making an award; unfortunately, one of the factors is not the financial situation of the municipality. A large award to police and firefighters in 1979 led Mayor Coleman Young of Detroit to lay off 690 police in 1980, most of whom were blacks and women (because of union rules requiring layoffs to occur in reverse order of seniority).

Because working conditions are a subject for collective bargaining, they are also subject to arbitration. In Battle Creek, Michigan, a tinderbox of bad racial feelings, a white police officer was suspended for harassing a black citizen. An arbitrator reduced the suspension and required the city to pay the officer for the bulk of his suspension. The ruling upset local black leaders and heightened racial tensions. Arbitrators can ignore social and political factors in the community in their awards. Politicians are more likely to consider those factors, but they may lack the power to do so. What are Battle Creek blacks supposed to do? Vote against the mayor and city council in the next election? Democratic accountability has broken down, and a system of government by arbitration has replaced government by the consent of the governed.

Because of the increasing technical and legal problems associated with negotiating labor contracts, and because public employee strikes are, strictly speaking, illegal, courts have been asked to intervene in labor disputes. Generally, public officials will request back-to-work orders from judges. Such orders are generally issued, but they are generally disobeyed. It is possible for judges to find union leaders in contempt of court in such situations, and send them to jail, but judges have generally been reluctant to do so. Such actions often heighten tensions and do not hasten settlement (union members know the jails are not big enough to hold them all). Some judges have tried to act as mediators, with little success (see box 7.4).

In her study of collective bargaining between the United Federation of Teachers (UFT) and the New York City Board of Education, Sara Silbiger was struck by the variety of ways in which the collective bargaining process

Box 7.4: Judges and Teachers

Like many states, Michigan allows its teachers to organize and bargain collectively but prohibits them from striking. Nevertheless, strike they do, and the common practice is for school districts to sue in court to obtain back-to-work orders against the striking teachers. If teachers ignore these orders, they risk being found in contempt of court. If they are found in contempt, they may be fined or jailed; usually such remedies are directed at union leaders.

In the spring of 1980, a particularly ugly situation developed in the "downriver" working-class suburbs of Detroit. When the downriver teachers struck, the school district lawyers filed in Wayne County Circuit Court, part of the state court system, for a back-to-work order. Because the teachers were striking in four different districts, two different circuit court judges were involved. Judge Wise immediately got tough: he issued the injunctions quickly and sent nine union leaders to jail when the orders were disobeyed. But the Michigan Court of Appeals overruled his order on technical

Source: Various newspaper accounts; Judge Columbo's remarks were printed in an advertisement published by the Gibraltar and Woodhaven school districts and Michigan Association of School Boards in the Detroit *Free Press,* April 18, 1980.

---

determined educational policy. The UFT influenced "educational finance and productivity, management opportunities to improve the quality of service, and sociospatial patterns of resource distribution to various neighborhoods in the city."[19] Most of these influences on public policy were based in negotiations concerning employee work rules. Silbiger's study graphically demonstrates the power gained by city employee unions via the collective bargaining process. As unions gain influence over public policy, elected leaders lose control. Elections become weaker as channels for public influence on policy, simply because whoever is elected must abide by the collective bargaining process.

Public officials as interest groups

On September 5, 1980, eight mayors representing the United States Conference of Mayors, led by Richard G. Hatcher, Mayor of Gary, Indiana,

[19] Sara L. Silbiger, "Collective Bargaining and the Distribution of Benefits: Education in New York City," in *Urban Policy Making,* ed. Dale Rogers Marshall (Beverly Hills, Calif.: Sage, 1979), p.276.

grounds. Judge Columbo at first tried a gentler approach: he brought the parties together in his courtroom to negotiate. The negotiations made no progress, so the school districts requested an injunction. Judge Columbo denied the request, not because he sympathized with the teachers, but because he believed they would ignore his order. He expressed his frustrations in his legal opinion:

> I decline to join the foolishness of issuing another injunction that is going to be disobeyed and is going to be flouted by this irresponsible group of elitist anarchists who have no respect for the law, its institutions, or anything else. . . . This [the teachers] is already a well-paid group. The average one of them earns now about $25,000 a year. Had they accepted this order they would earn at the end of the contract well over $30,000 a year; far in excess of the median income of the communities which they are preying upon like vultures. . . .
>
> Collective bargaining was originally designed to help working people collectively bargain with their employer so that they could get a decent wage, have a decent roof over their heads and have decent food on the table for their family. This particular stoppage shows what a perverse reversal of those roles has occurred. Here we have this professional organization, already well paid and underworked, seeking to be overpaid and underworked at the expense of working-class communities that neither can afford it nor understand it.

asked President Carter to include more federal aid for cities in his proposals to Congress. Government was lobbying government, a pattern that has increased as the federal government has dispensed more and more money to local governments.[20] Other organizations of government officials that act as interest associations include the National League of Cities, the National Association of Counties, and the International City Managers Association. Many large cities also maintain full-time lobbyists in Washington, as well as in the state capital.

Associations of local government officials are concerned with all the things that traditional interest groups are concerned with: gaining benefits from government. They use the tools of traditional interest associations: letter-writing campaigns to influence members of Congress, public relations campaigns to influence the public, and support in election campaigns. They have come to play important roles in a very important policy system: the system responsible for dispensing federal grants to state and local governments.

[20] See Donald Haider, *When Governments Come to Washington* (New York: Free Press, 1974).

Public interest advocates and the bias
of the interest group system

Because groups possess different resources, and because some people are more likely to get together and organize than others, the interest group system is not representative of the public at large. Some interests tend to be omitted from the policy process because the groups representing them are often not well organized, or because they lack resources. Because the poor are less likely to organize, they are less likely to be represented in the policy process. The system is biased toward those who do organize.

Various programs, sponsored by both government and private groups, have attempted to open new avenues to encourage the representation of the unorganized—consumers, poor renters, minorities. A whole new profession has emerged, that of the public interest advocate. Lawyers, social scientists, and other professionals have intervened in the policymaking process on behalf of unrepresented interests, and on occasion have stopped highway construction, delayed urban renewal projects, organized rent strikes, and halted evictions from public housing projects. They have also lost numerous battles, but their existence as intervenors has changed the character of urban policymaking.

The problem with public interest advocates is that they are no more representative of the general public than are public officials or other interest groups. As the director of a group promoting greater citizen participation in policymaking has noted,

> In many ways, public interest advocates are as remote, paternalistic, and arrogant as the bureaucrats and regulators they criticize for these qualities. Very few of the public interest advocacy groups enjoy an active membership drawn from the general public. Deriving their support from foundations and lawyers' fees awarded by courts, they are themselves unaccountable to the public they purport to represent.[21]

Because public interest advocates tend to promote different policy positions than traditional interest groups, they have altered the configuration of opinions that are represented in the interest group system. Many policy systems have operated differently after the intervention of public interest advocates. In particular, traditional groups have been less likely to prevail on issues.

One of the most important consequences of the entry of public interest advocates into politics has been to delay or stop projects, such as highway construction, that previously plowed through neighborhoods and public

[21] Nelson Rosenbaum, "Grassroots for the Public Interest," *Citizen Participation* 2 (September/October, 1980): 23.

parks. In the past, policymakers thought little of the opinions of the poor and the "friends of the park" who objected, but when skilled public interest advocates press the case, they can no longer take that stance. It is generally easier for any group to block or delay projects than it is to start and implement projects. The public interest advocacy movement has strongly confirmed this long-standing observation of interest-group politics.

Concluding Comments: The Myth of the Independent Policymaker

If Americans harbor deep distrust of political parties, they harbor as deep or deeper distrust of interest groups. The term *special interest group* is an epithet that elicits strong disdain. There is even an interest group that lobbies against interest groups—Common Cause. At the state and local levels, as well as at the national level, numerous so-called reforms have been aimed at weakening the influence of interest groups, including requirements of registration of lobbyists, detailed filing of expenses used in attempting to influence legislation, and public financing of campaigns and elections.

Consider, for a moment, what a policymaker who did not respond to special interests would be like. Would he or she be the ideal of a century of reformers, the statesmanlike searcher for the common good? Perhaps, but what happens when there are two or more conceptions of what the common good is? Will the policymaker compromise? If so, he or she has become responsive to the demands of the special interests who press their claims. Will he or she stand on principle? What if the principle is wrong? It is easy to say that the voters will repay our policymaker for mistakes at election time, but what if election time is three years away? Interest groups and political parties have the resources to affect public policy between elections. But elections may be most important because they force elected officials to pay attention to organized citizen demands—organized through interest groups and the party structure—between elections. Not only do elections give the elected official reason to be responsive to group demands, they give him or her reason to respond to demands that are rooted in majority opinion.

In this book we have stressed the existence of two kinds of public policy issues with which the political system must deal. In the first, a public interest really does exist, either because government is asked to provide a collective good (in which everyone is genuinely better off) or because the benefits provided by the policy overwhelmingly outweigh the harms done. In facing the second kind of issue, the political system must deal with policies that will genuinely harm some people and genuinely benefit others; moreover, doing nothing will continue harms and benefits. Being an independent, noncompromising statesman may be fine for the first type of issue, but it can be actually harmful for the second. Indeed, the best kind of leader for the second kind of issue, in which conflict between groups must be faced, is one steeped in the arts of politics—compromise, conciliation, bargaining, and negotiation—with the power to enforce the bargains he or she strikes.

American democracy is built on the freedom to organize. But if politicians have no motive to pay attention to organization, then that freedom is meaningless. Elected officials—mayors, city councillors, governors, legislators, members of Congress, the president—are not judges, insulated from the fray of politics. Nor should they be, if democracy is to have meaning.

There is, however, a final possibility. It may be that neither groups nor parties nor elected leaders have much influence on the major directions of local public policies. A number of political scientists and sociologists have done research indicating that most policies are set by a small, unified economic elite. Others claim that, on the contrary, the interplay of groups and elected officials does determine public policies in cities. It is to the evaluation of these competing claims that we now turn.

CHAPTER 8

The Structure
of Urban Power

The owners and managers of major banks and corporations are the heart of an upper social class that can be considered a ruling class because it dominates all major aspects of American life.
—William Domhoff

The most lasting impressions created by a systematic analysis of New York City's political and governmental system as a whole are of its democratic virtues: its qualities of openness, its commitments to bargaining and accommodation among participants, its receptivity to new participants, its opportunities for the exercise of leadership by an un-matched variety and number of the city's residents, new and old.
—Wallace S. Sayre and Herbert Kaufman

In New Haven, as elsewhere, there exist significant inequalities in wealth, income, status, education, knowledge, access to the media and to organizations and in many other crucial resources. . . . The question arises, however, whether in the midst of inequalities like these it much matters if a regime is "democratic" or not.
—Robert A. Dahl

As the quotations indicate, nowhere in the study of humanity and the in-stitutions it has created are basic issues better conceptualized and joined in more vigorous debate than in the study of community power structures. For well over a quarter of a century, two loosely knit schools of thought have debated whether a small economic elite or democratic political institutions determine the public policies a community pursues.

The debate has been characterized by careful empirical studies of the configurations of power in a number of American cities, rigorous theorizing, and innovation in the methods and techniques of studying social power. At least twice researchers have reinvestigated communities studied earlier and have reported contradictory findings.[1] But the ongoing controversy has also been characterized by an inability of many researchers to see beyond the ideological blinders that often result from the fervent defense of a position, sloppy thinking, and occasionally, harsh personalizing of the issues. Although there is no sign that the differences between the contending parties have moved toward resolution, at least the areas of disagreement have been clearly delineated.

Power and Influence

Power is the ability of one person to get another to act differently from how he or she would have acted in the ordinary course of events. This can involve the performance of an act that would not have been performed ordinarily, but it can also involve nonperformance. If a person refrains from doing something because of the power of another person, he or she has been influenced by that person. (Influence is merely a weak form of power; it is a relationship in which one person's behavior is affected by another, but not determined by it.) A *power structure* is the regularized exercise of power within a social system. It is distinguished from single exercises of power in that it takes place repeatedly over time (is regularized) and involves a set of regularly interacting individuals (a social system).

Power and power structures are difficult to study for three reasons. First, there is a *baseline problem*. How do we know what the behavior of a person would have been in the absence of an influence attempt? The second problem is the problem of *observability*. We noted previously that a person may refrain from doing something because another person acts to prevent the performance of the act. There is no problem in observing a power relationship if the influencer does something, such as issuing a threat, in attempting to affect the behavior of the influence. But what if a person refrains from performing an act because he or she anticipates that the other person will react negatively? If, for example, a black family does not move into a white

---

[1] M. Kent Jennings, *Community Influentials: The Elites of Atlanta* (Glencoe, Ill.: Free Press, 1964), reports pluralism where earlier Floyd Hunter found elitism; and G. William Domhoff, *Who Really Rules? New Haven and Community Power Reexamined* (New Brunswick, N.J.: Transaction Books, 1978), found elitism where Robert Dahl found pluralism.

neighborhood because of fear of retaliation, has power been exercised? We observe no act, yet most people would infer a power relationship. How are we to infer anything from something we don't observe? On the other hand, if we do not root our study of power in observables, we will end up jumping to all sorts of unwarranted conclusions about why people don't act. The third problem in the study of social power is that of *structure*. Under what conditions are we entitled to infer the regularized relationships that constitute a power structure?

As we shall see, each of these problems has plagued the study of community power. Because of these difficulties, no single empirical study can possibly resolve the continuing differences of opinion among both scholars and lay people on the subject. The best that we can do is put forth the issues and indicate where our sympathies lie.

The Pluralists and the Elitists

The two schools of thought on the issue of community power structures are distinguished chiefly by how they view the distribution of power in society. They also tend to differ in the methods they use in studying power. The *elitists,* or stratificationists, view power as being narrowly held, generally by an economic elite, with political officeholders subservient to the economic power holders. The *pluralists* see power as being more widely spread among social actors, and see politicians as holding independent power. They believe that one major influence on the behavior of politicians is the electorate. Hence voters hold indirect power, because they have some influence over elected officials.

Nelson Polsby, a staunch pluralist, has detailed the basic tenets of the elitist approach:

1. The upper class rules in local community life.
2. Political and civic leaders are subordinate to the upper class.
3. A single "power elite" rules in the community.
4. The upper class power elite rules in its own interests.
5. Social conflict takes place between the upper and lower classes.[2]

With the exception of the last one, these propositions are self-explanatory. Elitists tend to accept the premise that enduring social conflict is based in the economic class structure, and that other forms of conflict, such as conflict between two working-class groups, are not enduring.

[2] Nelson Polsby, *Community Power and Political Theory,* 2nd ed. (New Haven, Conn.: Yale University Press, 1980), ch. 1. To our knowledge, no elitist has objected to Polsby's specification.

To Polsby's original formulation of the elitist position, we add a sixth, increasingly evident in the writing of elitists:

6. The local power elite is interlocked with a national power elite that controls all major aspects of American life.

To the elitist, then, the rich and varied group life described in the preceding chapter has little to do with the actual process of settling community policies. The "lower levels" of power are merely "fighting over the scraps" left by the power elite.

Pluralists generally reject the propositions set forth above. As is the case in the writings of the elitists, pluralists differ themselves on the various issues, but they tend to accept the following propositions:

1. Social conflict is organized around groups, only some of which are based on class membership.
2. Power must be distinguished from power resources. Not all resources are used to influence public policy.
3. Power resources are distributed unequally, so that some groups possess more of those resources than others.
4. Nevertheless, all groups can gain access to some resources.
5. Elected officials are independent actors (they possess power resources that they use to influence public policy).
6. Voters indirectly influence policy, because elections cause politicians to pay attention to them.

For the pluralists, then, power is more widely dispersed than for the elitists, social conflict centers in groups rather than class (although class membership is an important source of group conflict), and democratic institutions have the effect of making mass preferences felt in the policymaking process.

Methods and Findings

Three different methods have been used to study urban power structures: the *reputational approach,* the *positional-overlap approach,* and the *decisional approach.* Most studies of community power rely most heavily on one of the approaches, but several studies have used a combination of methods.

The reputational approach identifies the powerful by asking a panel of people who are presumably knowledgeable to indicate who the powerful are. This approach was used by the sociologist Floyd Hunter in his classic study of Atlanta.[3] Hunter solicited four lists of leaders from civic organizations: leaders in civic affairs, business and finance, local politics and government, and "society." Then a panel of fourteen judges from the community chose those they considered the top leaders on each list. Hunter's next step was to examine the extent of overlap among the lists. He concluded that power in Atlanta was in the hands of a very small group of business people, and that the political and community leaders were subordinate to this cabal.

The reputational method has been used primarily by sociologists and has tended to lead to the discovery of elitist power structures. This approach has been criticized on the grounds that it studies the reputation for power rather than the actual exercise of power. Obviously the results from this approach are highly dependent on the composition of both the initial lists and the panel of judges.

Researchers using the positional-overlap method develop two or more lists of individuals and examine the extent of overlap among the lists. The lists are based on the presumed power that the individuals hold, based on their positions within broad domains of social activity. One list, for example, may consist of the boards of directors of major banks and corporations in the community along with members of the community's most prestigious law firms. Such a list would presumably indicate economic power. A second list might consist of the past and present members of the city's major boards and commissions. If there were extensive overlap between these two lists, this would be evidence of an elitist power structure. If there were not significant overlap, either a pluralist power structure exists, or the economic elite doesn't bother with politics because it is not important.

The positional-overlap method, like the reputational method, has been criticized because it fails to investigate the actual exercise of power. It relies completely on the investigator's definition of what lists of positions are powerful. Perhaps most damning is the fact that corporate directors are not necessarily more powerful than politicians. Significant overlap between two lists is incomplete information, because the most powerful members of the two groups may not overlap.

Researchers using the decisional approach attempt to study power by examining specific decisions in which power can be presumed to have been exercised. By discovering who wanted what from whom, how the decision-making process took place, and who prevailed over whom, researchers deduce the configurations of power. This process involves discovering the attitudes and actions of participants in the decision-making process through interviews and direct observation. The decisional approach is the application

---

[3] Floyd Hunter, *Community Power Structure: A Study of Decision Makers* (Chapel Hill, N.C.: University of North Carolina Press, 1953).

of a much-used method in political science, the *case study* method, to the study of power. It has been used primarily by political scientists, and has tended to lead to the discovery of pluralist power structures.

Who governs?

In a classic study using a combination of the decisional method and the positional-overlap method, political scientist Robert Dahl presents a vigorous defense of the pluralist approach.[4] Dahl and his colleagues, Nelson Polsby and Raymond Wolfinger, studied decision making in three separate issue-areas in New Haven, Connecticut: urban renewal, nominations for political office, and public education. In each of the three areas, Dahl found that power was shared among various interested groups, and that groups interested in one issue were not generally interested in the other areas. The business community, for example, was quite interested in urban renewal, but it was not very active on the issue of education. The only actor who spanned all coalitions was Mayor Richard Lee: "Only the Mayor was a member of all the major coalitions, and in each of them he was one of the two or three men of highest influence."[5] Dahl terms this pattern the *executive-centered coalition.*

In many ways the issue of urban renewal is the most interesting of the three issue-areas studied by Dahl. In this area business owners, the group most often held up by elitists as the "power behind the throne," clearly had a compelling interest. For many years plans for redeveloping New Haven's downtown had been circulated, in both public and private circles. But, in Polsby's words, they were not "self-executing." Dahl says:

> Very little happened until redevelopment became attached to the political fortunes of an ambitious politician [Mayor Lee]. Redevelopment was not produced by a surge of popular demand for a new city, nor was it produced by the wants and demands of the Economic Notables, even though many of them believed that changes in the physical pattern of the city were necessary to their own goals.[6]

Mayor Lee was the classic policy entrepreneur. His motive was the furtherance of his political career. He constructed the coalition of business, labor, and political leaders that formed the blue-ribbon Citizens' Action Commission. It served to give legitimacy and acceptability to the redevelopment program. Still, all major initiatives came from the city government, particularly the city's redevelopment agency. Redevelopment was Mayor

[4] Robert A. Dahl, *Who Governs? Democracy and Power in New Haven* (New Haven, Conn.: Yale University Press, 1961).
[5] Ibid., p. 200.
[6] Ibid., p. 115.

Lee's ballgame. Other individuals and groups clearly affected the outcome and therefore exercised influence. But Lee was at the center of power, and he was clearly no mere pawn of the business community. He was serving his own interests, which often diverged from those of the city's business community. If his actions were limited by the business community, Lee was also constrained by his anticipation of what voters would accept. Lee, after all, was the one major actor who would have to stand for reelection on the record of redevelopment, which he had made a major priority.

Urban renewal in other cities did not originate from the political system, however. In Detroit, the impetus for the touted "Renaissance" came from the business community (see box 8.1).

The second face of power

The decisional approach has been criticized on a number of grounds. The most important objections include the selectivity of issues, the attention to what is actively controversial, and the potential of a "mobilization of bias," what has been called a non-decision-making process.

Issue Selectivity. The issues one chooses for study color the results one is likely to uncover. Elitists have attacked Dahl's choice of political nominations and public education on the grounds that the economic elite is not interested in such matters, because its members reside in the suburbs; thus, these issue-areas do not constitute proper tests of the power elite hypothesis. That this may be true does not make these issues unimportant. Indeed, public education doubtless touches more people's lives than does urban renewal, and in ways that are more enduring. And power was exercised in this domain—by different actors than in the domain of urban renewal, but exercised nevertheless. Indeed, it would seem to be necessary to examine a range of issues if one is interested in mapping a power structure for a community, not just issues that the researcher has predetermined will involve business interests. All of this does not mean that issue selection is not important; clearly it is. It does mean that the criticism that pluralists study unimportant issues is misplaced.

Controversy. Issues involve controversy. But attention only to what is actively controversial can focus attention away from two processes that are very important in the configuration of community power. In the first place, issues may not be raised by an individual who perceives that he or she is going to lose. Carl Friedrich has termed this process the law of *anticipated reactions.* The actions that people take are always conditioned by what they estimate the reactions of others are likely to be. In politics, this means that issues will not be raised, and hence will not become controversial, if potential

---

Box 8.1: Making It Happen
in Motor City

In the winter of 1970 twenty-one executives from Detroit's business community, along with the mayor of Detroit and the governor of Michigan, gathered at the suggestion of the president of the city's Chamber of Commerce. The aim was to "do something," something dramatic, that would revitalize Detroit's stagnating downtown district. In attendance were top executives from General Motors, Chrysler, and American Motors, the chairman of the board of the city's leading department store, and bankers, other business people, and financiers. Max Fisher, a financier and entrepreneur with ties to the Nixon administration, was there, as was Henry Ford II, chairman of the board of Ford Motor Company and head of the city's most famous family. The group agreed to form a "coalition" named Detroit Renaissance. Fisher was named chairman of the group.

The discussions quickly began to center on Detroit's riverfront. Ford said that he would take the lead in developing a major building project on the river. And major it was. By the time the Renaissance Center complex of a seventy-three-story hotel and four forty-story office buildings was completed, it was the largest private investment ever undertaken in a city—at a cost of $337 million.

It might be thought that if a group as powerful as Detroit Renaissance decided on a project, bringing it to fruition would be a simple matter. Quite the opposite was true. Investment was flowing to the suburbs, and reversing that powerful trend for what many

Source: See the pamphlet, *The Top Forty-Seven Who Make It Happen: A Study of Power.* A series of articles reprinted from the *Detroit News* (Detroit: The Detroit News, n.d.) Interestingly, this study makes the general case that the Detroit power structure is much more broadly based than in the past, now including many government officials rather than just corporate and business leaders. It also includes quite a few blacks, most in positions of leadership in government or labor. Negotiation continually occurs between the old, business-based elite of money and families and the new elite based on control of government and labor unions. According to the study, the negotiations result in coalitions that join members from both groups in pursuit of common goals.

---

policy entrepreneurs perceive them to be lost causes. Dahl noted this process at work in New Haven:

Politicians are wary of their [the Economic Notables'] potential influence and avoid policies that might unite the Notables in bitter opposition. Fortunately

saw as an enterprise doomed to failure was a difficult task. Henry Ford was the "point man" for raising the initial $134 million investment. Corporations with local interests were presented with arguments concerning civic revitalization and the importance of the central business district to the health of the metropolis, and corporations in competitive situations were played off against one another (each of the major metropolitan daily newspapers invested half a million dollars). Companies in direct business relationships with the automobile companies were prevailed upon to invest. ("We did it,"

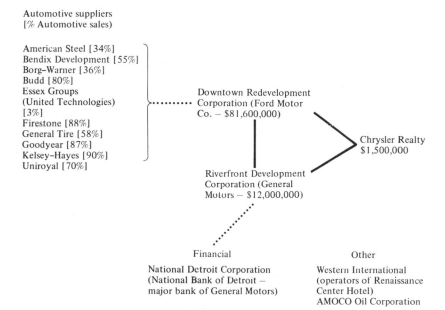

Automotive suppliers
[% Automotive sales)

American Steel [34%]
Bendix Development [55%]
Borg–Warner [36%]
Budd [80%]
Essex Groups
(United Technologies)
[3%]
Firestone [88%]
General Tire [58%]
Goodyear [87%]
Kelsey–Hayes [90%]
Uniroyal [70%]

Downtown Redevelopment Corporation (Ford Motor Co. – $81,600,000)

Chrysler Realty $1,500,000

Riverfront Development Corporation (General Motors – $12,000,000)

Financial
National Detroit Corporation (National Bank of Detroit – major bank of General Motors)

Other
Western International (operators of Renaissance Center Hotel)
AMOCO Oil Corporation

The Renaissance Partnership (Million Dollar Club; companies that invested at least $1 million in Detroit Renaissance).

Source: See the pamphlet *The Top Forty-Seven Who Make It Happen: A Study of Power*. A series of articles reprinted from the *Detroit News*. (Detroit: The Detroit News, n.d.)

for the politician, it is easy to avoid the implacable hostility of the Notables, for living conditions and the belief system of the community have not—at least so far—generated demands for local policies markedly antagonistic to the goals of businessmen and Notables.[7]

[7] Ibid., p. 84.

said one executive, "because Henry Ford asked us to. Ford and GM are two of our largest customers. What can you do when they ask? You have to come up with the money.") Many companies viewed the investment as a "charitable contribution" to the health of the city, and perhaps a payoff that would buy goodwill from a political structure that was clearly going to be controlled by blacks in the near future.

The biggest investments came from the automobile companies themselves. General Motors invested $12 million, but only after Henry Ford had made a personal visit to GM's headquarters. The lion's share of the initial investment, however, came from Ford Motor Company's real estate subsidiary—over $81 million. This investment has subsequently been severely criticized because Ford's automotive operations have lost money and the company has had difficulty in raising cash for retooling and modernization in recent years.

The initial investment was used to entice a consortium of twenty-eight banks to lend $200 million for construction. Long-term mortgage financing was obtained primarily from the insurance industry.

In terms of the aims of the Detroit Renaissance coalition, the building project has been a success. The office buildings are financially healthy, although the hotel has experienced operating losses. Small businesses, restaurants, boutiques, and so forth have sprung up in and around the glass-and-steel towers. New office towers have been constructed. Riverfront land prices have increased dramatically, and new construction projects are planned. But the investment itself has not returned a profit.

In the case of Detroit Renaissance, governmental involvement came late. Not surprisingly, city and state officials eagerly cooperated with the business community, helping with plans, permits, and site clearance. But, unlike urban renewal in New Haven, this project was put together by a private entrepreneur, not a public one.

Focusing on the actively controversial can also mean missing issue-areas in which a policy settlement has been put into effect. By a *policy settlement* we mean an issue that is no longer on the public agenda because one side won on the matter when it was actively controversial. If, for example, a public issue has proceeded through the policy cycle and has been implemented by establishing a governmental agency, controversy may no longer surround the issue. Nevertheless, decisions with important implications for public policy continue to be made. Policymaking is of the off-cycle variety, out of the limelight of public opinion. Yet such decision making is very important in the configuration of community power.[8]

Nondecisions. Studying issues that are on the public agenda ignores the mobilization of bias that is inherent in any political system. E. E. Schattschneider put the matter this way:

> All forms of political organization have a bias in favor of the exploitation of some kinds of conflict and the suppression of others because organization is the mobilization of bias. Some issues are organized into politics while others are organized out.[9]

What this means is that some groups will have an easier time than others getting their issues placed on the public agenda, where they will receive serious consideration. If an issue is perceived to be a legitimate matter for political action, it will have an easier time reaching the agenda than an issue that is not so perceived.

Because of this basic feature of political life, a strategy available to those seeking to maintain the status quo is to try to discredit the proposals by making them seem contrary to the general beliefs and values prevalent in the community. An even better strategy is to attempt to fortify community values in such a way that the offending proposals are never raised by groups that might want them. Bachrach and Baratz have termed such a mobilization of bias involving community values a non-decision-making process.[10] Decisions are not made because the issues never reach the public agenda for serious discussion; they are not taken seriously because certain groups are able to exert control of that public agenda.

Without a doubt groups do often pursue a non-decision-making strategy. The question is how often they are successful. Recent political history shows that many issues once thought to be off the agenda because they were kept off by powerful groups are now vigorously debated. As numerous groups

---

[8] By examining issue-areas, rather than single controversial issues, Dahl did incorporate in his study some features of that form of policymaking we have termed off cycle. Other students of particular issues have not been as careful to study such bundles of issues.

[9] E. E. Schattschneider, *The Semi-Sovereign People* (New York: Holt, Rineha•t and Winston, 1960), p. 71.

[10] Peter Bachrach and Morton S. Baratz, "Two Faces of Power," *American Political Science Review* 56 (December 1962): 947–52.

press their claims on government, many political scientists wonder if anyone can exert any control at all over the scheduling of issues for public debate.

Modern Elitism

In recent years, the writings of American social scientists who tend to accept the ruling-class tenets have become more theoretical and explicitly tied to the work of European Marxist scholars, scholars who accept the work of Karl Marx as providing the basic understanding of modern industrial society. Although elitists have always pointed to domination by business elites as characterizing American community power structures, recent writings detail the influence of the economic structure as a whole on power configurations. Michael Parenti, for example, has written:

> A capitalist economic system creates a capitalist-dominated society and . . .
> the ruling-class interests, by virtue of their control of wealth and production,
> insinuate themselves into almost all areas of ideology and institution, exercising
> not just economic power, but social, cultural, and political power. This fact is
> the overriding condition of the existing social structure.[11]

Modern elitists, such as Parenti, do not deny that there exist numerous groups of citizens with different interests in America, but they note (correctly) that the mere existence of groups does not indicate a dispersion of power. The elitists see power resources as so concentrated that meaningful exercise of power by nonelites is impossible.

Modern elitists see culture as an instrument of class dominance, manipulated by economic elites to ensure the subjugation of masses through acceptance of symbols of the legitimacy of the capitalist economic system. Culture and the institutions rooted in culture, including liberal democratic institutions such as representative government, are used by the ruling class to get the powerless to accept the system. Elections primarily perform such a legitimizing function; they are expressions of support for the existing order rather than instruments of popular control of the governors by the governed.

The use of the institutions and symbols of culture are not unintended consequences of the operation of the social system, but conscious and deliberate manipulations. Parenti, again, denies that culture is "merely an accidental accretion of time and habit," but is a "*product* and *instrument* of class control." The ruling elites of capitalist society "*consciously* try to keep tight

---

[11] Michael Parenti, *Power and the Powerless* (New York: St. Martin's Press, 1978), p. 215. The term *elitist* is perhaps unfortunate. Writers like Parenti do not like the domination by elites; indeed, they are politically left, generally styling themselves radicals or socialists.

control over the command positions of social institutions and over the flow of symbols, values, information, rules, and choices which are the stuff of culture.''[12]

Saving elitism from itself

One of the major problems with elitism as a description of the exercise of community power is its paranoid quality. Elitists argue over and over that the economic elite *consciously* control things. Although the members of the upper economic strata clearly possess more power than you or I, to impute total control over economics, politics, culture, and ideology to them, as some modern elitists have done, is not reasonable.

Recognizing this, Clarence Stone has developed a theory of power that, in essence, saves elitism from itself by doing away with the necessity of postulating elite cabals. Stone's theory, which he terms *systemic power,* stresses that elected leaders, even when they are elected by a coalition composed disproportionately of lower-class voters, are pushed into the arms of the community elite because of forces beyond the control of leaders. Public officials operate ''under *dual pressures*—one set based in electoral accountability and the other based in the hierarchical distribution of economic, organizational, and cultural resources.''[13]

Elected leaders wish to further their careers by accomplishing things. They must marshal resources in order to accomplish public purposes. Only the economic elite has the organizational resources to accomplish the large public works projects that mark political success. The free mobility of citizens and capital means that high tax burdens have the potential to drive the economic elite and its investments out of town. Elected leaders, especially those of working-class origins, crave recognition. The cultural resources of the economic elite can provide that recognition. Thus politicians are dependent on elites because elites possess superior political resources, because they can move their business enterprises out of town if they disagree with community policies, and because they can confer status.

Hence, the elected leader has a motive to make common cause with the economic elite. Politicians certainly cannot ignore their electoral bases; however, neither can they ignore the economic elite. No one is consciously manipulating the elected leader; rather, the way in which the system operates forces this commonality. Elitism can be salvaged as a viable theory only if such systemic bases of power can be shown to be operating.

---

[12] Ibid., pp. 216–17. The italics for ''consciously'' are added.
[13] Clarence Stone, ''Systemic Power in Community Decision-Making: A Restatement of Stratification Theory,'' *American Political Science Review* 74 (December 1980): 984.

Modern Pluralism

Pluralism and elections

The loosely knit camp of scholars termed pluralists also accept that economics is the root of many of the interests and groups that characterize modern American society. But they do not see political resources as being as concentrated as do the elitists (although they do take note of the vast inequalities that permeate American society), and they view the resources as being to some extent noncumulative. No group can effectively "corner the market" on power resources. Even the members of the economic elite possess different interests, with corporate managers often having different interests from bondholders, and bankers having different concerns from manufacturers. Moreover, other interests exist independently of economic interests—regional, ethnic, religious, and so forth. The cultural differences that lead to the emergence of these interests are not mere expressions of class antagonisms, nor are they irrelevant to the structure of power.

Perhaps the key element in the pluralist conception of American society is the role of elections. For the pluralists, elections do not serve merely an expressive purpose, although they do serve that purpose. Elections, when they are conducted in a reasonably free and open manner, provide the incentive for elected officials to pay attention to mass preferences. The claims of interest groups cannot be ignored, because such groups are potential sources of electoral opposition. In elections numbers are more important than money; money may be used to buy votes, certainly, but at base votes, not dollars, are counted.

Elections thus have the effect of broadening the universe of potential political resources. Not only do numbers become important in power calculations, but skill in mobilizing citizens also becomes a resource. Because of elections, political resources are much more widely distributed than are economic resources.[14]

Normative pluralism: The balance wheel

Pluralism is primarily an empirical theory of government (as is elitism). It claims to describe and explain the manner in which public power and influence are exercised in the process of policymaking. There is, however, a normative aspect to pluralism. Many pluralists have contended that the system of government they describe is in fact the system most likely to reach

---

[14] No better explication of this system exists than the writing of Robert Dahl. In addition to *Who Governs?* see his *Preface to Democratic Theory* (Chicago: University of Chicago Press, 1956).

public policy settlements that are in the public interest. This is because pluralism includes several ways in which interests are balanced so that no single interest can completely dominate the policy process. Two aspects of this balance stem from free elections and the freedom to organize.

First, the wider dispersion of political resources, made possible primarily by the existence of free and open elections, means that there will be a potential check on the domination of the economic elite. Leaders can always mobilize voters, forming electoral coalitions capable of defeating the elite. This will not always happen, but the potential limits what elites can do.

Second, pluralism provides a weighting scheme for preferences. Elections are based on the principle of one person, one vote. Yet some people have a greater stake in politics than others, and some people have a greater stake in a particular issue than others. Parents with school-age children, for example, have a more compelling interest in educational policy than do citizens who do not have children. Pure electoral democracy contains no way to weight interests for their intensity; a person who feels intensely about an issue is granted one vote, as is one who doesn't care much about the issue. The weighting scheme of pluralism stems from the necessity for organization. Organization is crucial in making preferences known to policymakers. Yet effective political organization is difficult; it requires time, energy, and money, resources that might be used by an individual in pursuing other goals. Only when a person feels intensely about an issue will he or she organize. This fact of pluralist life leads to a weighting of preferences toward those who feel strongly about the issue.

The existence of elections and the necessity of organizing serve as the balance wheels of pluralism. So long as the basic constitutional freedoms of a democratic society exist, in the thinking of pluralists, the realization of public policies in the public interest is most likely.

Attacks on the balance wheel

The arguments between the elitists and the pluralists have centered primarily on the very existence of pluralism, not on its advantages or disadvantages. Indeed, a reading of the elitist objections to the pluralist model gives one the impression that the elitists would not be uncomfortable with pluralism if it could be shown to exist. Four serious objections to the advantages of pluralist government have been put forward, however: three claiming that it is not democratic enough, the final claiming that it is, in essence, too democratic.

Citizen Passivity. The first objection notes that pluralism has relegated the average citizen to an almost totally passive role. By emphasizing the roles of elections, interest groups led by a small number of political activists, and the professional politicians, pluralism has left the citizen nothing more than to come out periodically to cast a vote, then go home and ignore political affairs until election time rolls around again. This relegation has led to calls for an expanded participatory role for the citizen in the policymaking process through such mechanisms as neighborhood government, citizen-advisory panels for government, and a stronger voice for workers in the running of factories. It has been claimed that such participation better integrates the citizen into the governing process, and makes government more democratic.

Manipulated Elections. A second criticism of the pluralist balance wheel is that elections are not, in fact, vehicles for the expression of citizen interests. Rather, they have become popularity contests among candidates who use image rather than issues to distinguish among themselves. Candidates are more packages created by campaign consultants than political leaders. Just as advertising has been used to sell product images, so do political consultants sell candidates. And just as advertising has been used to challenge the economists' model of the freely and independently acting consumer who is so crucial to the existence of a properly operating free market economy, so has the manipulation of campaigns negated the democratic function of elections. The choices reflected in elections are irrelevant, because candidates and media professionals have concentrated on the image rather than the issues.

The Bias of Organization. The necessity for political organization weights preferences. It weights preferences according to intensity, but it also weights preferences toward those citizens who possess the skills for organization. Those skills are disproportionately concentrated among the middle and upper classes. Hence, there is a built-in bias in relying on organization to weight political preferences. The necessity of organizing in order to make an interest felt in the policy process means that preferences will be weighted (1) according to the intensity of preference, and (2) according to the class background of the organizers.

Pluralism's Excesses. The final objection to pluralism is that it has gotten out of hand. In the words of Frederick Wirt, we have in many cities a "politics of hyperpluralism" in which many groups place demands on government, and the government lacks the means or the will to resist any of the many conflicting demands that barrage it.[15] Because government is so diffuse, trying to placate disparate demands, no coherent policies can be put in place. Government does not set goals and rationally try to implement

---

[15] See Frederick M. Wirt, *Power in the City: Decision-Making in San Francisco* (Berkeley, Calif.: University of California Press, 1974).

those goals. Strong politicians in the tradition of New Haven's Mayor Lee who are able to set priorities and hold to them by keeping other issues off the public agenda have all but disappeared from the modern political scene. Rather, all demands reach the public agenda; there is no way of setting the agenda for rational public discussion of the issues. There is no time to see that the decisions are properly implemented, because elected leaders are too busy hurrying to meet the next explosion of demands. All sorts of groups that in the past had trouble getting their demands considered seriously now easily place their demands on the public agenda. In this view, nobody controls the agenda.

The most graphic description of this process has been given by Douglas Yates. Yates calls the system "street-fighting pluralism":

> Urban policy making is itself fragmented and unstable. Most especially, it is reactive; urban policy makers are constantly rushing from one small crisis to another. In their reactivism they bounce from one hopeful policy response to another, constantly remake and undo decisions, and often search blindly for some solution that will work.[16]

Acceding to the numerous demands that various groups direct at government is expensive. In those cities where elected officials give in to the new demands coming in to the political system, budgets grow, and they grow faster than the city's tax base. Movement of people, jobs, and industry to the suburbs and to the Sunbelt causes the tax base in many cities to shrink, in real (noninflated) dollars. Elected officials face a growing gap between the demands of groups for public goods and services and the resource base that can be used to satisfy them. If leaders increase the tax bite taken by local government, they are sure to increase the flight to the suburbs and the Sunbelt. If they do not increase the resources available to government by increasing taxes or finding more state and federal aid, they have to take away something from groups who already have a share of the pie, and politics is bound to get more rancorous. In many cities, fragmentation of governmental authority (discussed in chapters 9 and 10) means that no urban politician holds the power necessary to curtail demands and enforce a political settlement.

Hyperpluralism—a pluralism without central leadership strong enough to enforce bargaining and compromise among competing interests—has been the result of the weakening of the institutions that had the potential to control demands. The most important institutions that once acted to control the flood of demands on government are the political party system and the strong chief executive, both of which have been weakened by local government reform movements. Local government has been unable to resist the

---

[16] Douglas Yates, *The Ungovernable City: The Politics of Urban Problems and Policy Making* (Cambridge, Mass.: MIT Press, 1977), p. 15.

flood of demands, and this is a major component of the urban fiscal crisis now plaguing many cities.

The failure of many city governments to handle the demands of hyperpluralism has led some political scientists to reexamine the doctrines of pluralism from a different perspective—that some limits on pluralism might be desirable. The notion of many pluralists that the free play of organized political groups would lead to the realization of the public interest has been vigorously attacked. Political scientist Donald Haider comments that this failure

> presents a rebuff to the prescriptive pluralists who in the fashion of the classical economists, envisage the general good as being advanced to the extent that society's organized groups achieve the status of formal participation in the political decision-making process.[17]

In the absence of creative leaders with the formal and informal tools to enforce policy settlements among conflicting interests, the advantages of pluralism in advancing the public interest are limited.

System Transformation

Political systems are conservative. They admit new participants only grudgingly. It is entirely possible for one set of political groups to engage in bargaining and compromise with one another while other groups are effectively shut out of the process and watch from the sidelines. These groups lack the power to force the issues that concern them onto the existing political agenda.

Then, for a combination of reasons, the excluded groups are able to bring their demands to policymakers in such a way that they must be considered seriously. Generally, this occurs for three reasons. First, the groups excluded experience a growth in their political resources. This happened for urban blacks, for example, when their numbers swelled northern cities during the 1950s and 1960s. Second, leaders representing the excluded groups skillfully exploit the growing resources. Third, there is weakness in the existing system, and political leaders are unable to contain the exploding demands. Suddenly the demands of the excluded are treated seriously, and the entrepreneurs who bring the demands are allowed to participate in the policymaking process as representatives of legitimate demands.

The entry of new groups into the political arena transforms the very

---

[17] Donald Haider, "Sayre and Kaufman Revisited: New York City Government Since 1965," *Urban Affairs Quarterly* 15 (December 1979): 143.

nature of the system. The relationships among the participants change. New relationships are established, and new alliances are made.

Perhaps the clearest example of such system transformation occurred in the South in the late 1960s with the entry of blacks into the southern electorate. Even where blacks were a minority, they were courted by white politicians. The politics of race-baiting disappeared within a few years; it made no sense to engage in rhetoric that promoted racial polarization and turn over to your opponent a sizable bloc of voters. Different alliances were forged in city councils and state legislatures. The three largest cities of the deep South, Atlanta, Birmingham, and New Orleans, all elected black mayors.

But system transformation has also occurred in large nonsouthern cities. Wirt has described a process of change in San Francisco that involved a movement from a system of power in which local businesses (and to some extent labor leaders) predominated to a system of many participants. The two groups that were important in the new system that had not been active in the old were neighborhood groups and outside business executives concerned with constructing corporate headquarters in downtown San Francisco.[18]

It is also possible for political systems to contract, either abruptly or slowly. Groups that earlier participated in the pluralist bargaining process may be forced out, and their demands treated as taboo. This seems to have happened to some extent to the demands of minorities in New York since the 1975 fiscal crisis in the city. As resources became tight, the political system became less open to the demands of such groups. A last-in, first-out principle seems to have been operating (see box 8.2).

External Influences on Local Politics

Local power structures are intimately tied to trends developing at the national level. One does not have to accept William Domhoff's view that there exists a national system of class dominance that controls the local system of power to recognize the importance of these trends. The American economy has become increasingly centralized in the hands of a number of large corporations. Oligopoly rather than open competition characterizes many industries, and these industries include many of the most important: steel, automobiles, energy, and communications. Many industries respond to a national market and, increasingly, an international one. Television and other mass media outlets have proved to be powerful centralizing and standardizing forces. Partially in response to these national trends, federal government programs have been developed to deal with what are increasingly perceived as national problems. Even urban renewal in New Haven was made possible by federal programs.

[18] Wirt, *Power in the City,* ch. 3.

Box 8.2: Political Contraction
in New York

In 1975, New York City experienced a severe financial crisis. Committed expenditures were so much greater than revenues that the city could no longer meet its payroll. Many have pointed to the city's shrinking revenue base and the movement of jobs and industry to the suburbs and to the Sunbelt, but some political scientists have offered a different interpretation. Martin Shefter writes that the New York fiscal crisis was "above all a political crisis," having its roots in political changes, not just demographic changes. These changes were an explosion of demands on the city's political system, demands from city employees, minorities, and the recipients of city services such as welfare and education. The city's weakened political system could not withstand the onslaught, and resorted to financial gimmicks to maintain the fiction of a balanced budget. In 1975 the financial house of cards collapsed, and the system was again transformed.

In 1959, Wallace Sayre and Herbert Kaufman published *Governing New York City,* still the most comprehensive study of a single city's government and politics. In 1965 they updated their study, finding few changes from their earlier interpretation. In brief, Sayre and Kaufman found an extreme form of pluralism in New York: a pluralism of independent power centers that jealously resisted encroachment from other political actors. They called these power centers *islands of power.* These numerous power centers coexisted in a political system with weak citywide political institutions. The

Sources: See Martin Shefter, "New York City's Fiscal Crisis: The Politics of Inflation and Retrenchment," *The Public Interest* 48 (Summer 1977): 98–127; and Donald Haider, "Sayre and Kaufman Revisited: New York City Government Since 1965," *Urban Affairs Quarterly* 15 (December 1979): 123–45.

The increasing importance of such national trends has had a powerful influence on the character of decision making in local political systems. Wirt studied community decision making in two very different locales: San Francisco, with its reputation as perhaps the most urbane of American cities, and Panola County, Mississippi, a rural region in the Mississippi Delta country south of Memphis. Wirt commented on the diversity he observed, but he also noted an important similarity, the necessity of responding to powerful national trends:

As removed as sophisticated San Francisco and bucolic Panola County are—in distance, climate, history, resources, social structure (and cuisine)—they also

mayor of New York shares power with various independent boards and commissions, such major public authorities as the Port Authority, and the Board of Estimate. The weak party system, perhaps never as strong as the legends about Tammany Hall would suggest, offers little centralizing influence. In the period of political quiescence and growing resources that characterized New York during the 1950s and early 1960s, this system worked well. During the late 1960s, however, the demands of new groups put a severe strain on this system of dispersed power.

Donald Haider sees three periods of political change following this period of stability. From 1965 to 1970 a period of *extreme pluralism* existed. Many new demands reached government. Weak leadership in the central government was unable (or unwilling) to limit governmental response to the demands of hyperpluralism. Great growth in government took place. From 1970 to 1975 abrupt *resource contraction* took place, and the islands of power reestablished themselves and fought to protect gains made in the period of resource expansion. After 1975 participants had to face the specter of bankruptcy together. A new force entered the political arena: the holders of the city's bonds. Fearing that the city might default on its obligations, banks and other lending institutions demanded—and got—a restructuring of city government that would ensure political stability and financially responsible government. This meant in practice that limits were put on responding to the demands of claimant groups. The state of New York created the Emergency Financial Control Board to oversee the city's finances, a board dominated by executives from big business. If the city was not to be run in the interest of the bondholders, they were at least to be strongly represented in the councils of government. A new system of government was in place.

---

demonstrate surprising similarities in their reactions to recent national events. While different in the complexity of their response to those events, both are alike in their inescapable necessity to respond. These responses are filtered and conditioned by differences in their history, group life, and so on. But the sultry rural Delta and cool urbane San Francisco are as one in having to reverberate to the fact of their membership in a national system of governance and economics now being swept by massive social and political changes.[19]

The study of community power has increasingly become the study of just how local decision-making systems respond to trends rooted in national

[19] Ibid., p. ix.

economic and political systems. Concerning the federally funded urban renewal in New Haven, pluralist Nelson Polsby points out that the existence of a facilitating federal program fails to explain why massive urban renewal took place in New Haven and not in Hartford or somewhere else. Local decision making increasingly involves response to economic, demographic, cultural, and political trends that impinge on the local community from outside, but this has not eliminated local discretion or the opportunity for the exercise of local leadership.

Perhaps this has always been the case. Community power systems were heavily influenced by the great waves of immigration at the turn of the century; affected again by the Great Depression of the 1930s and the federal programs established to deal with it; altered significantly by the internal migration of blacks and the stormy politics of the 1960s.

> Major forces of growth and decay, affluence and bankruptcy, are as difficult to pin on the explicit choices of individually powerful local actors today as they were fifteen years ago. Some decision-makers, to be sure, give the appearance of riding the tiger of demographic trends, whereas others fall off. . . . It is still true of course that significant functions remain in most communities and likewise some degree of freedom in managing sources and achieving outcomes.[20]

No community anywhere is an isolated island, free to pursue its political policies oblivious of demographic, economic, and political trends. But neither is any community a simple pawn in a game played on a national board. Just how local communities respond to the stimuli provided by these national trends, and just how they manage the resources they control, have an important bearing on the future of the community. The study of local systems of power and decision making thus remains an important part of the study of urban politics.

Conclusions

Some of the most important questions of political science cannot be answered with finality. However, careful reasoning about an issue almost always helps to clear away the underbrush of fuzzy thinking. Robert Dahl has put the issue as clearly as anyone: "In a political system where nearly every adult may vote but where knowledge, wealth, social position, access to officials, and other resources are unequally distributed, who actually governs?"[21] We would actually add only one phrase to this formulation of the problem: and in whose interest do they govern?

[20] Polsby, *Community Power,* p. 237.
[21] Dahl, *Who Governs?* p. 1.

There is no disagreement on many of the essentials of the problem: vast inequalities of wealth and other resources do exist in urban America; such inequalities are often transferable into politics, resulting in unequal power among individuals; national trends limit the discretion of local decision makers. There are, however, two key issues that remain unresolved between elitists and pluralists. The first concerns whether elections are meaningful instruments of popular control and the second concerns just how cumulative power resources are. Do elected officials condition their actions on what they expect the electorate to do, or do they merely respond to what a power elite wishes? Second, are resources too tightly concentrated in the hands of an elite to make this exercise of the franchise meaningful?

There is no single answer for all political systems at all times. American cities today vary in their power structures. Some are dominated by a power elite. But some suffer a second grievous ill: pluralism run amok. In the absence of some leadership, too much responsiveness to too many conflicting demands can result in incoherent public policy, and put severe strain on community resources. Some political scientists see the problems of cities today as stemming not from tight control by a power elite, but from an inability to control incoming demands, a situation that has been called hyperpluralism.

Many cities today face declining resources, and this state of affairs has limited the ability of political leaders to satisfy new demands. Hence, in many cities system contraction is occurring, and demands from minorities, city workers, and neighborhood organizations are being treated as heresies. There seems to be a new political order emerging in American cities, one rooted in economic development and appeals to business interests. This new order is gradually replacing the hyperpluralism that characterized many cities in the 1960s and 1970s, and has important implications for the study of urban power.

PART III

Local Government Structures

Local governments in America have evolved over time into a rich variety of forms. Some city governments encompass virtually all their metropolitan regions. Other metropolises are composed of numerous municipalities. States treat their local governments differently, some allowing municipal governments to provide many services, others creating all sorts of special-purpose governments to accomplish the same goals.

The diversity in form does not stop there. City governments themselves have all sorts of different structures: some have strong mayors; others have mayors with no executive functions. Some city councils possess numerous powers; others are almost completely subservient to the mayor. And so on.

This diversity in structure is important because different structural forms can lead to strikingly different public policy outcomes. Some governmental structures are biased toward the production of certain types of policies—those favoring business, for example. Other forms facilitate the smooth implementation of whatever policies are adopted; still others virtually make certain that implementation problems will occur. The two chapters that compose this section focus on the variety of urban governmental forms, and trace the implications of these forms for the urban policymaking process and for our five core issues.

CHAPTER 9

The Metropolitan
Public Economy

The typical American metropolis is overlaid with numerous governments, each responsible for policymaking as well as the provision of routine services. This governmental fragmentation results in fiscal disparities among communities and differences in abilities to finance policy initiatives, hampers governmental solutions to metropolitan problems, and imposes a severe burden on citizens searching for the locus of responsibility for a governmental function. But it also promotes a choice of alternate "policy packages" for citizens. In this chapter we investigate this complex *metropolitan public economy*.

Governmental Complexity

The land-use pattern of the modern American metropolis increasingly has come to resemble the multiple-centered nuclei model discussed in chapter 4. On this complex land-use pattern is superimposed a variety of governmental units. If one looks at a typical map of a metropolitan area, one will see various towns and cities delineated, perhaps distinguished by different colors. These governmental jurisdictions are the *municipalities* of the metropolis. They are general-purpose governments, responsible for providing a range of policies and services to citizens, and possessing substantial autonomy or independence from other governments. They have, that is, significant policymaking responsibility.

Municipalities are not the only general-purpose governments in the typical urban region. *County* governments provide a range of policies and services to all citizens in their jurisdictions, but they generally provide more services in areas that are unincorporated (that is, not served by a municipal government) than in incorporated areas. A metropolitan area may be contained within a single county, or it may sprawl over several counties. The functions of counties are often distinct from those of municipalities. Some functions are, however, performed by both counties and municipalities, and jurisdictional problems do occur. Both the counties and the municipalities of many metropolitan areas provide police services, road and street surfacing and repair, health services, and court systems. In the southern states the county is generally a more important governing unit than in the rest of the country, but everywhere the county adds to the governmental complexity of the metropolis.[1]

A final general-purpose governmental unit that operates in the Northeast and Midwest is the *township*. Although their functions vary from state to state, townships primarily provide a limited range of services to unincorporated rural areas.

General-purpose governments are not the only governments that exist in the city. Many *special-purpose* governmental units also operate there but do not appear on the map. Sometimes these special units of government are larger than general-purpose governments; sometimes they are smaller; sometimes their boundaries correspond exactly to those of other governmental units. Often they cut across several separate general-purpose governmental jurisdictions. These special-purpose units are responsible for a limited number of functions, and lack the broad policymaking responsibility of general-purpose governments. Some examples of these special-purpose governments are school districts, water and sewer districts, park districts, and transportation authorities.

Fragmentation

Each governmental unit in the metropolis has the responsibility for providing certain services for citizens, and has the authority to tax citizens to

---

[1] County governments do not exist in Connecticut or Rhode Island; in Louisiana they are called parishes, and in Alaska, boroughs. In some cases, cities have been consolidated with the county, and a single government performs both kinds of functions; St. Louis is an example.

finance those services. The overlapping jurisdictions of governments mean that the typical citizen is receiving services from several units of government, and is paying taxes to these separate units. Governmental *fragmentation* refers to both the number of separate governmental units within an urban area and the degree of overlap of the various units of government. This overlap can occur with respect to both geography and function. *Geographic fragmentation* means that a single neighborhood is served by many different units. *Functional fragmentation* means that the various units are responsible for performing similar governmental functions, as would be the case if both a municipality and a county provided health services.

The degree of geographic fragmentation can be gauged by examining the number of distinct governments that have taxing power over the typical taxpayer. Table 9.1 lists the separate taxing units that a taxpayer in Western Springs, Illinois, a suburb of Chicago, has to pay. (To make the process as painless as possible, the Cook County tax collector collects the taxes owed and distributes the money to the various jurisdictions, so the taxpayer gets a single tax bill.) The list of taxing jurisdictions includes three separate school districts (elementary, high school, community college); three general-purpose governments (county, village, and township, with two special funds earmarked for township activities—road and bridge and general assistance, a form of government transfer payments to the poor); the metropolitan sanitary district; a mass transit district; a couple of health-related governmental enterprises; and a mosquito-abatement district.

Table 9.1. Governmental units that have taxing authority over a suburban Cook County, Illinois property owner

School District #101
Lyons Township High School #204
Community College District #502
Forest Preserve District of Cook County
Suburban TB Sanitarium
Township of Lyons
Road and Bridge—Lyons Township
General Assistance—Lyons Township
Metropolitan Sanitary District of Greater Chicago
Des Plaines Valley Mosquito Abatement District
Western Springs Park District
Village of Western Springs
Lyons Mental Health
West Suburban Mass Transit District
County of Cook
Hospital Governing Commission

Separate policy cycles

Each of these taxing jurisdictions engages in policymaking processes. Each must deal with the various stages of the policy cycle: agenda setting, enactment, implementation, and impact. Each also .engages in off-cycle policymaking—those policy activities that occur well out of the limelight of local public scrutiny, primarily the provision of routine services.

Perhaps most important, each engages in actions that influence the problems and opportunities faced by other units of governments that occupy the metropolitan landscape. In engaging in their roles as producers of policies and services, governments perform actions that inadvertently affect other units of government. These effects are called *policy externalities,* or *spillovers.* But policies are not the only things that spill over. Problems are often larger than governments, and this means that communities must cooperate in order to solve them.

Externalities are especially severe at the local level, because the coequal governmental units that exist in the typical American metropolis have no authority to order one another about. If a suburban school board runs into difficulties with policies pursued by a municipality, it cannot rely on lines of authority to straighten things out. It must either engage in negotiation with the municipality or turn to another level of government that does have the legal authority to solve the problem—the state government, the federal government, or the federal or state courts.

The Legal Status of Local Governments

All types of local governments are subdivisions of state governments. Legally, they do not possess independent policymaking functions unless that power is granted by the state constitution or state legislature. The legal status of local governments is very different from that of the states in the federal system, because states are not subdivisions of the national government. Rather, they have an independent constitutional existence.

Dual role

The subordinate status of municipal governments means that these governments have a dual role. They are, first, governmental devices for satisfying the demands of local citizens for government services, and, second, administrative units for carrying out state policies. Special-purpose local governments also find themselves in this dual role. School districts, for example, are supposed to provide educational programs that correspond to the wishes of local voters, and local voters must approve property taxes to support their local schools. Yet school districts must abide by myriad regulations set by the state government that mandate the length of the school year, acceptable curricula, special programs, teacher qualifications, and so forth. Moreover, state governments have increasingly provided financial aid for local governments, so that finances for local services are as confusing as the division of responsibilities.

This dual role for local governments leads, not surprisingly, to numerous conflicts over the rights and responsibilities of the state and its local governments. These conflicting roles are further examined in Part IV.

Courts have taken a strict view of this subordinate status of local governments. The legal scholar John Dillon, in a doctrine that has been adopted by both federal and state courts known as *Dillon's Rule,* commented that municipalities possess only three kinds of governmental power. First, municipalities can exercise those powers that are granted *in express words;* second, those that are a *necessary implication* of express powers; third, those that are *indispensable* in carrying out local government responsibilities; "not simply convenient, but indispensable."[2]

Local governments, being legal creatures of the state, can, at least in theory, be abolished, consolidated, or altered in a multitude of ways by act of the state legislature. In an early case, the Supreme Court stated that local governments are "created as convenient agencies for exercising such of the government powers of the state as may be entrusted to them. . . . the territory over which they shall be exercised rests in the absolute discretion of the state."[3]

Municipalities are brought into existence by the process of *incorporation.* The residents of an area must *petition* the state legislature in order to incorporate, and a referendum vote on the issue is held. The new municipality is issued a *charter,* and may exercise all governmental powers provided by the state in its laws governing municipalities.[4] The charter specifies the governmental form of the municipality and issues a limited grant of local governmental authority to the new government.

Home rule

The stringent judicial application of Dillon's Rule kept state legislatures busy with local and special legislation. As urbanization continued apace, carrying with it increased demand for governmental intervention in society,

[2] Quoted in Sho Sato and Arvo Van Alstyne, *State and Local Government Law,* 2nd ed. (Boston: Little, Brown, 1977), p. 82. Dillon first formulated the rule in 1868, while serving as the chief justice of the Iowa Supreme Court.

[3] Hunter v. City of Pittsburgh, 207 U.S. 161.

[4] Sometimes municipalities are created by a *special act* of the state legislature, which serves as the city's charter. A good discussion of the process of incorporation can be found in Charles R. Adrian and Charles Press, *Governing Urban America,* 5th ed. (New York: McGraw-Hill, 1977), ch. 8.

involvement of state legislatures in local policymaking increased. Moreover, virtually all action taken by municipalities was subject to court challenges on the grounds that appropriate state statutes did not exist to support the action. The *home rule* movement was an attempt to reverse Dillon's Rule and allow local governments substantial authority to act without the need for specific approval of the state legislature. Home rule was initiated in the Missouri Constitution of 1875, and today a majority of states have some provision for home rule for at least some of its municipalities (and occasionally counties). Home rule provisions adopted recently include those in Massachusetts in 1965; in North Dakota in 1966; in Florida, Pennsylvania, and Judge Dillon's home state of Iowa in 1968; in Illinois in 1970; and in Montana in 1972.[5]

Home rule seeks to grant a measure of policymaking power to municipalities and to obtain general authority to undertake and administer local programs in matters not dealt with in legislative statutes. If, however, a policy enacted by a home rule municipality is within a field that has been dealt with by state law, however inadequately, the courts are likely to invalidate the municipal action. Moreover, states continue to supervise their municipalities fairly closely, by, for example, continuing in force limitations on the tax and debt limits of local governments. In Michigan the Municipal Finance Commission must specifically approve borrowing by local governments in excess of limits specified by the state constitution. In Illinois, the 1970 constitution allows the state legislature to impose debt limits for home rule counties by simple majority vote.

There is a vast amount of state-to-state variation in the meaning of the term *home rule*. Some states supervise their local units of government so closely that self-government is a sham. In other states, home rule grants important self-governing power. Whatever the case, not all municipalities in a state have home rule status. In Illinois, for example, the 1970 constitution granted home rule automatically to all municipalities with populations of more than 25,000; smaller municipalities may obtain home rule status by petition and referendum. Home rule powers may also be withdrawn by referendum. This provision has led some citizens to seek revocation of their municipalities' home rule charters. Most of these attempts have been stimulated by a desire to limit the taxing power granted under home rule authority.

For cities not possessing home rule (and for those home rule cities in states that keep a tight rein on their local governments), a working relationship must be maintained with the municipality's state legislative delegation. The representatives and senators within whose districts the municipality falls will generally be responsible for carrying the local bills of interest to the

---

[5] Sato and Van Alstyne, *State and Local Government Law,* p. 135.

municipality. The necessary intergovernmental cooperation has led, in the minds of some observers, to an extraordinary degree of caution on the part of municipal officials in meeting the problems that face them. Because local bills seldom receive the full attention of the legislature, they may also be poorly drafted or ill adapted to the local problem.

Home rule conjures up visions of local autonomy and self-rule, but many commentators have viewed it as a mixed blessing. Legal scholars Sato and Van Alstyne offer four reasons that broad grants of policymaking authority to local governments ought not be embraced uncritically:

1. Most of the significant problems of local government today are not of local concern alone, but reach beyond artificial political boundary lines.

2. Home rule tends to proliferate disparate local policies addressed to problems of common regional concern, where uniformity of standards and practices may be most desirable.

3. Home rule tends to be politically unrealistic to the extent that it places policy-making responsibilities in the hands of local officials, since local fiscal resources are seldom equal to local needs.

4. The plea of "home rule" within the states—like that of "states' rights" within the federal system—may well prove to be an excuse for . . . inactivity when affirmative governmental action is urgent.[6]

Governmental Structure of the Metropolis

A metropolis consists of an economically integrated system with numerous governmental jurisdictions superimposed on it. The relations among these jurisdictions are termed *horizontal intergovernmental relations; vertical intergovernmental relations* refers to the relationships among local, state, and federal governments. The key issue in the study of horizontal governmental relations is: How can coordination of policymaking and service delivery be achieved in the governmentally fragmented metropolis?

A variety of possible coordinating mechanisms exists, and most have been tried by one or more cities at some time or another. One may think of the coordinating structures of a metropolitan political economy as falling along a continuum (see figure 9.1). At one end of the continuum lie no formal coordinating mechanisms, a situation that is the governmental analog to the free market economy. At the other end of the continuum lies a single, consolidated government that governs the entire metropolitan region—*unigov,*

<hr/>

[6] Ibid., 143.

Figure 9.1. Alternative structures
of the metropolitan political
economy.

as it is sometimes called. Between these two extremes lie several other possible coordinating mechanisms, ranging from the most voluntary to the most coercive. Finally, it is possible to decentralize further—to the neighborhood level. Advocates of community control in large cities are in favor of this type of organization.

The Market Solution

The most spirited defense of the fragmented, decentralized metropolis has been made by the *public economists*. Because it emphasizes choice among alternatives by citizens, this approach is sometimes termed the *public choice approach*.[7] Essentially, the public economists see in the fragmented metropolis a reflection of the free market, in which numerous producers of goods and services compete for the loyalties of many independently acting consumers. The various governments offer *policy packages* to citizens; each policy package differs in its mix of service level and quality. The citizen decides how to spend his or her tax dollar by deciding which of the many policy-producing units to move to. In the view of the public economist, the fragmentation, duplication, and lack of formal coordination among local governments in the metropolis are not to be decried. Rather, such a system will provide the best match between citizen preferences and public policies by providing a variety of policy packages for the citizen to choose from.

---

[7] A good summary of this approach may be found in Robert Bish, *The Public Economy of Metropolitan Areas* (Chicago: Rand McNally, 1971); a less technical presentation is Robert Bish and Vincent Ostrom, *Understanding Urban Government* (Washington, D.C.: American Enterprise Institute for Public Policy Research, 1973).

The Tiebout thesis

The intellectual roots of this approach may be traced to an article written in the mid-1950s by Charles Tiebout.[8] Tiebout showed that, under certain very stringent conditions, public goods provided by local governments can be allocated efficiently. If the conditions are met, the various expenditures for local functions such as police, fire, sewerage, building and zoning, and so forth can be allocated to match citizen preferences exactly. Let us take fire protection as an example. All citizens probably want excellent fire protection, but not all citizens are willing or able to pay for it. Those willing to pay can move to a community offering excellent fire protection, but taxes are high in that community to support the good service. Those willing to risk poorer service, along with those unable to afford better, will gravitate toward a community spending less on fire protection. This example may be generalized to policy and services packages, the mix of all locally provided public goods. A citizen seeks out the mix of services that best satisfies his or her preferences, given the amount he or she is willing to pay in local taxes. This match, in total, is called an *economically efficient* allocation of local public services.

Many of the conditions of the Tiebout thesis, as it has come to be called, are not fulfilled in actual cities. The conditions include, for example, the assumption that citizens are fully mobile. This will not be the case so long as there is racial discrimination in the real estate market. Other assumptions include full knowledge by citizens of policy package differences among communities and choice of residence community by citizens based only on differences in policy offerings, not, for example, on the length of home-to-work trips. Citizens, not commercial and industrial concerns, are assumed to pay taxes. Finally, no service spillovers occur. (Service spillovers occur when services produced by one municipality can be enjoyed by residents from other municipalities; for example, if one community maintains an art museum that residents of other communities enjoy.)

Each of these basic assumptions is violated in practice, but that does not necessarily vitiate the entire Tiebout model. It depends on how much each is violated in practice. Regardless of the exact fit of the model, it does capture certain behaviors of citizens. People do move in search of better schools, more open space guaranteed by zoning laws, more recreational opportunities. By "voting with their feet," they endorse certain "preferred states of community affairs" and reject others.[9]

[8] Charles B. Tiebout, "A Pure Theory of Local Expenditures," *Journal of Political Economy* (October 1956): 416–24. See also Vincent Ostrom, Charles M. Tiebout, and Robert Warren, "The Organization of Government in Metropolitan Areas: A Theoretical Inquiry," *American Political Science Review* 55 (December 1961): 831–42.

[9] The term is from Ostrom et al., "The Organization of Government," p. 833.

Income redistribution

In the analysis of the urban public economists, policy packages are matched to citizen preferences only to the extent that citizens are willing and able to pay for them. Elinor Ostrom of Indiana University has commented that "in their normative analysis, most political economists will use as a first maxim that those individuals who receive services should pay for them."[10] The effect of this assumption is to take the existing metropolitan income distribution as given. An *income distribution* is the way in which total income is divided up among people. Income distributions may be *equal,* in which case each 10 percent of the population would receive 10 percent of the income. More generally, however, they are *skewed,* such that the poorest 10 percent of the population receives far less than 10 percent of the income, and the richest receive far more. In the United States the distribution of income is heavily skewed. In 1977, the 5 percent of Americans receiving the most income had a median income of almost $32,000; the lowest twenty percent earned but $6,500. The distribution of *wealth* is even more heavily skewed: the top 1 percent of wealth holders control 20.1 percent of the nation's wealth.

In the model developed by the public economists, local services will go to those who have the income to pay for them and are willing to do so. Metropolitan fiscal disparities result from this feature of the model. Local policy packages are not *redistributive:* the poor do not receive more and the rich less of the services and policies produced by local government. Hence, the system will not improve the real income of the poor or subtract from the real income of the wealthy. In essence, taxes are collected from citizens, and services are provided in direct proportion to the amounts of taxes taken from citizens. It is not that the public economists are necessarily against the redistribution of income. It is just that they believe that any redistribution ought not take place at the local level (or even at the state level). Redistributive policies ought to be pursued only at the federal level. If local units engage in redistribution, wealthy citizens will, once again, "vote with their feet," moving away from communities that engage in redistribution. Similarly, poorer citizens will gravitate to those units that practice redistribution, putting a severe burden on the fiscal capacities of those jurisdictions.

Gary Miller contends that the California property tax revolt is not new. It has been going on for at least twenty-five years in Los Angeles, but that it had been expressed by exit from high-tax jurisdictions. Citizens "voted with their feet for low taxes, low levels of bureaucratic activity, low levels of government spending, . . . they did this by choosing to live in those municipalities that offered this mix of policies." Because it is the wealthy

---

[10] Elinor Ostrom, "Metropolitan Reform: Propositions Derived from Two Traditions," *Social Science Quarterly* 53 (December 1972): 483.

who leave, however, "fragmented government introduces an explicit bias in favor of upper-income groups who move to favorable jurisdictions," an option they would not have in the absence of fragmentation.[11] Metropolitan fragmentation and freedom of mobility definitely disadvantage the poor who are increasingly concentrated in resource-poor jurisdictions.

Collective goods and the scale of production

Many of the services provided by local governments are collective or public goods. Recall from chapter 3 that a collective good is a good or service whose benefits cannot be denied any citizen, if the good or service is produced. It is entirely possible that some communities will engage in policy actions that are, in essence, collective goods. In this case, it will not be possible to deny benefits to those living outside the jurisdiction. People outside the jurisdiction will benefit without having to contribute taxes to support the activity. An excellent example of this is public health. If a jurisdiction engages in a public health effort to eradicate a contagious disease, people outside the jurisdiction are less likely to contract the disease. More subtle examples occur when a central city provides police protection, sewerage capacity, road and bridge repair, and other services for commuters who pay their taxes in their bedroom suburbs. These benefits that spill over from one community to another are called, appropriately enough, *service spillovers* or, sometimes, *external policy effects*. On the other hand, a jurisdiction may be so large that many citizens are being taxed for services they are not receiving. Should, for example, the citizens of a large city be taxed to provide water and power services for a new subdivision? All are taxed, but only the subdivision benefits.

Public economists argue that the size of governmental jurisdictions can be adjusted to minimize such problems. As Elinor Ostrom has put it,

> Whenever a political jurisdiction is larger than the group receiving benefits, some individuals may pay for benefits which they do not receive. On the other hand, whenever a political jurisdiction is smaller than the group receiving benefits, some individuals may receive benefits and not pay.[12]

Service spillovers and external policy effects vary from service to service and from policy to policy. Hence, one size jurisdiction may not be appropriate for all kinds of services. Political economists recommend that a variety of sizes of governmental units be used; they are not troubled at all by the increase in overlap and fragmentation that would result from the use of such a variety of governmental jurisdictions.

---

[11] Gary Miller, *Cities by Contract: The Politics of Municipal Incorporation* (Cambridge, Mass.: MIT Press, 1981), pp. 8 and 197.

[12] Ostrom, "Metropolitan Reform," p. 483.

An issue closely related to service spillovers is that of the *scale* of production. Some municipal services require large capital expenditures: water and sewer facilities are prime examples. Small communities cannot afford the start-up costs of such systems. Spread over a large number of citizens, however, the unit cost is much reduced. Hence, such capital-intensive services must be undertaken by larger units of government. Again, public economists argue that the optimum scale of production varies by service. As in the case of service spillovers, they keep one principle in the fore: assign a governmental function to the smallest unit possible, and don't worry too much about duplication, overlap, or governmental fragmentation. It is possible, however, for economic efficiency (matching citizens' willingness to pay) and service efficiency (producing the most service at the lowest cost) to deviate, because the former favors small jurisdictions and the latter large ones (see box 9.1).

Box 9.1: Economic Efficiency and Service Efficiency

Economic efficiency exists in the urban public economy when citizens' effective preferences (that is, their preferences backed up by their abilities to pay) match the level of services provided by the various governments in the metropolis. Political economists argue that economic efficiency occurs when there are numerous small units of government, each serving a relatively homogeneous citizenry. *Service efficiency,* however, means something different. It implies that public services are produced at the lowest per-unit cost to the taxpayer possible. Because there are some economies of scale in the production of most services, there exists some minimum size of governmental unit below which service efficiency does not exist.

In Detroit, for example, water and sewerage are provided by the central city through a contract arrangement with the suburbs. Many suburban officials believe their rates are too high, and they would like to opt out of the system. That would involve, however, building a new sewerage treatment plant—a prohibitively expensive proposition. Such capital-intensive services are strongly affected by economies of scale, but all services are affected to one degree or another.

That economies of scale exist does not imply that large cities are more efficient. For most services the threshold size necessary to achieve economies of scale is fairly low.

Interjurisdictional Arrangements

The problem of metropolitan government organization can be seen as the necessity to minimize service spillovers, maximize efficient service production, and maximize local control of policymaking simultaneously. This probably cannot be done all at once for all services, but the attempt has led to a variety of different intergovernmental arrangements in the cities of the United States.

One way a community can deal with the problems of service spillovers and inefficiencies associated with small scale and at the same time retain local control is by contracting with other governmental jurisdictions to produce the desired services. *Production* of services is in effect severed from *provision*. The community provides by taxing its citizens and paying the larger jurisdiction to produce the service. This kind of service arrangement has two variants. In *service contracting* a smaller suburb will contract with a larger unit of government, generally the county or the central city, for the provision of the service. The city of Detroit, for example, provides water for the entire metropolitan region on a contractual basis, and allows suburban representation on the water board. In the second variant, *service agreements,* two or more units of government will agree to provide jointly for service that neither could afford alone.

The Lakewood plan

Service contracting has become most prevalent in the Los Angeles metropolis. There the state of California has provided enabling legislation that has encouraged service contracting. In southern California there is a unit of government that has aggressively pursued this option—Los Angeles County.[13] In 1912, the state of California authorized counties to provide a wide range of services to unincorporated areas, and Los Angeles County did such an effective job that many of the advantages of incorporation were eliminated. Even though the population of the metropolitan area grew steadily, there were almost no incorporations between the mid-1920s and 1954.

That year the small, affluent unincorporated area of Lakewood was threatened with annexation by the city of Long Beach. Lakewood quickly incorporated, and immediately contracted with Los Angeles County for a full range of services. Lakewood became "the city without a payroll"; the provi-

[13] On interjurisdictional arrangements in Los Angeles, with a comparison with St. Louis and Detroit, see David R. Reynolds, "Progress Toward Achieving Efficient and Responsive Spatial-Political Systems in Urban America," in *Urban Policymaking and Metropolitan Dynamics,* ed. John S. Adams (Cambridge, Mass.: Ballinger, 1976), pp. 463–538; see also Miller, *Cities by Contract.*

sion and production of services were entirely separated. When it became evident that a community could enjoy the benefits of incorporation without having to assume the burdens of service production, numerous unincorporated communities quickly incorporated and contracted with the county.

David Reynolds, a student of service contracting and interjurisdictional arrangements, believes that, properly utilized, these forms of intergovernmental cooperation can go a long way toward solving the "metropolitan problem":

> [Interjurisdictional cooperative efforts] have been successful in terms of allowing a high degree of local autonomy while permitting the realization of economics of scale in service provision and the realization of higher services levels. . . . The existence of a politically fragmented metropolis need not imply that mutually satisfactory solutions to nonlocal and even areawide service problems cannot be reached.[14]

Special Districts

Special-purpose districts are governmental units established to perform a single function. In many cases special districts were established to deal directly with the three problems of metropolitan governmental organization: local autonomy, productive efficiency, and service spillovers. Fire protection districts, water supply and sewerage districts, park and recreation authorities, hospital districts, and library districts are all examples of districts established to deal with these problems. Such districts can allow economies of scale, eliminate service spillovers by making the service delivery unit correspond to service beneficiaries, and still allow municipalities autonomy to deal with other, more localized problems.

Many special districts, however, were established with other purposes in mind. School districts, of which there were some 16,548 in 1977, were established independently of municipal governments in order to free education from partisan political concerns. Other special districts were established to circumvent limitations on the extent to which municipalities could employ the property tax and engage in borrowing. These limitations are often written into state constitutions. Local building authorities, for example, can issue bonds to finance a variety of government buildings desired by local governments; this allows the local governments to remain under mandated debt limits.

A major reason for the extreme governmental fragmentation that exists in Illinois is that state's large number of special districts. A provision of the 1870 state constitution placed limits on the extent to which local govern-

---

[14] Reynolds, "Progress," p. 495.

ments were permitted to go into debt, and it also required that taxation be uniform throughout the taxing jurisdiction. This meant that counties and cities could not provide special services needed in only part of the jurisdiction, taxing only those benefiting from them. The response to these two limitations was a proliferation of special districts. The constitution of 1970 eliminated these provisions, too late to prevent the development of 2,745 special districts to get around these constitutional limits.

It is worthwhile to compare the experience of Illinois with that of California and Michigan. In Michigan, the municipality remains the primary unit of service delivery and local policy production. State laws have permitted a variety of interjurisdictional arrangements to deal with the problems of local autonomy and productive efficiency. In California, state law has facilitated the service-contracting arrangement, a system in which the county has assumed a more important role as service producer. In Illinois, restrictive state law has resulted in a multiplicity of special districts, most of which operate out of the light of public scrutiny. The importance of state constitutional provisions and legislation to the metropolitan public economy is highlighted by these three examples.

The Illinois example illustrates another point. Even if governmental fragmentation can facilitate competition and citizen satisfaction, it can also become downright pathogenic. This is not proliferation of government to deal with the very real problems of local autonomy and service spillovers. It is a response to antiquated constitutional provisions. The constitutional provisions were honest attempts to deal with real problems: governmental bankruptcy and inequitable taxation. But they were not wisely drafted, and had the unanticipated consequence of increasing governmental fragmentation.

Accountability

When fragmentation becomes extreme, especially when there is a great deal of functional fragmentation, accountability suffers. *Accountability* is the ability of citizens to hold government responsible for what it does. But if numerous, functionally specific governments provide specialized services, it is very difficult for the typical citizen to know which unit is responsible for the public policy that is of concern. A key assumption of the Tiebout thesis has broken down: citizens do not have "perfect knowledge," nor, under normal circumstances, could they be expected to.

Accountability can break down for a second reason. The governing boards of special districts are often appointed, not elected. This means that citizens cannot "throw the rascals out," even if they determine exactly who is responsible for the mess. Elections are imperfect instruments of popular control, but in the case of many special districts, they are absent (see box 9.2).

Box 9.2: The Public Authority and Robert Moses

The *public authority* is a governmental form that resembles the private corporation but is granted certain public powers by government. Usually these powers are the authority to construct public improvements, such as bridges or water systems, and to issue bonds to finance the improvements. In order to pay off the bonds, the public authority can charge the public for the use of the improvements. The public authority was created in England during the reign of Queen Elizabeth I, but it was used sparingly in the United States prior to 1921. In that year, the Port Authority of New York was established by an interstate compact between the states of New York and New Jersey.

The early pattern in the United States was to establish a public authority to build and operate one public improvement. Bonds were issued for a specific period, and when the bonds were paid off, the authority would turn over the improvement to a general-purpose government and go out of existence. The Port Authority of New York broke with this tradition by gaining the authority to operate several public improvements simultaneously, and to pool revenues

Source: See Robert Caro, *The Power Broker: Robert Moses and the Fall of New York.* (New York: Vintage, 1974).

Councils of Governments

Because the various units of government within the metropolis operate independently and none is subservient to any others (although all are subunits of the state), they must engage in bargaining, negotiation, compromise, and conciliation to achieve common ends. Occasionally this system of negotiation breaks down, and rancorous conflict can occur between the central city and its suburbs, between suburbs, or, not infrequently, between a special district and a general-purpose government.

This process has led Matthew Holden to liken relationships among governmental units in the metropolis to those among nations in the international sphere.[15] Each unit possesses sovereignty, and units must engage in di-

[15] Matthew Holden, "The Governance of the Metropolis as a Problem in Diplomacy," *Journal of Politics* 26 (August 1964): 627–47.

from the various bridges and tunnels that the authority operated to pay off bond issues. Robert Moses further exploited this device.

In the words of his biographer, Robert Caro, Robert Moses was "America's greatest builder." In the forty-four years he held public power, from 1924 to 1968, he never earned a regular salary, yet he became a major political force in New York. He built highways, bridges, public housing, parks, and playgrounds, as well as a dozen mammoth urban renewal projects. His projects dispossessed hundreds of thousands of people, mostly poor; his highways gave the automobile its premiere position in the transportation system of New York; his opposition to planning allowed his projects to proceed unconstrained by rational considerations of what the future New York metropolis would look like. His bitterest critic, Lewis Mumford, said that "in the twentieth century, the influence of Robert Moses on the cities of America was greater than that of any other person."*

Moses held numerous positions during his long political career, but the bedrock of his power was the Triborough Bridge Authority. That public authority was created to construct a bridge connecting the boroughs of Manhattan, the Bronx, and Queens; the original idea was that the authority would go out of existence when the

*Quoted in Robert Caro, *The Power Broker: Robert Moses and the Fall of New York* (New York: Vintage, 1974), p. 12.

plomacy or open conflict to achieve ends. In the metropolis, as among nations, some governments are strong and some are weak, but none is able to exert total control to achieve its ends, and there is no formal mechanism for ensuring cooperation and coordination of policymaking.

The analogy, of course, is not complete. There are other superordinate governments in the metropolis—the state government and, increasingly, the federal government—that have impact on areawide problems.

Just as the United Nations, and the League of Nations before it, were established in an attempt to promote cooperation among nations and keep world peace without member nations having to sacrifice their sovereignty, so have metropolitan-wide coordinating agencies emerged to deal with regional problems. These agencies resemble nothing so much as councils of ambassadors from independent nations; indeed, they are called *councils of governments,* or COGs. The various units of government are represented in

bridge was completed. Robert Moses was appointed head of the authority.

The tolls from the Triborough Bridge proved to be far more than estimated, and the authority was netting almost $1.5 million a year by 1938. These revenues could be used in only one way—to retire the authority's bonds faster. In 1938, however, Moses, the classic policy entrepreneur, invented a gimmick that would allow his authority to last forever, at least theoretically. He persuaded the New York legislature to amend the Triborough Bridge Authority Act to provide for reissuing the authority's bonds. Moses now had the ability to reissue, say, forty-year bonds every thirty-nine years. And no government—not state, not local, not federal—could interfere with his operation. Because bonds are contracts between seller and buyer, they fall under Article 1, Section 10 of the United States Constitution, which provides that no state shall engage in any action "impairing the obligation of contracts."

Moses' power base remained secure until he encountered a political operator even more politically astute than he—Governor Nelson Rockefeller. Rockefeller forced a merger between the Metropolitan Transit Authority (MTA) and the Triborough Authority, primarily in order to use Triborough profits to help cover the deficits run up by the computer railroad system operated by the MTA. Moses was forced out of a meaningful role in the merged operation.

COGs, with seats reserved for cities, villages, counties, townships, and school boards.

COGs began as metropolitan planning commissions, and there were few of these units as late as the mid-1960s. Those that did exist were on shaky financial ground, possessing no firm source of funds and no mechanisms to enforce cooperation among governments. The federal government provided both in the 1960s. The 1965 Housing and Urban Development Act provided funds for regional planning agencies. Today, COGs remain heavily dependent on federal funds for their activities. The Southeast Michigan Council of Governments (SEMCOG), for example, receives 62 percent of its funds from the federal government; the remainder comes from the state of Michigan and membership fees.

In 1966, Congress required in the Model Cities Act that many federal grants to local governments be approved by metropolitan review agencies, providing a potential enforcement mechanism. The operating procedures for this review process were specified in a memorandum, or circular, put out by the Office of Management and Budget (OMB) in 1969. The review power is termed A-95 review, after the designation of the OMB circular.

The use of the A-95 review process varies among metropolitan areas, as does its effectiveness. Although some observers have seen it as a rubber stamp for projects that the various units of government want to undertake, this is not entirely the case. What it has become in many instances is an arena for the local units of government to oppose one another when they disagree over the desirability of projects. The review power allows the council of government to veto projects initiated by one local government that would harm citizens of a second local government (the classic policy spillover). It is not a method for securing metropolitan cooperation on needed projects; it is, rather, a way of settling conflicts among localities.

Federation, or Two Tiers of Government

Some urban problems affect neighborhoods; others spill over into the entire region. Because urban problems differ in their geographic extent, some governmental reformers have called for a *federated* or *two-tier* form of government.[16] In such a form, a metropolitan government would assume responsibility for regionwide functions such as sewer and water systems and transit planning, and local governments would continue to control functions that are primarily local in nature, such as garbage collection. Some functions, such as police protection, would be shared.

This federated structure has been most thoroughly implemented in Canada: in metropolitan Toronto, Ontario, and Winnipeg, Manitoba. In Toronto, the Ontario provincial parliament created a Metropolitan Council in 1953, with representation equally divided between the city of Toronto and suburban communities. The council is responsible for providing regionwide services; the incorporated municipalities continue to provide local services.

In the United States, Miami has a modified form of federated structure, set up in 1957 using existing governmental units. Dade County serves as the regional government, providing such areawide functions as public health, mass transit, and some police and fire services. Municipalities and special-purpose districts continue to provide education and police and fire protection, and engage in zoning and land-use planning, although the county has the power to set minimum standards in these areas. In the unincorporated areas of the county, Dade County performs all functions.

[16] These reformers include the prestigious Committee for Economic Development. See *CED, Reshaping Government in Metropolitan Areas* (New York: CED, 1970). See John J. Harrigan, *Political Change in the Metropolis* (Boston: Little, Brown, 1976), pp. 232–38, for a discussion and evaluation.

The Miami structure has engendered bitter conflicts between the municipalities and the county, even though, in the words of John Harrigan, "the functions that had the most highly prized social amenities of the region—public education and residential location—remained in the control of the local governments."[17]

Annexation

One solution to the metropolitan problem is to put the region under the control of a single governmental unit. One method for achieving this is *annexation,* in which one local government, usually the central city, takes into its boundaries unincorporated areas.

During the late nineteenth century, most cities grew by annexation, but this trend slackened after the Second World War, at least for cities in the older urbanized areas. During the 1960s, the larger cities in the East grew by less than 20 percent, but the cities of the South and Southwest more than doubled their populations through the use of the mechanisms of annexation. Annexation is related to the age of the city, with newer cities annexing more. Annexation is also more likely when residents of the center city and the suburban fringe resemble each other in class and in ethnic and racial characteristics. Finally, in some states, laws facilitate annexation.[18]

Generally, municipalities may annex only contiguous areas. If a municipality becomes surrounded by other municipalities, its opportunities for annexation are effectively eliminated. The first city in the United States to lose the power of annexation was St. Louis. In 1876, voters in St. Louis and the remainder of St. Louis County approved a provision for the city to withdraw from the county and perform its own county governmental functions. Just prior to the separation, the city annexed enough rural territory to triple its area. Once the city of St. Louis became a separate county, it could not impinge on the territory of other counties.[19] Growth occurred far beyond the established boundaries, and St. Louis became the first city surrounded by suburbs. Other center cities in the urbanized East and Midwest also became ringed by suburbs, sometimes because of decisions by the central city, sometimes because of action by inhabitants of the fringe, and sometimes because of action by the state legislature.

There are four basic ways in which cities annex: by legislative determination, by judicial determination, by popular determination, and by unilateral municipal annexation.[20] In legislative determination, the state legislature re-

---

[17] Harrigan, *Political Change,* p. 234.
[18] Advisory Commission on Intergovernmental Relations (ACIR), *Substate Regionalism and the Federal System,* vol. 3 (Washington: U.S. Government Printing Office, 1974), p. 82.
[19] Reynolds, "Progress," p. 474.
[20] ACIR, *Substate Regionalism,* p. 93.

tains control over annexation. In judicial determination, state courts decide whether a proposed annexation will take place. Virginia is the state that relies most extensively on judicial annexation. In popular determination, annexation can proceed only if the citizens in the area that is to be annexed (and, sometimes, in the annexing jurisdiction) approve. This process is used in about 60 percent of the states, and it has prevented annexation in many instances. Both fringe residents, fearing consolidation with the central city, and center city minorities, fearing dilution of their political power, have rejected annexation.

Finally, in some states municipalities can annex unilaterally. In Missouri, all home rule cities have this power. In Texas, state law provides home rule cities with the option to annex unilaterally, and, just as important, prohibits incorporation of new municipalities within a three-mile limit of a municipality possessing annexation powers without permission of the unit. This provision has retarded the development of suburbs, but has led to explosive growth of major Texas cities (but see box 9.3). Such cities as Houston and San Antonio continue to include most of the metropolitan area in their boundaries, unlike the suburb-ringed cities of the North. Table 9.2 presents

---

Box 9.3: Annexation Hardball

Houston is not the only city to engage in annexation hardball. In the early 1900s, Los Angeles constructed an aqueduct to import water from the Owens River to the metropolitan area. During the twenty years following, the city pursued an aggressive policy of territorial expansion, using its monopoly on the water supply for the arid region to club fringe areas into submission. But by the mid-1920s, Los Angeles began to anticipate water shortages, and began investigating the possibility of importing water from the Colorado River.

Because of the manner in which Los Angeles had used its water monopoly, suburban municipalities opposed an extension of the monopoly. Because the project required both federal and state approval, Los Angeles was forced to enter into a cooperative arrangement with several counties and municipalities to form the Metropolitan Water District, which built the aqueduct and sold water to governments in the region. The end of the water monopoly spelled the end of the period of large-scale annexation. Since 1930 Los Angeles has annexed only a few square miles of area along its fringes.

Table 9.2. Center city population as a percentage of metropolitan (SMSA) population, selected cities, 1970

City	Percentage Center City Population
Chicago	44
Detroit	29
Houston	62
Los Angeles	39
New York	73
Philadelphia	41
St. Louis	26
San Antonio	77

Source: U.S. Bureau of the Census, *Statistical Abstract of the United States, 1979* (Washington, D.C.: U.S. Government Printing Office, 1979), tables 20 and 24.

the percentage of metropolitan area population that is concentrated in the central city for selected large cities. As can be seen, only New York City contains as high a proportion of its region's population as Houston and San Antonio.

Consolidation

Consolidation occurs when two or more units of government merge to form a single jurisdiction. This kind of governmental reform has been accomplished a number of times in the United States, the most common consolidation being between school districts. From 1967 to 1972, over 27 percent of all the school districts in the country vanished; most of this decline represented consolidation in rural areas.

Several municipal consolidations occurred in the nineteenth century, the most important of which created New York City. Prior to 1874, New York was Manhattan; Brooklyn was a separate municipality. In 1874 and 1895, New York annexed the two townships that today make up the Bronx; then, in 1898, New York and Brooklyn were consolidated, along with Queens and Richmond (Staten Island). This created essentially a two-tier government, with both the municipality of New York and the five borough governments performing public functions. As with many policy changes, a policy entrepreneur supplied essential energy. Andrew Haswell Green worked tirelessly for some thirty years, keeping the issue of consolidation on the public agenda. A second crucial actor was Thomas C. Platt, New York State Republican leader, who used his party position to get the new city charter through the state legislature.[21]

However popular consolidation has been for rural school boards in recent years, it has uniformly been rejected by voters as a solution to metropolitan problems. Between 1949 and 1974, some forty-seven referenda were held on consolidating a metropolitan county with its municipalities, and only twelve passed. Only three of these involved major cities: Nashville consolidated with Davidson County, Tennessee, in 1962; Jacksonville consolidated with Daval County, Florida, in 1967; and Indianapolis unified with Marion County, Indiana, in 1969. Nearly all the attempts were concentrated in the southeastern states; successes were even more concentrated there. When measures were defeated, the margin of defeat was generally large.[22]

The strongest opposition to consolidation referenda generally comes from suburbanites, who fear that the consolidation is an attempt by the central city to tap their relatively sound tax bases. (One of the complaints that governmental reformers lodge against the fragmented metropolis is center city–suburban fiscal disparities, so this perception is not totally incorrect.) Opposition also comes from central city and suburban political officeholders who see in the consolidated system a threat to their influence. Increasingly, center city minorities have eyed consolidation with suspicion, viewing it as an attempt to dilute their power.

For municipalities, consolidation has not been a popular mechanism for solving the "metropolitan problem." Indeed, most citizens do not seem to be particularly troubled by the existing arrangements. When problems of coordination or fiscal disparities have become particularly severe, generally solutions other than consolidation have been utilized: annexation, special districts, or funding from the state or federal government. The unpopularity of consolidation and the availability of other approaches to metropolitan problems lead to a poor prognosis for future attempts at consolidation.

Decentralization

The city of New York has about as many people as Sweden. If Sweden lacked local governments, says political scientist Robert Dahl, we might ask,

> Where . . . are your local governments? But should we not ask the same thing of New Yorkers? Where are your local governments? For purely historical and

---

[21] Wallace S. Sayre and Herbert Kaufman, *Governing New York City: Politics in the Metropolis* (New York: Norton, 1965), pp. 11–15.

[22] John J. Harrigan and William C. Johnson, *Governing the Twin Cities Region: The Metropolitan Council in Comparative Perspective* (Minneapolis: University of Minnesota Press, 1978), p. 11.

what seem rather irrational reasons, we continue to regard the government of the giant metropolis as if it were a local government, when we might more properly consider it the equivalent of a state or provincial government—and hence badly in need of being broken up into smaller units for purposes of local government.[23]

Dahl is centrally concerned about the problem of democracy: Can the large city be democratically governed? Public choice theorists Robert Bish and Vincent Ostrom go further, suggesting that the so-called urban crisis may be blamed, in part at least, on the lack of ability of large, bureaucratic city governments to solve neighborhood problems:

> The urban crisis has reached its most critical proportions in big cities, not in suburbia. . . . The absence of fragmented authority and multiple jurisdictions within large central cities is the principal source of institutional failure in urban government. The absence of neighborhood governments makes it difficult for residents of urban neighborhoods to organize so that common problems can be handled in routine ways.[24]

Municipal decentralization may be defined as "the physical dispersal of governmental structures in such a way as to increase the residents' access to governmental officials and their influence on governmental operations."[25] Decentralization of large city governments represents an increase in fragmentation of the metropolitan public economy, and thus is the opposite of metropolitan consolidation as a solution to urban problems.

Eric Nordlinger has distinguished between two dimensions along which decentralization can occur: the political and the administrative.[26] *Administrative* decentralization involves moving some bureaucratic functions to the neighborhood level. Major policymaking functions remain at city hall, but administrative units are placed in the neighborhood. Because significant discretion exists at the lower levels of most municipal bureaucracies, this decentralization can result in tailoring services to communities in better ways than can be accomplished from city hall. *Political* decentralization is the transfer of some decision-making functions to the neighborhood level. Such decentralization can vary from an information-advisory capacity to a control capacity.

Because decentralization can vary along both of these dimensions, any actual attempt at decentralization will involve a mixture. Detroit's mini–police

[23] Robert A. Dahl, "The City in the Future of Democracy," *American Political Science Review* (December 1967): 968.

[24] Bish and Ostrom, *Understanding Urban Government*, p. 95.

[25] Eric Nordlinger, *Decentralizing the City: A Study of Boston's Little City Halls* (Cambridge, Mass.: MIT Press, 1972), p. 6.

[26] Ibid., pp. 8–41.

stations, for example, are purely administrative units; neighborhoods have no policymaking input in police policies. Boston's Little City Halls involve both some administrative decentralization and some political decentralization. New York's community planning districts have some policymaking responsibilities, but do not deliver services and hence do not involve administrative decentralization. In Chicago, Dick Simpson, a political scientist and former alderman, has advocated ward assemblies and community zoning boards to plan land-use strategies. These proposals involve significant political decentralization.[27]

The politics of decentralization

Decentralization became a major issue in urban politics in the mid- to late 1960s, when blacks and other minorities were just beginning to flex their political muscles. As a consequence, the issue of decentralization became closely identified with the political goals of blacks. Indeed, no idea ever becomes prominent without a specific group to carry it. More specifically, we are always able to identify a small number of policy entrepreneurs who are most important in developing the issue and making demands on government.

An idea becomes prominent in political discourse to the extent that a group (or group leaders) perceive group gain in the idea. Generally, an idea is most successful when it carries with it symbols that are strongly rooted in American culture. Decentralization of large-city government was just such an idea. Not only was it perceived by many black leaders in cities as a key to increased political power, but it carried with it such connotations as self-government, anti-big-government feeling, and the sanctity of neighborhood. Moreover, many whites saw decentralization as a counterweight to increases in black political power. If blacks could control their neighborhoods in the face of white control of the major institutions of urban government, the thinking went, so could whites. Such control had the potential to block school integration, in particular.

Because the issue of decentralization appealed to a substantial number of both blacks and whites, and because it fitted in with a number of American cultural precepts, it became an important force in the politics of many large cities. Many of the attempts at decentralization were unsuccessful, because of the opposition of important interests. These interests included big-city politicians, who saw a threat to their power bases, and interest groups organized at the citywide level, such as teachers and workers in municipal bureaucracies. These groups opposed decentralization because it threatened the prevailing arrangements worked out between them and city government.

[27] See Dick Simpson, Judy Stevens, and Rich Kohnen, eds., *Neighborhood Government in Chicago's 44th Ward* (Chicago: Stipes, 1979).

Nevertheless, there were decentralization victories, including neighborhood city halls in Boston and Detroit, school decentralization in Detroit, and community planning districts and the Office of Neighborhood Government in New York City.

Because ideas directed at governmental forms, such as decentralization, tend to be carried by certain groups, they often get bound up with other aspects of the ideological component of group struggle. The Fainsteins have identified two separate ideological frameworks structuring the arguments in favor of community control. The first, which they refer to as the *democratic model,* is exemplified by the comments of the political scientists quoted at the opening of this section. It emphasizes popular control and self-rule. The second ideological framework, which the Fainsteins refer to as the *race-conflict model,* "stresses the utilization of the homogeneous black neighborhood as a vehicle for the mobilization of black power."[28] In their interviews with minority and white community leaders in New York, the Fainsteins found that black leaders were somewhat more supportive of community control in some form or another, but that almost all leaders, white and black, adopted the democratic ideology to rationalize their support. Indeed, 80 percent of minority leaders opted for the democratic ideology.[29]

[28] Norman I. Fainstein and Susan S. Fainstein, "The Future of Community Control," *American Political Science Review* (September 1976): 907.

[29] Ibid., table 2.

Box 9.4: The Ocean Hill-Brownsville Controversy

Perhaps the most spectacular conflict centering on community control occurred in New York City's Ocean Hill–Brownsville community. In 1967, the New York Board of Education created three experimental school districts in black areas; one of these was in Brooklyn's Ocean Hill–Brownsville district. The teachers in that district were about 80 percent white, and most of these white teachers were Jewish. When the local district board transferred some of the teachers, the United Federation of Teachers (UFT) protested, and the teachers struck the district. The conflict quickly spread citywide, and the battle lines were drawn: white professional educators versus a board composed of members of the minority community. The teachers demanded autonomy to determine educational needs, and demanded that politics be removed from education. The UFT called for local boards that possessed advisory

Source: See Murray S. Stedman, Jr., *Urban Politics,* 2nd ed. (Cambridge, Mass: Winthrop, 1975), pp. 249–56.

However, in their operational beliefs, race made a difference: blacks were more supportive of decision making, as opposed to advisory powers, at the neighborhood level, and supported the decentralization of more services. The Fainsteins concluded that agreement on ideology masked large operational differences. This is to be expected when a political idea, such as decentralization, broadly appeals to American cultural precepts, but is perceived to benefit some groups more than others. It also explains why we can all agree on a course of action but "can't agree on the details"—the details are often more crucial than the generalities. This is clearly the case when everyone agrees on decentralization; when the discussion turns to the question of whether communities ought to have decision-making power or advisory power, the concensus collapses. That the details are by no means trivial is shown by the school decentralization controversy in New York City (see box 9.4).

The Optimum City Size

In dealing with the problems of metropolitan coordination, we face a key question of political theory: What is the optimal size for a governmental unit? If a government is small, its citizens will probably be fairly homogeneous in their demographic characteristics as well as their political

---

powers only, with most policymaking authority remaining with the central board. The district board stood for community control of local institutions. Ideologically, each side adopted a stance that conformed to American cultural precepts.

After a year of protracted conflict that involved no fewer than three separate teacher walk-outs, the New York legislature passed a law providing for local school boards to have some decision-making authority, with the central school board continuing to control many policy functions. In the reorganization, the three special districts lost their special status.

Clearly, this controversy involved much more than a disagreement about two exemplary principles of government: local control and educational professionalism. At root, this was a struggle for the control of the New York educational establishment. The UFT represented a predominantly white teacher corps in a city with a growing minority percentage in both its neighborhoods and its schools. These teachers feared for their jobs if the power to hire, fire, and transfer were granted to the community boards. Moreover,

interests. Florissant, Missouri, is more homogeneous than St. Louis; the citizens of Homewood, Alabama, are more similar to one another than those of Birmingham; the citizens of Wilmette, Illinois, have more in common than do the citizens of Chicago.

As a group gets larger and more heterogeneous, the degree of coercion necessary to enforce a decision increases. In large groups, some minority must be forced to accept the will of the majority on most issues, although the coerced minority may vary from issue to issue. There are, then, very substantial costs of making decisions in large, diverse governments. Those costs have to do with the number of people who will be losers on a public policy issue and the degree to which they will have to be coerced to get them to accept the decision that has been made.

If one wants to minimize the coercive potential of government, it would seem that one ought to favor small units of government. Suburbs, for example, ought to be preferred to large, diverse cities. Unfortunately, the smaller the governmental unit engaging in decision making, the lower its ability to make meaningful decisions. Suburb A might, for example, be downwind from a heavily polluting factory that is just over the border of a separate jurisdiction. Yet the suburban government would lack the authority to deal with the problem. On the other hand, the citizens living in Suburb B might be quite happy with their factory, fearing loss of jobs if they were to prod their government into acting to regulate the pollution. Here is the dilemma. In

---

the UFT had substantial organizational interests. If decisions on salaries and working conditions were decentralized to the community boards, the UFT would probably lose the power it had in citywide bargaining. To defend these prerogatives, the UFT stood for central personnel control and rigid rules specifying work conditions and hiring and firing. These positions were justified in terms of their contribution to acquiring and maintaining a competent, professional teacher corps.

The forces of decentralization realized that, to the extent that these positions were adopted, the local boards would lack any real policy authority. Only if they could match local needs with the proper curricula and personnel could local autonomy become meaningful. Here, too, there was an underlying political current. Many blacks had come to see stringent civil service requirements concerning hiring, firing, and transfers as barriers to increasing the number of jobs for black teachers. Local control of educational policy was one tool that could be used to achieve that goal.

Suburb B, citizens are unanimous in wanting no regulation that might interfere with the operation of their local industry. No one is being coerced. In Suburb A, everyone is in favor of pollution control. Were the city to enact a stringent pollution control ordinance, no citizen of Suburb A would rise to speak in opposition. Yet the government of Suburb A is powerless to act against the major source of pollution.

Clearly, a metropolitan-wide government could deal with the issue. But—and here is the rub—such a government must coerce someone. Either the citizens of A or the citizens of B will lose on the issue, and the large government will be able to decide. (One tendency in all of this is to deny that any costs will be imposed. Pollution controls will not cost any jobs and will clean up the environment. One may also believe in the tooth fairy.)

A second problem in the ability of governments to deal with such problems is financial. Certain social problems, such as poor housing, may be concentrated in jurisdictions that lack the financial resources to deal with them. Center cities tend to suffer concentrated social problems—crime, poverty, and congestion, as well as poor housing—yet lack the financial resources to deal adequately with these problems. Suburban communities may have the financial resources yet lack the problems. Once again, a metropolitan government would have the ability to transfer the money to where the problems are, but not without the use of coercion. Suburbanites are not likely to view benignly the high taxes that would be necessary to deal with center city problems.

If government does nothing about a social problem, this does not mean that coercion is absent. The residents of Suburb A are being coerced, but they are being coerced by a private institution (the polluting factory) rather than by government. It may be somewhat more difficult to see the coercion that exists implicitly in the concentration problems in the center city, but coercion is there, especially when racial discrimination operates to impose poverty disproportionately on the minorities that tend to concentrate in central cities.

The major issue in the debate over the proper size of local government may be viewed as the attempt to minimize coercion, whether it be public or private. Figure 9.2 graphs the situation. On the horizontal axis is the number of homogeneous neighborhoods that can be combined to form units of government in the metropolis. The more neighborhoods that are combined, the larger the units of government must be. They must also be more heterogeneous. The smaller the number of neighborhoods combined, the more local governments there will be in the metropolis. If zero neighborhoods are combined to form governments, each neighborhood will be a separate government.

As we move to the right on the graph, then, the number of governments in the metropolis decreases. But the amount of public coercion increases,

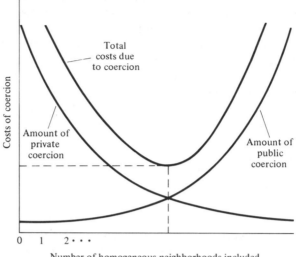

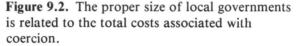

Figure 9.2. The proper size of local governments is related to the total costs associated with coercion.

because the larger the government, the more diverse minorities will have to be suppressed in the decision-making process. At the same time, however, the amount of private coercion will decrease, because the larger the governmental unit, the more social problems it will be able to deal with. Curves representing the amount of private and public coercion are drawn on the graph.

If these two curves are added, we have a total coercion curve, or, as it is labeled on the graph, the *total costs due to coercion.* As can be seen, this curve reaches a minimum where the private and public coercion curves cross. At this point total coercion will be as low as possible. Unfortunately, the exact point of minimum coercion depends on the shape of the curves, and we don't really know that. All we really know is that the proper size of local governments is somewhere between the metropolitan form and the neighborhood; the former coerces too much, and the latter lacks the resources to deal with the numerous social problems that would cross jurisdictional boundaries, leading to private coercion.

Robert Dahl puts the problem in this manner:

> The logic seems unassailable. Any unit you choose smaller than the globe itself . . . can be shown to be smaller than the boundaries of an urgent problem

generated by activities of some people who are outside the particular unit and hence beyond its authority. Rational control dictates even larger units. . . . Yet the larger the unit, the greater the costs of uniform rules, the larger the minorities that cannot prevail.[30]

Dahl suggests that the optimum city size may be in the range from 50,000 to 200,000 residents, an intermediate range in general suggested by figure 9.2. Yet the important variable here is not the absolute size of the city, but its heterogeneity. Size and heterogeneity correspond in general, but not always.

Conclusions

In this chapter we have examined the governmental confusion that is the metropolitan political economy. The fact that there are numerous governmental jurisdictions in the typical American metropolis, each with significant responsibility for providing services and each with policymaking authority, leads to five separate problems which, in sum, are often referred to as the metropolitan problem:

1. *Fiscal disparities.* Some governments are wealthy, others are poor. Those that are poor have problems but few resources; those that are wealthy have resources that could be tapped to solve problems but have fewer problems.

2. *Problem spillovers.* Problems are often larger than the governmental units that are supposed to solve them.

3. *Policy spillovers.* Policy actions engaged in by some governments cause problems for other governments.

4. *Accountability.* The multiplicity of governments puts a severe strain on the mechanisms that are supposed to hold governments accountable to citizens.

5. *Autonomy.* Attempts to solve metropolitan-wide problems inevitably affect the abilities of local communities to govern themselves.

Solutions that have been suggested range from metropolitan consolidation into a single municipal government to more decentralization. In general, there is a tradeoff that is difficult to avoid: as the governmental unit gets larger, there are fewer fiscal disparities, spillovers, and problems with accountability. However, these gains tend to sacrifice local autonomy and end up coercing minorities more.

[30] Dahl, "The City in the Future of Democracy," p. 959.

In the United States, federalism may be seen as an attempt to get around this Hobson's choice. If financing and spillovers can be handled by the state or federal government, while policy responsibility remains at the local level, then municipalities may be able to have their cake and eat it too. We examine this alternative in detail in chapter 13.

CHAPTER 10

The Structure
of Municipal Government

All human organizations possess structure. Formal organizations, such as governments, possess formal structures. In this chapter we describe the formal structure of American municipal governments, explain how that structure developed, and sketch the influence that governmental form has on urban policymaking. We are interested in both the *causes* of local government form in urban America and the *consequences* those forms have for the policymaking process.

Government Structure
as Policy Parameter

A *formal government structure* is the manner in which authority and responsibility for performing public functions are arranged. The formal structure is codified in a constitution, a charter, or a statute. It is the legal arrangement for conducting government.

There exists alongside the formal structure an informal structure, often not written into law but exerting much influence on the way in which authority and responsibility for governance are arranged. Party systems, interest groups, and the informal arrangements among politically active citizens all affect the exercise of authority and responsibility in American cities, yet they are not written into the formal governmental structure. This does not mean that formal structures are unimportant; quite the contrary. A number of studies by political scientists have indicated that the formal structures of municipal government have important consequences for policymaking. The formal structures of government work in tandem with the informal structures, so it is necessary to take both into consideration when studying urban policymaking.

The formal structures of government generally may be viewed as the parameters of public policymaking. By *parameters* we mean the relatively unchanging aspects of the policy process. The parameters of policymaking do change, but when they do the whole process of policymaking is also altered. This is because the formal structures of government condition the way in which policy is made but do not provide the immediate causes of policy. The changes in, for example, the level of expenditures of a city for police protection may be caused by changes in demands by citizens for police protection. But the way in which those demands are processed is conditioned by the form of government. Some types of formal government may *facilitate* the translation of those demands into increased expenditures; others may *inhibit* the translation of those demands.

An example of a governmental form that was designed constitutionally to inhibit the translation of demands into public policy is the federal government of the United States. The drafters of our Constitution deliberately designed a governmental form with an intricate system of divided powers and checks and balances in order to halt hasty action by government in response to immediate but short-term changes in public opinion. Although many of those retarding factors have long since been discarded (indirect election of senators) or modified (the electoral college), many features of this system remain, and still act to stymie positive governmental action.

A Systems Perspective on Local Government

Political scientists employ a *systems perspective* when examining the effect of governmental structure on public policymaking. A system is an entity composed of interdependent parts, that is circumscribed by a boundary that distinguishes the system from its environment. The boundary may be very concrete, as is the case for an automobile (that system of personal mobility), or it may be more arbitrary, as is the case for the "line" that separates political systems from their social and economic environments. In either case, the system accepts inputs from its environment and translates these inputs into outputs, which it delivers to the environment. The environment may react to these outputs and add inputs to the system, and the cycle starts anew.

The inputs to political systems are the demands of citizens and groups for policy actions, and the resources, financial and otherwise, that are available for use in producing public policies. The outputs of the political systems are public policies, which may be assessed by the degree of effort the government is using to achieve a policy end. The most common measure of municipal policy outputs has been expenditures. The systems perspective on the policy process can be diagrammed as follows:

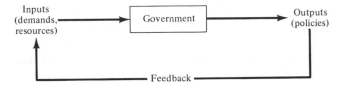

This systems perspective is quite similar to the policy cycle approach of chapter 2. Indeed, in the systems perspective policy outputs are simply the sum of on-cycle and off-cycle policies. If we had adequate measures of each, we could simply add them to find the total policy effort of government. Thus, the systems approach is more general than the policy cycle approach, but using the policy cycle approach helps us understand just how political systems translate inputs into policy outputs.

Responsiveness and Performance

We are now in a better position to understand this idea that governmental structure conditions the policy process. Some forms of government are like well-oiled machines; they translate citizen inputs into public policy effortlessly. We say that such forms of government are *responsive*. Other forms of government tend to blunt the translation of demands into policy outputs. They will produce policies, but it will take a stronger force from the environment to get them to move. These systems of government are less responsive.

It is also possible for different governmental forms to respond to different kinds of demands. Some forms of government may be more responsive to business interests; others may be more responsive to the demands of municipal unions. If such differential responsiveness of governmental institutions exists (and it almost always does), we say that the governmental structure is *biased* toward a particular group or interest.

It is important to note that bias refers to the long-term tendency of a governmental form. In the short run, a group or party may capture control of a government and act in the interests of those who elected them. If Democrats are elected instead of Republicans, we expect more sensitivity to the demands of workers and somewhat less sensitivity to the interests of business. Only if one form of government *consistently* benefits a group that other forms do not do we speak of bias. Bias can be demonstrated only by comparing two different governmental forms in two basically similar situations. Fortunately, a variety of governmental forms exist in metropolitan America, and political scientists have done these comparisons, as we shall see shortly.

Responsiveness is only one dimension of governmental performance. Two other dimensions of governmental performance are efficiency and effectiveness. *Efficiency* concerns the relationship between resources that a government uses and the outputs that it produces. One government is more efficient than another if it produces more services per dollar of tax money spent. *Effectiveness* is the degree to which government accomplishes policy goals—the extent to which it successfully solves the problems confronting it.

These three dimensions of governmental performance—responsiveness, effectiveness, and efficiency—are often in conflict. In particular, when a government takes on a new function or a number of new functions simultaneously, it performs the new functions less efficiently than those it already performs. Hence, in responding to demands to new problems—in trying to be more responsive and effective—government often becomes less efficient. To complicate the situation, in periods when government is growing and taking on new responsibilities, corruption tends to increase—primarily because opportunities for corruption increase.

This happened during the rapid growth of American cities during the early twentieth century. As cities grew, local governments took on a variety of new functions, providing for transportation, sanitary sewerage, street lighting, police protection, and building regulations. Although city governments, often run by political machines, effectively provided the necessary policies to transform America's cities from commercial centers to industrial giants, they did so inefficiently. City governments responded to the demands of both industrialists and immigrants but tolerated substantial corruption in the process.

No single change in government structure is likely to facilitate responsiveness, effectiveness, and efficiency simultaneously. A challenge for governmental reformers is to face the tradeoff squarely, without avoiding the issue.

The Changing Patterns
of Governmental Structure

Throughout American history, a variety of local governmental forms have been tried; some have been kept and some discarded. The history of the development of governmental forms can be viewed as a continuing attempt to find the proper mix of responsiveness, effectiveness, and efficiency in the face of the often rapid social change that keeps urban America in constant flux. Because the social and economic environment of American cities is continually changing, so are the problems faced by government. Institutional forms that worked satisfactorily in a previous era may prove to be archaic when facing new problems.

Because of these changes, performance gaps develop. A *performance gap* is a difference between how people expect a government to perform and how it is actually performing. Performance gaps stimulate a search for a governmental form that works better.

Performance is defined along all three dimensions, and it is unlikely that performance will decline along all three dimensions simultaneously. A decline in efficiency may occur at exactly the same time as increases in responsiveness. If a new governmental form is introduced, it may result in more efficiency but less responsiveness. Because some people value responsiveness over efficiency, and perhaps because the system is biased toward their types of demands, these people will not gladly embrace a proposed institutional change that would improve governmental efficiency at the expense of responsiveness. Such opponents will be joined by people who have a more immediate stake in the existing governmental form; they have jobs with the government, or have contracts with the government, or otherwise are receiving government benefits.

Here, then, is the way that change in municipal government form occurs. A formal structure of government faces new problems. Performance gaps occur along one or more of the dimensions of governmental performance. Groups of governmental reformers begin to demand new forms to replace the poorly operating existing forms. When the dissatisfaction becomes widespread among political activists, governmental reform has reached the policy agenda. Now the policy cycle begins to operate, in a manner similar to its operation on substantive policy issues. As the issue of reform heats up, individuals who perceive benefits from the current governmental structure rush to defend the current forms. During this period the performance gap increases, adding to the ire of the reformers. Then either the reformers win, replacing the existing forms of government with new forms, or their power declines and the status quo is maintained.

Even if the reformers win, their proposed reforms will be adopted more completely in some places than in others. In some cities the opponents of reform will prevail; in others they will have to give only a little ground. Older forms will remain as the *institutional residue* of earlier reform movements.

Often reformers are able to alter the entire manner in which people think about government organization. In this case, when new governments are established, they will embody the reform proposals. At any one time, then, there will be three kinds of municipal governments: those that remain unreformed by the reform movement; those that were changed from the old form to the new form; and those that were established since the reform movement, and are reformed from the start.

From Town Meeting
to Representative Government

Colonial towns were established and generally governed on the principles of local autonomy and grassroots participation in government, participation at least by those allowed the franchise. This group was composed of free, white males over twenty-one who owned property—a small proportion of all residents of the community. Settlements were isolated, and the homogeneous nature of the communities and the holders of the franchise led to general agreement on the political issues of the day. Although legal theory stressed the dependence of municipalities on grants of power from colonial legislatures, in practice the towns and cities of colonial America were self-governing. In New England, citizens gathered in town meetings to exercise direct democratic control over government. In other parts of the colonies, localities did not govern so democratically. Nevertheless, local control was the order of the day in all the colonies, with the partial exception of South Carolina, where the colonial legislature was continually interfering in the affairs of Charleston. Robert Wood has described local government in colonial America this way:

> From the middle of the seventeenth century to well into the nineteenth, local communities in America ran their own affairs, by and large, and ran them by a popular political process. The manageable size of even the largest colonial city and its relative isolation allowed the town fathers to behave both decisively and responsibly.[1]

[1] Robert Wood, *Suburbia: Its People and Their Politics* (Boston: Houghton Mifflin, 1958), p. 23. In this classic book, Wood argues that the search for this ideal of self-government initiated the trend toward separate suburban governments in the metropolis. At base, suburbia is an attempt to reestablish small-town life and government in the diverse, complex metropolis.

For all its local autonomy, the self-governing colonial town had its less pleasant underside. The majority of residents did not participate, either because they were excluded by law or because they lacked interest in participation. The communities tended to be intolerant of new ideas, and were capable of punishing deviance severely. In many communities, although local autonomy was strong, democracy was not. Many of the middle colonies employed *closed corporations* for governing purposes. In this form of government, the principal municipal officials held long terms of office and could appoint their successors. Philadelphia used this form of government. New York, on the other hand, used the *open corporation,* in which the major officers of government were elected.

Whatever its merits, autonomous small-town government prefaced on direct democracy was dependent on a rural America composed of isolated communities. As the cities along the Atlantic seaboard grew, and commerce among the major cities increased, the colonial form of municipal government became less and less satisfactory. In 1822 Boston reluctantly capitulated, and abandoned the town meeting for representative government.

In colonial America, and for a number of years after the ratification of the federal Constitution, cities in America were governed by unitary councils. After about 1820, many cities began to implement the doctrine of separation of powers by electing the executive (mayor) separately from the legislature (council). Some cities even copied the federal plan of a bicameral, or two-house, legislature, a system that was to prove exceedingly clumsy and inefficient in governing cities. By 1900, about one-third of the cities with over 25,000 population had bicameral councils, and such large cities as Boston and Philadelphia had divided legislative authority into a select council, or upper house, and a common council, or lower house.[2] Some municipal lower houses were quite large; Philadelphia's common council, for example, had 149 members. Councilmen were elected from single-member districts, and, because there were numerous councilmen, there were numerous districts, each relatively homogeneous.

To complicate things further, in many cities executive departments were run by boards whose members were sometimes appointed by the state government (particularly in the case of the police department), sometimes appointed by the mayor, and sometimes elected by the citizens of the city. This board system resulted in a municipal government whose major functions were in the hands of boards largely independent of both the city council

[2]Edward C. Banfield and James Q. Wilson, *City Politics* (New York: Vintage, 1963), p. 79. See also Frank J. Goodnow, *City Government in the United States* (New York: Appleton-Century-Crofts, 1904).

and the mayor. It continues to characterize county governments in many states today.

The Municipal Reform Movement

At the turn of the century, city governments were characterized by separated powers, large councils, independent executive departments, and weak mayors. Local policymaking authority was tightly constrained by state government. The result was government characterized by confused lines of authority and numerous independent centers of power. This situation made it extremely difficult for municipal governments to act effectively.

At about the same time, American cities were going through great changes associated with industrialization and immigration. The ineffective governmental forms had to deal with problems on a scale never before experienced in America. As factories were built, housing had to be built for the immigrant masses. Some system of transportation had to be developed, and technological advances made public transportation a realizable goal. Sanitation and public health, always problems in cities, became more serious problems as immigrants crowded into the tenements of New York, Philadelphia, Boston, and numerous other urban centers.

Political changes were occurring also. The immigrants quickly captured those city council districts that were in the growing ethnic areas of the city. The small size of the districts meant that they rapidly fell into the hands of the immigrants, but it also meant that each immigrant group could have its own bloc in the city council. The city councils of many large cities quickly became as ethnically diverse as the cities themselves.

The middle-class Anglo-Saxon Protestants who had occupied the cities prior to the onslaught of immigration viewed with disdain the lower-class Catholics who were rapidly invading the cities. Many felt that the immigrants were parochial and unsophisticated and could not possibly understand the complex art of government. They viewed with apprehension the increasing political power of the ethnics.

Municipal reformers, already concerned about the ineffectiveness of municipal governments, began to argue that the existing forms of government encouraged the representation of narrow and parochial interests by giving disproportionate power to councilmen elected from small districts. Small districts meant that councilmen were unlikely to perceive and act upon citywide interests. Moreover, the structure led to bargaining and deal making among the various ethnic blocs on the council. The mayor could represent citywide interests, because he was elected from the city as a whole, but his powers were not sufficient to overcome the parochial council.

The immigrants were also having an influence on the political party system. Most municipal governments at the time operated on the patronage system, with the party in power rewarding its followers with government jobs and other favors. With the growth of city government during the period of industrialization and immigration, many more jobs were available. The urban political machine, as developed by politicians of immigrant (particularly Irish) background, was rooted in specific material inducements. Often a political boss emerged with enough power to exercise control over the various elements in the party structure. The boss could centralize power in the city by trading favors with leaders of the diverse elements of the party, and, because he could centralize power, he could often accomplish things that were impossible under a more decentralized system. But there were obvious losses in efficiency, since the boss was heavily dependent on the patronage system for his source of inducements.

The *municipal reform movement* was a response to these rapid developments. The movement was staffed disproportionately by middle-class Anglo-Saxon Protestants with professional and business backgrounds. It was a reaction to the growing power of Catholic immigrants, the inefficiency of government, and the corruption associated with boss rule; but it also represented a defense of a philosophy of government that seemed to be threatened. That philosophy emphasized that the practice of government was a reasoned search for the common good (or public interest) rather than the resolution of competing interests, a role often performed by the political boss. As historian Samuel Hays has noted, the movement embodied the idea of scientific and technological progress as the means for this search, with public decisions flowing from expert analysis.[3] If only political organization could be rationalized, thought the reformers, and modern technology applied to urban government, then the correct public policy to deal with the problems facing the city could be found and implemented. They conceived their task as developing and implementing new governmental forms to replace the archaic system of decentralized power that characterized municipal governments at the turn of the century.

Ethos theory

Edward Banfield and James Q. Wilson have argued that the new working-class immigrants and the more established middle-class Anglo-Saxon Protestants held (and to some extent continue to hold) two distinct philosophies about the manner in which government ought to operate.[4] The middle-class Protestant (and, to a great extent, the Jewish) ethos stresses representing the entire community in decisions through a rational search for the common

[3] Samuel P. Hays, "The Politics of Reform in Municipal Government in the Progressive Era," *Pacific Northwest Quarterly* 55 (October 1964): 157–89.
[4] Banfield and Wilson, *City Politics,* pp. 38–43.

good, and then efficiently implementing the discovered policy by a professional and neutral bureaucracy. The ethos disdains partisan politics, lauds the role of experts in government, and stresses honesty, integrity, and efficiency. Banfield and Wilson term this the *public-regarding* or *unitary* ethos.

The immigrant ethos, based in the personalistic and familial relationships that European immigrants brought with them to America, stresses group and individual gain, and politics as a resolution of competing interests. Banfield and Wilson term it the *private-regarding* or *individualist* ethos.

What is most important about these orientations toward government is that they imply the adoption of certain municipal government forms. The implied institutional forms of the unitary ethos are the strong executive (especially the council-manager form); at-large representation on the city council, in which all councillors run from a district that consists of the entire city rather than from individual, single-member districts; nonpartisanship, in which political parties play no role in nominating and electing candidates for office; and a strong civil service system to replace patronage. Banfield and Wilson believe that the struggle over the adoption of municipal government reforms that began in the last quarter of the nineteenth century, intensified during the first quarter of the twentieth, and continues in muted form today reflects the conflict between these two philosophies of government.

According to Banfield and Wilson, these two orientations toward government may be discerned in the voting behavior of city dwellers today, as well as in their responses to public opinion questionnaires.[5] They found that voters in some political districts tended to vote for public expenditures that conferred no direct benefits on them but would cost them something in taxes. These districts had higher incomes, and they contained higher proportions of Anglo-Saxon, Jewish, and black residents. In a study of the attitudes toward government of a sample of Boston homeowners, they found that proponents of a unitary ethos tended to be Yankee or Jewish and have higher incomes and more schooling than those homeowners adopting an individualist ethos or holding no coherent ethos. This latter group was most of the sample, however, indicating that few Boston homeowners have a coherent ideology about government. Banfield and Wilson claim that in times past the orientations were probably held more widely and in more complete form, but in light of the prevailing educational levels and generally lower levels of political sophistication, this is very unlikely. They also suggest that the importance of ethos did not depend on widespread acceptance in the electorate.

> In many cities two small cliques, one of Yankee businessmen and professionals and the other of working- and lower-middle class politicians of immigrant

[5] James Q. Wilson and Edward C. Banfield, "Public Regardingness as a Value Premise in Voting Behavior," *American Political Science Review* 58 (December 1964): 876–87; and Wilson and Banfield, "Political Ethos Revisited," *American Political Science Review* 65 (December 1971): 1048–62.

origins, have, first one and then the other, exercised power that was largely independent of the opinion of the ordinary citizen.[6]

These two small cliques were the carriers of the ethos, and these were (and are) the citizens who participate disproportionately in civic affairs.

Ethos theory has been criticized on three grounds. First, critics have suggested that Banfield and Wilson's original terms, *private regarding* and *public regarding,* depict immigrants as selfish and Yankees as good-hearted. Second, critics have noted that Banfield and Wilson are not clear about whether ethos is rooted in class or in ethnicity. Is it being middle class that makes one public regarding, or is it being Anglo-Saxon? Finally, and most importantly, critics have questioned whether the public-regarding ethic is merely a smokescreen for self-interest. It is a common trait of humans to justify self-interest in broad philosophies that emphasize the contribution of what they want to the common good. Better-educated people are more adept at this, and are therefore more likely to cloak motives based in self-interest in appeals to the common good. The Anglo-Saxon middle class had a clear interest in altering municipal government forms: they were losing power to the immigrants. Public regardingness was a justification for the changes they sought to make.

Each of these points is valid. Generally, however, Banfield and Wilson are correct in pointing to the existence of two broad orientations about government, one emphasizing the search for a common good and the other emphasizing the role of government as a mechanism for deciding whose interests are to prevail when those interests conflict. Indeed, these orientations parallel the distinction we made early in this book between government as a provider of collective goods, which will not be produced without government action, and government as a mechanism for deciding who is to be coerced when externalities exist (see chapter 3). Banfield and Wilson are also correct in emphasizing that these orientations imply different governmental forms. Finally, the ideology of reform is at least as important as class or ethnic interest in motivating reform behavior. Although doubtless rooted in class and ethnic background, the unitary or public-regarding ethos on which the municipal reform movement was based had an independent influence on the actions of the reformers.

The Prescriptions of the Reformers

The reform movement generated several specific proposals for structural change, many of which were adopted and some of which continue to be topics of debate in cities.

[6] Wilson and Banfield, "Political Ethos Revisited," p. 1062.

The strong mayor

The formal authority of a mayor may be viewed as a political resource. Not all powerful mayors operate in a system of government that allots them extensive formal powers. Yet where the mayor possesses extensive formal authority, the mayor is more likely to become a powerful political actor.

The municipal reformers believed that strengthening the formal powers of the mayor would help offset what they felt was a pernicious system of bargaining and logrolling among the various municipal officers, particularly the city councillors elected from small, homogeneous wards. Moreover, granting sufficient formal authority to the mayor would allow "accountability at the top." Voters could vote for a candidate for mayor and the programs he or she proposed with the knowledge that the candidate, if elected, would possess the authority to implement them. Hence, the reformers proposed the *strong mayor* system. In this system, the mayor shared policymaking power with the city council. For example, the mayor would be responsible for developing the city budget, and the council would have the power to approve or reject the budget. The mayor could propose ordinances, but the council would have the power of enactment. The mayor could veto ordinances passed by the council, but the council would possess the authority to override the veto.

Under the strong mayor system, the mayor would have the primary responsibility to appoint and terminate the administrative officers and department heads of the city, with the council having the power to reject appointments. This, the reformers felt, would increase accountability and efficiency. It would increase accountability by allowing the mayor to get rid of appointees who refused to implement his or her programs. It would increase efficiency by centralizing administrative authority and eliminating duplication.

Not all cities have adopted all of the recommendations for strengthening the power of the mayor. Many cities continue to elect such municipal officers as the city clerk and the finance officer. In Milwaukee, the city council participates directly in the preparation of the budget. In many smaller cities, the mayor is a member of the city council and has few formal powers, and the administration is in the hands of a manager appointed by the council (another innovation of the municipal reformers).

Today there is no clear dividing line between strong and weak mayor systems. Strong mayors generally have primary appointment power over city administrators, possess significant budgetary authority, and have the power to veto city council measures. Weak mayors lack these powers, but there is much variability in the nature and extent of these powers among cities. Generally, larger cities have tended to adopt proposals for strengthening mayoral power, and smaller cities have tended to resist them.

Nonpartisanship

Municipal reformers, repeating the credo that "there is no Republican or Democratic way of sweeping the streets," advocated a nonpartisan ballot for the election of municipal officials. In a nonpartisan electoral system, party designations of candidates do not appear on the ballot. The intent of this reform was to remove partisan considerations from municipal administration, thereby weakening urban political machines. By removing this source of cleavage and conflict, the reformers hoped to make municipal government an exercise in the disinterested search for the common good.

The effect of the nonpartisan ballot varies from place to place. In general, nonpartisan systems may be grouped into three categories. In the first the parties operate just as they do under a partisan system, with parties endorsing candidates and working for their election. Chicago's city council (but not its mayor) is elected on a nonpartisan ballot, and this does not prevent the strong Democratic party organization from nominating and generally electing candidates.

In the second group of nonpartisan communities, other organized groups perform the functions of nomination and election that parties perform in partisan systems. In the past, a segment of the Los Angeles business community met regularly to endorse, finance, and elect candidates for mayor and council. Between its inception in 1954 and the election of 1973, San Antonio's Good Government League (GGL) was successful in electing seventy-eight of the eighty-one local council members it endorsed. According to one student of politics in San Antonio, the Good Government League was a "formal, permanent organization, with stable leadership, solid financing, and an elected board of directors."[7] The bedrock of support for the GGL was Anglo business elites, but the organization regularly slated candidates from the Mexican American and black communities in an exercise of coalitional politics that is reminiscent of party organizations. During the early seventies, the GGL suffered a series of electoral setbacks, and it closed its doors in December 1976.[8]

Occasionally organizations become such regular participants in elections that they may be called local parties. Cincinnati's City Charter Committee, for example, has a partylike structure and regularly and systematically nominates candidates for local office.

The final pattern that emerges in nonpartisan systems is a fluid group system, in which ad hoc campaign organizations centered around specific

[7] Robert L. Lineberry, *Equality and Urban Policy: The Distribution of Municipal Public Services* (Beverly Hills, Calif.: Sage, 1977), p. 56.

[8] L. Tucker Gibson, Jr., "Mayoralty Elections in San Antonio," paper presented at the Annual Meeting of the Southwestern Political Science Association, Houston, Texas, April 12–15, 1978.

candidates emerge and last only as long as the candidate is electorally successful. Other, more stable interest groups endorse and donate time and money to candidates, but they operate through the candidate's organization. This is the pattern in Detroit. There, Mayor Coleman Young has developed a strong electoral organization, but the organization does not endorse other candidates, even for municipal office (although the mayor may make his preferences known). The campaign organizations of mayors and city council members crumble as soon as the electoral ambitions of the officials end, and new groups emerge to support new candidates. The organizations are not continuous, but exist for the purpose of electing one and only one candidate. This pattern is probably most typical of nonpartisan cities.

Today most municipalities use the nonpartisan ballot—almost three-quarters of cities of over 25,000 population, according to a 1977 study. The partisan ballot is popular only in the Northeast; it is seldom used in the West or South.[9] Whatever the form, nonpartisanship has the effect of (1) lessening popular control of public policy and (2) uncoupling local and national policymaking. The latter was an explicit goal of the reformers. Political parties give voters a regular organization to hold accountable, and the partisan ballot gives them a method for accomplishing this. The party label also links local officials with national ones. Truly nonpartisan systems break both links.

At-large districting

When city council members run from a single district encompassing the entire city, the representational system is termed *at-large districting*. When each member represents a separate district, the system is termed *single-member districting*. The single-member district is generally termed a *ward*.

An innovation proposed by reformers to overcome the parochialism of city councils, the at-large system has proved immensely popular with cities, especially those that incorporated after the high tide of the municipal reform movement. Today about 64 percent of all cities with over 25,000 population employ an at-large system, with 36 percent using a ward system or a combination of ward and district systems in which some council members are elected from wards and others are elected by a citywide constituency. Ward systems are most prevalent in large cities and in the Northeast and Middle West. They are used less extensively in the South and West.[10]

Minorities. In recent years, at-large districting has come under fire by modern municipal reformers, spokespersons for minority interests, and, in

[9] Heywood T. Sanders, "Government Structure in American Cities," *Municipal Year Book 46* (Washington, D.C.: International City Manager's Association, 1979): Table 4/2.
[10] Ibid.

the South and Southwest, the federal government. It is believed that at-large systems disadvantage minority group members, who must present their candidates before a predominantly white electorate. If a city were 35 percent black, for example, it is possible that no black council members would be elected in an at-large system. This assumes, of course, that whites vote their racial prejudices (or perceive themselves as having different political interests from blacks). In a ward system with, say, twenty wards, it would be virtually impossible to exclude blacks completely from the council.

A number of recent research studies have examined the validity of this political wisdom. Most of these studies have concluded that the district election system facilitates the election of blacks to city councils. Delbert Taebel, for example, concludes that both at-large election systems and small city councils operate to limit the election of blacks and Hispanics. Taebel speculates that whites may be more willing to support blacks for office in large cities, where there are numerous "slices of the pie" to be divided up.[11]

It is possible that black underrepresentation is caused by other characteristics of cities, such as the size of the black population or the education level of the city's population, and these characteristics are also related to at-large systems. In this case, there would be no direct, or causal, relationship between black underrepresentation and type of election system. In such a situation, we would say that the relationship between election system and underrepresentation of blacks is spurious. To check for this possibility, Robinson and Dye examined black representation as a function of district type and other characteristics of cities that might also be related to black representation. Such a *multivariate* analysis, in which there are several independent variables (or possible causes) and one dependent variable (result), controls for the possibility of a spurious relationship. These researchers found that at-large elections had a strong, direct effect on black underrepresentation. Indeed, election type was the single most important variable in explaining black underrepresentation, and the authors comment that "the single most important obstacle to equity in black representation on city councils is the use of at-large elections."[12]

Although the general thrust of the quantitative studies is that at-large elec-

---

[11] Delbert Taebel, "Minority Representation on City Councils: The Impact of Structure on Blacks and Hispanics," *Social Science Quarterly* 59 (June 1978): 142–52. See also Clinton Jones, "The Impact of Local Election Systems on Black Representation," *Urban Affairs Quarterly* 11 (March 1976): 345–56; and Albert Karnig, "Black Representation on City Councils," *Urban Affairs Quarterly* 12 (December 1976): 223–42.

[12] Theodore P. Robinson and Thomas R. Dye, "Reformism and Black Representation on City Councils," *Social Science Quarterly* 59 (June 1978): 140. See, however, the contrary findings by Susan MacManus in her "Election Procedures and Minority Representation," *Social Science Quarterly* 59 (June 1978): 153–61. MacManus concludes that systems using a combination of at-large and district plans are most equitable.

In all of these studies, the extent of black disadvantage is overestimated, because black population, rather than black registered voters, is used as a basis of comparison.

toral systems do disadvantage blacks, it is important to emphasize that many other factors influence the extent of black representation. For example, where blacks are a majority of the voting population, at-large systems may actually give them an advantage. Where parties or other organizations regularly slate candidates, they may slate blacks to balance the ticket and then "sell" them to the electorate. If white voters scatter their votes while blacks "bullet vote" for a limited number of candidates, they may be able to elect more candidates than expected. Black candidates may be able to attract support from white trade unionists or liberal professionals, and this possibility often depends on the caliber of the opposition.

In recent years, the at-large electoral system has lost some of its popularity, and several cities, including San Antonio, have voted to go to a ward system (see box 10.1). Other cities, including Dallas, Houston, and Mobile, have been required by federal courts to institute some district representation. Although the Supreme Court has ruled that at-large electoral systems are not discriminatory unless intent to discriminate can be shown, several federal district judges have found that intent.[13]

Council-manager government

In 1914, the city of Dayton, Ohio, became the first sizable city to adopt the council-manager governmental form, perhaps the most innovative of the proposals of the municipal reformers. For a century American cities had strictly observed the separation of legislative and executive power introduced in the federal Constitution. Now, with the council-manager form of government, the municipal reformers were proposing a return to a unitary council, but with an added feature. A professional city manager, hired by the elected city council and serving at the pleasure of that council, would manage the delivery of services and attend to administrative duties. The manager would make all administrative appointments, and department heads would serve at the city manager's pleasure; he or she would prepare the municipal budget. The city council would set overall policy, and the city manager could make policy recommendations to the council, but he or she was not to be primarily responsible for policymaking. The mayor would be a member of the council, and serve primarily a ceremonial role.

Although council-manager government bears a resemblance to parliamentary government, it is modeled on the American business corporation. In the corporation, a board of directors serves to set company policy, but salaried managers are the primary decision makers on a daily basis.

---

[13] Federal courts now look carefully at any electoral arrangement that dilutes the power of minorities. This includes, in particular, at-large electoral systems and annexation of predominantly white outlying areas by central cities. (Recall the liberal annexation powers that the state of Texas grants its cities.)

Box 10.1: Charter Reform in San Antonio

From 1914 until 1951, San Antonio operated under a commission form of government. Reformers began to challenge this form in the 1930s, but it was not until 1951 that the council-manager form was adopted. Under this charter, the nine members of the city council were elected at large, and the council chose the "weak" mayor.

The adoption of the reform charter coincided with the rise to power of the Good Government League, an organization of business and professional people who kept a tight rein on San Antonio politics and government for a quarter of a century. During this period, city government was run as a closed corporation, generally for the benefit of downtown business interests. Endorsement by the GGL was virtually essential for victory in the citywide council races.

By 1970, San Antonio was 52 percent Mexican American and 9 percent black, but these two minority groups made up only about 46 percent of the city's registered voters. The GGL regularly slated two Mexican Americans for the council and, after 1965, also slated a black. Nevertheless, the city's minorities became increasingly restless under this system of government, which they felt was paternalistic and unresponsive to their interests. Indeed, minority neighborhoods regularly voted against GGL slates, but had not been able to crack the solid electoral front presented by Anglo voters supporting GGL candidates. According to Tucker Gibson, the success of the GGL

Source: See L. Tucker Gibson, Jr., "Mayoralty Elections in San Antonio," paper presented at the Annual Meeting of the Southwestern Political Science Association, Houston, Texas, April 12–15, 1978.

The council-manager form is based on a strict distinction between policymaking and administration. Policymaking was conceived by the reformers (and is conceived by many political scientists today) to consist of setting broad guidelines or directions for government action. Administration involves the implementation and routinization of these broad guidelines. In the council-manager form these functions were to be rigorously separated.

Note how different the theory of government underlying the council-manager form is from the separation-of-powers doctrine that is embodied in the federal structure, state governments, and the mayor-council form of municipal government. Although there is a general separation of functions into legislative (policymaking) and executive (administrative) in the separation-of-powers form, the theory behind this separation has nothing to

depended on "the consensus of the Anglo community elites, the higher rates of participation among Anglo voters, the cohesion among Anglo voters, and the lower rates of participation among Black and Mexican-American voters."

In 1973 an important election took place. GGL council member Charles Becker bolted the organization when he was not slated as its mayoralty candidate, and ran as an independent. The GGL endorsed a Mexican American to head its ticket, hoping to forge a coalition between the Mexican American community and the loyal portion of the Anglo community. The attempt failed, Becker was elected, and independents captured a majority of the council. Becker had carried the traditional Anglo GGL precincts, and the GGL candidate had swept the Mexican American community. Ethnic loyalty was apparently a more powerful reason for voting than the endorsements of organizations.

The power of the GGL was broken with this election, and shortly thereafter it closed its doors. In the meantime, a whole series of issues that the GGL had managed to keep off the civic agenda emerged during the ensuing period of political turmoil. Broad support for charter revision, including single-member districts for council members, began to emerge. A charter commission was formed, and submitted its proposals to the voters in 1974. The most important provision, single-member council districts, lost, but it garnered 48 percent of the vote. The vote split along ethnic lines, with the greatest support coming from Mexican American precincts and the most intense opposition coming from Anglo voters.

After the vote, independent council members, lacking organiza-

---

do with the separation of policy from administration. Indeed, the associated doctrine of checks and balances ensures that the executive will perform policy functions, and in modern times the executive has assumed an increasingly large role in the initiation of policy proposals. Nobody expects, nor did anyone ever expect, the chief executive in the separation-of-powers model to refrain from engaging in policymaking. But reformers expected city managers to refrain from doing so, and the credo of the International City Managers' Association, the trade association of the city manager profession, continues to stress this.

Politics. Where does politics fit into the schema of the advocates of the city manager plan? The answer from the reformers is that it was not sup-

tional support for a citywide race, continued to attack the at-large system, while the weakened GGL endorsed it. But it was clear that the independents had the best of the philosophical argument, and they hammered away at the unfairness to minorities of the at-large system.

In 1975, Texas came under the provisions of the federal Voting Rights Acts, and the independents and minorities of San Antonio challenged the legality of the at-large electoral system in court. In 1976 the city council appointed a second charter revision committee. In 1977 a single-member district plan, with the mayor elected at large, was submitted to the voters, and it was approved by 51 percent; the voting again fell along ethnic lines. Of the ten council members elected in 1977, four were Anglo, five were Mexican American, and one was black.

The electoral, public policy, and governmental reform victories won by independents and minorities in San Antonio were facilitated by a deep and irreparable split in the city's governing coalition. When Becker bolted the GGL, he took with him those community elites who were dissatisfied with the slowness of industrial and commercial development in San Antonio and the parochial nature of its leadership. This split gave immediate advantage to the minority community. In the ensuing period of political turmoil, many issues, including the issue of governmental reform, reached the policy agenda—issues that had been kept off the agenda previously by the prevailing configuration of political forces. When political change came to San Antonio it came rapidly, but this is at least partially due to the lack of change in the previous quarter of a century.

---

posed to enter at all. Politics as the competition of differing interests to determine public policy was supposed to be replaced by a rational search for the common good. If coalition building and bargaining were to occur, they were to occur among city council members, not within the city's administrative machinery. Yet anyone who has ever worked in a public agency, or has observed one closely, knows that politics takes place continually within the agency as well as between one agency and another. Moreover, the general direction of government action is often determined in this interplay, rather than by some vague guidelines issued by the city manager or city council.

The idea that the city manager is not to engage in politics, if strictly followed, would mean that the manager would be unable to build support for his or her programs by building a coalition on the council. This is a very unrealistic role for an administrative leader to play, especially in a city of any size, where numerous opinions or differences of opinions about what direction local government ought to take exist. This may well account for the widespread unpopularity of the council-manager form in large cities: only 21 percent of cities of over 500,000 population use the council-manager form of government.

In small cities and towns, however, where the political culture is homogeneous and few major cleavages exist, the division between policy and politics on the one hand and administration on the other may work very well. If community values are set and unquestioned, then the city council can easily reflect them without having to resort to bargaining and compromise. And the manager can easily administer the programs the community wishes to see implemented. This description may tend to overemphasize the nonconflictual nature of small-town life, where lack of political discord can mean that major cleavages are being suppressed rather than indicate a basic consensus on political values. Nevertheless, the council-manager form has proved far more popular with small communities than with large ones: a majority of cities with populations smaller than 100,000 have adopted the form. Moreover, Dye and MacManus report that ethnicity, measured as the percent of foreign-born in a city's population, is the best predictor of whether a city has a mayor-council form.[14] Ethnicity is a measure of heterogeneity and an indicator of social cleavage and likely political conflict.

The evidence suggests that the mayor-council form is best at reconciling conflicting political interests and marshaling power to achieve public goals. The council-manager form, however, may be well adapted to small, homogeneous communities where basic social conflicts are at a minimum.

A final form of municipal government is the *commission* form. In the commission form, voters elect a small commission that is responsible for both policymaking and administration. Each commissioner is the head of one or more city departments. Once embraced enthusiastically by municipal reformers, the commission form has lost favor, and it is employed by less than 6 percent of cities with populations of 20,000 or more.

Civil service

The dismantling of the patronage system, in which the victorious party in an election replaced government employees with their own supporters, had been on the agenda of government reformers for years before the high tide of municipal reform. In 1888, the federal government passed the Pendleton Act, which set up the federal civil service. But at the turn of the century many

[14] Thomas Dye and Susan MacManus, "Predicting City Government Structure," *American Journal of Political Science* 20 (May 1976): 257–72.

cities still used the patronage system, or, as it was sometimes called, the "spoils system." The lifeblood of the political machine was patronage; if the patronage system could be dismantled, reasoned the reformers, so could the machine. Hence, they kept civil service as an important item on their agenda.

In a civil service or merit system of employment, government employees are recruited and certified for employment by a board or department that is supposed to ignore political considerations in the employment process. The civil service board was conceived as a semiautonomous unit that set requirements for government positions, administered objective tests for the positions, and forwarded the results to department heads, who were supposed to choose the best qualified for the position. Promotions were to be handled in the same neutral, nonpolitical manner. The board was also to hear employee grievances. In many cities today, the semiautonomous civil service board has been replaced with a department of personnel, but its functions remain the same.

In cities where civil service systems have been implemented and rigorously administered (and that includes almost all medium-size and large cities), the political party structure generally has been weakened. Indeed, civil service is probably the most important structural change accounting for the decline of the urban political machine. Without the jobs and potential for career advancement once controlled almost completely by the party, the machine cannot offer the specific material inducements that are its mainstay. The precinct captains and ward heelers had little reason to continue the tiring work of maintaining contact with voters and intervening on their behalf with government agencies unless party bosses had control over their future employment and potential for advancement. And without this grassroots work, machine-backed candidates lost their advantage over other candidates.

Machines have sometimes managed to avoid the full implications of civil service reform by using a civil service classification termed *temporary* or *provisional* to carry their appointees. All civil service systems use such classifications to fill positions until employment can be certified. The difference is that machines have been able to extend almost indefinitely the time employees spend on temporary status. This means that such employees have no job protection, and may be let go for failing in their political duties. In Chicago, a new personnel code limits the amount of time an employee can spend on temporary status, but the city council has delayed implementing this provision.

Tradeoff. Recently federal courts have ruled that the firing of most public employees for political reasons is unconstitutional. In 1976, in a case involving the Chicago Democratic machine, the U.S. Supreme Court ruled that municipal employees cannot be dismissed on the grounds of party loyalty (or lack of it).[15] In that case, the Court specifically permitted the firing of "policy-making" employees. But in a 1980 case that involved a newly elected Democratic public defender's firing two Republican lawyers to replace them with members of his own party, the Supreme Court decided that even employees exercising some policy functions have a right to employment.[16]

Finally, a recent federal district court decision has prohibited the Chicago Democratic organization from using political work as a criterion for *hiring* city employees.[17] It has been appealed; if the case is affirmed on appeal the assault on patronage systems by the federal courts will be completed.

Civil service systems and the recent federal court decisions are based on the old policy-administration dichotomy that is one of the mainstays of the reformer's ideology. Administrators are supposed to be neutral implementers of the policies set by policymakers. Yet we have already noted that this separation is a false one. What happens when bureaucrats "stonewall" the implementation of programs with which they do not agree? Unless they are unusually clumsy, they can easily avoid getting fired for their actions.

Once again we see a tradeoff, this one between responsiveness and efficiency. Theoretically, government will operate more efficiently under a civil service system; there will not, for example, be wholesale turnovers in the personnel of an agency. But responsiveness of government suffers a double blow. In the first place, policymakers elected by the voters cannot fire employees who are resisting their policy innovations. If policymakers cannot implement their programs because of recalcitrant civil servants, it is difficult (logically, at least) to hold them accountable for the programs they advocate. In the second place, responsiveness declines because the neighborhood loses an important advocate in government—the party precinct captain, whose job tenure is dependent on how well he or she satisfies the demands of the residents of the precinct. Although merit systems lead to stable careers and efficiency in government operations, they also detract from responsiveness and accountability.

Affirmative Action. Merit systems of employment and advancement have recently come under fire from urban minorities, especially blacks. As blacks came to power in major cities, they quickly found that they could not replace the white bureaucrats with their supporters. This led some blacks to complain that whites had captured city bureaucracy using the patronage system, then had sealed themselves into it by installing the merit system. Moreover, many blacks believed (correctly) that the civil service examina-

---

[15] *Elrod* v. *Burns* 427 U.S. 347 (1976).

[16] *Branti* v. *Finkel* 445 U.S. 507 (1980).

[17] *Shakman* v. *Democratic Organization of Cook County* 481 *F. Supp.* 1315 (1979).

tions were not related to successful job performance and rewarded middle-class verbal skills, skills that poor minorities were unlikely to possess. Indeed, many blacks felt that a route of upward mobility that the European ethnics had used—government jobs—was closed to them just as they began to wield political power. This system of white control in black cities made city bureaucrats even less sensitive to the needs of urban blacks, and it led to deteriorating relationships between the community and city bureaucrats, especially the police.

The response of black politicians and their allies was to develop *affirmative action* programs, which gave blacks an advantage in employment and advancement they would not have received under civil service systems. In some programs, for example, a set percentage (say, 50 percent) of jobs are given to minorities passing a civil service examination.

Some social scientists argue that the potential of upward mobility reduced class antagonisms in urban America by moving potential leaders from the proletariat into the middle class. European working-class ethnics were far more successful in capturing political control in cities than they were in securing economic advantage. The patronage system allowed the immigrant masses to advance relatively rapidly in at least one sphere: politics. Blacks have found this route more difficult because of civil service systems that tend to perpetuate advantage. Affirmative action may perhaps best be seen as the black alternative to the patronage system.

Recall, referendum, initiative, and short ballot

Reformers also advocated a number of electoral reforms for both state and municipal governments. The major measures were the recall, the referendum, the initiative, and the short ballot. The *recall,* first adopted in Los Angeles in 1903, gives citizens the power to petition for an election to determine whether an official should be removed from office. It can be a powerful device for enforcing strongly held citizen preferences. A number of school board members, for example, have been removed by angry white voters in several states for supporting integration plans.

The *initiative* is a process by which voters propose legislation and force its consideration by the city or state. The *referendum* is a process by which a legislative proposal is brought before the voters for their approval or rejection. Used in tandem, the initiative and referendum have been used to bring a number of tax and expenditure limitation proposals before voters in a number of states.

Finally, the *short ballot* sought to simplify the number of offices voters were required to fill. Normally, this requires increased appointive powers for executive officers (that is, the mayor or governor).

The Policy Consequences
of Reformed Government

Because the various structural proposals of the reformers were aimed toward an interrelated set of goals, political scientists think of them as a package. Cities adopting these reform proposals are called *reformed;* those resisting the demands of the reformers, clinging to the mayor-council form, partisan ballot, and ward elections, are termed *unreformed.* Many governments adopted some of these proposals and rejected others; these governments may be categorized as more or less reformed, depending on how many of the structural reforms they have adopted.

Responsiveness

The municipal reformers expected certain consequences from their innovations. In particular, they expected that reformed governments would be less responsive to cleavages among the citizenry and more responsive to the public interest, however defined. How have reformed governments fared? Lineberry and Fowler subjected this prediction to empirical test. Employing the systems perspective discussed at the beginning of this chapter, these researchers measured policy outputs as the levels of expenditures and taxation of cities. Then they assembled data on certain socioeconomic characteristics of cities, assuming that such characteristics would indicate urban social cleavages and the demands on government that come from these cleavages. They related these inputs to policy outputs (expenditures and taxation). But (and here is their key prediction) unreformed governments should reflect the relationship between social cleavages and policy outputs more strongly than reformed governments. In other words, unreformed governments should facilitate the translation of demands from citizens into policy outputs. Lineberry and Fowler conclude that, indeed, "the goal of the reformers has been substantially fulfilled, for non-partisan elections, at-large constituencies and manager governments are associated with a lessened responsiveness of cities to the enduring conflicts of political life."[18]

Bias

Lineberry and Fowler treated responsiveness as a general characteristic of political systems, and found more of it in unreformed cities than in reformed cities. William Lyons has gone a step further and treated the problem of governmental form as one of bias. Lyons argues that unreformed cities

---

[18] Robert L. Lineberry and Edmund P. Fowler, "Reformism and Public Policies in American Cities," *American Political Science Review* 61 (September 1967): 715.

should be more responsive to demands for increased spending for public ser-vices, but that reformed cities should be more responsive to demands for decreases (or slower growth) in expenditures. So he classified variables as leading to heightened demands for city services (such as increases in the percentage of nonwhite citizens), leading to increases in resources available (such as increases in intergovernmental aid), or leading to increases in demands for lower spending (changes in the percentage of owner-occupied dwellings, under the theory that homeowners tend to demand less spending than renters). He then related these variables to expenditure changes between 1962 and 1972. As expected, unreformed cities tended to increase expen-ditures more rapidly in response to changes in resource opportunities and demands for increased expenditures, but reformed cities were more respon-sive to demands for reduced spending.[19]

Lyons's results indicate that certain municipal government forms predis-pose policymakers to respond to certain kinds of demands. In particular, unreformed cities are willing to increase their public sectors by increasing ex-penditures more in response to changes in resource opportunities. This situa-tion can be depicted as follows:

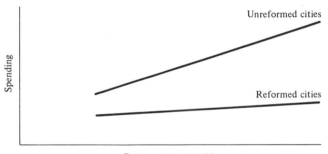

In the diagram it can be seen that both kinds of city increase spending when more resource opportunities exist. But unreformed cities do so more rapidly—they are more responsive to changes in revenue opportunities. Unreformed municipal structures seem to facilitate the translation of revenue opportunities into spending for services, and the same seems to be true of demands for increased spending.[20]

[19] William Lyons, "Reform and Response in American Cities: Structure and Policy Recon-sidered," *Social Science Quarterly* 59 (June 1978): 118–32. Lyons's work was based in a period of generally increasing resources for cities: the 1960s. Intergovernmental aid was increasing, cities were growing, and real income was increasing. Were unreformed cities less willing to cur-tail spending in the face of declining resources during the 1970s?

[20] One caution must be entered here. Wolfinger and Field noted that reformed governments are disproportionately distributed among the regions of the country, with southern and western cities most likely to possess reformed structures (see Raymond Wolfinger and John Osgood

Expenditures are not the only way of measuring policy outputs, yet most of the policy output literature has used these measures. In one study of governmental form, a different measure of policy output was utilized. Albert Karnig found that, as hypothesized, civil rights groups were more successful in obtaining favorable policy measures in unreformed cities than in reformed cities.[21] Karnig's study contains a second important feature. Instead of relying on social and economic characteristics of cities to assess demands for public programs, he counted the number of active civil rights groups in the cities he studied, on the assumption that the black community is better organized and more effective in presenting demands where there are numerous organizations. The number of civil rights groups was related to the number of programs that could be judged favorable to them, and the relationship was stronger for unreformed cities.

Conclusions

Governmental structure is the framework within which public policy is made. The translation of demands for public action occurs and the resources necessary to translate that action into public policy exist within the formal arrangement of authority that we call the structure of government. Some forms of government facilitate the translation of demands into policy, and others inhibit that translation.

Three dimensions of government performance exist: responsiveness, efficiency, and effectiveness. Some governmental forms encourage responsiveness; others favor efficiency or effectiveness. Indeed, a tradeoff exists. *It is not generally possible to maximize responsiveness, efficiency, and effectiveness within a single governmental structure.* Ward constituencies, for example, facilitate responsiveness to neighborhood-based interests but tend to inhibit efficiency in government.

Demands for structural change generally occur when some individuals perceive performance gaps along one or more of the basic dimensions of governmental performance. When a sufficient number of political activists perceive performance gaps, governmental reform has reached the political agenda, and the policy cycle begins to operate. Even though structural

---

Field, "Political Ethos and the Structure of American Government," *American Political Science Review* 60 [June 1966]: 306–26). If southern and western cities are less likely to respond to demands for spending than are northern cities and this tendency is independent of municipal structure, the effect will be wrongly attributed to structure. Although regional controls have been deprecated in this literature, the conclusions from it would be much stronger if such controls had been used.

[21] Albert Karnig, "Private Regarding Policy, Civil Rights Groups, and the Mediating Impact of Municipal Reforms," *American Journal of Political Science* 19 (February 1975): 91–106.

reform has far-reaching consequences for the operation of the policy process, it can be understood in terms of the policy cycle approach we have used throughout this book.

Two conceptions

Two broad conceptions of government exist. One views government primarily as a mechanism for discovering and implementing the public interest. In this view, governing is an exercise in technology. Public goods do exist, and public policies can be devised and implemented to realize the common good. Governmental coercion is merely a way of achieving the ends that individuals in voluntary cooperation cannot achieve. The second conception of government views public power as a way of resolving competing interests. Numerous externalities, or harms done inadvertently by one person to another, exist in modern urban life, and this situation gives rise to competing claims on government. Government must decide who is to be coerced, and whether the private coercion that exists is to be replaced by public coercion. Hence, government is an arbiter of the competing claims, and, because each side is often able to exercise some degree of influence, government is the institution within which bargaining and compromise occur among the competing interests.

It has been our position throughout this book that the issues facing government are a complex mix of these two kinds of situations: collective goods, in which everyone benefits (or at least no one is harmed), and competing interests, in which someone is going to be coerced, and government decides who and how much.

The two differing philosophies about government led to different prescriptions for governmental structure. The municipal reformers of the progressive era, who tended to see government as a mechanism for the rational search for the common good, advocated a set of reforms they thought would eliminate the conflict and discord that characterized urban (and especially ethnic machine) politics. These reforms included a strong chief executive, preferably a professional city manager or, if this was impossible, a strong mayor. In either case, city departments were to be organized hierarchically under the chief executive, and he or she was to have appointment power of all municipal administrators. The reforms also included at-large districts for city council elections, nonpartisan elections, and strong civil service protection for municipal employees.

Recent quantitative studies by political scientists suggest that reformers' proposals that embodied a middle-class ethic about the operation of government had their desired effects. In reformed cities, taxing and spending decisions are less responsive to demands stemming from social cleavages. Moreover, reformed structures tend to disadvantage minorities, both because they lessen their chances of election to the city council and because they reduce governmental responsiveness to their demands.

Reformed structures probably operate best in homogeneous communities with few enduring social cleavages; unreformed structures are probably most effective in large, heterogeneous cities where diverse interests must be represented and compromised.

PART IV

Urban Policymaking
in a Federal System

Local governments interact with citizens on a day-to-day basis far more frequently than do state governments or the national government. They must, because in the federal system they have been assigned the function of delivering services and, since the 1930s, implementing national urban policies. National policies have replaced, completely or in part, the traditional local role in the areas of social services, housing, and tranportation. Emerging relations among local, state, and federal governments have reflected a tension between the increasingly national scope of urban problems and the necessity of maintaining local flexibility.

Local governments nevertheless have the responsibility of raising much of the money that finances service delivery, so revenue considerations are never far from the minds of local public officials. Moreover, local governments bear the primary responsibility for regulating the use of land in this country. Little land-use planning and regulation take place at the state or federal level. Finally, local governments must staff and supervise the service delivery organizations that provide all essential urban services: police, fire, education, public sanitation, streets.

In this section we study the complex mix of responsibilities that characterizes the formation and implementation of urban policies: financing activities, implementing federal domestic policies, delivering public services, and regulating land use.

CHAPTER 11

Urban Public
Finance I:
Raising Revenue

At midnight on Friday, December 15, 1978, Cleveland became the first United States city to default on its loans since the Great Depression. Mayor Dennis Kucinich stormed out of an emergency city council meeting that night, a meeting in which the city council rejected the mayor's last-minute plan to save the city from default, predicting an "urban apocalypse." He said that the rejection of his plan meant that Clevelanders faced "six months of chaos because of one night of shame," and declared that he would be forced to cut services in half.[1] Because of the default, Cleveland was unable to borrow needed money for almost two years.

Three years before Cleveland's slide into bankruptcy, New York City teetered on the brink of a catastrophic bankruptcy and was pulled back only by massive state and federal loan guarantees. On October 19, 1979, Wayne County, Michigan, third most populous county in the nation, became the first county in the country since the 1930s to be unable to meet its payroll.

[1] William Griffin, "Cleveland City Services to Be Cut, Kucinich Says," *Chicago Tribune,* December 17, 1978.

Chicagoans read with some sense of smugness of the happenings in New York and Cleveland; certainly, they thought, it couldn't happen here. For years Chicago had enjoyed the reputation of financial stability. Its credit ratings were excellent (governments, like individuals, borrow money, and their abilities to borrow depend on their credit ratings). Then, in November 1979, the Chicago School District failed to meet its payroll, and teachers, administrators, and other school district workers went home without their paychecks.

In this chapter we will examine the problems of financing urban governments. How do local governments raise the money they spend? How do they spend the money they raise? Why do some cities spend more than others? Lurking behind these innocent-sounding questions, like Banquo's ghost in *Macbeth,* is the specter of default. Although nothing political leaders do can make the financial problems of their cities disappear, their political and managerial abilities can affect the fiscal stability of the cities they govern. The financial decisions they make also affect the distribution of public resources. Hence, city finances have both an economic and a political component.

Fiscal Stress

During the 1970s, for the first time since the Depression, many local governments began to experience severe financial strain. Some, such as Cleveland and Wayne County and the Chicago School District, defaulted on their obligations. Others made deep service cuts, not just eliminating fat but, as one mayor said, cutting to the marrow. Still others, such as New York, resorted to fiscal gimmicks and financial chicanery to balance budgets on paper, hoping that something—anything—would change and solve the problem.

It is easy to blame political leaders for the financial crises that many cities experienced in the 1970s, and, indeed, in some cases leaders did act irresponsibly. But in many other cases mayors found themselves forced to deal with declining resources during a period of rapid inflation and substantial increases in demand for vital services. The roots of the urban fiscal crisis include the changes in the structure of the American economy discussed in chapter 4, especially the movement of industry, jobs, and people to the suburbs and to the Sunbelt; increases in the concentration of the poor in center cities; increases in demands of municipal workers; and inflation. Because these changes do not affect cities equally, not all cities are experiencing severe financial strain. The urban fiscal crisis is concentrated in the older center cities of the Northeast and Midwest; many smaller cities and some larger ones are experiencing few financial difficulties. Although Buffalo,

Cleveland, and Philadelphia are experiencing severe financial stress, Phoenix, San Diego, and Nashville are on a much sounder footing.

Several urbanists have used various criteria to classify the degree of *fiscal strain* experienced by cities. One of the most comprehensive studies compared *social* needs, based on the social and economic status of resident population; *economic* needs, based on characteristics of local businesses; and *fiscal* needs, based on the tax and expenditure characteristics of local governments.[2] Table 11.1 reproduces that study. Need scores range from 0 (least need) to 100 (most need).

Table 11.1. Social, economic, and fiscal need for forty-five cities

City	Social Need		Economic Need		Fiscal Need	
	Score	Rank	Score	Rank	Score	Rank
Northeast						
Albany	n.a.	...	59	21	28	28
Boston	45	15	74	8	72	2
Buffalo	61	6	77	5	44	13
Jersey City	48	13	78	3	47	8
Newark	100	1	84	1	65	4
New York	41	21	80	2	67	3
Patterson	n.a.	...	72	9	45	.12
Philadelphia	49	12	70	12	53	6
Pittsburgh	43	20	71	10	37	18
Rochester	44	19	70	11	36	19
Midwest						
Akron	37	25	64	17	27	29
Chicago	46	16	76	6	n.a.	...
Cincinnati	45	17	65	16	44	14
Cleveland	67	2	78	4	42	16
Columbus	34	26	51	28	28	26
Detroit	62	4	66	15	46	9

(continued)

[2] Peggy L. Cuciti, *City Need and the Responsiveness of Federal Grant Programs,* report prepared for the Subcommittee on the City, Committee on Banking, Finance, and Urban Affairs, U.S. House of Representatives, 95th Congress (Washington, D.C.: U.S. Government Printing Office, 1978). This study is fully discussed in George F. Break, *Financing Government in a Federal System* (Washington, D.C.: Brookings Institution, 1980), pp. 193–97. Other studies of urban fiscal stress are Richard P. Nathan and Charles Adams, "Understanding Central City Hardship," *Political Science Quarterly* 91 (Spring 1976): 47–62; David T. Stanley, "Cities in Trouble," in *Managing Fiscal Stress, ed.* Charles Levine (Chatham, N.J.: Chatham House, 1980); *The President's National Urban Policy Report,* 1980, (Washington, D.C.: U.S. Department of Housing and Urban Development), Ch. 6; Terry N. Clark, "Cities Differ—But How and Why," unpublished manuscript, University of Chicago, 1976; Roy Bahl, ed., *The Fiscal Outlook for Cities* (Syracuse, N.Y.: Syracuse University Press, 1978); Robert W. Burchell and David Listokin, *Cities Under Stress: The Fiscal Crises of Urban America* (Piscataway, N.J.: Center for Urban Policy Research, Rutgers University, 1981).

Table 11.1. (*continued*)

City	Social Need		Economic Need		Fiscal Need	
	Score	Rank	Score	Rank	Score	Rank
Midwest						
Gary	58	8	58	22	31	24
Indianapolis	21	35	37	37	22	32
Kansas City	29	30	56	24	n.a.	...
Milwaukee	37	23	64	18	n.a.	...
Minneapolis	20	37	62	20	23	31
Oklahoma City	30	29	34	39	n.a.	...
St. Louis	64	3	74	7	61	5
South						
Atlanta	47	14	45	30	n.a.	...
Baltimore	55	9	63	19	52	7
Birmingham	51	11	45	31	46	10
Dallas	11	39	35	38	n.a.	...
El Paso	n.a.	...	30	41	34	21
Houston	21	34	26	43	n.a.	...
Louisville	45	18	51	27	35	20
Miami	60	7	42	34	31	23
New Orleans	61	5	53	26	45	11
Norfolk	30	28	40	36	44	15
Tampa	51	10	29	42	29	25
Washington	n.a.	...	54	25	84	1
West						
Anaheim	n.a.	...	31	40	10	38
Denver	20	36	41	35	33	22
Los Angeles	27	31	57	23	18	34
Phoenix	24	32	16	45	18	33
Sacramento	40	22	43	33	24	30
San Bernadino	n.a.	...	49	29	28	27
San Diego	30	27	43	32	17	35
San Jose	37	24	24	44	12	37
San Francisco	22	33	68	13	39	17
Seattle	16	38	66	14	13	36

Source: Reprinted from Peggy L. Cuciti, *City Need and the Responsiveness of Federal Grants Programs,* report prepared for the Subcommittee on the City, Committee on Banking, Finance, and Urban Affairs, U.S. House of Representatives, 95th Congress, 1978

Two things are noteworthy in this study. First, there is a definite regional concentration of the need scores on all three dimensions. The northeastern cities tend to score high on all three dimensions, the western cities low. Second, there are very few cities that are in desperate situations on all three dimensions. Only Newark and St. Louis score in the top ten cities on all three rankings. A number of cities, however, score in the top ten on two dimensions: Boston, New York, and Jersey City are in both fiscal and economic need. Buffalo and Cleveland were ranked high in economic and social need, but this is a particularly unstable category. Urban fiscal systems cannot long remain sound when the economy and social structure have gone sour; Cleveland's relative fiscal soundness rating did not long outlast the study.

Local Government Revenue

The fiscal health of local governments is intertwined with the state of their economies and social structures. This is so because governments extract a large proportion of the resources they consume in providing public services from the residences and businesses within their jurisdictions. If the economy of a city is impoverished, so will its fiscal system be.

Governments get the money they spend in four ways: taxation, borrowing, charges for services, and intergovernment transfer payments (transfers of revenue from one level of government to another). The mix of revenue-raising vehicles varies considerably by level of government, each level tending to specialize in characteristic revenue-raising vehicles. This can be seen most clearly in the case of taxation. Local governments rely heavily on the property tax to support their activities. In 1978, 80 percent of all local government tax revenue was generated by the property tax. State governments, once also heavily reliant on the property tax, have turned to sales and income taxes as primary revenue-generating devices. In 1978, 48 percent of state taxes came from general and selective sales taxes; another 26 percent came from income taxes. Eighty-eight percent of the federal government's revenue comes from individual and corporate income taxes, and payroll taxes (which fund Social Security) collected from employees and employers. The tendencies of the federal government to rely on income and payroll taxes, state governments on sales (and, to a lesser extent, income) taxes, and local governments on property taxes is called *tax specialization*.[3]

A second way governments raise money is through borrowing. Governments issue *bonds,* which promise to repay the purchaser the face value of the bond, plus interest. Most borrowing by local governments is for capital improvements, such as roads, schools, and fire stations.

A third way that governments raise money is via *service charges.* Local governments are particularly reliant on this nontax revenue source, charging

[3] U.S. Advisory Commission on Intergovernmental Relations, *Significant Features of Fiscal Federalism, 1978-79 Edition* (Washington, D.C.: U.S. Government Printing Office, 1979). See Break, *Financing Government*, and James A. Maxwell and Richard Aronson, *Financing State and Local Government,* 3rd ed. (Washington, D.C.: Brookings Institution, 1977), for good discussions of financing state and local governments.

for water, sewer service, city inspections, licenses and permits, and other city services.

Finally, both state and local governments rely on governmental *transfer payments* from higher levels of government. States receive federal grants for fairly specific purposes. For example, the federal government pays a certain proportion of state welfare expenses, and that amount is determined on the basis of the number of welfare recipients in the state.

State governments also help to fund local programs. They make *grants* for specific purposes (or tie transfer payments to the performance of certain functions), such as special education for the handicapped. State governments also *share taxes* with localities, by collecting taxes in the jurisdiction and sending back a proportion to the jurisdiction. (Such shared taxes are sometimes called *pass-throughs,* because the collecting jurisdiction just passes the funds through to the receiving jurisdiction.) State governments often share sales taxes and state income taxes with their local governments, and there are generally no restrictions concerning how the local government spends the shared funds. The state also shares some taxes and restricts the use of the revenue to specific purposes, a practice called *earmarking.* State motor fuels taxes are often shared with municipalities, with the provision that the proceeds be used for road construction, for example.

The federal government has become increasingly important in the revenue considerations of both state and local governments. Few areas of state and local government activity are not touched by federal action, either by grants or by requirements that imply expenditures by state and local governments (or, most commonly, by both).

Sources of City Revenue

Revenue diversity: The case of Chicago

The complex system of raising revenue means that the revenue sources of local governments are quite diverse. Figure 11.1 gives the revenue sources for Chicago, exclusive of most federal grants.[4] The figures for Chicago reflect local customs and political conditions, of course, but they are probably fairly representative of the revenue structures of America's larger cities. The tax sources include both the locally imposed taxes (the property tax, the utilities taxes, and various miscellaneous taxes such as cigarette taxes, hotel occupancy tax, and taxes on such transactions as the recording of deeds) and state pass-through taxes from the sales tax and state income tax. In addition,

---

[4] Only general revenue is presented. Categorical, block, and project grants from the federal government are dealt with in a separate process, and therefore do not show up in the regular budget/revenue figures. See chapter 13 for a discussion of these federal grants.

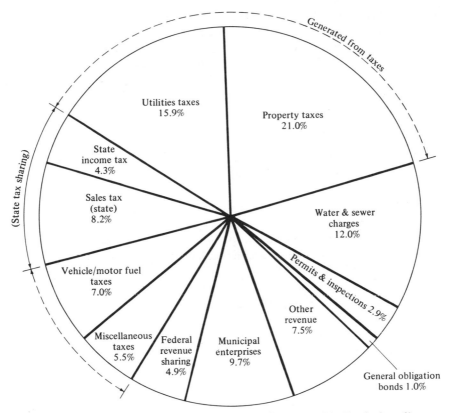

Figure 11.1. Sources of revenue, City of Chicago, 1980. Excludes all grants from the federal government for specific purposes (both categorical and block grants).

Source: Constructed by the author from figures in *The Annual Appropriations Ordinance of the City of Chicago for the Year 1980,* December 12, 1979.

the state shares taxes from motor fuels and vehicle taxes, which are earmarked for the repair and maintenance of streets and highways.

The city also receives revenue from water and sewer charges, and from issuing building permits and conducting for-fee inspections. Municipal enterprises such as O'Hare Airport and the Calumet Skyway Bridge yield substantial revenues, but most of the revenues are earmarked for those projects. During 1980 Chicago anticipated issuing only $11 million of general obligation bonds, but the year before issued over $31 million. Because revenue from such bonds goes primarily for capital projects, such as new libraries or fire stations, the number of bonds issued depends on the need for capital improvements as well as the state of the bond market and the city's credit. The size of the issue will thus vary considerably from year to year. Such sources as reimbursements from other governments, the independent school district, fines and forfeitures, and sales of city properties accounted for some of Chicago's revenue in 1980. Federal revenue sharing accounted for almost 5 percent of the money budgeted for 1980, but other federal grants, budgeted separately, funded many other activities.

Intergovernmental aid

During the fiscal year 1979, municipalities in the United States received $80.1 billion from all sources of revenue. Total revenues had grown steadily over the previous ten years, as figure 11.2 attests. That figure breaks down total revenue (except borrowing) into the four major sources we have discussed (property taxes, nonproperty taxes, intergovernmental revenue, and charges and miscellaneous). Although each source has grown, the dramatic increase has taken place in the dependence of municipalities on intergovernmental aid. In 1979 almost 40 percent of the total revenue of municipalities came from intergovernmental sources, with about 15 percent coming from federal grants and 22 percent from state grants and tax sharing. Property tax revenues have grown in dollar amount over the last decade, but they provide a smaller proportion of total revenues today than before. In fiscal year 1979, property taxes provided only about 23 percent of total local revenue, down from 34.5 percent in 1969, even though the property tax was the primary source of locally generated revenue. Note the sharp drop in property tax revenue in 1979, probably caused by the property tax limitation measures in vogue that year.

The increasing reliance on intergovernmental fiscal arrangements implies (1) a *centralization* of the revenue-raising function and (2) a *separation* of the responsibility of raising revenue from the authority to spend it. These changes have important political consequences, as we shall see.

There is great variation among cities in their reliance on the various sources of revenue. Table 11.2 presents the percentage of general city revenue derived from intergovernmental aid for selected cities in fiscal year 1978. Although many believe that aging northern cities have become heavily reliant on grants from the federal government to support their activities, table 11.2 indicates that this is not necessarily so. The Sunbelt cities of Houston and Dallas receive higher proportions of their revenues from the federal government than does New York City. Chicago and Detroit are less dependent on federal aid than El Paso and Corpus Christi.

It is true, however, that many northern cities have become far more reliant than other cities on state aid as a source of revenue. In 1978, 38.5 percent of New York City revenue came from New York State; Dallas got but 1.3 percent from Texas. Detroit received 24.2 percent of its money from

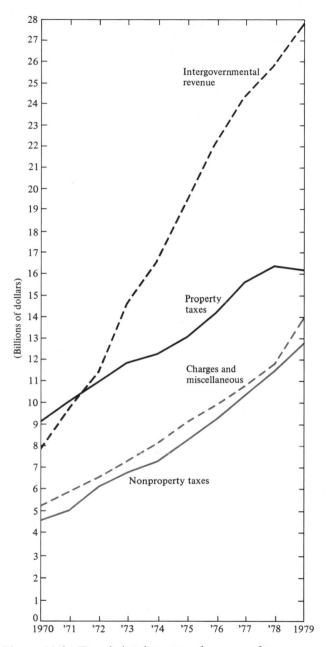

Figure 11.2. Trends in city general revenue from major sources, 1970–79.

Source: City Government Finances in 1978–79 (Washington, D.C.: U.S. Bureau of the Census, 1980), Figure 1.

Table 11.2. Percent of general city revenue derived from intergovernmental aid, 1978, selected cities

	Total intergovernmental	From state governments	From federal government
New York			
New York City	46.3%	38.5%	7.8%
New Rochelle	25.0	16.3	8.7
Rochester	34.4	28.6	5.8
Troy	75.2	30.2	45.0
Michigan			
Detroit	47.4	24.2	23.2
Dearborn	30.4	19.2	11.2
Ann Arbor	42.6	20.0	22.6
Illinois			
Chicago	40.8	13.4	27.4
Evanston	23.1	15.6	7.5
Decatur	28.5	13.3	15.2
Texas			
Houston	15.3	2.3	13.0
Dallas	12.6	1.3	11.3
Corpus Christi	32.4	1.6	30.7
Garland	9.2	1.4	7.8
El Paso	33.9	2.7	31.2

Source: City Government Finances, 1977–78 (Washington, D.C.: U.S. Bureau of the Census, 1980).

Michigan, but Corpus Christi got only 1.6 percent from the state. Many state governments in recent years, especially in the Northeast and Midwest, have begun generous aid programs to their distressed municipalities. Sunbelt states have been less willing to share taxes with their municipalities, but the generous annexation provisions in such states as Texas and Oklahoma (see chapter 9) and the generally healthier economies of these cities have meant that there is less need to do so.

The property tax

The property tax, the mainstay of local governments, is undoubtedly the most controversial of the taxes that governments levy. The controversy stems from the very nature of the tax, as well as the way it is administered in many jurisdictions, and has erupted into "taxpayer revolts" in California, Massachusetts, and other states. In many jurisdictions property tax limitation provisions have been enacted.

The types of property subject to tax and the rates at which they are taxed vary a great deal among different states and jurisdictions. Unlike sales and income taxes, property taxes are levied on estimated values, not actual transactions. A government official must estimate the value of property, an estimate that is termed the *assessed valuation*. The assessed valuation is supposed to be the market worth of the property. The tax is collected on the estimated value, so that local governments must employ both tax assessors (to arrive at the estimated values) and tax collectors. A property owner's tax bill is derived by multiplying the *tax rate* (a certain percentage) by the assessed value of the property.[5]

State governments have traditionally placed stringent limitations on the tax rates that local jurisdictions may impose without a vote of the citizens of the jurisdiction. What is different about the recent rash of property tax limitation proposals is that they limit the growth in assessed valuation that may be imposed. A citizen's property tax bill can get larger not only because government increases the tax rate, but also because the assessed valuation has gone up. The assessed valuation goes up when the property is appreciating in value. Because in recent years inflation in the real estate market has been greater than in other sectors of the economy, many people have seen their property tax bills go up faster than their incomes. Thus the property tax takes a greater proportion of income. Some municipalities experiencing increases in the assessed valuation of property in their jurisdictions have actually lowered the tax rate, proudly announcing this accomplishment to taxpayers. But this is small comfort to the taxpayer who sees a tax bill go up nevertheless, because the assessed valuation of the property has gone up faster than the tax rate has gone down.

Inequity. The growth in tax bills caused by growth in assessed valuation without an increase in the tax rate has led to the proposals to limit growth in assessed valuation. Several have been passed. But these provisions add an element of inequity to the property tax structure. Assessed valuations are supposed to reflect market worth, but if the growth in assessed valuation is limited, the assessed valuation can no longer represent market worth for those properties that are growing faster than the limit. The result is that properties that are rapidly growing in value will be undertaxed.

Indeed, a major source of inequity in property taxation occurs because assessed values do not equal market values. Property tax assessment is an inexact science at best; as practiced in some jurisdictions, it is neither an art nor a science. The major reason that assessed values diverge from market values is that tax assessors do not always update the estimated values for the properties in their jurisdictions. Properties do not increase (or decrease) in value

[5] Some states provide that only a proportion of the assessed valuation be subject to tax, so that the nominal tax rate may not be the real tax rate.

uniformly. If such changes are not regularly taken into account, properties that were taxed at the same real rate (the tax rate relative to market worth) five years ago will not be taxed at the same real rate today (except in the unlikely event that their market values have changed in exactly the same ways). (See Boxes 11.1 and 11.2)

Box 11.1: Property Taxes in Elmville

Inequities in property taxation occur for a number of reasons. One major reason is that assessed valuations do not reflect market values. To understand how this happens, let us take a hypothetical city: Elmville. Elmville is divided into two sections: rich and poor. In the poor section, there is no growth, or decline, in property values. In the rich section, property values are going up by 10 percent a year.

Let us take two homes in Elmville, one on Elm Street in the poor district, the other in affluent Druid Hills. The former sold in 1975 for $10,000, the latter for $100,000. Hence, we know that these were their true market values in 1975. Let us assume that the tax rate in Elmville is 0.02 (2 percent) per year. Let us further assume that there are no administrative shenanigans in the Elmville assessor's office, and the assessor reevaluates properties every five years (in 1975 and in 1980). Because the property owner's tax bill is calculated by multiplying the tax rate (.02) times the assessed valuation, in 1975 the tax bills of the two properties would be:

Elm Street property: (.02)($10,000) = $200
Druid Hills property: (.02)($100,000) = $2000

The Elm Street property's tax bill is 10 percent of the Druid Hills property tax bill, as it should be since the Elm Street property is worth one tenth the value of the Druid Hills property.

In 1978 the Elm Street property is still worth $10,000, but the Druid Hills property has appreciated 10 percent per year and is now worth $133,100. But the property tax bills are unchanged, because the assessed values are unchanged. The Druid Hills home is being undertaxed relative to the Elm Street home. The real tax rate is still 0.02 for the Elm Street home, but is $2,000/$133,000 = 0.015 for the Druid Hills home. The *assessment lag,* the period between assessments, causes inequities in the property tax structure such that properties increasing in value are undertaxed, and properties that are stable in value (or are declining) are overtaxed.

Box 11.2: Confusion and Taxation

The complex nature of property taxation invariably means that many who pay taxes do not understand exactly why they must pay. They brag to friends and neighbors about how much their houses have gone up in value, but they are not so pleased to find out that their property tax bills have gone up in proportion to the increase in the houses' selling prices.

When the Detroit tax assessor attempted to justify increases of almost 80 percent in tax bills in some neighborhoods, she commented that the only standard was selling price. "The big question—the only question—is would he [an angry taxpayer] sell his house for $62,500 [the original assessed valuation]?"

The taxpayer answered: "The question is not really how much I would sell my house for. The question is what is actually the real property value of my property. The selling price is irrelevant to property value." What the taxpayer fails to understand is that an assessment is nothing more than an estimate of what the property would sell for if it were sold.

Source: Carey English, "Complaints about new assessments deluge Detroit office," *Detroit Free Press,* February 10, 1980.

In order to correct disparities among taxing jurisdictions, many states have instituted programs to ensure that the aggregate assessments made by jurisdictions do, in fact, equal the market value in the jurisdictions. The state studies the ratio between the assessed values of properties and the selling prices of properties that have sold recently in the jurisdiction, and prepares *assessment-sales ratios* for taxing jurisdictions. If the assessing process is correct, this ratio should equal 1.0. Based on these figures, the state sets a *state equalized value* (SEV) that adjusts every property owner's bill up or down depending on whether the jurisdiction is underassessing or overassessing. This process equalizes taxing practices between municipalities, but it will not equalize treatment of different properties within a single municipality (because every owner's property is adjusted according to the SEV).

Intrajurisdictional inequity can also occur because of the difficulty of assessing some types of property. Assessing the worth of an industrial plant or a railroad or a skyscraper can be very difficult, especially if the property has not been sold recently. Some jurisdictions have purposely kept the assessments of such downtown commercial properties low in order to forestall the loss of industry and businesses to suburbs or other regions.

A final source of intrajurisdictional inequity is the existence of tax exemptions for many kinds of property. Property owned by governments, religious groups, and nonprofit, philanthropic, or educational organizations is exempt from property taxation. One might be sympathetic to tax exemptions for a church, but not so sympathetic about a tax exemption for an office building run for profit by a church. Nevertheless, under the laws of most states, such property does qualify for an exemption. Property tax exemptions reach truly massive proportions in many states. A Michigan report estimated recently that $29.4 billion worth of taxable property that would have yielded nearly $1.6 billion in property taxes fell under various exemptions in 1979.[6] Such exemptions can increase fiscal strain on municipalities where exempt property is concentrated.

Tax Incidence. The *incidence* of a tax is on whom the burden of the tax falls in the final analysis. Many taxes are levied on people or businesses who are able to pass the burden along. A property tax levied on the owner of an apartment complex is generally passed along to the tenants. In this case the incidence of the tax falls on the renter, not the landlord or landlady.

A major issue in the study of tax incidence is the degree to which a tax is progressive, regressive, or proportional. A *progressive* tax is one whose real tax rate increases as the income of the taxpayer increases, so that higher-income taxpayers pay higher percentages of income (not just greater dollar amounts) in taxes than lower-income taxpayers. A *regressive* tax is one whose real tax rate increases as the income of the taxpayer decreases. A *proportional* tax has a constant tax rate for all income classes.

Traditionally, it was thought that the property tax is regressive in its incidence because low-income families pay a higher proportion of their incomes for housing than do middle- or high-income families. Because the property tax rate is constant for all values of property, the poor end up paying this rate on a higher proportion of their income. Consequently, the property tax would be regressive relative to income.

Changes in the housing market, changes in state tax laws, and recent economic analysis have brought this view into question. Middle-income people seem to be increasing their income share going toward housing, because housing is seen by many as both a home and an investment. This has narrowed the gap between the poor and the better off in the proportion of income spent for housing. Moreover, many states have begun to give tax breaks to the poor and the elderly, in the form of homestead exemptions from the property tax which reduce taxes for poor and elderly homeowners, and *circuit breakers,* which grant income tax relief to taxpayers whose property tax exceeds a certain proportion of income. Finally, recent

---

[6] *State of Michigan, Tax Expenditure Report of the Governor, 1980* (Lansing, Mich.: Office of Management and Budget, 1980). Exempt organizations sometimes pay in lieu taxes to help compensate for the services they consume, but in lieu taxes never yield as much as the true tax rate.

economic analysis brings into question whether the property tax was ever as regressive as the older view suggested.[7] Those changes that have tended to make the incidence of the property tax proportional are somewhat offset by assessment practices, which add an element of regressivity to the property tax structure. At present, however, the prevailing academic wisdom is that the property tax is neither regressive nor progressive, but is approximately proportional at all levels of income.

Tax Delinquency. An increasingly severe problem in many urban areas is property tax delinquency, in which owners default on the taxes due on their property. This default robs the city treasury of needed tax dollars and leaves the city as a major landowner as it takes title to delinquent parcels. Disposing of property thus acquired can become a major undertaking, and often results in property's remaining unproductive while the city follows legal procedures for acquiring private property.

Robert Lake, of the Center for Urban Policy Research at Rutgers University, has completed a thorough study of the factors leading to delinquency. Lake reports that the average annual uncollected property tax for the period 1970–74 in the forty-eight largest cities varied from 14.8 percent in Chicago to almost nothing in Birmingham, Alabama. He found the following factors to be associated with delinquency: large populations, rapid increases in rents, high vacancy rates, and low birth rates. Lake comments that delinquency "tends to be highest in large cities with high vacancy rates, where there is a withdrawal of low value units from the occupied housing market, and with a lack of young families in the childbearing years who might sustain a viable level of demand for housing."[8] These are factors associated with urban *disinvestment*. Tax delinquency is most problematic where owners can no longer get satisfactory rates of return on their investments. But Lake's data also suggest that management and governmental factors are at work, because cities in equally dire economic straits have very different delinquency rates. The Frostbelt cities of Newark, New Jersey, and Chicago have high rates of delinquency, but so does the booming Sunbelt city of Houston (9.4 percent). Detroit collects all but 2.5 percent of its real estate taxes, Philadelphia all but 3.4 percent.

Lake also conducted a sample survey of property owners in Pittsburgh. He found that tax delinquency was related to the owner's decision to abandon the building's title to the city, and that both were related to the quality of the building and its vacancy rate (which, of course, indicates the building's

[7] See Henry Aaron, *Who Pays the Property Tax?* (Washington, D.C.: Brookings Institution, 1975).

[8] Robert W. Lake, *Real Estate Tax Delinquency: Private Disinvestment and Public Response* (New Brunswick, N.J.: Center for Urban Policy Research, 1979), p. 72. Interestingly, Lake found no association between tax rates and delinquency.

profitability). Landlords were more likely to relinquish title to their property than were owner-occupants. Because of the intimate relationship between profitability and tax delinquency, Lake notes, the city "can expect to obtain the worst of its housing stock through tax sale and acquisition."[9]

Tax delinquency is thus both an indicator of urban decay and a cause of revenue problems for cities. It also means that more property will fall into the hands of city government, causing administrative headaches in managing and disposing of the property, a task few municipalities are equipped to handle.

Tax Expenditures for Economic Growth. One increasingly large expenditure of cities comes in the form of property tax abatements for commercial and industrial firms that will locate a new facility in the city or refurbish an old one. City officials have become so concerned with rebuilding the economic bases of their cities that they have begun to compete with one another for needed private investment. By reducing the property tax bills of firms, officials hope to attract needed additions to the tax base. Most studies on the subject indicate that taxes are not a major reason that firms relocate. Even so, if two cities are otherwise equally attractive, a firm will locate in the one offering the tax break. So once tax abatements are offered by one city, they tend to spread to others.[10]

The effect of such *tax expenditures,* or expenditures accomplished by reducing taxes rather than allocating money raised from taxes, will be to increase the local tax burden on residences and existing business enterprises not receiving abatement. And if all cities offer tax abatement programs to attract industry, the net result will be nonexistent. No industry will be attracted to a locality by a program.

Cities then, are caught in a severe bind. Not having programs to attract industry means that a city will not be competitive with those that do, yet having such programs will not guarantee success. If tax abatements are granted to firms that would have located in the city anyway, the result is to impose heavier tax burdens on residences and existing firms, increasing the probability that they will relocate elsewhere.

Borrowing

There are two kinds of local government budgets: the *operating* budget, for on-going expenses such as personnel and maintenance, and the *capital* budget, for facilities whose expected life is relatively long—highways, police stations, sewerage systems, for example. Cities are authorized to borrow

---

[9] Ibid., p. 174.

[10] For a review of the existing literature, see Lynn W. Bachelor, "Urban Economic Development: Issues and Policies," *Urban Affairs Quarterly* 16 (December 1981), pp. 239–46.

Many cities have granted property tax reductions or abatements to businesses and industries to attract development. Detroit city councilman Kenneth Cockrel displays his displeasure at a proposal for a tax reduction for a developer.

Source: Detroit Free Press, June 5, 1981.

only to fund the capital budget and to meet short-term operating obligations. They are not authorized to borrow to fund the operating budget—only the federal government can do that.

Local governments borrow by issuing bonds. Bonds are promises to repay loans, with interest, within a specified time span. Bonds are bought and sold in the bond market, so that the ability of local governments to borrow money is conditional on investors' evaluations of the future financial stability of the government. Although Cleveland was in technical default of its bond obligations in late 1978, no city has fully defaulted on its bonds since the 1930s.

Cities have defaulted on their bonds in times past, however, and investors in the bonds lost money. During the depression of 1873, as many as 20 percent of local governments defaulted, leading to state-imposed limits on the amount by which municipalities can go into debt, usually in the form of a debt-to-assessed-valuation ratio.[11] These limitations did not prevent local debt from increasing, however, and by 1978 municipalities in the United States had over $78 billion of debt outstanding. The typical municipality has an outstanding bonded debt approximately equal to its yearly expenditures.[12]

Long-Term Borrowing. Local governments issue bonds primarily to finance capital expenditures. Such debt is termed *long term,* because payment to creditors is stretched out over a number of years. Most of this debt is in the form of *general obligation bonds,* which puts the "full faith and credit" of the municipality behind the bonds. This means, practically, that if the municipality goes bankrupt the obligations to the bondholders will be satisfied first. To circumvent state limitations on borrowing, however, many cities have issued *nonguaranteed bonds.* Because state limits on municipal borrowing vary considerably from state to state, the amount of nonguaranteed bonded debt varies from city to city. Los Angeles, for example, had over $2.7 million in debt outstanding, and all but $122,000 of it was nonguaranteed. Over half of Houston's almost $1 billion of debt is nonguaranteed. On the other hand, less than 14 percent of New York City's debt is of the nonguaranteed variety. Nationwide, 45.5 percent of the long-term debt of municipalities is nonguaranteed. The effect of this massive issuance of nonguaranteed debt is to vitiate the debt limitations established in times past by state governments. This is often accomplished with the complicity of state government officials who do not wish to initiate the necessary state constitutional change in the debt limits (state officials also wish to keep the revenue issue off the public agenda).

A broader point ought to be made here. Although Dillon's Rule operates legally to constrain municipal policy initiatives, in practice local and state officials often act to allow more local discretion than a strict reading of the law would suggest. This has obviously occurred in the case of municipal borrowing. Between 1977 and 1978, long-term debt outstanding for municipalities increased 9.8 percent, while revenues from all sources increased only 8.6 per-

---

[11] James A. Maxwell and Richard Aronson, *Financing State and Local Governments,* 3rd ed., p. 190.
[12] *City Government Finances in 1977–78* (Washington, D.C.: U.S. Bureau of the Census, 1980).

cent (and local tax revenues increased only 6.8 percent). Municipalities are often unwilling to increase taxes, but they seem far less reluctant to increase debt.

Most nonguaranteed debt is in the form of revenue bonds. *Revenue* bonds are bonds that pledge the revenue from the earnings of a specific enterprise funded by the bonds toward the repayment of the principal and interest of the bonds. Because general revenues are not involved, the municipality need not pledge its "full faith and credit" toward repaying them, and therefore the bonds do not fall under state-imposed debt limitations. Revenue bonds have been used recently to make loans to private industry to finance construction costs for new facilities. City officials have justified such loans (at bargain rates) on the grounds that the increased jobs and tax revenues from the project provide public benefits. Nevertheless, such uses have been criticized as "giveaways" to private industry.

Short-Term Borrowing. Because property tax bills come due once a year, local government income is not synchronized with the necessity to meet payrolls and other expenditures. At some times local governments have an embarrassment of riches; at others they cannot meet payrolls even though plenty of money will be forthcoming shortly. This situation leads to special relationships with local banks. Local governments deposit large amounts of money with banks at tax time, often in non-interest-bearing accounts. Clearly the favored banks stand to make considerable money by investing these funds even for short periods.

When the accounts are depleted, local governments must turn to lenders to finance their operations for the remainder of the fiscal year. This is termed *short-term* borrowing. Local governments' *notes* promise repayment for these loans, and these notes go by a variety of names: *tax anticipation notes,* which pledge future taxes toward repayment; *revenue anticipation notes,* pledging unspecified future revenues; and *bond anticipation notes,* which pledge revenues from future bond issues. (These notes are known as TANs, RANs, and BANs, respectively.) Purchasers of such notes are promised repayment plus interest.

Tax-Exempt Bond Market. Unlike bonds issued by private corporations, the federal government does not tax the interest on state and local bonds through the income tax. This provision was included when Congress passed the original act taxing individual income in 1913 and has never been removed. Because of this exemption, state and local governments can sell their bonds at interest rates considerably below the rate prevailing for taxable bonds. Because investors know that they will not be taxed on the interest income from state and local bonds, they will accept lower interest. The tax exemption amounts to a subsidy of state and local bonding capacity by the federal government, thus providing an incentive for state and local governments to borrow.

Changes in the federal tax laws passed by Congress at the urging of the Reagan administration in 1981 have had the effect of making the municipal bond market less attractive to the high-income investor traditionally purchasing such bonds. Lowered tax rates on high incomes and the creation of new tax shelters mean that the tax shelters offered by the municipal bond market are less useful to the high-income investor. Consequently there is less money flowing to the municipal bond market, and therefore less money available for borrowing by cities.

Banks and insurance companies, like individuals, can lower their tax liabilities by purchasing municipal bonds. In 1973, over 50 percent of tax-exempt securities were held by commercial banks, and insurance companies held another 18 percent. After 1973, however, banks bought fewer municipal bonds, although they still served as *underwriters,* or brokers, for the bond issues. Richard Morris, a critic of the relationship between banks and city governments, has termed the decision of banks to withdraw from the municipal bond markets a "bank boycott" against the cities.

> No longer were cities able to borrow directly from local banks; banks were no longer buying city notes and bonds as part of their commitment to their home city. Rather banks had abandoned the city. They become headquarters-less, international institutions without roots and without loyalty.[13]

Yet Morris himself notes that banks had found other ways to shield their income from taxes and that corporate bonds had become relatively more profitable. A more likely explanation than a "bank boycott" is that the banks' changing investment patterns involved standard investment decisions—albeit decisions with important implications for the structure of the municipal bond market.

The ability of municipalities to issue bonds, and the interest rates they will have to pay in order to market the bonds, are strongly affected by ratings issued by bond-rating firms. The ratings issued by these New York firms are supposed to indicate the ability of cities to meet the interest and principal payments on their bond obligations, and serve as a signal of investment desirability to potential investors. The lower the bond rating the more speculative the investment, and the higher the interest rate that the city will have to pay in order to market its bonds.

Only two firms issue tax-exempt bond ratings: Moody's Investors Service and Standard & Poor's Corporation. The existence of only two firms in the bond-rating "market" means that there is a "shared monopoly" of ratings

---

[13] Richard S. Morris, *Bum Rap on America's Cities: The Real Causes of Urban Decay* (Englewood Cliffs, N.J.: Prentice-Hall, 1980), p. 56.

that have important consequences for cities and the taxpayers who must pay for increases in interest rates that are dictated by bond ratings. Especially crucial is the decision of the two rating firms to rate bonds as "below investment grade." If the ranking is low enough, a local government may be completely denied access to credit markets, and a financial crisis will be precipitated.

Such a downgrading of rating by Moody's for tax anticipation notes issued by the Chicago Board of Education in November, 1979, precluded the sale of the notes, and led directly to the financial crisis experienced by the board. Although the Chicago school board case indicates the power of the rating services, it is also true the board richly deserved the lower rating by engaging in poor financial practices. The board was "rolling" its notes, a practice in which a government uses the money from one bond or note sale to pay off bonds or notes *maturing,* or coming due. In other words, debt is used to finance debt, a situation analogous to a consumer's taking out a loan supposedly to consolidate debts. Moreover, the board was using money deposited in a "sinking" (or reserve) fund earmarked to repay bonds for operating expenses, another accounting practice that is indicative of impending financial doom.[14]

User fees

Many of the services provided by municipal government can be priced directly. Municipal water departments commonly charge fees based on the amount of water consumed rather than drawing on tax revenues to support their operations. Some economists have urged expanding this practice to many other urban public services.[15] Mushkin and Vehorn argue that setting a price for public services would guide the city in its production of services, because the city could produce just enough of the service to equal the amount for which citizen-consumers were willing to pay.[16] This is exactly the manner in which municipal water departments operate; indeed, this is how most private firms operate. User fees implement the *benefit principle* that those who benefit from government services ought to pay for the services—a principle that economists tend to favor.

In the case of many services, however, user fees are not reasonable. The primary reason is that the user and the beneficiary of the service are not the same, as would be the case when the police arrest a robber, for example. In

[14] The information on the Chicago Board of Education case comes from "The 1979 Chicago Board of Education Financial Crisis—A Continental Bank Review," Continental Illinois National Bank and Trust Company of Chicago, April 26, 1980.

[15] See Selma J. Mushkin, ed., *Public Prices for Public Products* (Washington, D.C.: Brookings Institution, 1972).

[16] See Selma J. Mushkin and Charles L. Vehorn, "User Fees and Charges," *Governmental Finance* (November 1977): 42–48.

other cases, user fees may be unfair. If people had to pay for fire services, the poor, living as they do in older, substandard dwellings not constructed by modern methods, would pay far more than the better off living in safer homes.

Government tends to take over the responsibility for providing services when the private market has failed. Such market failure occurs when the provision of collective goods is involved. For example, intracity bus systems are usually municipally owned because fares charged do not pay for the cost of the system. Nevertheless, all citizens benefit from a public transportation system because of the less crowded streets and reduced pollution that result from having fewer automobiles downtown. In such cases user fees are not going to work, or will pay only part of the cost of the service.

Many services, however, have been provided only after a political struggle. These services were adopted at the insistence of groups lodged within isolated policy systems; the costs of such services are passed on to the taxpayer at large. Such policy solutions may have been adopted in times past, when city budgets were less strained. The issue of whether to charge a user fee for a service can serve as a reevaluation of whether the service should be paid for by beneficiaries alone, or whether the public interest requires a continuation of a subsidy from general tax revenues in light of the fiscal strain experienced by many cities.

The Politics of Municipal Revenue

In the private sector, a consumer knows exactly what a desired item costs. He or she demands an item only if it can be paid for. When the citizen turns to government, however, there is no set price for service or commodities. This does not mean that there is no cost for the public service, only that the cost is covered through taxes (and other public sector revenue-raising techniques) rather than prices for the service. A citizen's taxes go to pay for police protection, fire protection, and street repair, but he or she does not pay for each call to the police department or fire department.

There is nothing inconsistent about wanting lower taxes and more service (so long as you are willing to cut the service someone else wants). Indeed, because of the organization of people into interest groups and issue publics, the costs a citizen is willing to impose on the general public by demanding government action does not necessarily show up on his or her tax bill. What any group demanding government action is doing, in effect, is trying to gain benefits from government within its limited policy system, and transferring the costs onto the general tax system (which, of course, does not impose costs on all citizens equally).

Today, many local governments find their resource bases shrinking, or at least growing at a slower rate than the costs of the services they provide. This means that taxes (or other revenue sources) must be increased just to maintain existing services. Politics is fought over a shrinking pie.

This situation generates interesting politics. Government officials are faced with numerous demands for increased intervention, yet they also face citizen hostility over increased taxes. This leads to a cardinal rule among political leaders: if at all possible, *keep the revenue issue off the political agenda.* This rule applies with special force to the property tax. If citizens become conscious of tax increases, they may be mobilized against such increases and vote either against the politicians supporting tax hikes or in favor of tax limitation proposals.

The Revenue Subsystem. In his excellent book on revenue politics in Oakland, California, Arnold Meltsner describes a *revenue subsystem* complete with operating rules and different parts with different revenue interests.[17] Similar arrangements exist in most other cities. The main components of the revenue subsystem included the following:

1. *The city council.* The city council members in this at-large city were, at the time of Meltsner's study, responsive primarily to taxpayers rather than to city employees or other groups demanding increased spending. City council members needed only to be gently dissuaded by the city manager if they contemplated increases in spending.

2. *The service departments.* City service departments were not revenue conscious, and were concerned primarily with providing service. Quality service costs money, so the service departments indirectly put pressure on the revenue subsystem through their budget requests.

3. *Tax publics.* Oakland's tax policies are salient to small, attentive publics that coalesce around the taxes that concern them. There is a cigarette-tax public, a hotel-occupancy-tax public, and so forth. Lurking behind these specialized tax publics is a quiescent majority, unaware of taxes, but capable of being aroused if a tax issue becomes salient.

The primary problem for officials in Oakland and elsewhere is simply to maintain the current payroll. A declining tax base (along with inflation) creates *fiscal atrophy.*[18] Even with no new demands, many older cities like Oakland face severe fiscal problems. Officials also face considerable uncertainty in their decision-making environment. In particular, two types of uncertainty concern them: (1) the occurrence of expenditure demands that

---

[17] Arnold Meltsner, *The Politics of City Revenue* (Berkeley, Calif.: University of California Press, 1971).
[18] Ibid.

cannot be avoided and will require new sources of revenue, and (2) the threshold beyond which opposition to changes in the tax structure will emerge.[19] Obviously an increase in demand and a low tolerance for tax increases by taxpayers will cause severe problems for city officials.

Officials enmeshed in such a subsystem are likely to pursue two strategies. First, they will search everywhere for revenue sources that are not visible to the tax public—they may tax automatic amusement machines, increase service charges, increase the taxes on liquor and cigarettes, start a lottery, open gambling casinos. A tactic employed by Mayor Daley of Chicago was to assemble a complex package of revenue-raising devices in order to be able to announce a small decrease in the property tax rate. Second, local decision makers may demand that the state or the federal government increase its support for local services. In the process of searching desperately for new sources of revenue, local officials are often willing to give away decision-making authority to other units of government in order to escape the burden of raising the tax rate.

Policy Implications
of Revenue Arrangements

One of the primary driving factors for increasing governmental centralization in the United States is the desire of local officials to escape their revenue problems. Local officials often argue that their cities lack the fiscal capacity to deal with the problems and service demands facing them, and they demand that a higher level of government assume responsibility for financing some services.

Transferring a governmental function to a higher level of government removes two constraints on the growth of government activity, however. First, moving from a jurisdiction to escape high tax burdens is no longer practical for the taxpayer if the state or federal government provides the service (or the financing for it). Hence, governments lose an important constraint on the growth of taxes: the need to compete for a robust tax base by attracting and retaining jobs, industries, and residents. Although a few of America's largest cities pursue liberal policies (New York City is the outstanding example), most cities are fiscally quite conservative. The major reason is the fear that high taxes will drive the most productive businesses and citizens out of the city. Because a sizable proportion of city revenues is locally generated, the loss of citizens and businesses puts further strain on the tax base. This city officials wish to avoid.

In the second place, the institutional structure of local governments tends

[19] Ibid.

to favor the representation of taxpayer interests, especially where reformed governmental structures exist. At the state and particularly the national level, other interests tend to be more important, and these interests often wish increases in governmental spending.

Because of these factors, a change in the location of a governmental function from a lower to a higher level in the federal system tends to benefit liberals (more particularly, those wishing increases in governmental spending). The use of intergovernmental fiscal transfers increases this tendency, because such transfers separate the government responsible for raising the money from the governmental unit with the authority to spend it. (Spending someone else's money is particularly easy.)

Changing the fiscal capacity of a government to deal with a problem by moving financing to a higher level of government increases the likelihood of (but of course does not ensure) a liberal approach to the problem. Political conservatives tend to favor local control and (to use an obsolete term) states' rights. Liberals tend to favor heavier reliance on the federal government. Their reasoning may be rooted in a preference for a particular institutional structure, but it is more likely that the institutional structure they advocate facilitates their policy proposals. In general, smaller units of government tend to promote fiscal restraint and conservatism in public policies, and larger governmental units promote the increased use of government to solve social problems.

Revenues and expenditures are inextricably linked. Revenue problems and fiscal stress occur because cities feel the need to spend more money than they are receiving through taxes, intergovernmental aid, and fees. The next chapter focuses on the expenditures of local governments—why some cities spend more than they used to, and what cities spend their money for.

CHAPTER 12

Urban Public
Finance II:
City Expenditures

The other side of the urban financial equation is expenditures. The pattern of public expenditures is a guide to the priorities established by a community in past policy settlements. Expenditures measure government efforts to achieve goals, although they do not indicate the degree to which those goals are accomplished. Hence municipal budgets record, in dollar terms, the public priorities established by past political actions and present governmental attempts to maintain and improve community conditions.

In the 1978 fiscal year, American municipalities spent over $77 billion for a variety of functions. Different cities spent very different proportions of this total figure, proportions that were not related directly to city populations. To illustrate, New York City, with an estimated population of 7,297,787 in 1978, spent $12,365,256,000, or $1,694 per resident. But Houston spent only $267 per resident, and Chicago only $406. Before jumping to the conclusion that New York is a fiscal wastrel, note that New York City spends over 22 percent of its budget for education, whereas Houston and Chicago spend very little.[1] This is because public school education is handled through independent boards of education in Houston and Chicago, but in New York it is part of municipal government. There are other reasons for expenditure differences that have little to do with the financial responsibility of the city government; it is a fallacy to compare city expenditures without examining the reasons for the differences in expenditures.

Some American Cities
Spend More Than Others

There are four basic reasons for variability in expenditure patterns among cities: need, demand, resources, and functional inclusiveness. Numerous studies by political scientists, economists, and sociologists have investigated the relations between these factors and spending levels; we summarize the general findings of these studies below.[2]

Need

Some cities spend more than others because of the need to do so. The most obvious need factor is city size. All other things being equal, a large city must spend more to provide services than a small city. Some other factors associated with the need for higher spending are specific to certain services. For example, a rapidly growing city must expend more to establish its capital infrastructure, such improvements as water mains, sewer systems, streets, sidewalks, and street lighting. Such cities do not have to spend more than cities of comparable size on police or fire protection. Cities with old housing stocks must spend more on fire protection and building inspections. Density of population is associated with higher expenditures for police, fire, and sanitation.

Central cities spend more per capita than suburbs, for two basic reasons. First, the concentration of social problems that has come to be known as *the* urban problem affects core cities much more intensely than suburbs. Second, central cities must provide services for people who work or shop in the city, but who do not reside and pay property taxes there. This consumption of police protection, sanitation services, and so forth, by suburbanites has

---

[1] *City Government Finances in 1977–78* (Washington, D.C.: U.S. Bureau of the Census, 1980).

[2] An excellent review of the expenditure determinants literature is John A. Foley, *A Comparative Study of the Determinants of Public Policies: A Review of Two Decades of Multidisciplinary Quantitative Research* (Ithaca, N.Y.: Program in Urban and Regional Studies, Cornell University, 1978). Most useful of recent studies of expenditure differences is Mark Schneider and John R. Logan, "Fiscal Implications of Class Segregation," *Urban Affairs Quarterly* 17 (September 1981): 23–36.

been called *suburban exploitation.*[3] As the metropolis has become more dispersed, however, there are fewer suburbanites who make trips to the center city and more center city residents who travel to suburbs (consequently exploiting suburban services). Moreover, state and federal aid has become more targeted to central cities over the years, helping to compensate for suburban exploitation. Michigan, for example, several years ago adopted a Detroit Equity Package, designed to help pay for services and facilities that were maintained by Detroiters but used by citizens from all over the metropolis—the zoo, the art museum, the main library. Changes in aid packages, as well as changes in the dependency of suburbs on the central city as a place of employment and shopping, have all but eliminated the problem of suburban exploitation in many cities.

Demand

Citizens of some cities demand more services from their local government than others. This can occur even though such cities do not experience any greater need for service than do other cities. For example, one community may pride itself on its schools, and demand higher-quality schools than surrounding communities. Owner-occupancy is inversely related to city expenditures—the higher the proportion of homeowners in a city, the lower the city expenditures. This is probably related to the tendency of renters to demand more services than owners, because homeowners feel they must bear the brunt of the city taxes that would go to pay for expanded service.

Demands or services may not come from the citizenry at large. One interesting finding reported by Terry Clark of the University of Chicago is that the proportion of citizens of Irish stock is positively and strongly associated with city expenditures, even with other factors held constant.[4] This finding is probably related to the patronage-run city machines established and run by European immigrants, particularly the Irish. The demands involved were less for specific city services and more for city jobs—the jobs that lubricated the urban machine. Expenditures went up because of the wish by the ethnics to build larger political organizations, which necessitated more jobs and a larger local public sector. More generally, demands may not be related directly to citizens' desires for services but to the interests of elected leaders in building and maintaining electoral organizations.

In recent years, the party organization has declined as a source of political demands, and city employee organizations have increased. Although we have no hard evidence, it is likely that city expenditures will be higher where city employees are organized and bargain collectively.

---

[3] See William B. Neenan, *Political Economy of Urban Areas* (Chicago: Markham, 1972).
[4] Terry Nichols Clark, "The Irish Ethic and the Spirit of Patronage," *Ethnicity* 2 (1975): 305–59.

Resources

Some cities spend more than others because they can afford to. This is particularly true for amenities services such as recreation facilities, libraries, and parks. Studies consistently show that communities of citizens with high incomes spend more on city services than those with low-income citizens. This may reflect demand, but it also undoubtedly reflects ability to pay. Moreover, the amount of state and federal aid is associated with higher spending, again indicating that when resources are available, they will be utilized. Intergovernmental aid reduces the fiscal disparities between rich and poor communities that would result from relying solely on a local tax base.

Functional inclusiveness

Some municipalities provide a wider range of services than other cities. This does not mean that services are not delivered in the latter cities. Rather, other governmental units provide the services. As noted previously, some municipalities are responsible for education, but in other cities public schools are run by an independent board of education. The number of separate governmental functions that are performed by municipal government is known as the *functional inclusiveness,* or *functional scope,* of the government. Two students of functional inclusiveness have written that "city governments may be comprehensive organizations providing a broad range of services, or they may be very specialized organizations providing a narrow range of services."[5] Some cities perform what are called the *core functions* (police, fire, sanitation); others provide many other services, such as education, health services, hospitals, sewerage, welfare, and libraries.

There is a clear tendency for cities in the Northeast to perform more services than those in other regions (see table 12.1). Moreover, these extra functions, such as welfare and education, tend to be very expensive. Western cities in particular tend to have governments of very limited purpose. This means that cities in the Northeast are likely to have to spend more than cities in other regions of the country, because they are doing more.

The functions performed by municipalities in the Northeast are performed by a variety of governmental arrangements in other sections of the country. The functions may be performed by the state, by other established units of government such as the county, or by special districts and authorities. Whatever the arrangement, the power of municipal governments as policymaking mechanisms is more limited where functional scope is

---

[5]Thomas R. Dye and John A. Garcia, "Structure, Function, and Policy in American Cities," *Urban Affairs Quarterly* 14 (September 1978): 103. See also Roland Liebert, *Disintegration and Political Action* (New York: Academic Press, 1976).

Table 12.1. Functional inclusiveness for central cities of SMSAs

Region	Average number of functions	Percentage of Cities with Responsibility for					
		Education	Welfare	Hospitals	Housing	Libraries	Health
Northeast	10.6	73.6	64.2	43.4	81.1	83.0	86.8
South	9.6	24.4	31.4	33.7	45.3	73.3	65.1
Midwest	9.6	17.7	21.0	30.6	64.5	54.8	82.3
West	8.9	12.2	14.6	17.1	51.2	82.9	43.9

Source: Reprinted from "Structure, Function and Policy," by Thomas R. Dye and John A. Garcia, in *Urban Affairs Quarterly,* pg. 107, 1978, with permission of the publisher, Sage Publications, Beverly Hills/London.

293

narrow. Where special districts and authorities are used to deliver services, the power of the municipality is particularly circumscribed. When citizens turn to the mayor, who is generally the most visible local official, to solve their problems, they may find that he or she lacks the jurisdiction to handle the problem (see box 12.1).

Why Do Cities Spend More
Than They Used To?

Each year the budgets of most cities increase. The major cause of increases in spending is inflation. City governments find that each year the costs of labor, materials, and equipment they must use to produce public services increase. As inflation has intensified in American society, it has steadily pushed up the budgets of local governments.

Municipal governments are subject to a particularly virulent form of inflation. Governments are generally labor intensive, which means that the costs they incur in producing services are primarily labor costs. In the private goods-producing sector, increases in *productivity* can help offset increases in labor costs. When automation is increased in an automobile assembly plant, labor costs decline (and they decline faster than the increases in costs for the capital improvement, or automation would not have been profitable). This means that fewer workers can do the same job, increasing productivity per worker.

Such productivity gains cannot be made in municipal governments, because labor costs are tied to the quality of the service. If one lays off teachers, for example, and increases the size of classes taught by the remaining teachers, few would claim productivity gains. But there is a further catch. Workers in local government view their wages as tied to wages in the private goods-producing sector. Private firms can afford to pay higher wages after automation, because, at least until recently, productivity gains often outstrip cost increases. But teachers, for example, relate their salaries to those of factory workers, even though they have experienced no productivity gains, because of the nature of the "industry" in which they work. Hence, wages of municipal employees are pushed up by wage increases in the private goods-producing sector even in the absence of productivity gains. This catch is known as *Baumol's disease,* after the economist who first looked seriously at the problem.[6] All of this does not mean that productivity gains cannot be made in local government. There are many places where productivity in local government can be improved. It does mean that such productivity will be harder to achieve than in the private sector, however.

[6] William Baumol, "The Macroeconomics of Unbalanced Growth," *American Economic Review* 57 (June 1967): 415–26.

Box 12.1: Leadership and Functional Authority

During the 1960s many federal officials assumed that mayors would be in a position to provide leadership on urban problems, problems that were not adequately being addressed by the state, if only the federal government would provide the financing. During hearings of a Senate subcommittee, Senators Robert Kennedy and Abraham Ribicoff were startled when Mayor Samuel Yorty of Los Angeles testified before a U.S. Senate subcommittee that he lacked the authority to take advantage of many federal programs, because the municipality of Los Angeles performed so few of the governmental functions performed in Los Angeles.

> *Senator Kennedy:* But are you not the mayor of all the people in Los Angeles?
> *Mayor Yorty:* Of the people of the city of Los Angeles, yes.
> *Kennedy:* Then if they have a problem, do they not look to you for some leadership?
> *Yorty:* Yes. . . . But whether or not I can solve a problem may depend on my jurisdiction.
> *Senator Ribicoff:* As I listened to your testimony, Mayor Yorty, I made some notes. This morning you have really waived authority and responsibility in the following areas: schools, welfare, transportation, employment, health, and housing, which leaves you as the head of the city basically with a ceremonial function, police, and recreation.
> *Yorty:* That is right, and fire.

Source: U.S. Senate Subcommittee on Executive Reorganization, *The Federal Role in Urban Affairs* (Washington, D.C.: U.S. Government Printing Office, 1966). Quoted in Roland Liebert, *Disintegration and Political Action* (New York: Academic Press, 1976), p. 9.

A second reason for increases in local government spending is that local governments perform more functions than in the past. Some of these functions have been adopted by innovative local governments, but most have been mandated by the state or federal governments or have been adopted because of the availability of generous grants from other levels of government.

At least some new programs have been adopted by cities to meet competition from other cities. This is particularly true of economic development policies. As their tax bases have shrunk, cities have searched for policies that would encourage new private investment. In the economic malaise that has characterized the late 1970s and early 1980s, private investment has been in short supply. Cities have begun to compete in an increasingly grim game with high stakes. City leaders have prevailed on state officials to permit them to offer a wide array of incentives for attracting private firms: property tax abatements, aid in site clearance for the new facility, loans from the sale of tax-exempt bonds, and outright grants. As a city adopts a new economic development policy, leaders of other cities feel forced to do so, lest they lose their competitive advantage in the race for private development.

One City's Budget: Expenditures
in Chicago

Because states allocate local functions differently among the various units of local government, expenditure figures for all cities lumped together can be misleading. Rather than examine aggregate expenditure figures, we will examine a single city's budget. Figure 12.1 breaks down appropriations made by the city of Chicago by function. The Chicago appropriations process budgets federal grants separately, so they are excluded from the figures. The largest budget portion went for police protection, with appropriations for streets and sanitation second. Employee pensions and debt service costs were also major items of expenditure for 1980.

Figure 12.1 gives one way to cut a budget pie. But, as figure 12.2 shows, budgets may be divided according to other criteria. Budgets may be divided by major function, as in figure 12.2(a), which indicates the parts of the budget that are controllable in the appropriations process. Cities as well as other governmental entities budget money for a specified period, usually a year; the appropriations period is called a *fiscal year*. But some expenditures must be budgeted for far longer than a year. For example, principal and interest on bonds must be paid during the current budget year regardless of the preferences of city officials. The same is true for pension fund payments to retired workers. Such long-term legally binding obligations are known as *uncontrollable expenditures*, because they cannot be limited in the current budgetary year.

Figure 12.2(b) cuts the city budget by object of expenditure. As is the case for most government budgets, the major portion of expenditures goes for personnel services in salaries and fringe benefits. Moreover, much of the money appropriated for contractual services is expended on personnel. Local government is labor intensive.

Finally, figure 12.2(c) divides the city budget by fund. Most expenditures come from the corporate or general fund, which includes most tax revenues. But some revenue sources are earmarked for special purposes. Revenues from the sale of water and sewer services, for example, are earmarked for expenditure by the city departments, and motor fuels taxes are earmarked for road construction and repair. Earmarking limits the ability of city officials

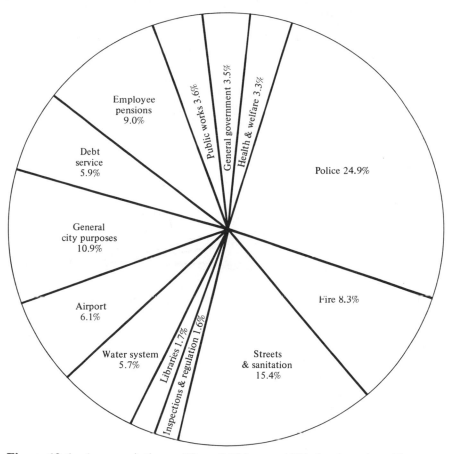

Figure 12.1. Appropriations, City of Chicago, 1980, by function. Excludes all federal categorical and block grants.

Source: Compiled by the author from figures in *The Annual Appropriations Ordinance of the City of Chicago for the Year 1980,* December 12, 1979.

to shift city revenues to areas where they think they are most needed. It limits their ability to set priorities based on current conditions. On the other hand, it also limits their ability to engage in financial shenanigans or to respond to short-lived fads (which is the rationale behind earmarking).

The Process of Public Budgeting

Public budgeting is the allocation of money to achieve public purposes. Although achieving public purposes is the result of public budgeting, it does not follow that public officials list the goals they wish to accomplish, list the

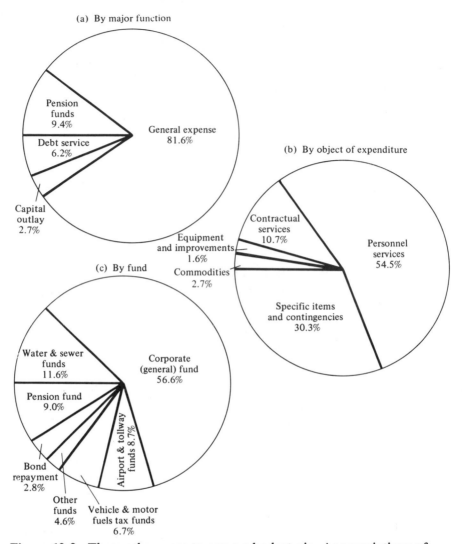

Figure 12.2. Three other ways to carve a budget pie. Appropriations of the City of Chicago, 1980.

means for accomplishing those goals, and budget accordingly. The *process* by which budgeting occurs is often quite different from the *outcome* of the budget process. Indeed, most students of government budgeting have concluded that the process tends to be heavily routinized, with few attempts to allocate funds according to community goals.

Rational budgeting

At first blush, explicitly allocating public funds according to how public activities affect community goals seems to be such a good idea that it is obviously the best way to proceed. But how would such a process work in practice? In the first place, officials would have to know exactly what the goals of government are, and the goals of government are not always clear-cut. The goals of private corporations are straightforward and easily measurable (they want to make a profit), but government's goals are not always so clear. Of course government exists to promote the common welfare, but how does one measure the common welfare? It is not possible to budget allocations to intended goals if the goals are not clear.

In the second place, even when goals are clear, the relationships between ends (goals) and means is not clear. Most people would probably say that the city police department, for example, is in the business of providing community security (perhaps measured by the crime rate—or the absence of crimes—as a baseline). Leaving aside problems of measuring community security by the crime rate (and there are many), budget officials would still have to face the problem of allocating money to police department programs in the absence of knowledge of how those programs affect the crime rate. If police officials knew just how each of their programs affected community security, and if community security were their only goal, they could allocate money among program activities to bring about the greatest degree of community security possible for the money that they had available (see box 12.2).

This approach to the problem of allocating public funds is called *rational analysis,* and public policy analysts at all levels of government have made progress in developing the tools necessary to relate public activities to community goals.[7] Public activities that are related explicitly to community goals are called *programs*. Because money is allocated according to programs rather than such standard accounting categories as salaries and supplies, such approaches to public budgeting are often called *program budgeting.* If we reexamine the various ways in which the city of Chicago's budget was broken down, we quickly see that none of the breakdowns in figure 12.2 are at all helpful in relating public activities to community goals, because none of the breakdowns relate to public goals. The breakdown in figure 12.1 is a start toward program budgeting but is far too crude to be helpful.

Rational budget analysis has been tried, in some form or another, in various governmental agencies at all levels of government. All forms involve relating budget allocations to goal accomplishment. Hence, one must both have clear measures of goals and know just how activities and programs are related to goals (that is, the ends-means relationship must be specified). This

[7] See, for example, Edith Stokey and Richard Zeckhauser, *A Primer for Policy Analysis* (New York: W. W. Norton, 1978).

Box 12.2: Rational Budget Analysis

To understand a little better the basic approach of rational budget
analysis, let us take the problem of relating community security to
two program activities: detective work and routine police patrolling.
Assume for the moment that (a) this is all the police department
does, and (b) we know exactly how each relates to community
security (measured, say, by the crime rate—or the lack of crimes—
based on some standard). Then examine the following diagram:

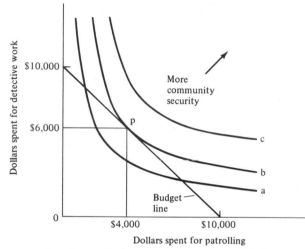

Assume that the police commissioner has $10,000 to spend be-
tween police patrolling and detective work. He wants to maximize
community security, which increases as one moves away from the

would end our problems if government pursued only a single goal, but
clearly it does not. When a government pursues multiple goals, as all but the
most single-purpose units do, the goals are likely to be *incommensurate,* or
not directly comparable. In such situations officials cannot compare benefits
accruing from expenditures aimed at one goal with benefits coming from expenditures aimed at another goal. The officials must decide which goal is
more important, and no rational budget analysis can do that. Finally, some
goals pursued by government are downright incompatible with one another.
Perhaps the most glaring example of incompatible governmental goals exists
at the federal level, where the Department of Agriculture funds tobacco subsidies and the Department of Health and Human Services funds antismoking

origin. The points on each of the curved lines represent equal amounts of community security. Because the commissioner doesn't care which activity he spends money on so long as he maximizes community security, the equal lines of community security are called *indifference curves.* What the commissioner wants to do is to move to the highest indifference curve possible; this maximizes community security. Indifference curves are concave to reflect the fact that each additional detective adds less to community security than the detective added before (and the same for the patrol units). The first detective solves the crimes easiest to solve, so the second must work harder on the crimes he or she solves, and so on.

Finally, the budget line specifies the tradeoff between patrolling and detection that the commissioner must make. He can choose, if he wishes, to spend $10,000 on detective work and nothing on patrolling. But this would be a very bad choice, because he can get more community security (move to a higher indifference curve) by spending less on detection and more on patrolling. Indeed, the best budget allocation occurs where an indifference curve is *tangent* to the budget line. This occurs at point p on indifference curve b. The commissioner cannot get to the better indifference curve c because he is constrained by the budget line. He would be foolish to drop back to indifference line a, because this implies less community security. As can be seen from the diagram, all of this implies that the commissioner should spend $6,000 for detective work and $4,000 for patrolling. This is the *optimal* budget allocation, in that it is the mix of program activities that brings about the largest impact on the agency's goal.

---

campaigns. Because of such problems, rational budgetary analysis does not work well in practice.

Budget actors

The budget process involves several different actors, each of whom often has interests different from the others. The major actors in municipal budgeting include the *chief executive* (mayor or manager), the *legislature* (the city council), the *service agencies,* such as the police and building departments, along with certain members of the *mayor's staff* who analyze the budget requests of the service agencies and provide the estimates of revenue that will be generated during the budget year. Coordination of these diverse actors can be difficult indeed, especially since budget allocation is often a *zero-sum game* in which anything won by one service agency will be a loss to the rest of the agencies.[8]

The budget process is *sequential*. One stage in the process cannot occur until all former stages are completed. Procedure differs from place to place, but at least the following must be accomplished: the agencies must forward budget requests to the chief executive; the chief executive must reconcile the requests with anticipated revenues and his or her own priorities; the chief executive must forward his or her budget to the city council, and the city council must produce a final balanced budget; and (in mayor-council cities) the mayor must approve the final budget. This process offers all sorts of places where disgruntled losers in an earlier stage of the process can act to reverse the earlier adverse decision. The ability to do this, however, is much more restricted in local governments than it is in Washington, because of the cursory treatment most city councils give to budget matters. Most councils lack the staff and the expertise to engage in budget battles with the chief executive. Hence, appealing over the head of the mayor to the city council may not be a useful strategy for an agency chief.

Budget routines

Because of ill-defined goals, lack of definitive knowledge about ends-means relationships, incommensurate and incompatible goals, and the necessity to coordinate the behaviors of many actors, rational public budgeting seldom occurs. The situation is far too complex and uncertain to rely solely on such tools, although they can be extremely effective in certain limited cases. It would be a mistake to conclude, however, that because the process of budgeting is nonrational that the results are therefore irrational. That is, the particular approach to budgeting known as rational analysis may not be particularly rational in an extremely complex and uncertain situation.

Most students of governmental budgeting have concluded that budgeting is *incremental*. Decision makers do not examine all public goals, all means to the goals, and budget accordingly; reality is simply too complex for such an evaluation. Rather they simplify budgetary complexity by adopting a set of routine operating procedures, the most important of which is to base this year's budget on last year's. John P. Crecine, in a careful study of budgeting

---

[8] The term *zero-sum game* is from the mathematical theory of games, which uses models in the form of games to explain human interaction. Chess is a zero-sum game, because every winner implies a loser; so are all sports contests. Providing collective goods, however, is what is known as a *positive-sum game*, because everyone is better off if the good is provided. Budget allocations are not invariably zero sum, because every agency can be made better off if revenues are growing faster than inflation, but in all large cities they clearly have a zero-sum character.

in three major midwestern cities, notes that mayors perceive the budget process as a continuing one. The mayor perceives

> this year's budget to be basically similar to last year's with a slight change in resources available (new revenue estimates) for dealing with a continuing set of municipal problems (police and fire protection, urban renewal, public works, transportation) augmented by a small number of partial solutions to old problems. In this context a logical way to proceed in solving the complex budgeting problem is to take last year's solution (current appropriations) and modify it in light of the *change* in available resources and the *change* in municipal problems and their available solutions, to obtain this year's solution. Very small portions of the budget are reconsidered from year to year and consequently, once an item is in the budget, its mere existence becomes its reason for being in succeeding budgets.[9]

The incremental approach to budgeting has several advantages. First, it obviates the need to evaluate all governmental goals at once. Second, it is perceived by most budget actors as being a reasonably fair method for handling the allocation process. Third, it stabilizes the allocation process by giving department heads and budget officials a set of expectations with which to guide their budget requests and subsequent decisions. Two expectations are particularly important: base and fair share. The *base* is the expectation that agency activities will be carried on at approximately the same level as the previous year. *Fair share* is the expectation that a department will receive a fair share of any increases (or decreases) in the overall city budget.[10]

A major disadvantage of incremental budgeting is that it does not allow for flexibility in responding to rapidly changing community needs or demands, or dramatic changes in revenues. Indeed, incremental budgeting based on bureaucratic routines means that expenditure levels will be set *within* government, with little influence from outside groups. The whole process is far off the policy cycle, governed by internal bureaucratic routines, such as incrementalism, with little interest or input from citizens.

It may be that public budgeting is not even as rational as the incremental model implies. Thomas Anton has complained that incrementalism means that budget makers have to engage in limited successive comparisons (at least last year's budget with this year's). For the most part, Anton claims, budget makers follow simple established routines. Because these routines are basically the same from year to year, budgets are basically the same. Anton describes a budget process that is even more bureaucratic than the incremental model, which, at base, does involve some decision-making discretion.[11]

[9] John P. Crecine, *Government Problem-Solving* (Chicago: Rand McNally, 1969), p. 41.

[10] These concepts are from Aaron Wildavsky, *The Politics of the Budgetary Process* (Boston: Little, Brown, 1964).

[11] Thomas Anton, *The Politics of State Expenditures in Illinois* (Urbana, Ill.: University of Illinois Press, 1966), p. 255.

In either case, the budget system is isolated from the political environment. However, two important constraints have the effect of linking this closed budget system to the environment of the political system. The first is the legal requirement of a balanced budget. All states require that their municipalities equalize expenditures and revenues; unlike the federal government, they cannot engage in deficit financing of *operating* expenses (they, of course, do borrow to finance capital expenses). This means that in an economic downturn during which revenues decline, a municipality will have to either cut expenses or raise taxes. The economic environment can thus have an impact on the levels of service provided by the city. The second constraint is a political one: the belief among most city administrators that the property tax should not be raised except in the direst circumstances. This leads to the attempts to find additional sources of revenue described earlier in this chapter, and, if all else fails, to the institution of service cuts. The twin constraints of a balanced budget and political limits to taxation tie budgetary decisions to revenue decisions. A budget decision cannot be made without revenue ramifications.

Budgeting and public policy

Two important implications emerge from the studies of governmental budgeting. First, the budgeting system is *semiclosed*. It is structured by rules and routines that provide stable expectations among the major actors—service delivery agencies, chief executives (mayors or managers), and legislatures (city councils). Incrementalism is the guiding principle, even when rational budgeting systems are employed. Allocations are tied to the present political environment via the "revenue constraints," the dual constraints of balanced budgets and fear of increasing taxes (see box 12.3).

In the second place, budget behavior of governmental officials is essentially conservative, in that they tend to conserve the programs that already appear in the budget. The budget process, based as it is on the internal rules and operating procedures of government, reflects past policy settlements. It is not a place where major policy initiatives take place. Nor, in the view of many political scientists, should it be. Such initiatives generally take place on the policy cycle, in the limelight of public opinion. Nevertheless, the budgetary process, because it allocates resources among government programs, has a strong impact on whether or not policies determined in the policy cycle can be carried out.

A final point about public budgeting ought to be mentioned. Although the process is rule bound and conservative, there is ample room for maneuvering. Skilled advocacy on the part of the head of an agency, support on the city council, and consistent action over several budget years by the mayor can result in important changes in the pattern of allocations. In-

Box 12.3: The Immutable Power
of Incrementalism

In New York, the administration of Mayor Abraham Beame (1974–78) had been deeply tainted by the financial crisis that broke in 1975. Mayor Edward Koch, who took office in 1978, has repeatedly claimed that he has "turned things around." Yet a recent study indicates that of that portion of the city budget left primarily to local discretion (that is, not strongly influenced by state and federal requirements), Mayor Koch's spending priorities have closely followed those of Mayor Beame's.

Percentage of Discretionary Budget

	1978	1982 (proposed)
Police	21.9	21.5
Fire	9.9	10.9
Sanitation	8.8	9.5
Administration	8.4	7.8
Transit	6.1	6.1

Source: See Clyde Haberman, "Koch's Priorities in Spending Are Held Similar to Beame's," *The New York Times,* 9 June 1981. This article is based on a report by the Citizens Budget Commission.

cremental changes are driven by human actions channeled by rules and procedures, and incremental changes can cumulate to result in important changes in policy directions.

The Anatomy of the Urban
Fiscal Crisis

Years ago the Texas legislature was embroiled in a raucous session, with most of the controversy centering on the passage of a tax increase. As the session drew to a close, the dialogue became more heated, and legislative leaders from the House of Representatives began to fault the Senate, while Senators blamed Representatives and the media criticized the governor and both houses. The normally reserved governor at the time, Preston Smith, said pointedly: "Don't push; don't shove; there is blame enough for everyone."

As many cities teetered on the brink of insolvency, struggling with the twin specters of default and severe cuts in service, the process of blame-fixing had begun. Some, including author Richard Morris and Mayor Dennis Kucinich of Cleveland, blamed the banks.[12] State and federal officials, the banks, and others blamed the politicians for giving in to more demands than cities could afford.[13] Local politicians blamed the municipal unions for failing to put citywide interests before union demands; state government, which was quite willing to add requirements to the services local governments have to perform but quite unwilling to help finance them; and the federal government, which never did provide as much money as financially strapped cities needed.

There is much truth in this finger-pointing exercise. There is plenty of blame to go around. But it is also true that many major cities have been swept by impersonal economic and social forces, forces that dwarf the abilities of political leadership to cope. These forces include the decline of central city tax bases caused by the movement of jobs, industries, and people to the suburbs and to the Sunbelt; the increase in demands by have-not groups, who targeted their efforts on sympathetic city governments; the rapid unionization of the municipal work force; and the inflation and economic decline that characterized the American economy in the 1970s. Speaking of these impersonal forces, David Stanley comments, "It is hard to do *anything* about the troubled cities. The basic cause of their difficulties, their withering economic bases, is also their most intractable problem."[14]

Nevertheless, certain political (as distinct from economic) factors are important in understanding the response of cities to their financial problems.

1. *Government by precedent.* Incremental budgeting and other routines used by local governments tend to maintain programs once they have been established. By virtue of once getting in the budget, programs acquire a legitimacy that allows their proponents to defend them even in the face of the severe financial situation facing government.

2. *Demands internal to government.* The demands that political leaders have the hardest time ignoring come from within government, from the municipal workers who want to keep their jobs and to stay even with corrosive inflation. Municipal workers become most vocal when they are threatened with loss of their jobs; hence, they become most active in times of fiscal crisis.

---

[12] Richard Morris, *Bum Rap on America's Cities: The Real Causes of Urban Decay* (Englewood Cliffs, N.J.: Prentice-Hall, 1980). Former Mayor Kucinich is at work on a book about his experiences with the banking establishment in Cleveland.

[13] See Charles R. Morris, *The Cost of Good Intentions: New York City and the Liberal Experiment* (New York: W. W. Norton, 1980).

[14] David Stanley, "Cities in Trouble," in *Managing Fiscal Stress: The Crisis in the Public Sector,* ed. Charles Levine (Chatham, N.J.: Chatham House, 1980).

3. *The tooth fairy syndrome.* Charles Levine, professor at the University of Kansas, notes that in the early stages of fiscal decline, few people are willing to believe that the crisis is real.[15] Just as many Americans reacted to the energy crisis of the 1970s as if it were an artifact of oil company manipulations, many citizens, municipal workers, and political leaders treat the early warning signs of fiscal decay with much less respect than is warranted. When there is so much need for service, and when so many people are demanding service, it seems a crime to deny them, especially in a rich country such as the United States. When an economic downturn occurs, leaders institute what they perceive as temporary measures, just until times get better, or until the federal government wakes up and takes over the welfare burden from the cities (a favorite tactic of New York City budgetmakers during the late 1960s and early 1970s), or until the tooth fairy comes.

4. *Financial mismanagement.* Here is where leadership matters. Some cities have managed their financial affairs in the face of economic decline better than others. Detroit, for example, was hit hard by the recession of 1980, and Mayor Coleman Young instituted severe service cuts. For several years he has maintained a posture of tough negotiation with city unions, which has led to a decrease in the growth of wage and salary packages, saving the city millions of ·dollars. Wayne County, Michigan, lacking strong executive leadership, has been far more generous with its workers, run up chronic budget deficits, and engaged in poor financial practices.

There are certain financial practices that are indicative of underlying fiscal difficulties, practices that are designed to stave off the day of reckoning in the hope that somehow things will improve. The practices include *rolling-over debt,* which is borrowing in order to pay back loans. This increases short-term debt, on which cities must pay high rates of interest. It is a way to finance operating expenses by borrowing and is, strictly speaking, contrary to state requirement that local governments balance their budgets. In 1974, as it rushed toward financial collapse, New York City had $13.5 million of debt outstanding; $3.7 million was short-term debt. This was over half the short-term debt outstanding for all municipalities in the country! By 1978, New York was deeper in debt (over $14 million), but less than $400,000 was short term. Indeed, New York was bailed out of its fiscal difficulties by the state and federal governments' aiding the city in transferring its short-term debt to long-term debt (and getting other governmental units to share the debt burden).

A second shady financial practice is using earmarked or reserve funds to

---

[15] Charles Levine, "More on Cutback Management: Hard Questions for Hard Times," in Levine, ed., *Managing Fiscal Stress.*

pay operating expenses. Often funds are reserved to pay interest and principal on bonds, but such funds are attractive targets for politicians searching desperately for cash.

A final practice that is sometimes used by local officials is mixing the *capital* and *operating* budgets. Capital budgets, funded by issuing bonds, are supposed to be used to fund improvements in the city's capital infrastructure—street construction, public lighting, and the like. But a dollar is a dollar, and there is always the temptation to postpone capital construction projects in order to pay immediate expenses.

Politics and economics

Both political and economic factors have contributed to the urban fiscal crisis. Any solutions will involve interaction between economics and politics. A key question is whether the aging industrial cities of America are able to revitalize their local economies. This depends in large measure on action taken by large national corporations and the federal government, but it also depends on what the leaders of local government and such community institutions as banks, local industries, and labor unions do. The economic trend is toward *deconcentration:* movement of productive capacity to the suburbs, to smaller towns, and to the Sunbelt. Any revitalization of central cities involves swimming upstream. To counteract deconcentration, public policies will have to be fashioned to lure investment back downtown. But first we ought to decide whether we want to fight deconcentration, and whether we can if we want to. If we do not wish to fight, then we need to fashion policies that will allow cities to shrink gracefully. Shrinkage of population is going to occur whatever we do; our only public policy choice is whether we want to allow the shrinkage of the economic, governmental, and political functions of central cities as well.

CHAPTER 13

Intergovernmental Relations and the Implementation of Federal Urban Programs

It is impossible to understand the failures and successes of America's urban policies without understanding federalism. Many federal domestic programs are enacted by the national government but implemented and subsequently administered by state and local governments. In the United States, state and local governments are not simply units of administrative convenience for the national government. Although local governments are legally subordinate to state governments (recall Dillon's Rule), the state governments are, legally at least, equal partners with the national government in the nation's constitutional structure.

In the last half-century, the federal government has come to dominate domestic policymaking. Nevertheless, the national government is not hierarchically related to state and local governments; it can seldom order them to implement national policy. Rather, the relationship between the states and the federal government is characterized by a great deal of bargaining and compromise. Federal programs are administered via a complex system of grants and incentives rather than by direct order and straightforward implementation. This important aspect of the policy implementation and administration process is termed *the vertical dimension of intergovernmental relations,* to distinguish it from horizontal intergovernmental relations, which deal with the relations between the various governments that operate within a single metropolis (see chapter 9).

Administration and Implementation

We have stressed in this book that most major political issues go through a sequence of stages termed the policy cycle. Implementation is one of the stages of that cycle. *Implementation* involves creating the institutional arrangements through which policy can be put regularly into operation. It can involve setting up a new agency, or requiring that the states and localities take on new functions. It can also involve more intensive use of old methods for achieving new objectives (the "new wine in old bottles" approach). What happens in implementation is that something distinctively different is done to put a policy into operation, and what is done follows directly from the enactment of the policy.

The *administration* of public policy is the off-cycle equivalent of implementation. Once a new method for delivering policy is established, the new method rapidly becomes a regular part of government. Newly created agencies adopt rules of procedure, and personnel fall into routines that structure the ways in which they go about the regular tasks they must perform to put the enacted policy into operation on a regular and long-term basis.

Supplemental security income

An example may help to clarify this distinction. In 1974 Congress passed an act providing for supplemental security income, or SSI. The act consolidated several categories of income security, grants from the federal government to the states (aid to the blind, aid to the disabled, and general assistance for the elderly), and transferred the responsibility for administering the program to the federal level. The various programs had been established in the 1930s, during the Great Depression. They had been funded by both the federal government (via intergovernmental grants) and the states. States were left to administer the programs as they saw fit, within general guidelines set by the federal government. Hence, the 1974 act transferred full responsibility for the programs from a state/federal partnership to the federal government.

Primarily because the social security system was perceived by Congress to be so well run, Congress gave responsibility for administering SSI to the Social Security Administration. Social Security is primarily a program of entitlements. Although the regulations are extremely complex, it is relatively straightforward to determine whether a person is eligible for benefits. The Social Security Administration, prior to 1974, was primarily in the business of determining the eligibility of persons who had stable working careers all their lives, and getting the checks into their hands. But SSI was something quite different. Social Security staff members were unaccustomed to dealing with welfare clients who were truly in need. In particular, they had little experience with clients who needed money, but who also displayed the other characteristics associated with poverty: poor health, poor education, and inability to deal with bureaucratic procedures.

In implementing SSI, the Social Security Administration had attempted to adapt its existing procedures to fit the new program. In essence, the agency had adopted an *incremental* solution to the problem confronting it: it changed its operating procedures only marginally. When it became evident that this strategy was not working well, more adjustments were made to fit the new circumstances. Gradually, implementation became administration as the agency settled down to a set of routines that dealt reasonably well with the new circumstances.

Supplemental security income represents a program whose locus of administration was switched from a federal/state partnership to the federal government alone; many more programs continue to involve both the national government and the state and local governments. The implementation and administration of these programs must, as a consequence, involve federal, state, and often local officials, and they involve regular contact among them. As Deil S. Wright has written, intergovernmental relations (IGR)

> are not one-time, occasional occurrences, formally ratified in agreements, or rigidly fixed by statutes or court decisions. Rather, IGR is the continuous, day-to-day pattern of contacts, knowledge, and evaluations of government officials.[1]

Intergovernmental Relations as a Bargaining Process

Perhaps the most important point to note about the complexity that characterizes the vertical dimension of intergovernmental relations is that the various participants have different goals. Often federal officials have in mind the more or less direct implementation of what they perceive to be national goals. The field offices of the various federal departments and agen-

[1] Deil S. Wright, "Intergovernmental Relations: An Analytical Overview," *The Annals of The American Academy of Political and Social Science* 416 (November 1974): 2.

cies may have strict directives from the Washington office, or they may have significant discretion. In either case, however, federal officials are likely to have one general goal in mind: getting the various state and local officials to cooperate in achieving national goals.

Local officials, on the other hand, bring different objectives to the intergovernmental partnership. Above all, they are interested in relieving their fiscal strain while avoiding as many "strings" from Washington as possible. The late Jeffrey Pressman has compared the intergovernmental grant-in-aid process to foreign aid among countries:

> The differences in perspective between federal and local bodies are due in part to their differing roles as donor and recipient in the grant-in-aid programs. As in foreign aid, a donor's perspective includes a preference for long-term plans, short-term funding, and a number of guidelines regulating how the money may be spent. The recipient's perspective, on the other hand, includes a preference for short-term plans, long-term funding, and relatively few guidelines on spending.[2]

The differences in objectives of the participants, as well as differences in background and training, mean that intergovernmental relations are bound to be fraught with misunderstandings and frustrations. Pressman notes:

> Federal and local officials, with their differing perspectives, career patterns, and associational experiences, sometimes find it difficult to understand each others' policy motives. . . . Because that problem [federal-city relations] involves *organizations with competing objectives,* more than computational or technical methods are required to solve it.[3]

Pressman goes straight to the heart of the matter. Because participants in the intergovernmental relations process come from different organizations (the federal government, or the state government, or city government; from the executive, legislative, or judicial or administrative branch), they will not agree on specific aims of programs. Because actors have incompatible policy preferences, their differences cannot be settled by urging them to "communicate" or "plan." (These are what Pressman means by technical methods.) According to Pressman, their differences can be solved only through bargaining.

> Donor and recipient need each other, but neither has the ability to control fully the actions of the other. Thus the aid process takes the form of bargaining between partly cooperative, partly antagonistic, and mutually dependent sets of actors.[4]

[2] Jeffrey Pressman, *Federal Programs and City Politics: The Dynamics of the Aid Process in Oakland* (Berkeley, Calif.: University of California Press, 1975), p. 11.
[3] Ibid., pp. 14 and 16.
[4] Ibid., p. 107.

There are two very distinct positions on this view of intergovernmental relations. Neither camp denies that bargaining exists, but the camps evaluate the process quite differently. One camp adheres to what has been termed the *cooperative-coercive model.*[5] Adherents to this view are concerned with the waste and duplication of effort that exists in the prevailing system in intergovernmental relations. They are concerned with coordinating the various federal initiatives and particularly decry the ability of state and local officials to deflect the accomplishment of national goals. They applaud the various strategies that have been implemented to try to coordinate the administration of the various federal programs at the local level (such as the A-95 review process, discussed in chapter 9), but they believe that the existing coordinating mechanisms have not gone far enough. One student of the problem has argued that coordination "requires a hierarchy of units wherein the coordinator exercises supremacy and, at least, tacit coercion against units lower in the hierarchy."[6]

In the other camp are such political scientists as Aaron Wildavsky, who has put the issue this way:

> Under a national regime, states and localities carry out national instructions. . . . In a federal regime, states and localities are disobedient. The operational meaning of federalism is found in the degree to which the constituent units disagree about what should be done, who should do it, and how it should be done. In a word, federalism is about conflict. It is also about cooperation, that is, the terms and conditions under which conflict is limited.[7]

Wildavsky calls this model of intergovernmental relations the *conflict-consent* model. He as well as other political scientists believe that this conflict and diversity of goals are not harmful—quite the contrary. In a diverse nation such as the United States, it is inevitable that different parts of the country or even parts of the same metropolitan area have different ideas about just what ought to be done at what level of government. Moreover, even when everyone is agreed about what general goals ought to be pursued by the nation, just how these goals ought to be implemented in the states and localities can be a source of severe disagreement. Such disagreements cannot be reconciled by urgings to "coordinate," to "communicate," or to "plan." As Pressman has noted, they can be resolved only by bargaining. Good faith bargaining at least provides a framework for forging agreement.

Perhaps the primary impediment to successful bargaining is that the participants tend not to perceive themselves in a bargaining situation. Many federal officials, in particular, do not understand why the localities cannot

[5] Aaron Wildavsky, *Speaking Truth to Power: The Art and Craft of Policy Analysis,* (Boston: Little, Brown, 1979), ch. 6.

[6] William Goodman, quoted in Ibid., p. 144.

[7] Ibid., p. 142.

just fall into line and help implement needed national goals. For their part, state and local officials complain continually that federal officials "just don't understand our problems here."

One final point: although it is useful to recognize bargaining as a tool for resolving differences among the various levels of government, its utility is limited by the vast expansion of federal programs during the past twenty years. As James Sundquist has pointed out, when the great expansion of federal programs occurred during the 1960s, no one had an overall plan for administering them.[8] The focus was on the immediate legislation, and similar programs were established with different administrative strategies. Had consistent administrative strategies been used, the process of bargaining would have stabilized in a limited number of arenas. But the federal programs of the 1960s did not always use the existing state and local governments to administer policies; they often set up new administrative units or forced severe modification of existing ones to administer the new policies. Too much was done in too little time using too many different administrative strategies to rely solely on conflict and bargaining to achieve consensus.

Sundquist notes:

> If total and perfect coordination could ever be achieved—which is not conceivable—it might prove stultifying. But how much chaos is "a little chaos" and how much is too much? . . . Is it possible to institutionalize . . . flexibility and responsiveness within a single system that is still *a single system* and an organizational strategy that is still a *single strategy?* How can the proper balance be attained between a little chaos and a little order?[9]

The Nationalization of Domestic Policy

During the past century, America experienced two long-term trends, both of which were accelerated by the Depression. The first is the growing intervention of all levels of government in all phases of society. The second is a change in emphasis by the federal government from defense to domestic policy.

Since 1950, the percentage of gross national product (GNP) consumed by government has grown from 22 percent to about one-third, as figure 13.1 indicates. The figure also shows that the greatest growth has been in state and local expenditures. This, however, underestimates the increase in the federal government's intervention in the domestic policy sphere. The federal

---

[8] James Sundquist, *Making Federalism Work* (Washington, D.C.: Brookings Institution, 1969), p. 13.
[9] Ibid., p. 28.

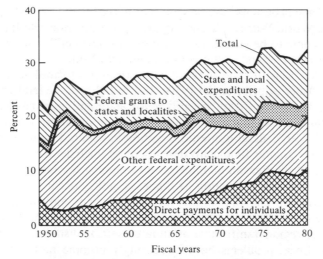

Figure 13.1. Government expenditures as a
percentage of gross national product (federal,
state, and local governments).

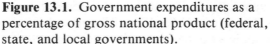

Source: "Special Analysis H: Federal Aid to State and
Local Governments," in *Special Analyses of the Budget of the
United States Government, Fiscal Year 1982* (Washington,
D.C.: U.S. Government Printing Office, 1981), p. 253.

government has, in effect, transferred effort from defense policy to domestic
policy in recent years. Expenditures for national defense have declined as a
percentage of federal outlays and as a percentage of GNP since 1966, and
have declined dramatically since the end of the Vietnam war. In 1966, federal
expenditures for defense were 7.6 percent of GNP; by 1976 they were 5.5 percent, and remained fairly constant through the remainder of the decade. Yet
during this period the whole federal government sector expanded from 18.7
percent to 22.6 percent of GNP. The net increase in domestic policy spending
was 6 percent of GNP.

What happened was a rapid increase of all governmental domestic expenditures from the end of World War II to the mid-1970s. From the mid-1960s
to the mid-1970s, there was also a rapid increase in federal intergovernmental grants to states and localities. The states and localities were becoming increasingly reliant on federal funds. During the same period, the federal
government took over complete control and financial responsibility for
several programs that were formerly financed jointly by the federal government and the states; these include the food stamp program in 1971 and
various welfare programs (SSI) in 1974.

Both the locus for new policy initiatives and the responsibility for financing established programs have tended to move to the federal level of government since World War II. This is why intergovernmental relations have increasingly come to be viewed as a process of implementing national goals. The notion of states and localities as implementing units, or even the federal government as a significant source of domestic policy formulation, was quite foreign to America prior to the 1930s. In the 1930s the federal government began to provide significant incentives for state and local governments to adopt certain policies that were seen as in the national interest. Since the Second World War, federal domestic spending has soared, and the states and localities have become financially dependent on the federal government. It is this trend that the Reagan administration hopes to reverse.

Why did this nationalization of domestic policy occur? There are three primary reasons. The first is that the country has moved quite quickly toward being a truly national society. Communication, technological changes, and regional shifts have attenuated sectionalism (but obviously not erased it). Local problems have increasingly become national problems. "Nobody," James Sundquist commented a decade ago, "says that if Los Angeles and Detroit and Newark and Cleveland have riots the problem is *local*." [10] Sundquist goes on to describe a process by which policy responsibility is transferred from local governments to the national government:

> As a major internal problem develops—or comes to public attention—public attitudes appear to pass through three stages. As the problem begins to be recognized, it is seen as local in character, outside the national concern. Then, as it persists and it becomes clear that the states and communities are unable to solve it unaided . . . the activists propose federal aid, but on the basis of helping the states and localities cope with what is still seen as *their* problem. Finally, the locus of basic responsibility shifts: the problem is recognized as in fact not local at all but as a *national* problem requiring a national solution that the states and localities are mandated . . . to carry out. [11]

The second reason for the increasing centralization of domestic policy in America is the general perception that the federal government's revenue system is both more productive and more equitable than state and local governments'. As we stressed in chapter 11, tax specialization among levels of government has occurred, with the federal government relying primarily on individual and corporate taxes, the states on a combination of sales and income taxes, and the localities on the property tax. The Great Tax Revolt of the late 1970s has been directed primarily at the property tax, adding to the perception of governmental officials that people don't like the property tax. Hence, many state and federal officials have demanded that the federal government shoulder a larger share of public expenditures.

[10] Ibid., p. 10.
[11] Ibid., p. 11.

There is little doubt that Americans do not like the property tax. But it is not clear that people like other taxes any more. In the recent past (as late as 1972), polls conducted by the Advisory Commission on Intergovernmental Relations (ACIR) indicated that the property tax was viewed overwhelmingly as the most unfair tax. Since then, however, the federal income tax has come to be viewed as the most unpopular tax. Table 13.1 reports the results of ACIR polls for several recent years.

These data suggest that the tax revolt is not as much a reaction to the unfairness of the property tax as it is a general discontent about the general level of governmental expenditures (at least among middle-income taxpayers). It may well be that one-third of GNP is about the limit of the public sector "take" that will be tolerated in the United States. If this speculation is true (and it is nothing more than speculation), then we have just about ended the period of the revenue shift from state and local government to the federal government—unless the states and localities are willing to reduce their expenditures in direct proportion to the increase in federal expenditures, something they have been unwilling or unable to do up to the present (see figure 13.1).

The final reason for the nationalization of domestic policy has been what E. E. Schattschneider termed "the expansion of conflict."[12] Activists ad-

Table 13.1. Changing American attitudes toward the unfairness of different taxes

Question: *Which do you think is the worst tax, that is, the least fair?*

	Federal/state income tax		State sales tax	Local property tax	Don't know
1972	19%	13%	13%	45%	11%
1973	30	10	20	31	11
1974	30	10	20	28	14
1975	28	11	23	29	10
1977	28	11	17	33	11
1978	30	11	18	32	10
1979	37	8	15	27	13
1980	36	10	19	25	10

Source: Data from the Gallup Organization. Table appeared in Richard Rose, "The Making of A Do-It-Yourself Tax Revolt," *Public Opinion* 3 (August/September 1980): Table 5, 17. Copyright © 1980 by the American Enterprise Institute. Reprinted by permission.

[12] E. E. Schattschneider, *The Semi-Sovereign People* (New York: Holt, 1960).

vocating that government do something about what they saw as pressing social problems were defeated time and time again at the state and local levels. Because of the disproportionate representation in state legislatures of rural and small-town interests that existed in most states until the intervention of the federal courts in the 1960s, liberal interests that favored governmental intervention in social problems almost always lost at the state level. Liberals could occasionally muster election victories in cities; indeed, Milwaukee was governed by socialists until 1960. At least some cities were ripe for liberal ideas, because of their concentrations of the poor, minorities, ethnics, and working-class citizens. But where electoral victories came, liberals quickly found there was little they could do. They ran squarely against the working-class citizen who owned a home and was quite willing to support liberal federal programs (in which case incomes would be taxed) but quite unwilling to support liberal local programs (in which case property would be taxed). Moreover, liberals in cities quickly found that their programs were "hostage" to the free movement of individuals and capital. If they raised tax rates too high, they found that industry, commerce, and individuals would move, thus shrinking the tax base further. If they expanded their public sectors too far, they found that they could be denied access to money for capital improvements in the bond market. (It is instructive that Milwaukee's socialists came to be known as "sewer socialists," because of their emphasis on basic city services and sound financial management.)

The situation dictated a change in strategy: expand the conflict by bringing in the federal government. The federal government had an untapped reservoir of fiscal resources (at least after Congress authorized the income tax in 1914). Direct election of senators and the fact that Senate districts could not be gerrymandered has meant that liberal interests were certain to be represented in that legislative body. The electoral college has given disproportionate weight to urban liberal interests, because large cities tend to be in large, populous states with a disproportionate number of electoral votes. This electoral structure has meant that presidents have reason to pay particular attention to urban interests. The House of Representatives, elected every two years, is the institution most sensitive to changes in popular opinion; such a change occurred during the 1930s when the Great Depression placed the issue of poverty caused by the failure of economic institutions (as opposed to the failure of individuals) on the public agenda.

Because of the structure of the federal government, liberals were able to win more political battles at the national level than in the states and localities, so that the decision to expand the conflict has worked well for liberals. In 1980, however, Republicans captured the presidency and the Senate, and established a working relationship with certain conservative southern Democrats (termed the "boll weevils"). Immediately Republicans began working to transfer as much policy authority as possible back to the states. They realized, quite correctly, that the federal government tends to be hospitable to liberal interests. Transferring power to the states, they hoped, would reduce the overall level of government in society.

The Impacts of Federal Policies

Federal programs affect local governments in three ways. One is through the *grant-in-aid* process, in which the federal government makes available funds to local governments. The second way is indirect, by providing for policies, such as housing and welfare programs, that have locational effects. By *locational effect* we mean that some localities are treated differently from others: small towns and rural regions are affected differently than large cities. Such policies do not have an equal impact on all locations, but affect some more intensely than others. As we noted in chapter 3, this locational effect is often an unintended consequence of a national policy designed to achieve national goals.

The final way that federal policies can affect local governments is through the *mandating* process. *Mandating* is demand by the federal (or a state) government that a local government perform some action. The demand may or may not be accompanied by funds to finance the mandated activity.

Grants-in-aid

The *grant-in-aid* process involves a transfer of money from the federal government to state and local governments. Grants from the national government actually predated the signing of the Constitution. They were, however, very small until the beginning of the twentieth century, and became a major aspect of domestic policy during the 1930s. During the Depression it became clear that the states were either unable or unwilling (many state legislatures were controlled by rural interests at the time) to provide much in the way of relief for the destitute. The federal government instituted numerous grants to the states for specific purposes (for example, general aid for the elderly). The money could be spent for certain objectives, and the state, as recipient of the grants, had to agree to certain guidelines.

Such grants are known as *categorical* grants. Since this early beginning, a variety of different grant arrangements have been tried (see box 13.1). The period since World War II has been an era of rapid growth in the use of federal grants to finance activities at the state and local level. In 1936, federal grants were 0.5 percent of the nation's GNP; by 1965 they were 1.6 percent of a much-expanded GNP; and by 1975 federal intergovernmental grants amounted to 3.6 percent of GNP. Since 1975, little growth has occurred.[13] In

---

[13] George F. Break, *Financing Government in a Federal System* (Washington, D.C.: Brookings Institution, 1980), p. 4.

Box 13.1: Classification of Grants

Today, the grant-in-aid process has spawned a complex system of relationships among federal, state, and local officials. Grants may be classified according to purpose; according to the nature of the stipulations attached to the grant by the grantor (federal government); and according to the method of award.

- *Purpose:* transportation, housing, general purpose, and so forth.
- *Stipulations*

    Categorical grant: A grant for a specific governmental purpose, such as special education or aid to families with dependent children. This is equivalent to earmarking in the budget process.

    Project grant: A grant for a specific project, such as a particular highway or subway system. This is the granting equivalent of capital expenditure in budgeting. Funds would be used for land acquisition and construction, but not for operating expenses.

    Block grant: A grant given for broad governmental purposes, but not any purpose. The donor attaches restrictions, but they allow the recipient government a great deal of leeway in spending the money.

    General revenue sharing: A grant with almost no strings attached. So long as the receiving government follows proper procedures, any legitimate governmental objective can be supported with these funds.

- *Method of Allocation*

    Formula allocation: The donor government allocates money to recipient governments according to prespecified formulas.

    Competitive allocation: The donor government allocates funds after judging the merits of applications filed by potential receiving governments.

1979 these expenditures were almost $84 billion, and consumed 16.8 percent of all federal government expenditures (22.4 percent of all domestic expenditures).[14]

[14] Office of Management and Budget, "Federal Aid to State and Local Governments," *Special Analysis of the Budget of the United States Government* (Washington, D.C.: U.S. Government Printing Office, 1980), p. 254.

About 40 percent of federal grants to states and localities are for payments to individuals. These grants are augmented by matching payments from the state or local government. This granting form has survived intact from the 1930s and now includes such programs as Medicaid (payments for medical care for the poor), income security programs (such as aid to families with dependent children), nutrition programs for children and the elderly, and housing payments. States and localities are essentially administrative units for the national government, and local government policy initiative centers solely on the size of the matching payment. Other federal grants go for service provision and capital improvement projects such as highways. Such grants involve more state and local policy discretion.

In recent years the state government has tended to assume the role of middleman in the intergovernmental grant structure. As George Break has noted, "The federal government has increasingly been in the business of providing aid, with local governments as major recipients, while state governments act as middlemen, both receiving and paying out large amounts of grant funds."[15] The state government passes through funds both to local governments and directly to individuals, but spends directly only a small portion of federal grants.

The Changing Grant Structure. As the federal government assumed an increasingly important role in the domestic life of the country, its relationships with the states and localities changed dramatically. This change is reflected in the intergovernmental grant structure. Not only have federal fiscal transfers to states and localities expanded greatly, but the objects of the expenditures have changed. Figure 13.2 depicts the percentage of federal intergovernmental grants going to various purposes in 1959, 1969, and 1979.

In 1959, over three-quarters of all federal grants to states and localities went for two purposes: income security (welfare) and transportation (primarily to build highways). Most federal money went to state government, where it was passed on as payments to individuals (income security) or was spent for capital improvements and maintaining services (transportation, education, employment, and social services). By 1969, the grant structure had altered considerably, with an infusion of funds for education, employment, social services, and health (primarily Medicaid). Income security took a smaller percentage of federal money, even though absolute expenditures were up. Community development, scattered among numerous categorical programs, consumed 5 percent of federal intergovernmental transfers.

By 1979 the grant-in-aid system had further evolved. The proportions of funds for transportation continued to decline, and mass transit projects competed with highways. *General revenue sharing,* a program that gave

[15] Break, *Financing Government,* p. 5.

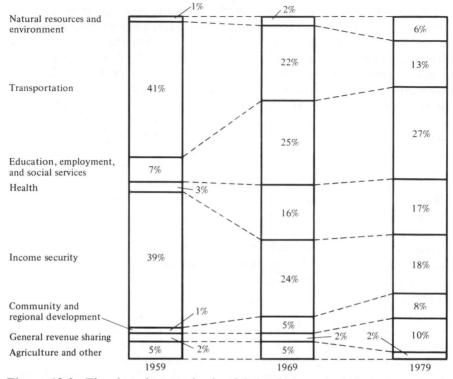

Figure 13.2. The changing emphasis of federal grants-in-aid.

Source: Drawn from Table H-4, *Special Analyses of the Budget of the United States, Fiscal Year 1981* (Washington, D.C.: U.S. Government Printing Office, 1980), p. 252. Percentages do not add up to 100% due to rounding.

communities almost unlimited freedom to spend grant money, was passed in 1974, and today consumes about 10 percent of federal intergovernmental transfers. The Housing and Community Development Act of 1974 consolidated seven previously existing categorical programs, including the urban renewal program and the model cities program, and gave communities more latitude in deciding how to spend funds. Both general revenue sharing and the Housing and Community Development Act were passed as part of President Nixon's attempt to consolidate the grant structure and give more discretion to states and communities in determining program priorities. (Recall that, on balance, states and localities are more conservative in their programs; hence, President Nixon and the Republican party hoped to accomplish more than a refurbishing of local policy discretion.)

In 1959, the federal government affected states and localities strongly in only two policy areas: transportation and income security. The 1960s, however, saw an active federal government intervene in many more domestic policy areas in many different ways. A fairly simple grant-in-aid structure has given way to an extremely complex one. It is this complexity that has generated the increasing necessity for state, local, and federal officials to enter bargaining arrangements to work out solutions to the problems this complexity has caused.

Locational effects

The second way the federal government affects localities is by establishing programs that have impact on cities disproportionately. Many federal programs involve direct *transfer* payments to individuals (with no state involvement). Estimates for the 1981 fiscal year are that 43 percent of federal outlays went for transfer payments. Most of these funds are for income maintenance (welfare) programs and social insurance (Social Security). With the concentration of the poor in central cities, clearly such programs have important implications for how cities are governed. Thus, direct payments to individuals have indirect effects on the structure and process of local government.

All sorts of other federal programs have locational impacts, often unintended. Some federal programs, such as highway programs, have inadvertently contributed to urban sprawl by giving suburbanites a system of the transportation that could move them from jobs in the central city to homes in the suburbs with reasonable speed. On the other hand, federal grants for mass transportation have tended to benefit central cities. Limitations on the level of air pollution set by the Federal Environmental Protection Agency have constrained the location of new plants. This has encouraged the suburban location of industry, because in at least some areas of most central cities no industry can be added that will add to the level of pollution.

Federal programs also have regional effects. Defense expenditures, for example, are concentrated in a limited number of states, particularly the Sunbelt states of California and Texas. Further, to the extent that federal grants are targeted toward the needy, as such programs as supplemental security income (SSI) and food stamps are, states with higher proportions of the poor will receive more federal grants. In the past, the Southeast has been the poorest region, but in the last quarter-century all regions have become more similar in their levels of wealth and income. In 1930, for example, the per capita income of the Mideast region (New York, Pennsylvania, New Jersey, Maryland, and Delaware) was 140 percent of the national average, whereas the income of the twelve states classified by the Bureau of the Census as the Southeast was just slightly above 50 percent of the national average. The average income in the Mideast was 2.8 times the average income in the Southeast. By the late 1970s this disparity was much attenuated, with the average income of the Mideast some 10 percent above the national average and the Southeast only 15 percent below.

Regional variation in federal outlays is extreme. Thomas Anton of the University of Michigan has prepared estimates for outlays for all federal programs on a regional basis. In 1977, the Mountain region received over one thousand dollars more per person in federal outlays than did the East North Central states that cluster along the Great Lakes. Table 13.2 presents estimates for all regions.

These data show quite clearly that no simple Sunbelt/Frostbelt difference exists. Although the East North Central region is dead last in the quest for federal dollars, the East South Central and West South Central do not fare much better. Increasingly it seems that the middle of the country fares most poorly in total federal outlays, with the West and East coasts and the Rocky Mountain states doing best.

Most of these regional differences reflect the unintended locational effects of various federal programs. For example, the Mountain states are first in federal outlays primarily because there are few people and long stretches of highways built with federal grants. It is not uncommon, however, for politicians to become aware of the locational effects of federal policies and to alter grant allocation formulas to reflect the locational effects. One very important example will illustrate. The Community Development Block Grant Program was established in 1974, consolidating seven existing categorical grant programs. Community development grants go directly to cities, bypassing the state completely. The method of allocation was by formula. Local governments were allocated these funds according to three factors: population, poverty (which was double weighted), and overcrowding.

Table 13.2 Per capita federal outlays, by region, 1977

	Outlay	*Rank order*
New England	$2,096	6
Middle Atlantic	2,362	4
East North Central	1,585	9
West North Central	2,111	5
South Atlantic	2,418	3
East South Central	2,061	7
West South Central	1,859	8
Mountain	2,596	1
Pacific	2,470	2
United States average	2,144	—

Source: Thomas Anton, "Outlays Data and the Analysis of Federal Policy Impact," in Norman J. Glickman, ed., *The Urban Impacts of Federal Policies* (Baltimore: Johns Hopkins University Press, 1980), p. 129. Reprinted by permission.

As many northern cities continued to lose population and housing over-crowding declined, officials from these cities became dissatisfied with the allocation formula. The formula seemed to favor the booming Sunbelt cities, with expanding populations and crowded housing conditions, more than their declining cities. In 1977 the formula was altered, using growth lag, poverty (weighted 1.5), and age of housing (double weighted). With their older housing stock and declining economies, northern industrial cities in-creased their take of the community development funds.

Mandating

It has become commonplace for state governments as well as the federal government to impose all sorts of requirements on local governments. Sometimes these requirements demand that local governments adopt certain programs. A state, for example, might require that a local school district provide for bilingual education. Other mandates require that local govern-ment activities be carried on in certain ways, by establishing reporting criteria or nondiscrimination in promotion and hiring, for example. The mandate may be imposed by direct order, or it can come in the form of a con-dition of receiving aid. Box 13.2 presents a classification of such mandates.

Mandates are a way of increasing control of local government activities by higher levels of government. They often impose significant burdens on local governments, sometimes without providing a source of funds to carry out the activity.

Often it is a court that mandates an activity, and because courts do not have the power to raise revenue, they cannot offer financial aid for the man-dated activity. One controversial mandate issued by federal courts to local school districts has been mandatory school integration. Such plans are often expensive, and courts sometimes find state governments at fault and order them to share the cost of the plan (local governments are, after all, the legal responsibility of states). But court mandates have not stopped there. The judge overseeing the Detroit school integration plan, recognizing the poten-tial impact of the plan on "white flight" from the school system as well as the general disruption to the educational process, ordered the Detroit School Board to take certain steps to increase the quality of education. These in-cluded vocational programs at certain locations, a teacher accountability plan, and a student code of rights and responsibilities. Whatever one thinks of the need for such programs, they have imposed significant expenses on the citizens of Detroit, and they have limited the policy discretion of the board of education. In Boston, school integration dominated the local policy agenda for years (see box 13.3).

Not surprisingly, local officials have complained bitterly about mandates. Edward Koch, mayor of New York, reports that New York City's budget is

Box 13.2: A Mandate Typology

I. Requirement mandates: Indicate what must be done.

    A. Programmatic mandates: Specify that a program must be adopted.

    B. Procedural mandates: Specify the manner in which a program must be performed by local government (for example, nondiscriminatory hiring, reporting procedures, planning requirements).

II. Constraint mandates: Limit the locally derived revenue that may be used by local government. These include limits on the tax rate and borrowing capacity normally imposed by state governments on localities.

III. Method of imposition: How the mandate is enforced by the higher-level government.

    A. Direct-order: A higher-level government directs a lower-level to do something (state-local relation).

    B. Conditions-of-aid: The mandate is a condition of receiving a grant from either the state or federal government.

Source: Max Nieman and Catherine Lovell, "Federal and State Requirements: Impacts on Local Government: Symposium Introduction," *The Urban Interest* 2 (Spring 1980); 46. Copyright 1980 University of Kansas. Reprinted with permission.

---

driven by forty-seven federal and state mandates. The mayor offers a "gloom and doom" estimate that the total cost of meeting these mandated requirements will be $6.25 billion in expenses, $711 million in capital expenditures, and $1.66 billion in lost revenue. Koch indicts Congress for imposing mandates in an unrealistic manner, stressing four points:

1. The federal government does not have to face the problem of the requirements it imposes, because it does not have the responsibility for final service delivery in such areas as education, transportation, and sewerage disposal.

2. Mandates attempt to impose a national solution on problems that have myriad different local manifestations.

3. Congress has imposed limitations on practices for which there are no feasible substitutes.

4. Mandates are infequently accompanied by adequate financial assistance.[16]

In a different guise, we again meet the primary problem of federalism: national problems existing in a system of divided powers. The current controversy over mandating is the most recent manifestation of an enduring issue: the proper division of authority and responsibility between the national government and the localities.

The Development of Federal Urban Programs

Stages in the development of intergovernmental relations in the United States have paralleled changes in the role of the federal government in domestic public policymaking. As the nation became more complex and interdependent, the federal government moved to deal with problems that were increasingly seen as national problems. But the states and communities, the traditional governmental units for dealing with domestic problems, had an independent, constitutional existence. They could not just be pushed aside, nor could they be ordered to carry out national policies. Hence, as the federal role in society grew, a change in intergovernmental relations necessarily followed.

We may divide recent history into five periods, corresponding to changes in the relations among the federal government, the states, and the cities: dual federalism (before 1933); basic formulation (1933–45); ordered growth (1945–64); the Great Society (1964–70); the New Federalism (1970–77); and Targeting (1977–81). President Reagan's intergovernmental proposals, many of which were implemented in the spring of 1981, indicate a new and radically different relationship between Washington and the localities.

It is dangerous to try to classify recent history. Dividing lines are never clear, and one period always carries over into the next. Most important, programs established in an earlier period almost always carry over into subsequent periods with their basic principles intact. The reasons for this are several: budgetary incrementalism, which tends to maintain programs from the past; a built-up bureaucracy that serves as an automatic defender of the program; congressional representatives who are sympathetic to the program (perhaps because they helped draft the legislation to establish the program years ago); and clients who have received the benefits from a program and want to continue doing so. Thus, programs and the agencies that administer them carry over the basic organizing principles from the past into the present. Even if new principles are used in establishing new programs, the old

[16] Edward I. Koch, "The Mandate Millstone," *The Public Interest* 61 (Fall 1980): 42–44.

Box 13.3: Busing in Boston

Since the Supreme Court's unanimous decision in *Brown* v. *Board of Education of Topeka, Kansas* in 1954, it has been unconstitutional for local school boards to create or maintain racially segregated school systems through their legal authority. On June 21, 1974, United States District Judge W. Arthur Garrity, Jr., issued his opinion in *Morgan* v. *Hennigan,* finding that the Boston School Committee had maintained through its legal authority a segregated school system. He ordered that Boston schools be desegregated by the fall term.

Judge Garrity's action came only after fifteen years of controversy over the schools. During the early 1960s, a reform coalition of blacks and liberal whites attempted to get the school committee to desegregate some schools; the committee refused. Their aims blunted, the coalition turned to the state legislature and in 1966 achieved a major victory: the *Racial Imbalance Act,* which mandated some desegregation for Boston. The school committee commenced to fight, delay, then fight again desegregation plans issued by the Massachusetts State Board of Education (when the school committee was unable to agree on a plan itself).

The Garrity decision meant that delaying tactics were no longer feasible, and a desegregation plan went into effect in the fall of 1974. But Boston's tightly knit ethnic neighborhoods were not ready

Source: See J. Michael Ross and William M. Berg, *"I Respectfully Disagree with the Judge's Order"* (Washington, D.C.: University Press of America), 1981; and Robert A. Dentler and Marvin B. Scott, *Schools on Trial* (Boston: Abt Books), 1981.

---

ones tend to survive along with them. Hence, the array of governmental programs that exists at any single time are characterized by a great deal of diversity. Old ways of doing things are never displaced by new ways; rather, the old and the new exist side by side.

Dual federalism (before 1933)

Prior to the Great Depression of the 1930s, the intervention of the federal government in domestic life was limited. As a consequence, interactions between the federal government and the states and localities were limited. The national government had provided land grants for public education in the

to yield. Violence broke out in South Boston, an Irish enclave. Black children, under judicial order to attend South Boston High School, were subjected to racial taunts and acts of violence. Not infrequently, they retaliated. To this day South Boston High remains a racial tinder box, a symbol of white resistance to court-ordered desegregation.

Politicians were elected again and again on one-plank platforms: fight busing. Louise Day Hicks, member of the school committee, member of the city council, and, finally, member of the United States House of Representatives, vituperatively attacked Judge Garrity and his decision; antibusing sentiment coalesced around her and other such outspoken politicians. No major white politician, including Mayor Kevin White, offered any more than grudging support for Garrity's decision (subsequently upheld by the United States Court of Appeals for the region).

As the level of disagreement grew and the school committee dug in its heels to try to subvert his decision in *Morgan* v. *Hennigan,* Judge Garrity issued judicial orders regarding all sorts of educational matters, many only tangentially related to desegregation policies. He ordered school district lines changed, student transportation plans implemented, the institution of "magnet" schools that were to draw students from across the city, teacher transfers, and a major school building program. He had to order police to enforce security in the disturbed high schools. Finally, the day-to-day operation of the school system was administered for all practical purposes in the courtroom of Judge Garrity. The recalcitrant school committee, still playing symbolic politics, had lost any ability to influence the course of Boston's educational policies.

Northwest Ordinance of 1787, which provided for government for the area north of the Ohio River. In 1862, Congress passed the Morrill Act, which granted states land for the establishment of agricultural colleges. These have become known as *land-grant colleges.* The grant-in-aid system which became firmly established during President Franklin Roosevelt's New Deal had its roots in early federal land policy.

In general, however, the period prior to the New Deal was characterized by *dual federalism.* This is the doctrine that the federal government and the states occupy separate and distinct policy spheres and should not intrude into each other's domains. The states, for example, were prohibited by the United States Constitution from engaging in foreign policy and coining money. The states seemed to have a certain policy responsibility reserved for them in the Tenth Amendment to the Constitution. Yet the Constitution, in Article 1, Section 8, gave Congress the power to regulate commerce among the states, and also granted Congress all powers "necessary and proper" for carrying out the powers granted by the Constitution to Congress (and therefore the national government). It was left to the Supreme Court to sort out the jurisdictions of state and federal government when there was a conflict.

At first the Court construed both the "necessary and proper" clause and the commerce clause liberally. Chief Justice John Marshall ruled in *McCulloch* v. *Maryland* (1819) that the United States government could establish a national bank, even though it was not expressly mentioned in the Constitution. In *Gibbons* v. *Ogden* (1824) Marshall ruled that the commerce clause did not prohibit the federal government from regulating commerce within a state, so long as the action regulated was part of an extended chain of actions that somewhere crossed state lines. This interpretation held sway during the nineteenth century.

During the period of rapid industrialization after the Civil War, the federal government limited its domestic activities to facilitating a domestic economic infrastructure by, for example, granting federal lands for railroad right-of-ways. The states, however, began to attempt to regulate some of the adverse effects of rapid industrialization. The Supreme Court became increasingly hostile toward such attempts, and in the case of *Lochner* v. *New York* (1905) declared unconstitutional a New York state law setting minimum hours of work for bakers. The Court reasoned that the law was a restraint of the right of contract. The United States Constitution had prohibited the federal government from interfering with the right of contract, but said nothing about state governments. The Court decided that the Fourteenth Amendment, which prohibited the states from denying citizens "life, liberty or property without due process of law," included a right of contract in its property provision. Justice Oliver Wendell Holmes wrote a stinging dissent, arguing that the Fourteenth Amendment did not enact substantive economic theories.

So the states were increasingly prohibited from interfering in economic life. Then in *Hammer* v. *Dagenhart* (1918), the court held in a five-to-four decision that the United States Child Labor Act of 1916 was unconstitutional. This was a regulation of *local* labor conditions, according to the Court, not interstate commerce under the doctrine of dual federalism, and was reserved to the states. But of course under the *Lochner* doctrine the states could not regulate labor conditions either. Dual federalism meant that some activities, primarily those that were designed by government to limit the adverse effects of unrestrained laissez-faire economic activity, could not be provided at all.

Basic formulation (1933–45)

With the doctrine of dual federalism firmly established in court decisions, and an activist Democratic administration under President Roosevelt pledging to get the country moving again, the stage for conflict between the executive branch and the Supreme Court was set. During the first few years of the New Deal, the Court repeatedly struck down as unconstitutional the actions of the federal government, often on the grounds that the activity was reserved for the states. After 1937, however, the court modified its position and upheld all major New Deal legislation. In the 1937 cases of *Steward Machine Company* v. *Davis* and *Helvering* v. *Davis,* the Court upheld the Social Security Act of 1935, including the grant-in-aid approach to welfare. This act continues to structure income security provisions today, and all changes in income security policies are approached as amendments to the Social Security Act.

In general, the period of the New Deal was characterized by an activist federal role and collaboration with the state governments, but with little direct involvement of local governments. Local governments were affected primarily indirectly, through the locational impacts of federal policies.

Ordered growth (1945–62)

During the first fifteen postwar years, the basic structure of federalism changed little. The roots of the two major urban policy initiatives, one in the field of housing and the other in the field of transportation, can be traced to the Roosevelt years. The number of grant programs grew and contacts among federal, state, and local government increased, but the growth for the most part was orderly. Federal officials emphasized professional standards of administration, and federal rules and standards increasingly accompanied grants to states and localities.

Housing and Urban Renewal. Major new federal initiatives occurred in the housing field with the Housing Act of 1949. To understand the impact of this act on urban areas, it is necessary to examine briefly governmental approaches to the housing problem.

The housing problem consists of three interrelated dimensions: supply, equity, and externalities. The *supply* problem is that not enough housing is being made available. The *equity* problem is that, when housing supplies are sufficient, the poor are housed in substandard buildings. The *externality* problem is one of public health and safety. The existence of slums threatens the safety of individuals not living in the slums: if the slums burn, the fire may spread to nonslum districts. Encroaching slums can also affect the property values of nonslum neighborhoods.

First governmental attempts to deal with housing attacked the externality problem. In the wooden cities of pre-twentieth-century America, the threat of fire was real, and municipal governments attempted to deal with the problem by specifying building standards. Housing reformer Lawrence Veiller reports that there have been laws regulating buildings in New York City since 1647.[17]

By the middle of the nineteenth century, housing reformers began to envision government regulation as a remedy for both the externality problem and the equity problem. American cities were rapidly becoming crowded with European immigrants; the unregulated building of tenements and the conversion of single-family dwellings to hotels clearly threatened the public health and safety. By the third quarter of the nineteenth century, public health professionals began to view disease and epidemics as controllable by preventive measures, and these professionals saw safe and sanitary housing as a key. In 1867, New York passed its first Tenement House Law. Although standards were low, the act established the principle of regulation of the housing industry.[18]

The housing reformers, however, wanted to solve more than just the externality problem; they wanted to solve the problem of slum housing for the poor by imposing standards of habitability on builders and landlords. In the minds of early twentieth-century housing reformers, housing regulation was an answer to the housing equity problem. In 1901, New York City passed a comprehensive tenement-house law and established a city department to administer it. Other municipalities quickly adopted tenement-house laws and, later, housing codes applicable to all housing. (This is a good example of the diffusion of a policy innovation.)

Although municipal housing ordinances have eliminated the worst slum housing, they have obviously failed to eliminate slums. The reason is twofold. First, housing codes have never been enforced systematically enough to bring up an entire city's housing stock to what most people would consider appropriate. The second reason is that slum housing performs a social function. In a country like the United States, where significant poverty continues to exist, the poor must live somewhere. Rigorous enforcement of housing codes invariably drives up the price of housing. If the poor cannot afford the better housing that is mandated by government regulation, the housing market will not provide it. Hence, the rigorous regulation of housing standards can have the unintended consequence of limiting the supply of housing for the poor.

The federal government's first involvement in housing policy was an at-

[17] Lawrence Veiller, *Tenement House Legislation in New York, 1852–1900* (Albany, N.Y.: Brandow Printing Co., 1900), p. 11.

[18] Roy Lubove, *The Progressives and the Slums: Tenement House Reform in New York City, 1890–1917,* (Pittsburgh: University of Pittsburgh Press, 1962), p. 27.

tempt to stimulate housing supply. In the Depression the housing industry had come to a standstill; no new housing was being built. To make matters worse, people were losing their homes as banks and other lending institutions foreclosed on mortgages in a desperate effort to stave off bankruptcy. The response of the federal government was the National Housing Act of 1934, which created the Federal Housing Administration (FHA). This agency was established to insure mortgages for single-family dwellings, and was willing to insure mortgages for longer periods than banks were (twenty to thirty years). Later, private lending institutions copied the long-term mortgages, making housing ownership possible for more people than previously (the monthly payments on a long-term mortgage are far smaller than on a short-term one).

This housing act did not affect cities directly. But it indirectly affected the spatial structure of cities—it encouraged suburban sprawl by insuring mortgages primarily on new houses in suburbs. After World War II the FHA was instrumental in alleviating the housing shortage that had developed during the Depression and the war, but its policies had the effect of encouraging outward growth and single-family living (rather than upward growth and apartment living).

The Depression saw a second approach to the housing problem, an attempt to deal with supply and equity. The Housing Act of 1937 created the United States Housing Agency and authorized it to lend money to local public housing authorities to clear slums and provide public housing.

The basic approach established in the Housing Act of 1937 was extended in the Housing Act of 1949. This act sought to deal with the vociferous opposition to the 1937 act from real estate interests, which opposed the building of public housing and argued that government should help the private sector to solve the problem. The 1949 act authorized purchase of land by local public authorities, who were to clear the land and sell it to private developers at a loss. The federal government would repay the loss to the local public authority. Private developers were to use the land for predominantly residential construction and were to provide some low- and moderate-income housing. The federal government was now involved in *urban renewal.*

This act employed direct federal-municipal contacts to deal with a major domestic policy problem. State governments were left only to pass enabling legislation. Henceforth intergovernmental relations were to become more complicated, with federal officials now dealing directly with local officials as well as with state officials.

The 1954 amendments to the Housing Act of 1949 permitted local public authorities to use federal grants for nonresidential building. The percentage allowed for non-residential building was increased in 1959 and again in 1961 (to 30 percent). Local officials perceived that urban renewal could be used to refurbish their declining tax bases, and thought that the best way to do that was to finance commercial building and middle- and upper-income housing. Replacing housing for the poor with housing for the poor seemed to many local officials an inadvisable strategy for renewing cities. They pressured Congress to permit more nonresidential building and increase the allowable proportion of middle- and upper-income housing. The objective of improving housing was being replaced by the goal of restoring the city treasury.

As is the case for many public policies, the housing and urban renewal policies of the 1950s and 1960s had important unintended effects. One objective had been to provide better housing for the poor. Yet in urban neighborhood after urban neighborhood, the poor were forced out of their homes with little thought about where they were to be relocated. Many cities did genuinely plan to relocate them in the long run, in some of the new housing that was to be built in the urban renewal area. But it proved difficult to get private developers to build low-income housing (indeed, this is the source of the housing equity problem). Moreover, few city governments spent much time considering the short-term relocation problems of the poor. In most cities housing was in short supply during the 1950s. Tearing down even substandard units was bound to increase the pressure on the rest of the housing stock, as displaced families moved in with relatives and friends. The result was the deterioration of "near slum" housing in many cities. Clearing slums had the effect of creating more slums.

Transportation. In 1944 Congress passed an act setting out in skeleton form the interstate highway system. In 1956 the Federal Highway Act was passed, financing the federal highway trust fund from federal gasoline taxes. The interstate highway system was funded through a grant-in-aid formula requiring the federal government to pay 90 percent of construction costs. For years thereafter a powerful policy system dominated federal transportation policy. This system was composed of the Federal Bureau of Public Roads, state highway departments, private highway contractors, and automobile associations, particularly the American Automobile Association. With more and more gasoline consumed each year in more and more vehicles, the road coalition could count on more and more funds from the highway trust fund, money that could be used only for highway construction. One observer called the fund an "ever-normal trough," a source of seemingly unending funds for rural-dominated highway interests.

When highway building did come to the cities, it encouraged suburban sprawl and robbed central cities of valuable tax-paying land. Building freeways in crowded cities also imposed severe social burdens on residents. In order to keep costs down, highway engineers planned their urban expressways to go through poor neighborhoods wherever possible. This imposed the social cost of relocation on those least able to afford it. City officials watched their mass transit systems deteriorate while the road coalition prospered.

The road coalition held sway over federal transportation policies until the mid-1970s, when a series of events weakened this seemingly invulnerable policy system. As gasoline prices rose, motorists drove fewer miles, cutting into revenue. Inflation damaged the purchasing power of highway dollars, but gasoline taxes were not increased. (Once a large percentage of the price of motor fuel was state and federal taxes, but today that percentage is trivial.) Finally, in 1973 Congress opened the highway trust fund to mass transit uses. Although the road coalition is still important in federal (and state) transportation policy, its influence is much diminished today.

The Great Society (1962–70)

When John Fitzgerald Kennedy came to the presidency in 1961, he inherited a domestic policy structure that centered on building highways and providing income security payments to the poor. Since World War II little thought had been given to the basic structure of welfare policy. Welfare was still conceived of as temporary payments to guard individuals against a poorly functioning economy. Yet it was becoming clear to officials in the Kennedy administration that many people never got out of poverty, with or without welfare payments. The *cycle-of-poverty theory* was born. Poverty was associated with certain characteristics, including lack of education and of employable skills. These characteristics were passed on from generation to generation, locking a segment of society into a permanent underclass.

To break this cycle of poverty, federal officials developed a *social services strategy* (see box 13.4). In addition to living expenses the poor would be provided opportunities to pull themselves out of poverty by such services as job training, day care for children, and preschool education. Policymakers forgot that the American economy, at its best, left about 4 percent of American job-seekers unemployed. The best that the services strategy could do was to shuffle around who was unemployed.

After the tragic death of President Kennedy, President Lyndon Johnson adopted most of the Kennedy domestic program and built his own policy agenda. The Johnson years saw the greatest domestic policy initiatives since the New Deal, initiatives that radically altered the structure of federalism.

The War on Poverty. The *Economic Opportunity Act of 1964* fully embodied the services strategy. It established such programs as Head Start, a preschool educational program, a Job Corps for the hard-core unemployed, and the Neighborhood Youth Corps. The War on Poverty also contained a second strategy. Those formulating the poverty program believed that if the programs were turned over to traditional government bureaucracies, the

Box 13.4: Uncontrollable Spending
for Social Services

In 1962, Congress passed amendments to the Social Security Act
that created categorical grants to the states for provision of social
services. The social service amendments joined the old age social insurance and the public welfare provisions of the Act, which had survived basically intact since the 1930s.

The public welfare sections of the Social Security Act had always
been open ended. Congress had authorized the federal government
to match state spending for public welfare regardless of the number
of recipients certified by the states. Such expenditure mandated by
statute is known as *uncontrollable spending,* because the amount of
money expended is out of the control of budget makers. (Of course
the law can be changed, so no spending is uncontrollable in the long
run.)

In the 1962 amendments, Congress adhered to past practice (an
incremental approach) and made the social service provisions open
ended. If the secretary of the Department of Health, Education and
Welfare certified that the services were needed by present or potential recipients of public aid, then the federal government would pay
75 percent of the cost of services for all clients enrolled by the
states.

For a variety of reasons, including changes in the Social Security
Act by Congress in 1967, growing welfare case loads, and internal
reorganization in HEW, the department lost control over the service
certification process, and began certifying all sorts of services requested by the states that were not anticipated by the framers of the

Source: See Martha Derthick, *Uncontrollable Spending for Social Services Grants*
(Washington, D.C.: Brookings Institution, 1975).

---

bureaucracies would be too cautious in developing needed innovative approaches. Moreover, there was a danger in putting the programs in the hands
of state agencies, as the traditional grant-in-aid programs had done. State
governments were simply too captive of small-town, rural, and suburban interests to deal effectively with urban problems. Neither were city governments likely to be instruments of innovative policy, dominated as they were
by local political forces.

This view of existing domestic programs led the President to propose, and
Congress to accept, establishing the Office of Economic Opportunity

1962 amendments. States began to perceive the amendments as a way of transferring to the federal government the burden of financing programs that had traditionally been the responsibility of the states. State and local officials began to pressure federal officials to certify the services that they wished to fund through the open-ended social service provisions. The large states were the leaders in this game of "creative financing": California used a variety of techniques to tap from 25 percent to 36 percent of all social service grants from 1967 to 1971; the Illinois welfare department began to purchase services from other state departments, thereby financing the services from the other departments by federal grants. New York went for certification of a wide array of services, including health, mental hygiene, education, correction, commerce, narcotics addiction, the office of aging, and the state university.

Finally the abuses became too great. Mississippi was requesting social service grants equal to half its yearly budget. Newspapers began to feature exposés on the situation; social services grants reached the public agenda. In 1972, Congress closed the loophole by placing a $2.5 billion ceiling on the program.

It would be easy to attribute this failure in implementation of a straightforward federal policy (the social services strategy) to a poorly drafted law. Indeed, it *was* poorly drafted. But the situation was much more intricate. Many officials in HEW wanted to expand social services in exactly the same manner that the states did, so that the first breakdown in implementation occurred in the federal bureaucracy. The second culprit was the federal system. State and local officials invariably have different interests from federal officials. The former see their primary problem as fiscal relief; the latter view the primary problem as one of putting federal policies into operation.

---

separate from the traditional departments of the federal government. At the local level, the act established *community action agencies* (CAAs) to mobilize community resources to attack poverty and provide services. The agencies were to be quasi-governmental organizations, consisting of government representatives (city government, school systems, and social welfare agencies), private groups (business, labor, religious groups), and neighborhood representatives, with "maximum feasible participation" by the latter. The community action agencies were to develop and administer community action plans for combating poverty.

Wide variability developed in the independence of the CAAs from city government, as well as in the extent of participation by residents. In some cities, such as Chicago, the CAA was tightly controlled by city government. In others, such as Los Angeles, the CAA operated quite independently of municipal government, further fragmenting service delivery in the city.[19]

Community action agencies became controversial in several communities, especially where CAA representatives engaged in protest activities and attacked local politicians and businessmen. The Nixon administration dismantled the Office of Economic Opportunity, ended funding for the CAAs, and placed the remaining War on Poverty programs in several traditional federal bureaucracies. In 1981, the Reagan administration abolished the remaining vestige of the community action approach to urban problems when it discontinued funding for the Community Services Agency.

The War on Poverty was an important special case in the development of American federalism. Distrusting both centralized solutions to urban problems *and* the ability of local governments to deal with the national problem of poverty, the Johnson administration tried to create new organizational forms that would simultaneously give the poor access to government and deliver the services they needed. The War on Poverty increased government fragmentation and complexity, but it also gave political access to individuals who had not experienced it previously.

Model Cities. Urban renewal had not salvaged the cities, but this failure had not quelled the hope that government could solve urban problems. In 1966 Congress passed the Demonstration Cities and Metropolitan Development Act, which was to be a bold new governmental initiative in a limited number of cities. Cities would apply for funds by identifying target neighborhoods that should be revitalized. Funds would be distributed directly to city governments, bypassing the states. President Johnson, however, abandoned the initial concept of targeting cities when it became apparent that Congress would refuse to fund a limited number of cities. In 1966, 63 cities were funded; in 1967, 150. Targeting had fallen victim to classic legislative logrolling. Money was distributed to such metropolises as Pikeville, Kentucky; Smithville, Tennessee; and Laredo, Texas, primarily to satisfy powerful members of Congress.

Housing. Major housing acts were passed in 1965, when the cabinet department of Housing and Urban Development (HUD) was created, and in

---

[19] See David Greenstone and Paul Peterson, *Race and Authority in Urban Politics* (Chicago: University of Chicago Press, 1976).

1968, when two major acts were passed. The Fair Housing Act prohibited discrimination in the sale of housing. The Housing and Urban Development Act inaugurated a new concept in dealing with the problems of housing supply and equity. Government would *subsidize* the purchaser of housing, thus stimulating demand and increasing equity simultaneously. The act contained provisions for *mortgage* subsidies for homeowners of moderate income and *rent* subsidies for renters. To stimulate new construction, the subsidies were made available for new or rehabilitated housing only.

In many cities the mortgage subsidy program was an abject failure. Unscrupulous contractors built substandard structures, bribed building inspectors to approve them, then moved in unsuspecting families. Banks and lending institutions failed to check the structures for which they were issuing mortgages, because their investments were insured by the United States government (another part of the program). Often the incomes of the people moved into the homes were not adequate to meet mortgage payments and provide for regular maintenance, even when the houses were sound. Because the program required minimal down payments from owners (as little as $100), it was easy for owners simply to abandon the houses. Hence, an unanticipated consequence of the mortgage subsidy program was housing abandonment. The program was ended by the Nixon administration, but the federal government continues to fund a variety of rent supplement programs.

Other Programs. The Johnson administration enacted a number of other urban-related programs, most of which increased contacts among state, local, and federal officials. In 1965 the federal government began to fund elementary and secondary education on a large scale for the first time. That same year, Medicare, a health insurance program for the elderly, and Medicaid, one for the poor, were established. These similar programs worked on different principles. The Medicare program was a national one, fully funded and administered by the federal government. Medicaid was a grant-in-aid program.

The Older Americans Act recognized the elderly as a significant national constituency. Later amendments to the act established a network of agencies at the state and local levels to provide and coordinate services for the elderly. As was the case for CAAs in the War on Poverty, there is great variability in the relationships between the area agencies on aging, which are established at the local level, and municipal governments. In some places the area agencies are departments of municipal government; in others they are quasi-independent agencies. In some areas they span several counties. Because of their powerful and politically acceptable constituents, the area agency network is alive, well, and contributing to intergovernmental complexity.

The new federalism (1970–77)

The election of a Republican administration in 1968 signaled a change in the national government's outlook on federal-local relations. President Nixon wanted to give as much leeway as possible to the states and localities in spending federal grants. Although he faced a Democratic Congress, he received powerful support from state and local officials. Nixon adopted a plan devised by economist Walter Heller in the 1960s. The Heller plan encompassed two strategies for rationalizing the complex maze of intergovernmental relations. *General revenue sharing* was to go to states and localities to be used entirely as they saw fit. *Special revenue sharing* was to consolidate many separate categorical programs into broad blocks, such as law enforcement, community development, and education, with few strings attached within categories. A local government could not, however, use law enforcement block grants to fund community development activities.

In 1972, Congress enacted general revenue sharing in the State and Local Fiscal Assistance Act. Forty percent went to the states, 60 percent to localities; apportionment was by formula based on population and tax effort. The Act was renewed in 1976, and again in 1980.

Nixon had less luck with his special revenue proposals. Congress modified them considerably but did consolidate several grant-in-aid programs in 1973 and 1974. The Comprehensive Employment and Training Act (CETA) consolidated manpower programs and decentralized their operation. Almost immediately a conflict developed between city governments, who tried to use CETA funds to supplement city payrolls, and the federal Department of Labor, which saw the purpose of CETA as training the "hard-core" unemployed and then getting them employment without federal subsidy. Again we can observe the classic conflict of federalism. Under President Carter the administration of this program was tightened considerably, eliminating major abuses. Nevertheless, the Reagan administration curtailed CETA funding dramatically and has seriously considered eliminating it entirely.

Even more important to municipal governments, the Housing and Community Development Act consolidated seven grant-in-aid programs, including model cities and urban renewal. Money was allocated directly to cities on a formula basis. Cities were required to spend funds on community development projects in low- and moderate-income neighborhoods.

Targeting (1977–81)

With the return of the Democrats to power in 1977, control of federal grants to states and localities was reemphasized. New procedural controls were instituted in many of the grant-in-aid programs, controls that have become known as mandates (see pp. 325–27). *Project* grants came into vogue, with the Urban Development Action Grant (UDAG) program a major example. The purpose of the UDAG program is to attract private redevelopment money to cities by using some public funds, a concept known as *leveraging*. In the UDAG program, cities must apply competitively for money, demonstrate that the project will revitalize a low- or moderate-income neighborhood, and prove that the project would not be completed in the absence of the public subsidy.

The Carter administration also proposed that federal urban programs be *targeted* at distressed cities. It supported changing the allocation formula for community development funds to the benefit of cities with declining economies. It suggested *countercyclical* aid, which went to places especially distressed economically, and a local public works program. President Carter initially opposed the renewal of general revenue sharing in 1980, because it conflicted with his targeting strategy by funding local governments regardless of need.

On March 27, 1978, President Carter announced what he hoped would be the basis for a national urban policy under the rubric of a "new partnership to conserve America's communities." He proposed increased coordination of federal urban programs, aid to local governments in employment and economic development projects, and improvement in community development projects. The new urban programs he proposed would have cost the federal government $11.5 billion in 1980.

The rapidly worsening economic circumstances beginning in 1978, portending huge increases in federal deficits, crowded the new partnership off the federal agenda and meant that resources for new programs would be far harder to generate. In his budget for the 1981 fiscal year, Carter projected a slowdown in the rate of growth of grants to states and localities. The major reason given was "the need for overall budget restraint as part of a major effort to hold down inflation."[20]

Back to the states: A Reagan revolution?

Urban policy priorities change with changes in control of the presidency. In November 1980, Americans elected Ronald Reagan to the presidency, a Republican who did not accept the basic tenets of the domestic programs established during the 1930s. Voters not only gave Reagan a solid electoral majority, they also gave the Republican party control of the Senate for the first time in a quarter-century.

President Reagan immediately set about formulating and presenting to Congress a set of proposals that would (1) reverse the increasing role of

[20] Office of Management and Budget, "Federal Aid," p. 239.

government in society, and (2) turn policymaking authority back to state and local governments. His proposals to restructure the intergovernmental grant-in-aid process would amount to a revolution in intergovernmental relations, if enacted intact.

Reagan proposed, first, cutting back on grant-in-aid funds significantly, and second, consolidating categorical project grants to states and cities in a small number of "superblock" grants that would go to the states only. The theory behind this proposal is that cities, being legal creatures of states, ought to turn to state governments rather than to the federal government for aid. Moreover, the proposals were designed to break up policy systems that were responsible for allocating large portions of federal domestic expenditures. The conservative Republicans staffing the Reagan administration reasoned that the "big spending" policy systems in education, welfare, and urban program areas would be far more difficult to establish on a state-by-state basis. Thus, the block grant proposals reflected far more than a philosophy concerning where the functions of government ought to take place. By changing the locus of governmental responsibility, Republicans hoped to reduce the overall level of governmental intervention in society. The only program that President Reagan has sponsored that would aid fiscally stressed cities is the "urban enterprise zone" program proposed by Buffalo Republican Congressman Jack Kemp. This consists of offering federal tax breaks for businesses that invest in qualifying central city neighborhoods. While the prospects for passage of the program are good, the prospects for a major impact on urban problems are very poor.

Mayors, urban congressional representatives, and black spokespersons were highly critical of the proposals, whereas state-level interests generally supported the proposed grant structure but criticized the funding cuts.

During the spring of 1981, President Reagan was able to push through Congress many of his intergovernmental proposals. Severe funding cuts for domestic programs were achieved, and a large number of categorical programs were combined into several block grants (see box 13.5). In 1982 President Reagan proposed, under the rubric of the "New Federalism," turning over even more programs to the states and localities.

Concluding Comments: Implementing Urban Programs in a Federal System

In the past few years political scientists have devoted considerable attention to the problem of implementation. This concern was stimulated by the recognition that federal programs often did not work the way their proponents had intended at the enactment stage. Some political scientists have tried to clarify the conditions under which smooth implementation can be

Box 13.5: The Reagan "Superblocks"

The Reagan approach to intergovernmental relations is to turn back significant responsibilities for social and urban programs to state and local governments. This approach has two prongs: a significant reduction in federal funds going to these programs (under the assumption that if the states and cities want them, they will fund them) and a consolidation of most categorical and project grants into a small number of block grants.

In his initial budget proposals for fiscal year 1982, President Reagan proposed establishing five major block grants; Congress altered the proposals in the Omnibus Reconciliation Act of 1981. The result was nine new block grants combining fifty-six previously categorical aid programs. They are:

Community Development

Community Services

Maternal and Child Health

Health Prevention and Services

Alcohol, Drug Abuse, and Mental Health

Social Services

Primary Care

Low Income Energy Assistance

Education

Source: See Bruce L. R. Smith and James D. Carroll, "Reagan and the New Deal: Repeal or Replay?" *PS* 4 (Fall 1981): 758–66.

---

achieved. Paul Sabatier and Daniel Mazmanian, for example, suggest that successful implementation is associated with (1) attacking problems that are tractable, or amenable to governmental solutions; (2) drafting a statute that is clear in its goals, unambiguous in its policy directives; (3) establishing implementing institutions with hierarchical arrangements among them and with sufficient financial resources to attain statutory objectives; and (4) having external conditions that favor implementation, rather than retard it (such as public and media support).[21]

[21] Paul Sabatier and Daniel Mazmanian, "The Implementation of Public Policy: A Framework for Analysis," *Policy Studies Journal* 8 (Special # 2, 1980): 538–59.

This is of course good advice. Yet certain features of the American system operate against such principles. The first is the tendency of legislators to compromise on statutory objectives. If goals are kept vague and policy directions are left up to administrators, conflict will be lessened during the policy enactment stage. This may displace the conflict from the enactment stage to the implementation stage, as actors find out that what they thought was a firm policy settlement was not that at all. But vague legislation does take advantage of an important facet of the policy process: the tendency of public attention to decline after enactment. Policy solutions can be worked out using off-cycle methods, rather than by trying to forge coherent public policy in the glare of public attention. Other reasons for less-than-clear statutory direction for public programs are the inability to foresee the array of outcomes generated by a policy and the pressures of time that preclude more extensive legislative investigation.

A second major reason that successful implementation of federal urban programs is an elusive goal is the federal system itself. We have repeatedly stressed in this chapter that federal officials and state and local officials have different goals in mind when they make contact to implement federal policies. State and local officials are not hierarchical cogs in a national bureaucracy. They have significant policy discretion themselves. Hence, the implementation process in a federal system must involve a considerable amount of bargaining and compromise on both goals and means. Yet what is too much bargaining (and, hence, too little coordination)? No one really knows. What we can say is that smooth implementation is really not to be expected in a federal system.

Finally, the national government's approach to implementing federal objectives has not been consistent. Democratic administrations have tended to stress implementation of national goals, but Republican administrations have emphasized local autonomy and the undesirability of nationalizing too many local functions. Even within administrations (and within Congresses), positions have not been consistent on this issue. Democrats have tended to favor aid to cities regardless of the mechanism, and Republicans have opposed it. So the Carter administration and most Democrats in Congress favored expanding the community development block grant program, even though it carried few mandates. (Several mandates have been added to the program, including nondiscrimination in administration, environmental impact statements, and historic preservation evaluations for projects involving major building or demolition.)

The result is a complex, ongoing intergovernmental process characterized by conflict, bargaining, and occasionally smooth implementation. Some people have become frustrated with this complexity and have called for coordinated implementation. This position stems in part from the belief that the policy enactment process has settled things by establishing a collective good that benefits everyone (or at least a good whose benefits far outweight costs). Yet officials in the hinterland may not view things that way. For them to conform to national objectives, either they must be coerced (by, for example, the mandating process) or they must be bargained with. So long as local and federal objectives diverge to some extent, there are no other choices.

CHAPTER 14

The Bureaucratic Connection: Delivering Public Services

Much of the public policy activity of municipal governments is administrative in nature. Most decisions are made within municipal service delivery agencies, and seldom do they bubble up to the surface to occupy the time of top government officials. Service delivery decisions take place far off the policy cycle, out of the glare of public attention. Decisions are bureaucratically determined, with only occasional intrusion by such directly political factors as interest groups and political parties.

Nevertheless, the numerous minor and mundane administrative decisions accumulate to have important policy consequences. Indeed, if public policy is what government *does,* the large number of service delivery decisions made by the various municipal bureaucracies *is* the urban public policy of America. Moreover, these decisions touch the lives of citizens more directly than any other aspect of the political process. In large measure, urban public services determine the quality of life city-dwellers experience. Urban service decisions are *individually* unimportant (except to the citizens who are directly affected) but *collectively* crucial.

The Norm of Neutral Competence

Gradually, throughout American history, the norm of neutral competence has become the most important value in American public administration. The norm of neutral competence is best summarized by the slogan, "Take administration out of politics and politics out of administration."[1] In this view, public bureaucracies ought to be neutral implementing mechanisms for policies determined by the political branches of government—chief executives and legislatures. Administration itself ought not to be influenced by partisan political considerations, and politicians should be able to count on neutral implementing agencies to carry out the policies they set.

The battle for a public bureaucracy free of politics was fought most intensely at the local level. Indeed, in some cities it continues to be fought. Civil service systems were instituted to replace the patronage system ("Take administration out of politics") and were gradually extended to apply to promotion and advancement within agencies ("Take politics out of administration").

Yet as politics, conceived as partisan political activity, was removed from municipal agencies, a new politics began to fill the vacuum. Agencies were no longer tools of party bosses, but they became political forces in their own right. Two new interests emerged on the urban political scene: agencies and city employees. The agencies had substantial independence from chief executives, because the mayor could no longer hire and fire anyone in the agency except the head of the agency and the chief assistants. This meant that a staff continued to operate reasonably sure that it would be around longer than the mayor. Staff members often developed into agency advocates, defending programs and agency prerogatives, often in opposition to the preferences of the mayor. Moreover, city employees have interests beyond those of the agency itself. Employees are interested in salaries, job security, and stable career opportunities. In many cities employee unions were formed to foster these goals. In the end, neither was administration removed from politics nor politics from administration. Rather, a new form of politics replaced the old form. In many cities, mayors no longer negotiate with party chieftains to achieve policy aims. Instead they negotiate with the heads of labor unions and the staffs of the various municipal agencies. City bureaucrats are often competent, but they are almost never neutral. Nevertheless, the norm of neutral competence is the most important guiding principle in American public administration. As we shall see in this chapter, it has tremendous influence on public service delivery in urban America.

[1] See Herbert Kaufman, "Emerging Conflicts in the Doctrines of Public Administration," *American Political Science Review* 50 (December 1956): 1057–73.

Five Key Issues

There are five key issues in the study of urban public services: responsiveness, effectiveness, efficiency, distribution, and internal control. Not surprisingly, these issues reflect the overlying issues of governance set out in chapter 1 in microcosm. *Responsiveness* involves the extent to which service delivery agencies are responsive to citizen demands, which are generally in the form of citizen-initiated contacts. *Effectiveness* concerns the degree to which urban services solve the problems faced by citizens. Is the urban service agency achieving its goals? *Efficiency* deals with the productivity of urban service agencies. How do service agencies translate their budget allocations into services? Are urban services too costly? Can productivity be improved? *Distribution* concerns which citizens get what levels of service. Do blacks get fewer (or poorer-quality) services than whites, for example? Finally, the issue of *internal control* concerns the way in which the individual worker in the service organization relates to central management. This is especially important in the case of urban service agencies, because the individuals who actually deliver services spend most of their time in the field, far from the overseeing eyes of supervisors. The policeman who spends most of his working hours patrolling and answering calls for service exemplifies the problem of internal control. As we shall see, the issue of internal control is closely associated with the governance issue of democratic accountability. Accountability breaks down if elected officials cannot control government workers.

Bureaucratic Responsiveness

Two separate issues are involved in a discussion of the responsiveness of urban service bureaucracies. The first concerns the responsiveness of service agencies to citizen-initiated contacts. When citizens complain, what do bureaucracies do? As we noted in chapter 5, citizen-initiated contacts provide an important channel of access for citizens to influence government decision making. But the effectiveness of this channel depends on how government responds to citizen complaints.

The second issue involves the degree to which elected officials actually can control what bureaucracies do. This is a more global conception of bureaucratic responsiveness. If elected officials cannot control bureaucracies, then electoral accountability cannot in the normal course of political events be established. In the absence of such control, elected officials will be unable to implement the policies preferred by citizens. The decline of the patronage system, the rise of the norm of neutral competence, and the emergence of employee organizations and unions have all operated against executive control of service delivery agencies. In this section we examine the responsiveness of bureaucracies to citizen contacts; we will explore the issues of bureaucratic control later.

Complaints

City bureaucrats are simply more attuned to respond to citizen complaints in some cities than in others. In many cities, service agencies attempt to investigate all citizen complaints. But some agencies seem to pursue the investigations more vigorously than others. In some cities, centralized complaint bureaus handle citizen complaints; often these agencies follow up on complaints to see what the responsible bureaucracy has done. In Detroit, for example, the Office of the Ombudsman accepts citizen complaints, contacts the responsible bureaucracy (sometimes repeatedly), and mails the citizen a written report of the action taken. In other cities, agencies harbor a more cavalier attitude toward citizen complaints. In Houston, one study showed that many citizen complaints were simply ignored by service agencies. Only a third of complaining citizens received a substantive response.[2]

Even when city service agencies investigate citizen complaints, they may not act on them. Whether or not a citizen receives satisfaction (beyond an investigation of the complaint) is related to (1) whether the complaint is valid; (2) whether, if it is valid, the city agency has the authority, legal or otherwise, to act; and (3) whether the agency has the resources to act. If, for example, a wife calls the police to intervene in a spouse-abuse case, the police officers who respond must decide whether the complaint is valid. If citizens complain about the poor quality of street surfaces in their neighborhood, the agency may find their complaints legitimate and may also have the authority to make repairs, but a tight budget may mean putting off the project for the present.

Production: Efficiency and Effectiveness

The twin issues of efficiency and effectiveness are key elements in the service production process. Urban public services are produced in a two-stage process. In the first stage, service inputs are transformed by the agency into ser-

[2] Kenneth Mladenka, "Citizen Demand and Bureaucratic Response: Direct Dialing Democracy in a Major American City," *Urban Affairs Quarterly* 12 (March 1977): 273–90.

vice outputs. In the second stage, outputs are transformed into service impacts. The process is diagrammed here.

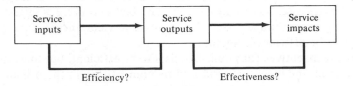

Service inputs are the resources allocated by government (the mayor and city council) to the service agency. These are the budget allocations to the agency. These resources are used to produce *service outputs,* the mix of activities used by the agency in attempting to accomplish its goals. A police department, for example, uses its budget allocations to hire patrol officers and detectives, buy equipment, and staff the crime laboratory. These outputs bear some relationship to *service impacts.* Impacts are the headway an agency is making on the problems that it is supposed to solve.

An *effective* agency is one that is making the largest impact possible with the lowest level of output possible. That is, effectiveness is the ratio of impacts to outputs. The higher this ratio, the better the agency is performing. An *efficient* agency is one that is producing a high level of outputs at the lowest possible cost of inputs. It is entirely possible that an agency may efficiently produce outputs that are ineffective in accomplishing goals. The fire department may get as many fire prevention inspections as is humanly possible out of its budget allocations, spending few dollars on administrative overhead. But if fire prevention inspections are not related to goal accomplishment, the agency is employing its resources ineffectively.

Efficiency

The *efficiency* of a service organization is the amount of output produced per dollar of resources allocated in the budget process.[3] In private firms, efficiency may be assessed either by dividing the number of units produced (the total output) by the cost of all units, or by dividing the dollar value of the output by the cost of the resource inputs. This latter strategy is possible because private firms must sell their products in the marketplace. Moreover, for private firms in truly competitive markets, there is an incentive for efficiency. Efficient firms are able to lower the price of their products below those of inefficient firms and still reap profits. If a firm is too inefficient, in fact, it will be driven from the marketplace (again, if markets are truly competitive).

[3] For a state-of-the art survey of issues in governmental efficiency, see George Washkins, ed., *Productivity Improvement for State and Local Government* (New York: Wiley, 1980).

City governments do not compete with one another in producing services for their citizens. Within its jurisdiction, a city government holds a monopoly in the production of many services—police, fire, streets, garbage collection, and other essential urban services. The fact that there is little competition among the producers of urban public services means that a major incentive to be efficient is absent.

There are incentives for public officials to be efficient, but these are quite different from the incentive produced by competition in the private sector. The two major incentives for public officials to be efficient are citizen mobility and taxpayer resistance to increased spending. Mobility means that citizens may move from a municipality that operates inefficiently to one that operates efficiently, receive the same in services, and pay less in taxes. Taxpayer resistance means that public officials cannot simply hike taxes in order to cover over inefficient operations.

These factors, however, often seem remote to city officials who must face the more immediate demands of citizens for more or better-quality services, and of public employees for higher pay or more favorable working conditions. Many of the working conditions established in the collective-bargaining process operate contrary to efficient service production. In many cities, bus mechanics receive overtime pay for working at night. Yet demand for buses is higher during daytime hours. In order to meet daytime demands, a city may have to get the buses fixed at night, even though the same mechanics who are earning overtime pay at night will be idle during the day. Such examples of service inefficiencies can be found in most cities.

Measuring Outputs. Public services are produced in a strikingly different environment from private services, and that environment makes the measurement of efficiency difficult. First, public services are not sold to the public. Occasionally there are user charges, but such charges almost never reflect the value of the service. So efficiency cannot be measured as the ratio of output to the cost of input. In the second place, there is a true unit of output for only a few services. A ton of refuse collected can serve as a unit of output for sanitation services, but what is a unit of police protection? Hence, in many urban service agencies it is difficult to assess efficiency by dividing the number of units of output produced by the cost of inputs.[4]

Indeed, when public sector managers do try to quantify outputs, they can generate bizarre behavior on the part of workers, who perceive that they are being evaluated by these measures. If a city manager were to try to assess the efficiency of police activities by adopting the clearance rate for crimes (that is, the verified crimes that have been cleared by arrest), he or she would run the risk of subtly influencing the behavior of police officers, who of course

---

[4] For some practical suggestions, see Harry P. Hatry, *How Effective Are Your Community Services?* (Washington, D.C.: Urban Institute, 1977).

want to look effective. They may drop work on the difficult murder cases and concentrate on catching "cat" burglars, who may confess to hundreds of breaking and entering crimes. This problem results because the measure (clearance rate) does not fully indicate all the complexity of police operations. If it did, the manager would be pleased to let police officers do whatever they could to produce "units of output."

A major problem in assessing outputs is that much service delivery activity takes place far from the central office of the agency. Welfare case workers, police, fire prevention inspectors, and health inspectors all operate in the field, in regular contact with citizens. The agency may have them fill out reports detailing what they have done, but many aspects of the service process are not indicated by the reports. Moreover, the correctness of the judgment of the "street-level bureaucrat" cannot be second-guessed by supervisors, simply because they were not there.

There are two basic sources of information on agency outputs. One is the records kept by the agency. Although these records cannot tell everything that is happening in the field, they are the most objective indicators of the service process. A major problem is the record-keeping habits of many service agencies. Some agencies are meticulous; others lack the staff, the expertise, and the interest to maintain complete records.

A second way to assess agency outputs is through citizen evaluation studies. Barbara Nelson has noted that clients of a service agency can provide three types of evaluation. *Problem-centered* evaluations concern direct judgments of the bureaucratic process itself. How efficiently does the client think his or her problem was handled? *Relationship-centered* evaluations are client judgments of how they were treated by agency personnel. *Outcome evaluations* concern the effectiveness or quality of the service rendered.[5] Stipak, however, has issued a number of cautions in using client evaluations to assess service outputs. First, there is a *halo effect* in client evaluations. Service recipients tend to be overwhelmingly positive in their evaluations of the services they receive. A manager of a service agency must have some basis for comparison before concluding that the performance of his or her agency is satisfactory. Second, the accuracy of client perceptions decreases for programs that do not involve close and regular client-agency interaction. Third, specific evaluations are more accurate than general assessments. Fourth, the evaluation may reflect citizen attitudes that are not directly related to program performance. Health clinics may receive higher ratings than garbage collection because people generally hold health professionals in higher esteem than sanitation workers. Finally, different client groups may have different expectations of service. Comparisons across client groupings can

[5] Barbara J. Nelson, "Client Perceptions of Officialdom: Assessing Citizen Encounters with Social Programs," paper presented at the Conference on the Public Encounter, Virginia Polytechnic Institute and State University, Blacksburg, Va., January 9–11, 1980.

be misleading. Two groups having different attitudes may offer different evaluations, even though they have been treated similarly in all aspects of the service delivery process.[6]

Cost of Service. Do public services cost more than comparable services in the private sector? This is a more difficult question than it first appears, for two reasons. First, many public services are produced by government because the private sector has failed to produce them in sufficient quantities. (Recall the discussion of collective goods in chapter 3.) In the second place, when public services are produced by a private company for a city government, the company is granted a monopoly and lacks the incentive of competition every bit as much as government itself. Such arrangements were once common for transit systems, but most cities have since taken over the responsibility for mass transit. Today, many communities contract with private firms for garbage collection. In those instances in which private production and public production can be directly compared, private services are generally cheaper. An evaluation expert for drug-abuse programs in a major city, in which some programs were run by the city health department and some were contracted out to a variety of private suppliers, commented to the author: "We have inexpensive private programs and expensive private programs, but we have only expensive public programs."

One urbanist who has systematically studied the cost of government services is E. S. Savas. Savas has studied refuse collection in a number of localities. His studies indicate that municipalities that contract out refuse collection have a lower cost of service than do those that provide the service themselves.[7]

Apparently, municipal budgets substantially understate the true cost of refuse collection service.[8] Not all the costs of sanitation services are charged to the sanitation department, for a variety of reasons. Cities often assign fringes, garage expenses, and some administrative and capital costs to other accounts than those maintained for refuse collection. Thus the sanitation department budget understates the true cost of service. This misleads policymakers into thinking that services are costing less than they actually are. But when a city contracts with a private firm for a service, it knows exactly what the service costs.

Savas believes that this situation, in which the budget understates the cost

[6] Brian Stipak, "Using Clients to Evaluate Programs," paper presented at the Conference on the Public Encounter, Virginia Polytechnic Institute and State University, Blacksburg, Va., January 9–11, 1980; Stipak, "Citizen Satisfaction with Urban Services," *Public Administration Review* 39 (1979): 46–52.

[7] E. S. Savas, "Public vs. Private Refuse Collection: A Critical Review of the Evidence," *Journal of Urban Analysis* 6 (1979), pp. 1–13.

[8] E. S. Savas, "How Much Do Government Services Really Cost?" *Urban Affairs Quarterly* 15 (September 1979): 23–28.

of service and municipal officials think they are spending less than they actually are, probably applies to other services as well. It must be pointed out, however, that the entire cost of public services is going to show up in the budget, unless municipal officials are engaging in true budget gimmickry. The numbers from the various accounts used by a municipal government must add up to a total sooner or later. The result is that citizens and officials do know the entire cost of all the services provided, but they may not know the correct breakdown for each service.

These and similar findings have led many urbanists to advocate a fuller use of contracting for those services that can be contracted to private firms. Although some core municipal functions, such as police protection, cannot be contracted, many others can. Savas says that "in many cases . . . the private firm can do the same work at lower cost."[9]

Effectiveness

An effective urban service agency is one that is accomplishing its goals. Put slightly differently, an effective agency is one that is making an impact on the problems that it is supposed to solve.

Service agencies accomplish goals by producing services, which in turn are supposed to solve problems and accomplish public goals. It is not always clear that the services produced help in solving problems. For example, fire departments generally engage in fire prevention and fire suppression activities. Fire prevention involves public education about fire risks and inspection of businesses, apartments, and homes for fire hazards. Fire suppression is putting out fires once they have started. Clearly, fire suppression is related to the goals of the fire department. But are fire prevention activities? How do we know whether fire prevention activities have any effect? Is the probability of fire lessened by these activities? The same questions can be asked of police patrolling. Does routine police patrolling deter crime? A major study in Kansas City indicates that it may not.[10]

Assessing Effectiveness. The advocates of municipal reform stressed that scientific management ought to be employed to analyze the delivery of public services. Only by using precise methods could it be determined whether services were being delivered effectively and efficiently. Today

---

[9] Ibid., p. 41. A second interesting finding from the study is that the budgets of council-manager governments stated costs more accurately than budgets of mayor-council cities. This was probably because smaller cities make more use of contracting *and* are more likely to have council-manager forms, but it also suggests that council-manager forms are more efficient in service provision.

[10] George Kelling, Tony Pate, Duane Dieckman, and Charles E. Brown,, *The Kansas City Preventive Patrol Experiment: Summary Report* (Washington, D.C.: Police Foundation, 1974).

many cities employ evaluators who try to assess the extent to which urban services are achieving goals. Evaluators employ a variety of techniques developed in such diverse academic disciplines as engineering, psychology, and business management. Assessing agency effectiveness involves measuring goals, measuring levels of service, and then examining the relationship between the two.

One cannot assess goal accomplishment without having a measure of the goal. Some goals are relatively easy to measure—for example, the goal of the city sanitation division is simply to collect and dispose of refuse. Other goals are abstract, vague, and difficult to measure. For example, the goal of police agencies is "community security," obviously an elusive concept.[11]

One can envision several measures of community security, including reported crimes (but citizens don't report all crimes), the subjective fear of crime among citizens (but such subjective feelings may be only tenuously related to objective conditions), and reported victimization rates in citizen surveys (but citizens may report incidents that are not legally crimes, or may fail to report incidences that are). All of these measures have been used, and they yield different results. Which is best? In general, some combination should be used. Using a combination of measures is called the *multiple indicator* approach, because each of the measures of community security (or goal of other agencies) indicates (rather than directly assesses) the goal.

In order to assess service effectiveness, program outputs must be linked to measures of the community conditions that agencies are supposed to affect. The major problem here is that many factors other than the outputs of government service agencies affect such community conditions. Elinor Ostrom, the political scientist who has contributed most to developing measures of police performance, comments: "A perplexing problem in conceptualizing the output of a police department is that while its activities contribute to the security of the community, *it is never the sole contributor to this state of affairs.*"[12] Rather, a whole set of institutional arrangements, including the state of the economy, housing markets, educational systems, community organizations, and the court and penal systems interact with the police to produce community security.

Because the activities of urban service agencies are never sole contributors to the goals that they are supposed to accomplish, it is very difficult to assess the precise contribution of the agency to its stated goals. Imagine that a police department is assessing its performance in relation to the reported crime rate, as verified by the department. If crime rates are declining, the police chief will surely claim credit. If crime rates are rising, it will either be because of community conditions (rising unemployment, for example) or

---

[11] Elinor Ostrom, "On the Meaning and Measurement of Efficiency in the Provision of Urban Police Services," *Journal of Criminal Justice* 1 (1973): 97.
[12] Ibid., p. 97.

because the mayor has cut the police budget. In either case, more police are needed. If the crime rate remains steady while the police are rapidly adding officers, things would have been worse had the buildup not occurred. In a situation in which it is unclear just how much police contributed to community security, no worthy police chief is going to miss an opportunity to claim credit, nor is he or she going to accept blame.

The only way to attribute community security to police activities is for the other factors contributing to community security to remain constant while police activity increases or decreases. In the constant flux of urban America, this is impossible. But if it could be done, and community security (however measured) changed, the change in community security could be attributed to the change in police activity.

Methods of Assessment. Social scientists have developed several ways to approximate this condition and thereby assess the effectiveness of public programs. All of these methods rely on comparisons. There are two basic kinds of comparisons: cross-sectional and time-series comparisons. *Cross-sectional* designs rely on comparisons between cities. In the simplest cross-sectional design, there are two groups of cities, one of which has programs (such as a special police detail to capture bank robbers) and the other of which does not. The two groups of cities are compared with respect to the goals of the program (how many robberies there are). In more complex designs, there are several groups of cities, ordered according to how much effort (such as expenditures) they provide for the program). *Time-series* designs involve comparisons of one city at several points in time, some before the program was introduced, some after.

So far we have not solved the problem of "sole contribution," the fact that other factors, termed *confounding factors,* also contribute to service agency goals. These confounding factors somehow must be controlled. This can be accomplished by three methods: true experiments, quasi-experiments, and statistical controls. In *true experiments,* confounding factors are held constant either physically or through a process termed *random assignment.* In the latter case, cities would be randomly assigned programs (for example, some cities would be assigned bank robbery programs and others would not be allowed to adopt them). By randomly assigning programs, the investigator would hope that the confounding factors will "cancel themselves out." Only in exceptional circumstances will the student of program effectiveness be able to find and measure such a situation.

In *quasi-experiments,* the investigator cannot control just when and where a program will be introduced by a service delivery agency. When the program is introduced, however, the investigator tries to approximate an experiment as closely as possible. Then he or she tries to rule out as many of the possible confounding factors as possible. The best quasi-experiment is called the *interrupted-time-series design with control series.* This design makes use of both cross-sectional and time-series comparisons. Let us say that City A establishes a special police bureau to catch bank robbers. We expect that bank robberies will go down after the program is adopted. But what if bank robberies were going to go down anyway (because of those bothersome confounding factors)? The best way to make sure this is not happening is to examine another city, one that has not adopted a bank robbery program (City B). If its bank robbery rate does not go down, City A's bank robbery program is effective (see figure 14.1).

The final method for studying the effectiveness of programs run by service agencies is the *statistical control (or nonexperimental)* design. In this design, the investigator must discover and measure all confounding factors. Then, in essence, he or she is able to subtract the effects of all these factors from the effects that can be attributed to the program. For the design to be correct, it is necessary for all relevant factors to be discovered and included. If any are missed, the estimates of program effectiveness will be wrong.[13]

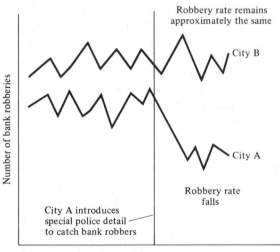

Figure 14.1. Interrupted-time series design to evaluate the effectiveness of a police program.

[13] The study of program effectiveness requires substantial knowledge of both statistics and social science research design. Courses in these topics are offered at many universities. For an introduction to these topics, see Laura Irwin Langbein, *Discovering Whether Programs Work* (Santa Monica, Calif.: Goodyear, 1980). More technical coverage is in Thomas Cook and Donald Campbell, *Quasi-Experimentation* (Chicago: Rand McNally, 1979).

Distribution

Urban public services are designed to solve collective community problems—the problems of crime, or urban decay, or growth management. Yet it is possible that the resources that cities commit to solving these problems can benefit some citizens more than others. The study of the manner in which service benefits go to different classes of citizens and their neighborhoods is called the study of *service distribution*.

There are five basic patterns of service distribution. Each depends on the correspondence between the social class composition of the neighborhood and the level of benefits received by the neighborhood. If service is identical for all neighborhoods, regardless of social class, the service distribution pattern is one of *equality*. If the poor receive more benefits than the better off, the service pattern is termed *compensatory,* because government benefits are compensating for the private disadvantages suffered by citizens in poor neighborhoods. If the better off receive better services and the poor receive worse, the pattern is *cumulative*. Finally, the pattern may be *curvilinear*. There are two possible curvilinear patterns. The first is a U-*shaped* distribution, in which the poorest and the best-off neighborhoods receive the most service benefits, the middle-income neighborhoods the fewest. The second is ∩-*shaped,* with the middle-income neighborhoods receiving the most service benefits, and both poor and wealthy receiving the least. Recall that citizen-initiated contacts are related to the social status of neighborhoods by such a ∩-shaped curve. Thus, if city service agencies simply respond to citizen-initiated contacts uncritically, a ∩-shaped curve of service benefits will result. Figure 14.2 diagrams the various patterns of service distribution.

The two tiers of service distribution

Service distribution in a metropolitan area is accomplished within a two-tiered structure. The first tier is an *inter*jurisdictional service pattern; the second is *intra*jurisdictional. *Interjurisdictional* service distribution refers to varying service levels among the various municipal governments within the metropolis. Some suburbs may, for example, have better parks or libraries than either the central city or other suburbs. This variability is a consequence of the differences in the ability to afford services and differences in citizen demands for services. (We have discussed these factors in detail in chapter 9.)

Intrajurisdictional service distribution refers to differences in service levels among neighborhoods within a single municipality. Neighborhood A may get more or better police service than Neighborhood Z, yet these dif-

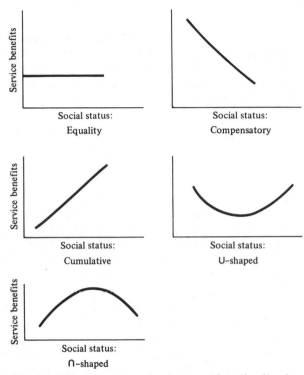

Figure 14.2. Patterns of urban service distribution.

ferences cannot be explained in the same manner as interjurisdictional variations can. The reason is that interjurisdictional differences are produced by
separately acting policymaking units (the municipal governments). Neighborhoods, on the other hand, are not independent policymaking units, and
must rely on city hall to deliver services.

The underclass hypothesis

In perhaps no other area of urban political inquiry have initial ideas of
political scientists been so incorrect as in the study of intrajurisdictional
urban service distributions. Fresh from the pluralist-elitist arguments about
power structures, many political scientists reasoned that regardless of which
position was correct, the poor should get fewer urban services. The consensus was that organization is crucial in politics, and the poor are notoriously
difficult to organize because of their lack of skills and resources. Hence,
even in a pluralist system, the poor should be able to claim fewer of the urban

services produced by cities than the better off. Add to this the fact of pervasive racial discrimination in society, the fact that the aging urban party structures were still in the hands of the European ethnics, unable or unwilling to organize the black ghettos, and it would seem that blacks would also be candidates for service discrimination. Robert Lineberry has termed this working hypothesis the *underclass hypothesis,* to stress that it was expected that blacks and poor would experience service discrimination.

Furthermore, several service equalization court suits were initiated in the late 1960s and early 1970s. The most celebrated of these suits resulted in the court case of *Hawkins* v. *Shaw, Mississippi* (1971). In this case, the United States Fifth Circuit Court of Appeals ruled that the town of Shaw had violated the equal protection clause of the Fourteenth Amendment to the Constitution by denying to black residents services that were available to whites. "The evidence established that nearly ninety-eight percent of homes fronting on unpaved streets were black-occupied; ninety-seven percent of homes not served by sanitary sewers were in black neighborhoods."[14] Many urbanists leaped to the conclusion that such pervasive, cumulative service discrimination was "also typical of much larger cities in the U.S."[15]

Unpatterned inequality

Armed with the underclass hypothesis, political scientists began to collect systematic data on service distribution in a number of cities. Sometimes the data indicated that the poor received poorer-quality services, but at other times it seemed that they received better services. Lineberry summarized the results from his San Antonio study as "unpatterned inequality." In none of the services he studied did he find an equal distribution of services. In every service, some San Antonio residents got better services than did others. But service benefits were not cumulative. That is, if one group got better library services, it was unlikely to get better police services. None of the distributions corresponded to political power configurations.[16]

Other studies of service distributions in other cities turned up similar results: in Houston, Detroit, Oakland, Boston, and Chicago, the pattern held.[17] In no case were there clear, cumulative service distribution patterns

[14] Robert L. Lineberry, "Mandating Urban Equality: The Distribution of Urban Public Services," *Texas Law Review* 53 (December 1974): 33–34.

[15] Kevin Cox, *Conflict, Power and Politics in the City: A Geographic View* (New York: McGraw-Hill, 1973), p. 74.

[16] Robert L. Lineberry, *Equality and Urban Policy: The Distribution of Municipal Public Services* (Beverly Hills, Calif.: Sage, 1977).

[17] *Houston:* Kenneth Mladenka and Kim Hill, "The Distribution of Urban Police Services," *Journal of Politics* 40 (February 1978): 112–33; George E. Antunes and John Plumlee, "The Distribution of an Urban Public Service," *Urban Affairs Quarterly* 12 (March 1977): 313–32; Kenneth Mladenka and Kim Hill, "The Distribution of Benefits in an Urban Environment: Parks and Libraries in Houston," *Urban Affairs Quarterly* 13 (September 1977):

Box 14.1: The Complexity of Service Distribution

A study of housing-code enforcement in Detroit measured five aspects of service delivery. Housing-code enforcement is a municipal service that attempts to maintain the quality of housing by initiating action against owners who allow their properties to deteriorate. The five aspects of service delivery are *routine inspections, response to citizen-initiated contacts, service intensity* (the number of follow-up site visits used by the code-enforcement agency in trying to get owners to comply to agency directives); *quality of service* (measured as time of response to citizen complaints) and *compliance of owners to agency citations.* Each aspect of the service delivery process was found to have a different distributional pattern. Routine inspections were conducted primarily in the poorest neighborhoods. Response to citizen-initiated contacts occurred disproportionately in low-to-middle-income neighborhoods (why?). Service follow-up site visits occurred disproportionately in poor neighborhoods, and the agency obtained the best record of compliance in the middle-class neighborhoods. Quality of service was lowest in working-class neighborhoods, and highest in poor and middle-income neighborhoods. Here, then, is a prime example of *unpatterned inequality.*

Source: See Bryan D. Jones, in association with Saadia Greenberg and Joseph Drew, *Service Delivery in the City* (New York: Longman, 1980), chs. 6–7.

benefiting the better off and harming the poor. To add to the complexity, some aspects of a single service might be distributed in one manner, other aspects in another (see box 14.1). Beyond a shadow of a doubt, the underclass hypothesis is incorrect for most services in most American cities.

The bureaucratic connection

If neither discrimination nor political action is responsible for observed patterns of urban service distributions, then what is? It has become increas-

73–94. *Detroit:* Bryan Jones in association with Saadia Greenberg and Joseph Drew, *Service Delivery in the City* (New York: Longman, 1980). *Oakland:* Frank Levy, Arnold Meltsner, and Aaron Wildavsky, *Urban Outcomes* (Berkeley, Calif.: University of California Press, 1974). *Boston:* Pietro Nivola, *The Urban Service Problem: A Study of Housing Inspection* (Lexington, Mass.: Lexington Books, 1979). *Chicago:* Kenneth Mladenka, "The Urban Bureaucracy and the Chicago Political Machine: Who Gets What and the Limits to Political Control," *American Political Science Review* 74 (December 1980): 991–98.

ingly evident that the standard operating procedures used by service agencies to deal with the routine tasks they perform are responsible for the observed patterns of service distribution.

Standard operating procedures, or *decision rules,* are routine ways of performing tasks. They emerge whenever an organization has to perform a repetitive task. Rather than treat each problem as a new decision that must be made, organizations employ *performance programs.* When a task must be performed, organizational personnel simply consult the performance program and do it the way it has always been done.

Any set decision rules are possible. An agency might, for example, serve all Democrats requesting a service and refuse to serve all Republicans. Or it might give quality service to whites, but not to blacks. That such decision rules are not usually employed by service agencies requires explanation.

Throughout the twentieth century local service agencies have become increasingly bureaucratic. We have emphasized that this involved "taking administration out of politics" by instituting personnel systems monitored by civil service systems. But it also involved adopting the norm of *universalism,* in which all citizens are served according to the problems they have, not according to their ethnic backgrounds, party affiliations, or political connections. This norm was implemented in public agencies by installing decision rules that were *procedurally* fair: Every citizen requesting a service is treated equally. Two examples of procedurally fair service delivery rules are waiting for service on a "first come, first served" basis, and delivering service according to the severity of the problem. Hospital emergency rooms, for example, use a combination of these procedures. You wait your turn unless your injury is particularly severe, in which case you are treated on a priority basis. Most people would not object to this system. But if patients were admitted more quickly because they knew the emergency room doctor, others might object.

Other bureaucratic operating procedures are designed to ensure fair treatment of service personnel. For example, job assignments are often based on seniority. When there is a vacancy, the person who has been with the agency the longest will be offered the position. If he or she refuses, it will be offered to the next most senior, and so forth, until the position is filled. When job assignments are based on seniority, members of service organizations are reassured that political favoritism is not playing a part in assignments. On the other hand, management is unable to choose the best person for the job.

Political scientists have long noted that the rules and procedures used to structure the policymaking process have the effect of benefiting some citizens and harming others. In chapter 10 we noted that the adoption of such governmental forms as the council-manager system have various unintended consequences, one of which is lessening participation, which works to the detriment of the poor. One might say that governmental forms have distributional consequences.

In light of this, it is perhaps not surprising that seemingly neutral bureaucratic procedures also have distributional effects. In their study of service delivery agencies in Oakland, California, Levy and his colleagues found that the procedures used in delivering services often harmed some citizens and benefited others. They comment that "somehow these benevolent norms . . . which ought to help everyone, end up helping some more than others. These rules, like many 'neutral' decision rules, are not neutral. They have a class bias."[18]

One should not infer from this statement that bureaucratic decision rules always benefit the well off. The distributional consequences of a bureaucratic decision rule depend on the nature of the rule. For example, consider the rule used by many agencies to render service in response to citizen-initiated contacts only. This will have the consequence of delivering the most service to neighborhoods that initiate large numbers of contacts. These neighborhoods, as we know, are not the best off, because those neighborhoods initiate fewer citizen contacts than working-class or poor ones.

On the other hand, consider the seniority-transfer rule for job assignments. In many school systems teachers are allowed to transfer according to seniority. Jobs in middle-class neighborhoods are generally viewed as more desirable than those in ghetto neighborhoods, because of both the home backgrounds of the children and the relative absence of disciplinary problems. Hence, it is common for the teachers with the most seniority (and thus those with the most experience and highest pay) to transfer to the better-off neighborhoods.

There are even rules that operate to benefit the poorest neighborhoods. One rule used by the Detroit Sanitation Division is to assign extra resources where there are alleys behind residences, because citizens are less careful about placing garbage in containers in alleys than they are when they must put it in front of their houses. Alleys, however, are located primarily in the older center city, where the poor live. A second rule, also from Detroit, is to inspect routinely all multistory buildings for housing-code violations. Again, these buildings are located primarily in the poorer sections of the city.

The common thread running through all these examples is that in each case a procedurally neutral decision rule has distributional consequences. The rule unintentionally treats citizens differently. Seldom do urban service agencies perform a *distributional analysis* for the decision rules that they adopt. The rule is adopted to cope with a particular problem, and no one in the agency ever asks just what distributional effects the rule is likely to have. Were they to do so, it might be possible to eliminate the more undesirable effects of some procedures.

---

[18] Frank Levy, Arnold Meltsner, and Aaron Wildavsky, *Urban Outcomes* (Berkeley, Calif.: University of California Press, 1974). p. 232.

Distribution: The individual dimension

In many cases, the bureaucratic decision rules established by a service agency are violated in practice. If a policeman refuses to take the complaint of a black as seriously as he would a similar complaint by a white, he has violated a basic principle of bureaucracy: the norm of universalism. The behavior of police and other so-called street-level bureaucrats may conflict with the norms established by agency personnel. We shall have more to say about this aspect of service delivery shortly.

A second way in which universalistic norms are violated stems from the unequal distribution of knowledge among citizens. Some citizens are just more adept at dealing with bureaucracies than others. The "court-wise" teenager who knows just how far she can go in the juvenile justice system without ending up in a reformatory exhibits this adeptness. So does the lawyer who owns a slum building and is under fire from the building department. In general, middle-class people are more adept at dealing with bureaucracies than are working-class or poor citizens. Such knowledgeables are able to use bureaucratic procedures to gain special benefits for themselves.

Finally, some persons or organizations may be able to get bureaucracy to afford them special treatment simply because they are powerful. Evidence from Chicago suggests that those Democratic ward organizations that are powerful within the machine are able to get special service from the city building department (see box 14.2).

Internal Bureaucratic Control

If democratic policymaking institutions are to be effective, the policies they enact must be carried out by bureaucracies that are accountable. "Accountability is the link between bureaucracy and democracy." [19]

Bureaucratic accountability to the elected branches of government means two things. It means, first, that the executives administering government service agencies are accountable to the elected branches of government. In the second place, it means that the behaviors of public sector workers are in conformity with the policies of agency executives. In other words, the elected branches must be able to control the behaviors of agency executives, and agency executives must be able to control the behaviors of the other members of the organization. This conception of democratic accountability has been termed *overhead democracy*.[20]

[19] Michael Lipsky, *Street-Level Bureaucracy: Dilemmas of the Individual in Public Services* (New York: Russell Sage, 1980), p. 160.

[20] Emmette S. Redford, *Ideal and Practice in Public Administration* (University, Ala.: University of Alabama Press, 1958), p. 89.

Box 14.2: A Tale of Two City Building Departments

Not all municipal agencies operate in an atmosphere free of partisan political concerns. In Chicago, the Democratic party can and does influence the service delivery process in some agencies. There, the norm of neutral competence coexists with the norm of response to political demands. In some agencies, particularly the police and fire departments, neutral competence in service delivery prevails. This does not mean that internal agency politics cannot be fierce; they often are. It does mean that calls for service, and the response of the police, are not normally affected by political considerations. In other agencies, such as the building department, political considerations exist alongside the norm of neutral competence, making a volatile mix.

In Detroit, the norm of neutral competence prevails in all city agencies. Again, internal agency politics can be fierce, but there are no strong party organizations to interfere with the procedurally neutral delivery of services.

It is interesting to compare the building departments of these two cities. In both cities, agency procedures prescribe a set of rules to be followed for one important part of the service process: responding to citizen complaints. The process works like this: characteristics of the buildings in a neighborhood, and the characteristics of citizens themselves, cause citizens to contact government regarding building-code enforcement. Generally, these contacts follow the model discussed in chapter 5, where we noted that citizen-initiated contacts stem from a need perceived by the citizen (deteriorated housing), and information about whom to contact to solve the problem. The rule in both Detroit and Chicago is to inspect in response to every complaint. Then the agency judges the severity of the complaint and acts accordingly. The least severe situations are not acted upon; more severe situations receive agency citations; and the most severe situations are sent to court. The actions of the agency are more or less effective in solving the citizen's problems, but no problems are

Source: See Bryan D. Jones in association with Saadia Greenberg and Joseph Drew, *Service Delivery in the City* (New York: Longman, 1980), chapters 6 and 7 on Detroit; Jones, "Party and Bureaucracy: The Influence of Intermediary Groups on Urban Service Delivery," *American Political Science Review* XX (September 1981): 688–700 on Chicago. See also Kenneth Mladenka, "The Urban Bureaucracy and the Political Machine: Who Gets What and the Limits to Political Control," *American Political Science Review* 74 (December 1980): 991–98.

solved unless the agency takes action. The process can be diagrammed as follows:

According to the formal agency rules, different city neighborhoods do not get preferential treatment because of their racial or class composition or because they are politically active. And that is largely how the process operates in Detroit.

In Chicago, however, the party organization influences *each stage* of the service delivery process. In those neighborhoods where the party is strongest, more citizen complaints are filed with the department; citizens get better service (in that the agency acts on more of the citizen complaints it receives, and acts more severely on them); and owners are more likely to comply to orders from the building department. Service impact is thus greater where the party organization is strongest. In Chicago, the situation looks like this:

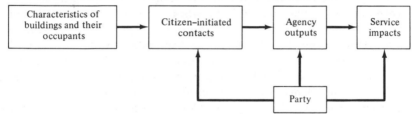

Which system is better? Most of us would probably say the process is fairer in Detroit, but we ought to stop and think. The party in Chicago is making more demands on the building department, in order to maintain the character of the housing stock (primarily through the precinct captains, who call in complaints to the department). It is also able to improve service for its citizens. Finally, the party is able to improve the impact of the actions taken by the building department by directly negotiating with landlords who refuse to comply. On the other side of the coin, the party does this by substantial interference with the norm of neutral competence. Bureaucrats seem to be more observant of building-code violations where the party is strong (concomitantly, they are less observant of them in neighborhoods where the party is weak). Here again is one of those tradeoffs that we meet so often in the study of urban politics: political responsiveness (and perhaps service impact) must be relinquished in order to gain procedural fairness and administrative neutrality.

In urban America, control of agency executives by local legislatures and elected chief executives does not always exist. We have noted in earlier chapters that the selection of agency heads is not in the hands of the mayor or the city council in many cities. In council-manager cities, the manager is formally responsible to the city council, but city council members are often part-time volunteers with little expertise in municipal government. The manager often acts as policy initiator, and his or her recommendations are usually followed by the council. This is a far cry from the theory of democratic accountability as normally stated.

We have also noted that agency executives cannot automatically control the behavior of the workers in the agency they are supposed to command. Workers are unionized; there exist work rules and ways of doing things that resist intrusion by agency managers. Many managers of urban service delivery agencies find that they must bargain with and cajole their employees rather than simply issue a command.

Street-level bureaucrats

Many of the conflicts in urban service delivery organizations occur between agency management and the workers responsible for delivering services directly to citizens—welfare case workers, police officers, municipal court judges, public health nurses, teachers, and building inspectors. These *street-level bureaucrats,* as they have been called by Michael Lipsky, are subject to intense job stress. This stress stems from a combination of factors.[21]

First, the problems faced by street-level bureaucrats often seem to be insurmountable. The intertwined problems of poverty, crime, deteriorating housing, poor health, and educational problems are obviously not dealt with adequately by the private sector. Indeed, the inequalities that exist in American urban society, inequalities that allow some citizens to reside in affluent suburbs and others to suffer in squalid slums, are in large measure *caused by* the private sector. Government service agencies often intervene to mitigate the harsh effects of unbridled private enterprise. But the cumulative effects of urban inequalities mean that the problems that are symptoms of urban poverty are almost intractable. The most that the street-level bureaucrat can expect is modest individual successes; large-scale victories almost never occur. Indeed, most of the situations that street-level bureaucrats are responsible for attacking—poor health, crime, deteriorated housing—are more responsive to large-scale social forces (such as improvements in national economic conditions) than to the efforts of the service bureaucrats.

The second factor contributing to job stress is the limited resources governments use to attack large-scale social problems. Limited resources mean that service agencies are continually rationing services, and that de-

[21] Lipsky, *Street-Level Bureaucracy,* ch. 3.

mand for services almost always exceeds supply. Few legal-service lawyers have the luxury of spending the time necessary to prepare properly the cases brought to them by the poor. Few teachers can spend the necessary hours instructing promising students when they spend most class time worrying about student discipline.

The third factor involved in job stress is that many street-level bureaucrats have professional training that emphasizes the quality of service and the exercise of professional responsibility. Imagine the shock of the nutritionist who goes out to center city day-care programs to instruct students and staff on proper dietary balance only to discover that three- and four-year-olds are not even being fed enough to maintain their energy during the day. Imagine the frustration of the drug-abuse worker who must contend with clients who have been referred by the criminal justice system, but who have no real interest in "shaking the habit." Service quality almost always takes a back seat to more pressing problems: discipline, obtaining and holding client interest in bettering his or her situation, getting clients to keep appointments, and, not infrequently, worrying about threats to one's personal safety.

Fourth, government service agencies are specialized. Nurses and doctors from the department of health deal with the health problems of city dwellers. Welfare case workers try to alleviate the immediate monetary problems of the poor. Housing inspectors try to improve the conditions of the buildings in which the poor are housed. Unfortunately, however, the problems of the poor are not so neatly segmented. Problems exist together as a syndrome, while government approaches are segmented. Perhaps no street-level workers realize this more than drug- and alcohol-abuse workers. If the treated patient returns to his or her former environment, the abuse problems almost invariably return.

Fifth, government services are difficult to measure. This means that the street-level bureaucrat has trouble knowing when she or he is performing well. If good teaching cannot be measured, how does one know whether one is a good teacher? Moreover, the problem of measurement means that agency executives have trouble knowing whether their workers are performing well. In the absence of such knowledge, rewards such as salary increases and promotions tend to be based on seniority. If it is not possible to measure performance adequately, how can promotions and raises be fairly allocated? Many street-level bureaucrats and their union leaders argue that seniority is the only way.

Coping

The street-level bureaucrat must deal with job stress that is invariably anxiety arousing. Just how the worker in the street handles this anxiety is very important in understanding how urban service agencies operate.

Lipsky has developed a theory of how this anxiety is handled, and what its implications are for bureaucratic accountability.[22] Lipsky contends that street-level bureaucrats develop *defense mechanisms* that allow them to cope with job stress on a day-to-day basis. These coping mechanisms work, in the sense that they allow the public service worker to function. And if the individual bureaucrat can function, then the agency can go on delivering services. But too much reliance on these coping mechanisms can extract heavy costs from both the psychological well-being of the street-level bureaucrat and the functioning of the service agency.

The cognitive shields that street-level bureaucrats use to defend themselves can take various forms. Moreover, they will be used more frequently in some service agencies than others. Three variables determine the frequency of use of bureaucratic defense mechanisms: the scarcity of resources available to the service agency, the frequency of contact with clients, and the proportion of clients who are poor. The scarcer the resources available to the agency, the more the agency must adopt a production-line attitude toward its service delivery responsibilities, and the more it must rely on routines rather than individual attention. The more street-level bureaucrats are in direct contact with clients, the more threatening the situation becomes, and the more they will rely on defense mechanisms. Finally, street-level bureaucrats are far more comfortable with the restrained, cooperative behavior of middle-class clients than the more volatile behavior of poorer clients, and are therefore less likely to rely on defense mechanisms.

In order for the bureaucratic coping mechanisms to work in defending against job stress, three separate elements must be in congruence: the *routines of practice* that develop in performing the job; the public service worker's *conceptions of the job;* and his or her *conceptions of the client.* In the normal course of events, routines of practice are forced on the worker in order to allow the bureaucracy to process large numbers of cases with a reasonable degree of procedural fairness. These rules, however, fly in the face of the professional training of the street-level bureaucrat, training that emphasizes individual attention and quality service. Slowly, the other two elements fall into congruence with the enforced patterns of practice. The worker develops a job conception that elevates coping to a higher level and lowers the ideals of quality service and goal accomplishment. Simultaneously, the street-level bureaucrat lowers his or her evaluation of the client. The client is often stereotyped as hostile, threatening, and uncooperative. Now all three elements, job conception, client conception, and bureaucratic processing routines, are in congruence. It will be very difficult to change just one. Indeed, bureaucratic change is often difficult because of the mutually reinforcing elements that form the basis of the street-level bureaucrat's coping mechanisms.

[22] Ibid.

Because of the manner in which these three elements interact, most training programs for public service workers are ill conceived. Most programs start with the premise that problems of police brutality or welfare case worker indifference stem from conceptions of clients. Street-level workers, so the theory goes, are hostile because they tend to be recruited out of the working class (which is true) and working-class attitudes are less tolerant of the poor than are middle-class attitudes (which is also true). Therefore, changing attitudes toward clients will improve the interaction between the public service worker and the client. This is most assuredly *not* true. The root of the problem is job stress, which leads to routinization, which in turn creates client conceptions. Altered client conceptions will not last long in this milieu.

Routines of Practice. The most important norm in modern public service bureaucracies is the norm of neutral competence. Its most important expression in dealing with clients is procedural fairness. Procedural fairness is supposed to ensure that all clients are treated the same (or at least in accordance with their condition, not their race, class, or political affiliation). In many service bureaucracies favoritism continues to occur, but it has been gradually replaced in most locales and in most agencies by procedural fairness.

We have already indicated that bureaucratic decision rules based on procedural fairness nevertheless have distributional effects. Some people are benefited more than others. But there is another aspect of patterns of bureaucratic practice rooted in procedural fairness: They operate against individual attention. Individual attention smacks of favoritism. The welfare case worker who acts as advocate for one case must neglect others. In a bureaucratic world of limited resources it cannot be otherwise. But why this one particular case? Is it the client most in need? Or is it the client who is most likely to benefit from treatment? Or perhaps it is favoritism.

Squeezed on one side by scarce resources and on the other by the norm of procedural fairness, street-level bureaucrats develop routines that will protect them from the resulting anxiety. Supervisors are not in a position to evaluate the quality of the work of the street-level bureaucrat, for two reasons: the lack of a measuring instrument and the fact that so much of the street-level bureaucrat's day is spent in the field away from the central office. But the supervisor can demand adherence to the norm of procedural fairness and the reality of scarce resources. Hence, street-level routines tend to conform to the norm of procedural fairness, but they often conflict with the professional norms of the helping professions. Such routines as queuing, service on a "first come, first served" basis, requiring client problems to fit standard forms, routine scheduling of field work and client visit, and the like all force clients to fit into bureaucratic categories. They offer procedural fairness, but they also ensure that clients are processed as cases rather than as

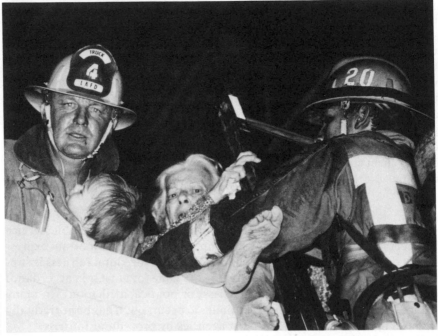

Wide World Photos

Los Angeles firefighters rescue residents from a burning apartment building. Although fire service is delivered according to standard decision rules, in this case response to citizen calls for aid, the actions of street-level bureaucrats such as firefighters on the scene involve discretion, judgment, and occasionally valor.

Source: AP Photo, *Detroit Free Press,* June 18, 1981.

human beings. Not incidentally, they protect the bureaucrat from the stress of having to deal with the client personally (as opposed to bureaucratically).

Client Conceptions. These routines conflict with the values of serving the public that attracted many public employees to their jobs. Something has to give; routines are incongruous with job conceptions and client perceptions. Gradually, clients come to be viewed as responsible for their fate, a bureaucratic disease known in its advanced stages as "blaming the victim." Clients are stereotyped, but they are also differentiated. The differentiation is simplistic: there exist the worthy (those who are cooperative and make the job of the street-level bureaucrat simpler) and those who are unworthy (those who are uncooperative and will not take responsibility for their condition). Housing inspectors, for example, may quickly classify tenants into those who are trying to maintain their apartments and surroundings and those who are filthy. The former deserve the services of the housing inspection department; the latter do not and are simply burdening the taxpayer and the landlord by complaining. Housing inspectors in Boston tended to "stigmatize clients and to approach the public with habitual scepticism," not an atypical client conception of police officers, public health nurses, and other street-level bureaucrats.[23]

As with all stereotypes, division of clients into responsible and irresponsible has a good deal of basis in reality. Some clients are more responsible than others. The danger lies in the crude categorization of clients, because, informally at least, the entire service agency tends to recognize the validity of the stereotype. Services can be denied to "troublemakers" and facilitated for the cooperative. If a street-level bureaucrat decides to withhold from a client information that he possesses but is not legally required to give, the client can have a much more difficult time receiving the service to which she is entitled. In coffee-break gossip sessions one often hears stories about how a public service employee gave a troublesome citizen the "bureaucratic run-around." Nothing illegal, just making sure the troublemaker finds out everything by himself. By the same token, the street-level bureaucrat can grant such information to clients whom he or she views as cooperative. Clients who are too passive, however, run the risk of being categorized as uninterested in the service, and may be stereotyped by the bureaucrat as not responsible.

Job Conceptions. Job conceptions change too. The ideal of public service through helping people fades: efficiency in processing clients becomes the ideal. Because success with clients is so difficult to achieve and to measure, other, more quantifiable goals come to the fore. In universities (yes, a professor is, for part of the day at least, a street-level bureaucrat) the quality of publications is difficult to assess, so the quantity of publications becomes the standard for success. Judges in urban courts are assessed, in part, by the number of cases they dispose of—a good judge is one who clears the docket. It is not uncommon for police commanders to assign a daily quota of traffic tickets—if officers are giving traffic tickets, at least they are not somewhere drinking coffee. Housing inspectors are assigned a specific number of buildings to inspect.

In each of these cases the incentives provided by management cause workers to concentrate on the quantifiable part of their jobs, often at the expense of quality. Their job conceptions change accordingly. The university professor is encouraged to write as many articles as he or she can; the quality of the work is a secondary consideration. Many urban judges who do not clear their dockets *are* inefficient. But those who do clear their dockets

---

[23] Nivola, *The Urban Service Problem,* p. 62. See also Peter K. Manning and John Van Maaven, eds., *Policing: A View from the Street* (Santa Monica, Calif.: Goodyear, 1978).

regularly may be ignoring many of the constitutional prerogatives of the defendants who appear before them. *Plea bargaining,* an arrangement by which a defendant agrees to plead guilty to a lesser crime than that for which he or she has been charged, is an excellent way to clear dockets. But it also can make a mockery of regular judicial procedures. The police officer writing traffic tickets cannot investigate more serious situations in depth. Superficial housing inspections, with many violations overlooked, are the inevitable result of trying to perform a set number of inspections.

Street-level bureaucrats come to evaluate themselves in terms of these goals. A productive university professor is one who publishes numerous articles. A judge who cannot keep his or her docket clear is a poor judge. Subtly, the street-level bureaucrat begins to evaluate himself or herself in terms of efficiency rather than quality and effectiveness. Any impediment to efficient processing of work flow may be resented. The judge may become impatient with the defendant who insists on a trial. The clinic doctor reacts negatively when the patient asks too many questions about the prescribed treatment. Job conceptions, client conceptions, and work practices now interlock, providing defense mechanisms against the stress that would exist without them.

Bureaucrats and public policy

The interactions between street-level bureaucrats and citizens are important because of the effect these interactions have on the formulation and implementation of public policy. Because in some situations street-level bureaucrats have a great deal of discretion in dealing with clients, the actions they take can actually become public policy. It is possible for the defense mechanisms of street-level bureaucrats to subvert policies formulated at higher levels of the service delivery organization. If the coping routines conflict with agency policies, something has to give. Because the coping mechanisms are so resilient, it is often agency policy that yields. Policy and practice diverge. Management either fights an all-out war on the coping routines of workers, rescinds the policy, or tolerates the divergence between policy and practice. In the last two cases, street-level bureaucrats have, in effect, made agency policy.

In this situation, internal bureaucratic control and accountability have broken down. Legislatures cannot be held responsible for public policies if they are subverted at the street level.

For the policies of agency heads to be thwarted by street-level bureaucrats is not rare, but neither is it the norm. Most agency policies are accepted by street-level bureaucrats. One reason that they are accepted, however, is that the policies are made with the full realization that street-level bureaucrats need coping routines to function. Any agency policy conflicting with such routines is likely to be discarded.

Not all street-level coping mechanisms operate in contradiction to the normal flow of public policy from legislature to agency head to street-level bureaucrat. An important coping strategy that aids in the establishment of internal bureaucratic control is the *denial of discretion* (see box 14.3). Street-level bureaucrats commonly deny that they have any discretion in dealing with a client. This shields them from having to take responsibility for the problem. In many service agencies, moreover, discretion at the street level is discouraged or even flatly prohibited. This pushes responsibility back up the bureaucracy to the top.

Indeed, if procedures are spelled out in enough detail, one can have a service delivery agency in which little discretion exists. Many urban service agencies regularly punish discretion on the part of their street-level bureaucrats, even when that discretion results in fairer treatment of clients. The result in such an agency is that all problems that do not fit the preexisting procedures and categories get pushed right to the top of the agency. The agency head spends most of his or her time dealing with problems that workers at the lower level should be able to handle.

Too much discretion by street-level bureaucrats can subvert democratic public policymaking by interfering with internal agency control. Too little discretion can also be harmful, by making agency executives deal in the details of client cases, spending little of their time on the overall policy direction of the agency. Very few service agencies are able to walk the thin line between too much and too little street-level discretion continually. Much depends on the task of the agency, the nature of its leadership, the resource constraints it faces, and the political context within which it exists.

The Role of the Agency Administrator

The administrator of urban service agencies possesses a great deal of discretion in setting policy. Although he or she is constrained by the routines of practice that develop at the street level, the agency executive has considerable latitude in directing agency efforts. Moreover, some evidence exists indicating that different administrators respond differently to identical conditions.

Decisions made by the director of an urban service agency are influenced by the following factors:

1. The *objective social conditions* into which service is delivered. Police departments facing high crime rates and a lower-income clientele tend

Box 14.3: Incident on a Montgomery Bus

In the 1950s, as for decades before, local ordinances throughout the South mandated segregation of the races in the use of public facilities. Although this practice was ruled unconstitutional by the Supreme Court in *Brown et al.* v. *Board of Education of Topeka, Kansas,* in 1954, municipalities were slow to comply (indeed, the court had not required immediate compliance). So the Montgomery, Alabama, city ordinance that required segregated seating on city buses was not unusual. Because the use of buses by the two races varied, the driver of the bus was empowered to demand that black riders move to the rear when there were no front seats for boarding white passengers.

Shortly after 5:00 P.M. on December 5, 1955, Rosa Parks, a seamstress and secretary to the local chapter of the National Association for the Advancement of Colored People, refused a bus driver's order to move to the rear of the bus. The driver left, to return with two white policemen. The following exchange took place:

*Policeman:*Why didn't you stand up when the driver asked you to?

Parks: Why do you all push us around?

Policeman: I don't know, but the law is the law and you are under arrest.

Rosa Parks' action sparked the famed Montgomery bus boycott by blacks, made the golden-tongued orator Martin Luther King, Jr.,

Source: See Gregory Skwira, "The Rosa Parks Story: A Bus Ride, A Boycott, a Beginning of History," *Detroit,* November 30, 1980, pp. 12–41.

to develop different policies than those located in quiet, upper-income suburbs.

2. The likely *reaction of significant others,* including street-level bureaucrats, employee unions, the mayor, the city council, and client organizations.

3. The director's *conception of his or her* own *role* as an administrator. Some executives are more forceful and directive than others.

Studies of police departments indicate that the decisions of police executives cannot be explained only by the first two factors. Wilson, for example, reports an enormous variation in the rate at which traffic tickets are

pastor at a small middle-class black church in Montgomery, a national figure, and resulted in the capitulation of the bus company (which derived 75 percent of its revenue from black riders). The civil rights movement was born.

But the incident on the bus also illustrates something about public bureaucracies. Michael Lipsky calls it the *retreat from discretion.* By replying "the law is the law" to Rosa Parks' question, the white policeman abrogated responsibility for what was happening, insulating himself from the obvious unfairness of the situation. The Montgomery city commission was responsible, not the individual policeman entrusted to carry out the law. The defense mechanism shielded the officer from the anxiety-arousing activity of examining the fairness of the law and using his discretion in enforcing it.

Such a retreat from discretion by the street-level bureaucrat enhances bureaucratic accountability. It ensures that the legal mandates of the policy branches of government will be implemented. But what if the policy branches are wrong? What if they are intentionally evil or misguided? Then the retreat from discretion ensures that bad public policies will be implemented. At the war crimes trials in Nuremburg, Germany, following World War II, Nazi after Nazi testified that he merely implemented the policies promulgated by higher-ups, and that he had no policy responsibility himself. Defendant after defendant pleaded that he was a mere cog in a bureaucratic machine.

The norm of neutral competence, the idea that bureaucracies are neutral instruments for implementing public policies made by legislatures and chief executives, clearly has limits as a guide for good bureaucratic behavior.

---

issued. "This variation is primarily the result of the policies of the administrator, not the characteristics of the community." [24] For example, in Syracuse the rate was ten times that in Albany, yet the social compositions and traffic patterns of the two cities were similar. The two major ways in which the police chief could increase the output of traffic tickets were creating specialized traffic units and inducing officers to write more tickets by instituting "quotas."

It is important to realize that most of the bureaucratic routines in service

[24] James Q. Wilson, *Varieties of Police Behavior* (Cambridge, Mass.: Harvard University Press, 1968), p. 95. See also John A. Gardiner, *Traffic and the Police: Variations in Law Enforcement* (Cambridge, Mass.: Harvard University Press, 1969).

agencies, even those that serve to protect the street-level bureaucrat, come from the policies set by agency administrators. Robert Yin has detailed the process by which a policy innovation becomes a bureaucratic routine.[25] In Yin's theory, a new policy must move through a series of "passages" in its life history. At each of these critical passages the supporters of the innovation must muster resources and support in order to get the policy through the critical stage. Suppose a service agency wishes to institute a computerized management information system. Passages on the route to routinization would include initial funding for computers, establishing new job classifications for the personnel who will run the system, and changing street-level procedures to fit what the computer can analyze (for example, reducing written reports to standard categories). At each stage supporters of the system must mobilize their resources to overcome the resistance that always appears to any proposed change.

It is not a foregone conclusion that all passages will be successfully navigated. If they are, however, the innovation becomes routinized in the standard practices followed by members of the organization.

Conclusions

This chapter has focused on the delivery of urban services and the problems of administering the agencies responsible for their delivery. Five key issues are important in studying urban public services: responsiveness, effectiveness, efficiency, distribution, and internal bureaucratic control.

The politics of government service delivery is a politics of administration. Interest groups, political parties, and even mayors and city councils are less important than agency executives, street-level bureaucrats, and bureaucratic routines. The link between local policymaking institutions (mayors and city councils) and the day-to-day delivery of services is not always strong. Elected policymakers cannot always control the behavior of agency heads, and agency heads cannot always control the behavior of street-level bureaucrats. This means that urban public policy will be strongly influenced by the procedures used by service delivery agencies in coping with their designated tasks, and many times these procedures affect policy in unanticipated ways.

Policies are made in a political milieu, so that initial goals are invariably compromised. Policy means are never directly related to goals, because no one is completely certain just how means and ends are related. Implementa-

[25] Robert K. Yin, *Changing Urban Bureaucracies: How New Practices Get Routinized* (Lexington, Mass.: Lexington Books, 1980).

tion of policies can proceed quite differently from the intentions of policy-makers, as agency heads and street-level bureaucrats struggle merely to cope. Nevertheless, urban policymakers are urged to "plan" so often that planning has become a major preoccupation of local governments. We examine this preoccupation in the next chapter.

CHAPTER 15

Planning and
Land-Use Regulation

In 1593, the English Parliament passed an act entitled "An Act Against New Buildings." Enacted to stem the explosive urban growth that London had experienced during the reign of Queen Elizabeth I, which had seen the city grow to a population of 120,000, the act forbade the construction of dwellinghouses in London and its environs. The act was repealed almost three hundred years later, when the population of London was about 4 million.[1]

Can the growth and spatial form of cities be planned successfully? Should they be planned? Any planning must be done by government, because only government has the power to see that the activities of private individuals conform to the plan. Hence, any meaningful plan for urban development carries with it an element of coercion. Moreover, the coercion has to be sufficient to channel private activities into conformity with the plan. The English dwellinghouse law provided a fine of five pounds as the penalty for building. Any

[1] Clifford Weaver and Richard Babcock, *City Zoning: The Once and Future Frontier* (Chicago: American Planning Association, 1979), p. 3. The authors attribute this without citation to M. B. Layfield.

developer who could expect a return of more than five pounds was not deterred from building. A meaningful urban plan must carry with it sufficient means of enforcement to ensure its implementation.

Under what circumstances are we willing to coerce privately acting individuals to conform to a plan for urban development? Under what circumstances *can* we do so? Or should urban planning be confined simply to providing information about present urban land use and projecting possible future land-use patterns? In this chapter we examine American attempts to plan for urban land use, and the regulations that have been used by urban governments to implement these plans. An overriding consideration in urban planning is the protection of the public interest within a system of private land-use development. Consequently we focus on the critical issues of defining the public interest and using coercion to further it.

Three Questions

The sprawling, unplanned, chaotic form of most American cities cries out for some form of meaningful urban planning. But planning raises three questions. First, who is to plan? Who is to say what form cities are to take? Different people have different values, and these values can imply vastly different urban forms. The power to plan and enforce the plan carries with it the power to coerce other citizens into conforming to the values of those who plan.

The second question concerns the ability to plan successfully. Can urban planners foresee all possible developments that ought to be incorporated into a plan? Clearly they cannot, so the plan must contain some flexibility. On the other hand, if the plan is altered to suit each and every claim then in effect, there is no plan. Any plan (or any plan that is enforced) will cause hardships to some people. Planning can also hamper economic growth (if growth is a desirable objective). Some investments in the city will be turned away, as, for example, when a private entrepreneur wants to build a highrise apartment in an area reserved for single-family dwellings. This means that the city will lose the investment and the increase in real value of property that would add to the property tax rolls. Should the land lie vacant until a developer who is willing to build single-family homes comes along? There is a conflict between the integrity of the plan and the growth of the city. One can envision a plan that would allow very little economic growth by placing so many restrictions on construction that no investor could expect a reasonable return on investment.

The final question involves limits on the use of government coercion. How much government coercion are we willing to use in a pluralistic, relatively open society in order to impose a plan? In making such decisions it must be noted that privately acting individuals often harm other people without meaning to do so. That is, a purely private system of urban development will involve private coercion. Hence, using government to coerce private individuals into conforming to a plan does not necessarily mean increasing the total amount of coercion that is practiced in society. What we have, then, is a tradeoff between private and public coercion. In some situations there will be a gain for society by imposing a plan; in others there will be a loss. Knowing which situation prevails is the problem.

This is another way of phrasing a key issue that this book has stressed: the issue of limited government. Some public policies will help more than they harm; others will harm more than they help. Moreover, there is no sure way of knowing which situation decision makers are facing. Because of this, urban planning is not a neutral enterprise, but involves key political issues of who is benefited and who is harmed by government policies.

Planning, Capitalism, and Pluralism

Any government planning involves placing constraints on the future use of both public and private resources. After the adoption of a plan for urban development, or an urban transportation system, or something as mundane as sewer-system extensions, neither private individuals nor governments are free to act as they did prior to the adoption of the plan. If, for example, a metropolitan planning agency draws up and implements a plan for a metropolitan waste-disposal system that prohibits sewer extensions in a northward direction, the municipalities to the north are effectively prohibited from growing (more people implies more sewers). Private developers cannot invest in subdivisions, or apartments, or even businesses in those municipalities.

Because planning puts constraints on future use of both private and public resources, it comes into conflict with two important urban systems: the capitalist economic system and the pluralist system of government. The capitalist economic system is based on the free flow of labor and capital. Investments go where they earn the highest rate of return for the investor. Planning constrains where investments can go. It does this by refusing some investments outright (a chemical factory in a residential community) and by making some more costly (by specifying very high standards of construction, for example).

Pluralism in government implies that government responds to the prevailing set of organized preferences for government action. Organization and participation have the effect of weighing preferences in the political system—the most active are the most heard. By responding to the most active, government provides public policies that are responsive to those who are willing to organize and express their preferences. In earlier chapters we have noted two major critiques of pluralism: that it is responsive only to elites, and that it is responsive to too many claims, a situation that has been termed *hyperpluralism*. Both of these critiques (which are themselves contradictory) imply that there exists a public interest and that the pluralist system of urban government is not achieving that public interest.

It is clear that both the capitalist system of urban development and the pluralist system of urban development can operate contrary to the public interest. Planning is an attempt to protect the public interest against encroachment by pluralist politics and capitalist economics. The problem with planning is the difficulty in knowing when one is protecting the public interest and when government is using its coercive powers to interfere with capitalist economics or pluralist politics in such a manner as to do inordinate harm to these systems.

The Private Development of American Cities

In the heyday of American urban growth, approximately from the turn of the century to the Great Depression, American cities developed within the framework of a more or less pure capitalist system. Few government regulations constrained the activities of the business people, real estate developers, and other private entrepreneurs who built houses, apartments, factories, and skyscrapers, and decided where to put them. These investors were driven by the profit motive. Vacant land would be developed if the entrepreneur could expect to receive a sufficient return on investment; otherwise it would not. City governments, often dominated by political machines, generally confined themselves to the provision of truly collective goods, those that obviously benefited all citizens but would not be provided by private entrepreneurs. Hence, city governments did provide the infrastructure that was necessary for development: streets, sewer systems, fire and police protection. But they did no planning of the future form of the city and precious little regulation of the kinds of buildings that private entrepreneurs were constructing.

Two problems

This system of private urban development results in the most productive use of society's resources. That is, the most total wealth is produced by private economic development. This is the case because each person is producing the maximum amount of wealth for himself or herself, and, when added up, this produces the maximum amount of wealth for society. There are, however, two major problems with unconstrained private development. The first is the problem of *distribution*. Although private development produces more total wealth than any other system of urban development, it does not necessarily distribute it fairly. Wealth and income can be concentrated in the hands of a very small number of very wealthy people.

The second problem is that strong negative *externalities* are often created. Negative externalities, it will be recalled, are situations in which some people are harmed by actions of other people who do not intend harm. Pure pursuit of private motives can often have negative consequences for others. Such externalities are particularly severe for land use, because once a piece of land has been developed, the use of the land has been determined for the foreseeable future. For example, consider the situation in which a coal-burning factory is built next to a residential neighborhood. Trucks now lumber down the once-quiet residential streets. Shift changes cause unmanageable traffic problems twice a day. Pollution now blackens houses. The factory owner, maximizing his or her own personal wealth, has created severe externalities for the residents of the neighborhood, externalities that can be measured in part by the decline in the value of the homes in the area, but which can also harm the health and general quality of life of residents.

Urban governments can do little about the problem of distribution. If they try to tax the wealthy and grant the proceeds to the poor, the wealthy will move. Taxing factories and commercial enterprises also has limits imposed by potential mobility. To the extent that the problem of the distribution of wealth and income is faced by the political system, it must be handled by the national government. Externalities, however, are localized and are best handled by local government.

Land-Use Planning: A Local Pastime

In the United States, little land-use planning takes place outside the jurisdiction of the municipality. Land-use planning and its handmaiden, the regulation of the structures that are placed on land, is almost completely a local prerogative. It is in this area that local policymaking is least constrained by state and national policies.

At the federal level, urban planning consists of, at best, collecting information about the urban impacts of federal policies[2] and trying to encourage states and governments of urban regions to engage in planning. Often this encouragement comes in the form of conditions attached to federal grants. The use of federally owned land is planned, although this planning has been attacked by two groups: environmentalists, who see the land managers as too willing to allow lumbering and other activities by private corporations on public lands; and many westerners, who want to see the vast western public land holdings sold to private individuals (this latter attack on land-use plan-

---

[2] Norman Glickman, ed., *The Urban Impacts of Federal Policies* (Baltimore: Johns Hopkins University Press, 1980).

ning has been called the "sagebrush rebellion," in honor of its western origin).

At the state level, little land-use planning occurs. After legislation was passed by Congress, states have taken more responsibility for managing coastal zones along oceans and along the Great Lakes. But for the most part state land-use planning has been limited to state forests and, to a lesser extent, navigable streams and rivers. Some states have also passed laws to protect farmland from encroaching urban sprawl. When states have attempted to move in the direction of statewide land-use regulations, they have met stiff opposition from two sources. First, the private owners of the land object to further regulation. Second, perhaps surprisingly, local land-use regulators strenuously object to state encroachment on their domain. When state land-use controls were proposed in Michigan, several years ago, all sorts of organizations of local officials opposed them, including associations of county officials, municipal officials, and township officials.

Several attempts at planning the direction of urban growth have been made at the regional level. Some of these plans have degenerated into primarily information-collecting and -disseminating operations, but others have begun to develop. Many have followed functional lines: transportation, water and sewer, and so forth. A second approach has been the councils of government approach (discussed in chapter 9). Regional planning has been most successful in the functional areas, primarily because the federal government has often refused to approve grants unless evidence exists of regional cooperation. Urban land use, although influenced by transportation and water systems, has been less affected by regional planning attempts.

Most land-use planning and regulation take place at the local level, and most municipalities are heavily involved in regulating the use of land and the structures placed on the land. This regulation forms a complex network of rules and restrictions that must be followed by any individual contemplating constructing housing or a factory or office building, or planning to change the use of a building from, say, office space to residential. Because each locality is responsible for regulations within its boundaries, nearby municipalities can have radically different building regulations. As one can imagine, this causes innumerable headaches for developers, architects, and builders. Representatives of these groups are constantly pressing for some standardization of land-use and building regulations at the state or national level.

Models of Planning

Planning as a profession had its roots in the housing reform movement of the late nineteenth and early twentieth centuries. The reformers stressed that housing conditions have a strong influence on a variety of other social ills:

crime, disease, poverty. Improve housing and you can improve the sorry state of cities. Urban planning came to represent the demand for rational, planned land use that would eliminate (or at least control) the various social ills that the housing reformers decried. To this day, urban planning stresses the rational use of urban space. Some planners, however, criticize this focus as too narrow, and believe that planning should deal with the broader social realities of cities. *Social planning* rejects the preeminent place of land-use planning in the planning profession, and views such factors as racial discrimination, class structure, and capitalist economics as important determinants of the quality of life in cities. Indeed, social planners see such factors as determining land use, and hence give land-use planning a secondary role in the planning process. Nevertheless, most urban planners today continue to hold to the traditional planning approach.

In 1909, the first conference on city planning was held, by New York City's housing reformers.[3] After that date city planning began to move away from its close association with the housing reform movement toward a separate professional identity. Most planners were architects and engineers, and were convinced that the public interest could be realized by applying scientific rationality to city land-use patterns. This orientation closely allied them to the municipal governmental reform movement, spearheaded by Richard Childs, an advertising executive who pressed incessantly for municipal reform. Indeed, planning came to be an integral part of the program advocated by the municipal reformers.

The classical model

Out of these roots came the classical model of urban planning. This model stressed rational decision making applied to land use. Its tenets included a deep belief in the existence of a public interest. The public interest was expressed in the *master plan,* a complete land-use plan for the entire city. All future land use was to be in conformity to the master plan; in a city that developed after the advent of planning, this could be the entire city. The master plan was to be developed by a planning commission, established independently of city government and composed of citizens who could perceive the public interest and would not be influenced by political considerations. Planners believed (and, indeed, most continue to believe) that politicians, with their penchant for negotiation and compromise, would be unable to recognize and abide by the public interest. The planning process was not to be entrusted to the politicans.

---

[3] Michael Vasu, *Politics and Planning* (Chapel Hill, N.C.: University of North Carolina Press, 1979), pp. 26–34.

Advocacy planning

Recently a school of thought has developed within the planning profession known as *advocacy planning*. Paul Davidoff, in a seminal article, rejects the notion of a unitary public interest that planners ought to try to discover. Davidoff sees the urban policy process as pluralistic, with each group professing a distinct conception of the public interest.[4]

To advocacy planners, rejection of a unitary public interest carries an implication for action. Planners ought to act as advocates for groups that are underrepresented in the urban policy process: the poor, minorities, the physically and socially handicapped. This would help ensure a fairer distribution of urban policy benefits. Classical planners disdained political involvement; advocacy planners relish it.

The depth of the influence of this view of the urban policy process can be discerned in a recent study of a national sample of urban planners by Michael Vasu. Almost 88 percent agreed with the statement that "no plan produced by a public agency is neutral but benefits some interests and discriminates against others."[5] This does not mean that most planners are willing to act as advocates, but it does indicate a rather thorough rejection of the basic tenet of the classical model of planning: the existence of a single public interest.

There is an essential contradiction in the advocacy planning model. Although it purports to reject a singular public interest, the model carries with it an implicit conception of the public interest. Advocacy planning does not advocate acting in the interest of planners, but in the interest of an adopted constituency. The implicit value judgment is that the existing political arrangements are not sufficiently attentive to the needs of the poor, particularly the minority poor. By possessing this view, advocacy planners have implicitly adopted a view of the public interest on which, presumably, they are willing to act.

Planners and the public

The substantive view of the public interest harbored by the urban planner, whatever his or her professional orientation, is quite different from that held by the typical American. This is to be expected: planners are an educated group of professionals whose careers depend on government. But the depth of disagreement between planners and the public is striking. Vasu reports profound differences between planners and the public in the willingness to take a liberal position on the involvement of government in such areas as

---

[4] Paul Davidoff, "Advocacy and Pluralism in Planning," *Journal of the American Institute of Planners* 31 (1965): pp. 331–38.
[5] Vasu, *Politics and Planning,* p. 73.

jobs, housing, and health care. Table 15.1, taken from Vasu's study, indicates that whereas half the sample of planners took a liberal position on these issues, less than a third of the sample of the American public did.

Land-Use Regulation

Municipalities enact various ordinances and codes (a collection of related ordinances) that regulate the use of land and buildings on land within their jurisdictions. It is possible to view these various regulations as implementing the planning process, but this is somewhat misleading, because most municipal codes and ordinances are enacted for reasons only distantly related to the master plan. Land-use regulation and urban planning, however, both are directed toward channeling the private use of urban land. Close examination of land-use regulation in any major city will reveal many changes in land-use plans made to reflect changing economic opportunities, as well as many changes in the plans of economic entrepreneurs because of the existence of municipal regulation of the use of land.

State enabling legislation

Because of Dillon's rule, state governments must pass enabling legislation to allow municipalities to regulate land use within their borders. Such enabling legislation specifies the procedures and standards to be followed in the ordinances that cities and towns may enact. The state legislation is enabling because it allows, but does not require, municipalities to engage in planning and land-use regulation. The state of New Jersey, for example, permits its municipalities to draw up a master plan for guiding land use. If a

Table 15.1. Comparison of planners and United States public on subjective political ideology

Political Ideology	Planners	Public
Liberal	50.5%	30.5%
Moderate	40.3	40.0
Conservative	9.2	29.5
Total	100.0%	100.0%

Source: From *Politics and Planning: A National Study of American Planners* by Michael L. Vasu. Copyright 1979 The University of North Carolina Press. Reprinted by permission of the publisher.

municipality does decide to write a master plan, however, it must contain a land-use plan, a transportation plan, a housing plan, and a utility service plan, among other elements.[6] Similar enabling legislation is required for other municipal ordinances.

Codes

The codes and ordinances enacted by municipalities to regulate land use include zoning ordinances, subdivision regulations, building codes, and housing codes. A *zoning ordinance* divides the municipality's land into zones and establishes regulations relating to the use of land and the size and height of buildings put on the land. It includes a map specifying the prescribed use of every parcel of land in the municipality. The typical ordinance divides the city into residential, commercial, and manufacturing districts. To build a factory in a residential district, for example, would be a violation of the ordinance. *Subdivision regulations* are local ordinances that specify the standards and procedures that must be followed when a developer divides up a large parcel of land into smaller parcels for development. Subdivision regulations specify minimum lot sizes, indicate what public services must be provided, and even set minimum depth of street pavement. *Building codes* specify standards for construction and construction materials. The building codes include electrical, ventilation, and plumbing standards as well as structural standards. One part of the building code, the *fire code,* is especially concerned with the use of fire-resistant construction techniques. *Housing codes* set maintenance standards for existing structures. Normally a building built before the adoption of the most recent building code does not have to conform to it, but it does have to conform to the housing code.

Development of Land-Use Regulations

Land-use regulations are adopted primarily to control externalities. The existence of such externalities was recognized in English common law, where the *nuisance doctrine* was developed long before the adoption of land-use regulation by municipalities. A nuisance arises when the owner of a piece of property engages in activities that cause damage, discomfort, or annoyance to owners of other properties. Courts may issue *injunctions* against the offending landowner, ordering him or her to cease the activity, or they may grant *damages* in the form of a monetary award to persons offended by the

---

[6] Jerome G. Rose, *Legal Foundations of Land Use Planning* (New Brunswick, N.J.: Center for Urban Policy Research, Rutgers University, 1979), pp. 54–55.

nuisance. Examples of nuisances include noise, smells, and dangerous conditions such as garbage, vermin, cesspools, and fire hazards.[7]

Early building codes primarily concerned fire safety. The first fire ordinance in America was enacted in New Amsterdam (New York) in 1647, when regulations specifying the construction of chimneys were adopted and building surveyors appointed.[8] The first detailed fire prevention law was adopted by New York in 1849. In 1867 the first tenement-house legislation in the United States was passed by New York, in response to lobbying efforts by housing reformers. This act regulated the maintenance of multiple-family residential structures. For the next half-century housing reformers pressed improvements and additions to both the building code and the tenement-house laws. Led by activist Lawrence Veiller, housing reformers began to advocate replacing tenement laws with comprehensive housing codes that would specify maintenance and occupancy standards for all existing buildings.

In 1916, New York City, the locus of most innovations in building and housing codes, enacted the first zoning ordinance. A major source of support for the ordinance was the city's upper class, who believed the exclusive Fifth Avenue shopping and residential district was threatened by the encroaching loft buildings of the nearby garment district. Developers were rapidly constructing both the loft buildings to hold the thousands of immigrants who cut and sewed the mass-produced garments, and the tenements that housed the immigrants.[9] Since one person's profit is often another person's externality, the city of New York agreed to a systematic land-use plan that would limit the free play of the private economic system. Henceforth, land use would not change except according to the city's specification of what was desirable. Clearly, however, what a city sees as desirable can easily be the preferences of the residents and merchants of Fifth Avenue rather than some nebulous conception of the public interest.

Deed restrictions

Today most cities have adopted zoning ordinances; Houston, Texas, is the major exception. This does not mean that Houston property owners can use their property any way they see fit. Many properties are encumbered with *deed restrictions* that limit the use of property to specified purposes (say, residential use). However, these deed restrictions were set for a specified period and are presently expiring in some parts of the city. Since property

[7] Ibid., pp. 62–64.

[8] Lawrence Veiller, *Tenement House Legislation in New York, 1852–1900* (Albany, N.Y.: Brandow Printing Co., 1900), p. 11.

[9] Dennis R. Judd, *The Politics of American Cities: Private Power and Public Power* (Boston: Little, Brown, 1979), pp. 182–83.

owners are not renewing the deed restrictions, owners are freer to alter the prevailing land use in many of Houston's neighborhoods.

Deed restrictions are a time-honored way of regulating land use without government. At one time such restrictive covenants were written to exclude blacks or Jews; such restrictions were ruled unconstitutional by the United States Supreme Court in 1948.[10] The problem with such regulatory tools, even when they are used in nondiscriminatory fashion, is that they rely on the cooperation of every owner in the neighborhood. If all owners write restrictions in their deeds, then the character of the neighborhood is protected. But if one owner refuses to do so and sells his or her property to an entrepreneur who opens a gas station, the residential character of the neighborhood is quickly destroyed. The gas station generates powerful negative externalities for the other owners.

Issues in Land-Use Regulation

Government can coerce all owners into maintaining a particular land-use pattern by adopting and enforcing a well-designed zoning law. This, in effect, suppresses the negative externalities that would result from nonconforming uses. Property owners are protected from changes in the value of property that would result from use changes. Other land-use and building regulations have similar justifications. A building code that is properly written and rigorously enforced can protect occupants of buildings from injury resulting from fire or structural collapse. That so many Americans die in fires each year regardless of building codes is indicative of the existence of many buildings not constructed to modern standards, lack of proper enforcement, and a technology that is far from perfect with respect to fire protection. What all land-use and building regulations have in common is the attempt to limit the harm done to innocent people by other individuals who do not actually intend to harm them. The architect who ignores fire prevention measures does not intend to kill people if her building burns down, but she realizes that cutting corners can make the construction project far less expensive. The building code makes construction more expensive for developers, but it protects occupants from fire hazards.

Side consequences of regulation

Land-use regulation, however, has several side consequences that may not be desirable from the point of view of urban society. These consequences have emerged as major issues in urban development. They include the issues of legality, equity, efficiency, and flexibility.

[10] *Shelly* v. *Kramer,* 334 U.S. 1 (1948).

Legality. Is it legal in America to tell the owner of private property what he or she can or cannot do with that property? In the landmark case of *Village of Euclid, Ohio* v. *Ambler Realty Company,* the United States Supreme Court ruled that the typical state enabling act and zoning ordinance were within the purview of the state's police power (the power to coerce for the public good) and were constitutional.[11] This does not mean that all zoning ordinances are constitutional; it is possible for a municipality to write an ordinance that is unduly harsh or discriminatory. Such an ordinance runs the risk of being declared invalid by the courts.

Equity. Some suburban communities have enacted zoning ordinances that have the effect of excluding "undesirable" people as well as undesirable land uses. Such practices are termed *exclusionary zoning.* It is possible to write a zoning ordinance, a set of subdivision regulations, and a building code that effectively price minorities out of the market. Such practices as requiring extraordinarily large lot sizes, excluding multiple-family housing, and setting unreasonably high construction standards can result in a homogeneous community of white upper-income families. For example, Bloomfield Hills, Michigan, the nation's wealthiest community, is zoned solely for single-family residences on two-acre lots. Zoning has been employed to manipulate the socioeconomic composition of the population.

Such zoning provisions have come into conflict with attempts by the United States government, as well as several state housing authorities, to disperse low-income housing throughout the metropolitan region, rather than concentrating it in the central city.[12] In 1975, the New Jersey Supreme Court ruled that municipalities would have to accept a "fair share" of low-income housing, based on the present and future needs of the entire region.[13] This decision heartened reformers seeking to eliminate exclusionary zoning. Then, in 1977, the United States Supreme Court issued an opinion that made it far more difficult to strike down exclusionary zoning. In a case involving the village of Arlington Heights, Illinois, the court ruled that plaintiffs (attacking a zoning ordinance as discriminatory under the Fourteenth Amendment) would have to show that policymakers *intended* discrimination, not just that the effect of the zoning ordinance was to discriminate.[14] Plaintiffs would have to get inside the minds of policymakers when the law was written, as well as show that the effect of the ordinance was discriminatory (since somebody must be harmed in order for the courts to consider a case).

---

[11] 272 U.S. 365 (1926).

[12] See Michael Danielson, *The Politics of Exclusion* (New York: Columbia University Press, 1976).

[13] *Southern Burlington N.A.A.C.P.* v. *Township of Mt. Laurel,* 67 N.J. 151 (1975).

[14] *Village of Arlington Heights* v. *Metropolitan Housing Development Corporation,* 429 U.S. 252 (1977).

Efficiency. The capitalist system can generate both income inequities and severe externalities that only government can correct. All government regulations, however, carry with them some expense, and therefore cut into the total amount of wealth produced. It is possible to enact a set of government regulations relating to urban land use that cost more (in lost wealth) than they are worth (in containing externalities). Such regulations are *inefficient.*

Government regulations that prescribe construction standards, for example, have a very real effect on the urban economy. Government regulations that add to the cost of construction without offering benefits at least equal to the increased cost have two consequences. First, they reduce the number of houses that will be built, because some people who can buy a new house at, say, $60,000 (the construction cost without the amount added by regulations) cannot buy one at $70,000 (the cost of construction with regulations). A pilot program sponsored by the United States Department of Housing and Urban Development indicated that builders could construct housing for 20 percent to 25 percent less where restrictive municipal building codes were relaxed and the process of enforcement (obtaining permits and scheduling inspections) was expedited. "We proved that a builder can go back into the inner city and be competitive," said one builder.[15]

In the second place, such regulations have the unintended effect of relegating the poor to poorer-quality housing than they would have access to in the absence of the regulations. If middle-income people cannot afford to move into new houses, neither can the poor (unless publicly subsidized housing is made available to them). Such, for example, is the result of enacting exclusionary land-use provisions that mandate construction standards that are higher than those necessary to protect the health and safety of the public.

Housing codes can have similar effects if they are too severe. A landlord of a central city apartment building must raise rents if he or she is to cover the costs of repairs or renovations mandated by the city housing code. If rents are raised too much, some people cannot afford to rent apartments in the building. If the vacancy rate in any given building is too large, the landlord cannot cover costs, and the building becomes a money-losing proposition. Many landlords in central cities, as well as in some suburban communities, have abandoned their properties in the face of mounting losses. Of course, housing codes are not the only factor in causing vacancy rates; the major factor is the decline in population in central cities. Nevertheless, housing codes do exert an upward pressure on rents, and high rents in poor districts do contribute to vacancy rates.[16]

[15] "Regulations Add Up, House Builders Say," *Detroit Free Press,* January 16, 1981.

[16] On central city landlords, see George Sternlieb and Robert Burchell, *Residential Abandonment: The Tenement Landlord Revisited* (New Brunswick, N.J.: Center for Urban Policy Research, Rutgers University, 1973).

Legal scholars have engaged in a vigorous debate over the benefits of housing codes. See

Flexibility. Can master plans and land-use regulations be drawn up in such a way that they adequately guide future city development but do not become roadblocks to progress? The requirements for proper land-use planning are indeed stringent. Jerome Rose lists the following requirements:

1. that planners can predict the nature and quantities of the community's needs with some precision and exactitude;
2. that planners can, with accuracy, convert the quantification of community needs into an allocation and designation of land use;
3. that the economic and political forces within the community will respond compliantly with these designations;
4. that the very act of designation of specified zones to prescribed uses will not undermine the achievement of other community goals and objectives.[17]

If these requirements cannot be met, then the planning process is likely to be counterproductive. It will be too rigid, and it will not correspond to community needs and future development.

Several devices exist to overcome the inflexibility of land-use planning. Indeed, such devices for flexibility are sometimes employed to such an extent that there is in effect no plan. If every property owner who objects to the land-use plan gets an exception, the zoning ordinance is meaningless.

A property owner who feels that he or she is being unduly harmed by the zoning plan has two options. First, the owner can get the city council to change the zoning category and allow him or her to use the land as desired. Such changes from the zoning ordinance are known as *spot zoning.* If a municipality allows much of this, its zoning map will soon take on a polka-dot pattern of varying land uses rather than orderly zones intended to direct development. Or the owner can take the case to the zoning board of appeals, which can grant a variance. A *variance* does not change the zoning law, but grants the owner an exception from the literal enforcement of the law. The owner must show that he or she will suffer "unnecessary hardship" if the variance is not granted.

There is a final, more unsavory, option for gaining flexibility. The owner may bribe the officials in charge of enforcing the building code or zoning ordinance to allow a nonconforming use. The more stringent the land-use codes, the greater will be the likelihood of corruption's entering the process. In some cities corruption in land-use regulation is a chronic problem.[18]

Bruce Ackerman, ed., *Economic Foundations of Property Law* (Boston: Little, Brown, 1975), pp. 160–217.

[17] Rose, *Legal Foundations,* p. 147.

[18] See the discussion of corruption in chapter 7.

Planning, Politics, and Decision Making

McClaughry's Law of Zoning: Where zoning is not needed, it will work perfectly. Where it is desperately needed, it always breaks down.[19]

Urban planning is a variant of rational decision making. Making a rational land-use plan involves the same elements as any rational choice.[20] In rational decision making, the decision maker lists the relevant alternatives available, identifies the consequences of each course of action, compares their relative costs and benefits, and selects the most desirable. There are two problems with such a procedure. First, searching through all the alternatives is itself expensive and time consuming. Decisions almost always must be made before all relevant information has been assembled. Second, it is impossible in most cases to forecast the consequences of each of the alternatives available. Urban futures are not easy to predict.

Once a rational decision has been made, or a rational land-use plan adopted, a third problem arises. How bound are decision makers to the plan? What if, some years in the future, circumstances change? Should the plan be altered? Circumstances, of course, are always changing. When are changes justified, and when are they unjustified? A final issue is who should be empowered to do the changing (see box 15.1).

Many political scientists, Charles Lindblom and Aaron Wildavsky among them, believe that urban futures are best left to a system of incremental change and mutual adjustments.[21] Such a system usually characterizes urban decision making, at least off-cycle decision making. Small changes that respond to the political and economic forces prevailing within the community do not commit a municipality to a course of action that can prove to be disastrous; in principle, at least, incremental changes are reversible. Because they do not involve whole-sale commitment of community resources, incremental changes will not necessitate a thorough evaluation of each available alternative.

The problem with incremental decisions is that they can add up to chaos. Undirected sprawl and wastefulness have characterized modern urban America. Pluralist politics, involving mutual adjustments among various

[19] Arthur Bloch, *Murphy's Law and Other Reasons Why Things Go Wrong* (Los Angeles: Price/Stern/Sloan, 1980) p. 29.

[20] Vasu, *Politics and Planning*, p. 90.

[21] Charles Lindblom, "The Science of Muddling Through," *Public Adminstration Review* 19 (1959): 79–88; Aaron Wildavsky, *Speaking Truth to Power: The Art and Craft of Policy Analysis* (Boston: Little, Brown, 1979). See also Lindblom, *Politics and Markets* (New York: Basic Books, 1977), ch. 23. Here Lindblom admits a limited role for planning within a pluralist system of decision making. He terms this type of planning *strategic* planning, and would limit the strategic planner's role to proposing solutions that would harm no one and benefit at least one. We have already noted that such situations are rare in urban America.

Box. 15.1: Shaping the Manhattan Skyline

It is no secret to real-estate developers, planners, and even most architects that they are not the real designers of midtown Manhattan. The people who write and amend and interpret the city's zoning ordinances have the real influence; they can do more to shape the core of the city than the developer who erects a dozen office towers or the architect who gives them form. For the zoning code, more than the wishes of the developer or the architect, determines how big a building may be, what shape it may have and to what uses it may be put.

Until recently, New York City had revised the original 1916 zoning ordinance only once—in 1961. The latest proposed revision was initiated to limit the soaring density levels of midtown Manhattan. The 1961 ordinance allowed extensive skyscraper construction. Moreover, the City Planning Commission has allowed many projects to exceed the specifications of the code, by declaring the project to be a "special zoning district." Such spot zoning caused one developer to complain, "During the past ten years the planning department has been the law, and the law has been whatever suited the fancy of the planners."

The proposed code revisions envision not only new height and space limitations, but also a geographic shift in construction of highrises. New York, through a change in its zoning code, is attempting to change not just what is built, but also where it is built.

Source: Paul Goldberger, "The Legal Hands That Shape the Manhattan Skyline," *New York Times,* July 17, 1980. Extracts © 1980 by the New York Times Company. Reprinted by permission.

---

politically active groups, can degenerate into hyperpluralism. Planning offers one possible mechanism to counteract such tendencies. But planning assumes that the planners can envision a rational urban future, and that they can impose on (coerce or convince) others to conform to the plan.

Most planners, however, believe all plans contain bias in favor of some urban groups and against others. They no longer accept the primary tenet of the classical model of urban planning: that the plan will embody the public interest. Indeed, urban planners are best viewed as an interest group, complete with professional ideology and a point of view substantially different from that of the American public.[22]

Even if urban planners could define a satisfactory community interest,

---

[22] Vasu, *Politics and Planning,* ch. 6.

City zoning and building codes regulate land use in the city. Massive construction of skyscrapers will be prohibited in certain sections of New York's Manhattan under a proposed zoning code.

Source: The New York Times, July 17, 1980.

Fred R. Conrad/NYT Pictures

there still would exist the issue of enforcement. Several studies have shown planners to be disdainful of the political process as practiced in urban America. Hence, they have passed up the opportunity to engage in politics to impose their plans. (Perhaps this is as it should be; planners have no electoral base whatsoever.) This makes it simple for politicians to ignore plans when the immediate situation so dictates. Few cities, especially cities beset with financial woes, can refuse private investments that offer the opportunity of revitalization. When major investors come forward with important projects, the zoning ordinance is no defense for those who oppose the project.

When General Motors recently offered to build a new assembly plant in Detroit if land could be found, land was found. That part of that land was zoned exclusively residential did not deter the plan at all; the city council quickly amended the ordinance. The key issue here is not just the change in the zoning classification. The real question is whether it was in the interest of the community to build the plant. The residents of Poletown, the neighborhood affected, thought not. City officials, and many city residents who thought the gain in jobs was important, thought so. General Motors really did not care; the plant would be greeted with open arms by many other communities. Zoning proved to be completely irrelevant to the ensuing conflict; nobody claimed that a zoning ordinance written years before had any bearing on the issue at hand. The site was cleared, the land was turned over to the company, and the residences, businesses, and churches of Poletown were replaced by an assembly plant.

Conclusions

A discussion of urban planning illuminates many of the issues stressed in this book. Unregulated capitalist economics can generate severe externalities that do substantial harm to residents. Pluralistic politics, with government continually adjusting to prevailing political circumstances, offers little opportunity to channel the social and economic forces that shape urban America. Urban planning and land-use regulation offer a method for limiting externalities and directing urban growth rationally, but planners may not be able to envision a public interest that is more than a reflection of one or more private interests. Plans and regulations, if enforced, can be inflexible, curtail growth, and generate undesirable side effects. If they are not enforced there is no plan.

At one time, many political scientists believed that a pluralist community politics constrained by frequent popular elections would automatically realize the public interest. Economists believed that any but the most limited interference in capitalist economics would be detrimental; left alone, the private economic system would produce "the greatest good for the greatest number." Urban planners and assorted reform groups believed that neither pluralist politics nor capitalist economics would result automatically in the realization of the public interest, but that technically trained experts could realize this goal. Today, the core beliefs of each of these groups has broken down. Many political scientists suspect that pure group politics cannot result in the common good, and they have begun to call for a strengthening of institutions to represent broader interests. Recent calls for strengthening political parties can be seen as a reaction to untrammeled group politics.

Economists for years have seen the importance of government in a nation in which the public sector consumes about a third of the gross national product. Urban planners believe that no plan can embody the public interest. Some still cling to utopian hopes for urban America, but most professionals observing modern American cities are not optimistic.

CHAPTER 16

Five Issues Revisited

Economic, social, and political forces have all profoundly affected the growth and development of American cities. Economic considerations dictated where cities were located and determined which cities would grow into metropolises. Over the years the economy became a national one, and advances in communication and transportation imposed a national culture and social structure on the country. As the economy and social structure became centralized, so too did the political system. Citizens increasingly looked to Washington for solutions to their problems.

Yet these national trends have not obliterated local distinctions. The United States possesses today a national economy, a national social structure, and a national political system, each linked to myriad local economies, social structures, and political systems. The dictum *e pluribus unum* continues to have meaning in the United States in the last quarter of the twentieth century.

The national economic and social trends that so strongly affect urban life, and the rapid pace at which these trends bring change, make all the more important the key issues of urban governance that have occupied us in this

401

book. Urban public policies, especially those policies that affect the location of citizens and the institutions they create—businesses, residences, and governments—are all the more crucial in a society where both individuals and institutions are geographically mobile. In this chapter we reexamine these basic issues.

Five general issues have guided our study of American urban politics. These questions concern how government power is to be used to structure human interactions in urban areas. The issues are:

1. *Limited government:* How much governmental intervention in society do we want?

2. *Local autonomy and effective government:* Can small local governments that possess substantial governing autonomy be effective in solving problems that are national in scope but nevertheless affect localities somewhat differently?

3. *Democratic accountability:* Can local political elites be held accountable to local publics for their actions (all of the time, some of the time, or never)?

4. *Efficiency and responsiveness:* Can we have efficient local governments that nevertheless remain responsive to the political forces that pluralist democracy fosters?

5. *Policy distribution:* To what extent are the benefits and costs of the urban policy process distributed in an equitable fashion to citizens? When and how is policy distribution accomplished through the manner in which urban physical space is used and the location of human activities in that space?

Some Selected Features of Urban Political Systems

Before we reexamine these key issues, it is worth reviewing several key features of urban political systems that bear on them.

1. Local governments are independent, policy-producing units. Although constrained legally by Dillon's rule, constitutional provisions, and federal mandates, the tradition of local autonomy is still important in urban America.

2. Local governments are administrative units for the implementation of state and, to an extent, national policies. They are thus both policy initiators and implementors of policies formulated at other levels of government, a dual role that inevitably leads to misunderstanding and conflict.

3. Marked economic inequality exists among citizens within a single municipality. Economic inequality also exists among municipalities.

4. The legitimacy of local governments rests on electoral accountability. Elections are rooted in political equality. Yet economic and social inequality means that potentially powerful private elites also exist in cities. To the degree that these elites use their private resources to influence public policies, they may be able to subvert popular control.

5. Because they are relatively small units of government, municipalities are affected strongly by forces far removed from their control. The most important are:

   a. The mobility of citizens and capital. Citizens and businesses can leave if they are unhappy with the policies pursued by a local government. Because the citizens and businesses most likely to leave are revenue producing, they can strongly affect a local government's tax base by moving. A reduced tax base means a reduction in the range and intensity of policies that the local government can pursue.

   b. The actions of other governments. City governments do not operate in a vacuum; they make policy in a world filled with other governments. They must compete for revenue-producing citizens and businesses with other municipalities in the metropolitan region. They are dependent on state and federal funding to finance their policies, programs, and services. And they must implement mandates coming from these levels of government, as well as from the courts.

The First Issue: Limited Government

The authority of governments is based on coercion. The actions they take rest, directly or indirectly, on their ability to use the implied threat of force to get citizens to obey.[1] Only when citizens change their behavior in accordance with new public policies can we say that policies have been implemented effectively. Because some degree of coercion, either direct or indirect, underlies all public policies, the issue of limited government becomes important.

Of course no government coerces all of its citizens directly. Rather, governments rely on a sense of legitimacy among citizens that they ought to obey the government. In America, most citizens feel most of the time that obeying government is the proper thing to do. Occasionally, however, this

---

[1] The view that governmental authority is based on the ability of government to use coercion comes from the writing of the German sociologist Max Weber. For a modern view that is different, see Charles Lindblom, *Politics and Markets* (New York: Basic Books, 1977), ch. 2.

sense of legitimacy has broken down in urban America, at least among certain groups. During the Civil War, the immigrant Irish rioted against the country's draft laws in New York. In more recent years, urban blacks have rioted; their grievances almost always include some complaints about the way public services are delivered. Breakdowns in the sense of duty to obey government are not widespread in the United States, but when they occur, it is almost always in cities.

One theory in current vogue would limit governmental action to the provision of collective goods. Collective goods, as we saw in chapter 3, are policies that exclude no citizen from the benefits produced by the policy. Yet many public policies coerce some citizens for the benefit of the rest. Some who are coerced are "free riders," who refuse to aid in a collective effort but want the benefits from the effort, which cannot be denied to them once the project is completed. Others, however, are coerced by government into acting contrary to what they believe to be their respective self-interests. They have lost in the policy process, and, as a result, costs are imposed on them.

Simply because some citizens have been coerced does not mean that government policies are unjustified. Much depends on the nature of the policy. This is particularly true for those policies that are not intended to promote collective endeavors, such as building a sanitary sewer system, but are intended to manage conflict among diverse groups of citizens. Policies forbidding gambling, the sale of alcohol or drugs, the use of certain building materials in construction, and the maintenance of private businesses in residential neighborhoods, as well as a host of other laws, ordinances, and court decisions, are not intended to provide pure collective goods. Rather, they impose the preferences of one group of citizens on others, even though they may provide benefits for a large number of citizens and coerce only a small number.

Many of these policies are enacted because of the externality effect. There exists considerable private coercion in all societies. Citizens, acting out of self-interest, often harm other citizens inadvertently. Such harms, called externalities, cannot be easily controlled by citizens acting privately. Yet in order to control externalities, government must coerce those who are producing the harm. Governmental action, then, is often justified as a necessary antidote to the excesses of private coercion.

Cities are ethnically, racially, and economically diverse. This mixture leads to more social conflict than occurs in rural regions, where values are both more certain and more stable. Because of this diversity, there is more need for government policies in an urban society than in a rural one. Yet when government acts, it almost always acts to enforce the values of one group in preference to the values of a second. Hence, the choices made by government are almost never neutral; they benefit some groups and deprive others. This does not mean that government action is unjustified. Often the interest that is promoted by the government is far and away more compelling than the interest that is not promoted. A large majority may support a particular policy, and a tiny minority oppose it. If the minority will not be inordinately harmed by the policy, it is quite appropriate for government to act. Such a policy would be in the public interest, even though not all citizens would support it. Such policies are proper governmental intrusions.

Policies, of course, do not readily sort themselves out as clearly in the public interest or not in the public interest. Many proposed policies impose substantial harm on a minority. Others benefit only a particular group, but are not really opposed by others; the majority is indifferent. In chapter 7 we saw that many policies are made within isolated policy systems, with little interference on the part of the majority of citizens, who understand little of the policy and care less. Yet the policies enacted and implemented by such isolated policy systems add up to large-scale governmental intervention in society. Finally, some policies grant substantial benefits to a bare majority, imposing costs on a sizable minority. It is very difficult for even the most objective observer to decide which policies are in the public interest and which are not.

No system on earth can operate perfectly all the time. It would be unreasonable to expect urban governments to yield policies in the public interest with perfect consistency. So the proper question is whether the existing political institutions and procedures of urban America are sufficient to produce policies that are *generally* in the public interest. Are these institutions and procedures effective in solving social problems? Do they provide for democratic accountability?

The Second Issue: Governmental Effectiveness and Local Autonomy

Small, autonomous local governments are not necessarily effective governments. As we noted in chapter 9, a small government is more likely to be able to put into force policies that conform to the wishes of its citizens, for two reasons: the wishes of the citizens are relatively easy to discern, and they are not likely to be in conflict with one another (small size and homogeneity tend to go together). Hence, various minorities are not as likely to be coerced by the majority, simply because minorities are less likely to exist. Where minorities exist, however, they may be coerced quite severely, as many a nonconforming resident of small-town America has found. Moreover, elite interests may be so overpowering, as is the case in many one-industry towns, that they stifle criticism. In other words, just because small jurisdictions *can* easily make and implement policies conforming to the wishes of citizens does not mean they *will* do so. Small jurisdictions are more responsive to local political forces, but those forces may not be democratic ones.

A major problem with using small, autonomous jurisdictions to deliver policies and services to citizens is the existence of problem spillovers from one jurisdiction to others. Urban problems do not respect jurisdictional boundaries. If problems are not contained within a governmental jurisdiction, then the government will lack the authority to deal with them. On the other hand, it is possible for a local government to produce a service that will benefit citizens who live in other jurisdictions. The citizens of one city will be taxing themselves to provide benefits for citizens of other cities; this is obviously inequitable. Small governments magnify these problems. In general, as the number of independent governmental units increases within a metropolitan area, the number of problems that cannot be dealt with through government action will increase, and the government policies that will benefit all citizens in the metropolis (not just in a single jurisdiction) will decrease. And overall governmental effectiveness will decline.

As we noted in chapter 13, the history of governmental relations in the United States has been a history of trying to deal with these problems through indirect means. A variety of special districts have been established to deal with problems that span local jurisdictions. State governments have provided all sorts of financial assistance to central cities lacking the resources to provide adequate services and meet the pressing social problems they face. The national government has provided aid directly to cities, and has imposed requirements for its use.

Although local officials have increasingly become bound up in the complexities of fiscal federalism, they continue to demand a significant amount of policy discretion and local autonomy. Intergovernmental relations thus come to be characterized by a large amount of conflict, bargaining, and compromise. The resulting complexity does allow the tension between local autonomy and governmental effectiveness to be dealt with on a continual basis. The complexity itself has become burdensome, however, and interferes with achieving the aim of efficient, coordinated government.

The Third Issue: Democratic Accountability

The modern pluralist/elitist dialogue set forth in chapter 8 basically concerns whether local democratic institutions are able to enforce popular control or whether private elites are able to brush aside these institutions and formulate and implement policies that are strictly for their benefit. Although the American political culture lauds local autonomy, many American political theorists have been pessimistic about the possibility of local democracy. James Madison believed that local governments tended to fall into the hands of special interests, which he called factions, because they failed to include a diversity of interests. Liberty could be protected, he felt, only by a political system that incorporated a range of factions, none of which could institute complete control.

Writing in 1919, two political scientists, Frank Goodnow and Frank Bates, also expressed skepticism that cities could nurture democracy:

> City populations . . . evidence an almost irresistible tendency to establish oligarchical or despotic government. They are apparently unable of themselves to organize a form of government under which the mass of the city population will not be exploited by the wealthy few.[2]

These authors were concerned about "boss rule," which they felt tended to be established in heterogeneous communities. Only by establishing tight limits on local autonomy could state governments prevent local oligarchy— states were more likely to reflect a unitary popular "will." Note how antagonistic this view is toward the heterogeneity of interests that Madison lauded. Although Goodnow and Bates also distrusted local governments, they did so because they thought the cities of early-twentieth-century America were *too* diverse in too small a space, encouraging the political manipulations of the boss. State control meant that this diversity could be diluted in a sea of homogeneous values.

Policy skew

Many political scientists today, siding with Madison, believe that popular control is most likely where a diversity of interests exists. Large governments will normally include a greater variety of interests, and they will promote conflict, compromise, and reconciliation among diverse interests. This system of pluralistic democracy yields less readily to the power of single-minded elites.

Yet even in large, diverse cities, some citizens possess more resources that can be converted into political power: wealth, education, and political skills. Perhaps the most potent resource that upper-income citizens possess is the ability to move when they do not agree with the public policies followed by city officials. Because of their concern with declining tax bases, city officials are extremely sensitive to the preferences of wealthy residents and the owners and managers of tax-producing business enterprises. This sensitivity skews public policies away from those supported by the general public.

Other forces also skew public policies toward the preferences of the mid-

[2] Frank Goodnow and Frank Bates, *Municipal Government* (New York: Century Company, 1919), p. 428.

dle and upper classes. The most important factor after mobility is the composition of the local electorate. As we noted in chapter 5, the poor vote at very low rates in local elections, leaving the field to middle- and upper-class voters. This tendency is especially pronounced in reformed cities without strong political parties. Not surprisingly, the officials elected by this constricted local electorate generally reflect the preferences of those who elected them.

Diversity also promotes the construction of separate, isolated policy systems that are only rarely penetrated by the general public. As the various elites compete, they stake out separate policy "turfs" that are left alone by other political actors. Hence, popular government can degenerate into an extremely fragmented form that is quite resistant to popular control.

The existence of policy skew in local communities does not mean that urban democracy is a sham. Indeed, the policies pursued by cities are different from what they would otherwise be *because of* the existence of democratic institutions. Unreformed cities, which make the expression of diverse preferences easier, pursue different (and more democratically responsive) policies than do reformed cities. What it does mean is that urban public officials are under dual pressures. One set encourages them to respond to democratically based electoral coalitions. The other set encourages them to respond to economic elites, who possess disproportionate power as a consequence of their access to political resources and their ability to move.

Public officials are responsive to citizen preferences because of electoral accountability. They are responsive to elite preferences because of the mobility and the superior organizational capacities of upper-income individuals. Just whose preferences prevail depends on a number of factors: the particular public policy in question, the leadership abilities of elected officials, national social and economic trends, and the composition of the local electorate.

Finally, where political parties are strong, popular control is most likely to be realized. Parties are the only institutions that have a stake in encouraging diverse interests to find solutions in the interest of the general citizenry. Indeed, where group demands are strong and political parties weak, politics degenerates into "hyperpluralism," an extreme form of undisciplined democracy.

The Fourth Issue: Efficient Government and Responsive Government

Recent research has documented the effect of certain forms of government on governmental responsiveness and efficiency. Although at first glance responsiveness and efficiency would not seem to be linked, they are related in an inverse fashion. To gain increases in efficiency one must sacrifice responsiveness. Moreover, certain forms of government promote efficiency, others responsiveness. The tradeoff is not absolute, however. Some governmental forms promote neither. Many county governments, still operating under the board form of government that was popular in the late nineteenth century, are neither responsive nor efficient.

Responsiveness concerns the extent to which a government translates the demands on it into public policies. Efficiency concerns the operation of government after its policy goals have been established. An efficient government performs the functions assigned to it with minimum use of taxpayer resources. As a government takes on more responsibilities, responding to demands for governmental outputs, its efficiency in performing functions tends to decline. More importantly, certain features of modern municipal governments, features that municipal reformers have insisted on, operate to enhance efficiency, but they also tend to blunt responsiveness. Such reforms as civil service systems, at-large districting, and nonpartisan elections do encourage the efficient delivery of urban services. But they also isolate government officials from political demands, and cause the government institutions that operate to be less responsive to these demands.

One reform encourages both responsiveness and efficiency: a strong chief executive. A mayor with extensive appointive powers and policymaking responsibilities will be visible to voters and will have the motive to respond to political demands because of the existence of the electoral sanction. To the extent that municipal government is under the mayor's control, the mayor can eliminate duplication and waste. The primary reason that county governments are everywhere inefficient is that they generally lack a central executive who can be held accountable by voters and can establish control over the various boards, commissions, and bureaus that make up county government in much of the country.

A final dimension of governmental performance discussed in chapter 10 is effectiveness. Effectiveness is the extent to which a government is achieving its policy goals. It is possible for a government to function smoothly in achieving its day-to-day tasks, yet make little headway against the problems facing it. It can also be highly responsive to demands for taking on new responsibilities, yet be ineffective in achieving its new goals.

The limited resources of local governments make the large-scale attack on urban problems very difficult. In the past, some federal programs have recognized the limited effectiveness of local governments. Urban programs of the administration of President Carter were supposed to be targeted toward areas of greatest need. Earlier programs that were supposed to concentrate resources in a limited number of cities in order to achieve maximum effectiveness were the model cities program of the Johnson administration and the urban renewal program. In all cases, however, resources have been spread around to too many communities in order to construct supportive political coalitions.

The classic case of political logrolling on a targeted federal program occurred in the model cities program. Established to demonstrate that federal aid, when intensively applied to a limited number of citiés, could be effective in revitalizing urban America, the program faced opposition from rural and suburban members of Congress. In order to construct a coalition that would support authorization and appropriation for the program, President Johnson expanded the program to include numerous small and medium-sized cities in the districts of key congressional representatives. With limited funds for each city, the program achieved its goal nowhere.

It is not clear that targeted urban policies such as the model cities program would have been effective even if sufficient funds had been available. One urban planner commented:

> Model cities didn't accomplish its goals anywhere in the country. It was a wonderfully honorable program in intent and it went down to a glorious defeat. It is not possible to solve basic social problems with a massive influx of money. Poor people are poor because they have a culture of poverty. You can't turn it around with a few classrooms or new buildings.[3]

The pessimism expressed in the above quote over the effectiveness of federal urban programs is widespread. It has led to funding cuts, and an increase in block grant funding, which allows more local discretion in the spending of funds.

Unfortunately, little research has been done that might clarify which forms of governmental organization encourage effectiveness. There seems to be a tradeoff between efficiency and responsiveness. We do not know, however, how effectiveness is related to these other two dimensions of governmental performance.

The Fifth Issue: Policy Distribution and Urban Location

Geographic space structures human interaction. It influences who buys what from whom. Slum dwellers pay the prices inflated by the high costs of doing business with the poor; suburbanites have access to higher-quality goods at

---

[3] Franziska L. Grieling, "Highland Park on the Brink," *Detroit News,* August 23, 1981. The quotation is from Michael Hickey, a planner for Highland Park, Michigan. For years, Highland Park received more federal grants, per capita, than any other city in the nation, yet the city in 1980 had the lowest per capita income in the Detroit metropolitan area—fully 40 percent below the average.

lower prices. Space dictates who will meet whom socially. Where people live and work affects their patterns of interaction with other people. And the way in which urban physical space is used profoundly affects the resources governments will have to solve social problems. The elementary fact that center cities have a preponderance of social problems and suburbs contain a disproportionate number of productive businesses and wealthy citizens means that some citizens can escape the burden of providing services for the less fortunate.

Yet there is a second side to the issue of the use of urban space. Humans use space purposefully to achieve certain patterns of human interactions. Homes for the wealthy tend to be clustered together, away from either working-class bungalows or slum tenements. Spatially separate governmental units called suburbs are established so that a relatively homogeneous citizenry can govern itself. As we noted in chapter 15, this homogeneous citizenry not infrequently enacts policies in the form of zoning codes and building restrictions that have the effect of keeping the community homogeneous. Alien elements, particularly the poor, are excluded. Humans, then, use space to structure human interactions by establishing governments and pursuing certain public policies.

Urban geography has not infrequently been used by policymakers to achieve certain political ends as a by-product of an announced policy. In many cities, highways have been located in order to accomplish slum removal as well as transportation objectives. The same is true of countless public works projects, from bridges to civic centers. And urban governments have approved of countless other private developments that resulted in the removal of the poor. Urban renewal policies, as we saw in chapter 13, were explicitly designed to remove the poor by removing substandard housing.

In other cases urban location has been responsible for policy outcomes that were quite unintended. Urban parks, established years ago, often serve an entirely different clientele than they did in an earlier period. As invasion and succession changed the ethnic and class character of neighborhoods, the characteristics of park users also changed in ways unrelated to the intentions of the original policy-makers. The same is true of some subway stations, recreation centers, and public hospitals.

Finally, local governments pursue policies that affect the location of citizens and businesses in other jurisdictions. Economic development policies and tax incentives, as we noted in chapters 11 and 12, are designed primarily to attract businesses from other locales, not to promote the establishment of entirely new enterprises.

In each of these cases, urban space is used to distribute the benefits and costs of the urban policymaking process to citizens. Distribution occurs in all spheres of public policymaking. What is unique about urban policymaking is that so much policy distribution occurs through the deliberate and inadver-

tent manipulation of how citizens, businesses, industries, and public institutions are located in urban space.

The National Interest

Even if community leaders were completely accountable to the citizens of the
local community, it would not follow that the national interest would be
served. What is good for the citizens of a single city and what is good for the
citizens of the country may be vastly different. Does the existence of independent policy-producing urban jurisdictions that are constrained by
citizen mobility and the actions of other levels of government yield urban
policies that are in the (national) public interest? There are three arguments
that hold that this system does *not* yield urban policies in the national
interest.

1. *The planning argument.* The existing system of numerous independently acting decision-making centers results in a hodgepodge of
   urban development characterized by unplanned sprawl. This is not in
   the public interest, for it results in wasted resources and a reduced
   quality of life for urban dwellers. Only land-use planning at the
   regional, state, or even national level can correct this situation.

2. *The liberals' argument.* The existing system of urban development has
   had the effect of separating *need* (in the center city) from *resources* (in
   the suburbs). The central city has the will to redistribute government
   benefits to the poor, but not the resources. The suburbs have the
   resources, but not the will. Only a national urban policy has the
   possibility of righting the imbalance, because only at the national level
   can the resources and the will be unified. The recent shift of jobs and
   people to the Sunbelt has simply magnified the need for a national urban strategy that takes account of both resources and needs.

3. *The conservatives' argument.* Cities are the home to the poor, yet there
   are limits to the extent to which government can or ought to intervene.
   Urban governments, and in particular New York City, have become
   hostage to urban "special interests." They find themselves in a situation where they must respond to the demands of the "urban constituency," which comprises the recipients of government benefits and the
   middle-class service providers who cater to them. Spending far exceeds
   the revenue that can be generated reasonably, and then the city government makes demands on state and federal government to bail it out.
   The existing system, consequently, does not work because city governments are *too* responsive to citizen demands.

On the other side of the coin, several political scientists have argued that the existing system of urban policymaking—which might best be characterized as a mix between local government actions, national policies and programs, and constraints imposed by the social and economic systems—does provide a method for arriving at urban policies in the national interest. The argument has three components.

1. In a diverse country, different localities will need different policies. Only local autonomy can provide that.

2. Nevertheless, there are national components to urban problems, and these aspects of urban problems can be solved only by the national government. Just what government will be responsible for what policies is never fixed in a federal system. Rather, the division of powers and responsibilities will be worked out on a day-to-day basis through negotiation and compromise.

3. Governments *ought* to be constrained by economic and social realities. It is entirely possible for governments to act in a manner that hinders the most productive use of economic resources. In attempting to pursue policies that serve the needs of the poor, governments can make society less productive (by, for example, setting such high tax rates that the incentive to work, invest, and save is hindered). The possibility of mobility limits this tendency. In a word, limited government is still a reasonable proposition.

The Limits of Change

Whatever the correct argument, one thing is clear. We will not move from where we are to an ideal urban future quickly, if ever. The urban future has been shaped by the past, and is being shaped by the present system of urban policymaking. That system of policymaking is complex and decentralized. Policymaking is often separated from policy implementation and administration. Numerous points exist at which change can be thwarted. Resource limitations at both the local and national levels virtually preclude any major urban initiatives.

Of course we hope that any change, even small, will move us toward a brighter urban future. Given the diversity of viewpoints in modern America, however, it is unlikely that we could agree on what a brighter urban future would look like, and we would probably be unable to recognize it if we got there. Such a statement ought not be viewed in an overly pessimistic fashion. Diversity has always been the most vibrant feature of urban America; that it also limits the possibility of change can be a source of strength.

INDEX